America's EDUCATIONAL TRADITION

America's EDUCATIONAL TRADITION

an
interpretive
history

WILLIAM M. FRENCH
Muhlenberg College

D.C. HEATH AND COMPANY Boston

PRINTED FEBRUARY 1967

COPYRIGHT © 1964 BY D. C. HEATH AND COMPANY.

Library of Congress Catalog Card Number 64-19012

Printed in the United States of America. (6d4)

Preface

At no time in the history of the United States has there been greater discussion of education and its relationship to the social, political, and economic order than at the present time. How unfortunate it is that much of this discussion proceeds without reference to the historical and sociological factors that have made American education what it is today. With this deficiency in mind, the author ventures to think that a history of the American educational system interpreted in light of our national aspirations and problems would be of considerable value to the prospective teacher and interested layman.

In his thirty years of teaching experience in the discipline of history of education, the author has seen certain movements, now particularly timely, generally neglected in conventional books in this field. The education of the Negro, the immigrant, and the handicapped are all noble parts of our educational story that ought to be told. Other important forces worthy of emphasis are the church, the state, and the nongovernmental agency.

The author is indebted to generations of students he has worked with who have brought a fresh viewpoint to his teaching and writing by their penetrating questions and arguments. The colleges and universities represented by these young people are: New York State College for Teachers at Albany (now the State University of New York), Muskingum College, Hastings College, Ohio State University, Macalaster College, and Muhlenberg College. Scores of the author's students have discovered gems of information in obscure books and local histories. He is further indebted to the late Dr. A. K. Beik of the State College at Albany who first awakened the author's interest in educational history and philosophy; and to Dr. John S. Brubacher, professor of education at the University of Michigan, who guided the author's study in this field. Credit and gratitude is also given to the United States Office of Education and the Research Division of the National Education Association for their wonderful generosity in supplying needed information. Appreciation is extended to the librarians at Muhlenberg College, to Peter Cistone, Robert Landis, and John Ponchak who read the manuscript and made helpful suggestions. Special acknowledgment is due to Mrs. Verra Mertz, the author's secretary, for typing the manuscript. Acknowledgment is due to the author's wife, Florence S. French, and to his son, Geoffry S. French, who sacrificed a certain amount of "togetherness" while this book was being written.

WILLIAM MARSHALL FRENCH

To Mabel I. Haupt, TEACHER
who encouraged me to write

Table of CONTENTS

1 In The Beginning   1

The English Heritage; People of the Book; The New England Primer; Apprenticeship; The Latin Grammar Schools; Reading and Writing Schools; Three Attitudes toward Schooling; Compulsory Maintenance Attitudes; The Parochial Attitude; Laissez-faire and Charity Attitude; New England Attitude Prevailed; The Colonial College; Three Levels Formed.

2 Colonial Latin Schools and Colleges   21

Education for a Minority; Four Types of Schools; The Latin Grammar School; The Boston Latin Grammar School; Other Latin Schools; Massachusetts Legislation; Latin School Students; The Curriculum; Method; Decline of Latin Schools; The First Nine Colleges; Founding of Harvard; Purposes of Colleges; Student Life in Colonial Days; All Small Institutions; Deism; A Venture in Faith.

3 Education in a New Nation   36

The Colonial Way Persists; Education and the Democratic Ideal; The Essayists; American Philosophical Society; Philosophical Basis of Essays; Education and the Constitution; Views of Founding Fathers; The Decline of Schools; The Decline in New England; The Town System; The Moving School; The District School; The First State Superintendent; Hawley's Achievements; Lack of Concern; Northwest Territory; Philanthropy in New York; Monitorial Schools; Toward a New Idea.

4 The Basis for Educational Reform   53

An Age of "Great Movements"; The Growth of Democracy; Education for Citizenship; Urbanization; Nationalism; The Religious Factor; Immigration; Attitude of Organized Labor; Humanitarianism; The Industrial Revolution; Rise in National Wealth.

5 Early Elementary Schools   67

The Colonial Heritage; New Texts by American Authors; Webster's Spellers and Readers; Morse's Geography; Grammars; Arithmetics; Histories; McGuffey's Readers; Other Subjects; The Teachers; The Schoolhouses; Attendance; Supervision; State Superintendent; The "One-Room" District School System; The Leaders of the Common School; The Elementary School.

6 Early Secondary Schools   87

New Type of Needs; Private Venture Schools; Franklin's Academy; Other Academies; Academies in New York; In Other States; Curriculum; Other Names; Method of Teaching; Influence of the Academies: Female Academies—Coeducation; Academies Today.

7 Development of the Common School   98

The Promise Incomplete; Aspects of the Reform; Demonstrating the Need; James G. Carter; Horace Mann; Other Massachusetts Leaders; Gideon Hawley; Henry Barnard; Thaddeus Stevens; Calvin Stowe; Murphey and Wiley; Other Leaders; The "Rate Bill" System; How the "Rate Bill" Worked; A Typical "Rate Bill"; The Cities Abolish "Rates"; Steps in Social Change; Free School Campaign; Propaganda Campaign; Free School Act of 1849; The Fatal Defect; Final Victory in 1867; The Victory Not Complete; Establishing Control; Compulsory Attendance; Extension of Program Upward.

8 The Changing Elementary School   127

The Traditional School; Ideas from Abroad; Pestalozzian Influence; Herbartian Influence; Froebelian Influence; Manual Training; Science Instruction; The Transformation; Dewey's Experiment; Other Experiments; Influence on Schools; Kilpatrick's Progressivism; Evaluation; Progressive Education Association; The Critics Attack; Growth in the Schools.

9 The American High School   143

An Extensive Institution; The First High School; Girls' High School
Massachusetts Law of 1827; Pennsylvania High Schools; New York Develop-
ments; Origins of High Schools; Union Free School Act; Western High
Schools; Southern High Schools; Legality of High Schools; The Kalamazoo Case;
Attendance Data; Lack of Uniformity; University Inspection; College Entrance
Examination Board; National Committees: Committee of Ten; Committee on
College Entrance Requirements; Economy of Time; Articulation of High School
and College; Commission on Reorganization; Changing High School Population;
Reasons for Increased Enrollment; National Survey of Secondary Education;
Issues of Secondary Education; The Depression of the 30's; American Youth
Commission; The Regents' Inquiry; Changes in Accrediting; Common Learn-
ings; Life Adjustment Curriculum; Reaction after Sputnik; The Conant
Reports; Junior High Schools; Vocational and Agricultural Education; The
Drop-outs; The Trump Plan; New Materials and Techniques.

10 The Growth of Colleges   173

Westward Movement; Motives for Frontier Colleges; "Union" Colleges; Petty
Restrictions; Who Should Control the Colleges? University of Virginia;
Western Universities; The Teachers College; Correspondence Study; Extension
Study; The College Curriculum; Persistence of Classics; The Enlightenment;
Method in Colleges; Realistic Studies; Morrill Act; Education of Women;
Accreditation.

11 Development of the Universities   195

What Is a University? The First American University; The Spirit Spreads; Role
of Philanthropy; Fund Raising Projects; A Social Protest; The Elective Principle;
Development of Science; Was Eliot Inconsistent? Proliferation of Courses; Some
Checks on Election; Growth in Enrollments; "The Tidal Wave"; The Changing
College; Growth in Research; Junior College Movement; Need for Further
Expansion; Education in the Professions; University Regalia.

12 The Education of Women   213

Few Have Opportunity; The Colonial View; The Female Academy; The Normal
School; Emma Willard, Mary Lyon; Catherine Beecher; Girls' High School;
High Schools; Expansion and Coeducation; Higher Education; Elmira College;
Oberlin College; Antioch College; Southern Colleges and State Universities; Cor-
nell University; A Matter of Degrees; Graduate and Professional Study;
Women in Medicine; Women as Lawyers; Present Status.

13 The Education of Teachers   229

What Teachers Were Like; Need for Teacher Education; Normal Schools Established; The Albany Normal School; More Normal Schools; The Reading Circle; Teachers' Institutes; Summer Sessions; Changing Concepts in Teacher Education; Repudiation of the Normal School and Teachers College; NCATE; New Plans in Teacher Education; The Conant Proposals.

14 Informal Education Agencies   257

Education Without Schools; Observation; Lecturers and Shows; War; Immigration; Magazines; Journals of Education; Specialized Magazines; Student Magazines; Significance of Magazines; Newspapers; Radio and Television; Motion Pictures; "Adult Education"; Libraries; The Arts.

15 The Non-Public Schools   275

A Persistent Question; Early Protestant Patterns; Early American Patterns; Proposal for National Schools; Protestant Parochial Schools; The Episcopalians; The Congregationalists; The Quakers; The Baptists; The Methodists; The Reformed Churches; Presbyterian Churches; Lutherans; Other Parochial Schools; Jewish; Secondary Schools and Colleges; Roman Catholic Position; Catholics and Public Schools; Catholic Parochial Schools; Hostility to Parochial Schools; Expansion of Parochial Schools; Renewed Hostility; Federal Aid to Church Schools? "Breaches in the Wall"; Unsettled Questions; The Supreme Court; A Completely Secular School? Secondary Schools; Independent Schools.

16 Incorporating the Minorities   295

Many Minorities in America; Education of the Negro; Freedmen's Bureau; Tax-Supported Schools; Philanthropies; Effects of Dual System; What Kind of Education? "Separate but Equal"; Supreme Court Decision, 1954; Great Number of Immigrants; The Early Immigrants; The Later Immigrants; Early School Leaving; Conflicts for the Children; Settlement Houses; Americanization; Americanization Schools; Educating the Handicapped.

17 Control and Administration   314

An Evolutionary Process; Simple Control and Administration; State School
Funds; County Superintendents; The City Superintendency; Professionalization;
Professional Literature; The Principalship; Expansion of State Departments;
Superintendents and Commissioners; Growing State Aid; U.S. Office of Edu-
cation; Federal Aid to Education; Who Controls Education? Principle of Lay
Control; State Sovereignty.

18 Professional Organizations of Teachers   328

Present Organizations; American Institute of Instruction; American Lyceum
Association; Two Other Associations; State Associations; National Teachers
Association; A Small Association; The National Education Association; Annual
Conventions; Proceedings; Affiliated Organizations; State Associations; Local
Associations; Zone Meetings; Legislative Activities; Committees and Com-
missions; American Federation of Teachers; American Association of Uni-
versity Professors; Insurance, Annuity, and Retirement Plans; State Retire-
ment Systems; Parent Teacher Association.

19 Freedom in Education   345

Security vs. Freedom; Colonial Religious Orthodoxy; Political and Economic
Pressures; Orthodoxy vs. Evolution; The Fear of Socialism; Teacher Tenure;
Censorship of Textbooks; Curriculum Controls; Loyalty Oaths; Reasons for
Restrictions; Personal Freedom of Teachers; Teaching about Communism; The
Vigilantes.

20 Today and Tomorrow   363

The Past as Prologue; Enrollment; Curriculum Development in the Elementary
School; Secondary School Curriculum; Methods of Teaching; Financing the
Schools; School District Reorganization; Diminution of Lay Control; The
Teachers; Continuing Education; Research in Education; Changing Economic
Viewpoint.

Index   393

"I know of no safe depository of the powers of society but the people themselves; if they are not enlightened enough to exercise their control with discretion, the remedy is not to take power away from them but to inform them by education."

—JEFFERSON

"They who teach young people well are more to be honored than they who produce them."
—ARISTOTLE

"A teacher affects eternity. He can never tell where his influence stops."
—HENRY ADAMS

"As is the teacher, so is the school."
—VICTOR COUSIN

1

In the Beginning

The English Heritage   In this day
of space exploration and projected space colonization, one might ask
what earthly institutions the pioneer space settlers might carry with
them to a new planet. One suspects that they would take a form of
government and, soon after they had built their homes, they would
doubtless establish houses of worship and start schools for the education of their children. All these—government, homes, churches
and schools—doubtless would, to a large extent, be patterned after
institutions these pioneers had known in their former homelands.
They would, in a sense, be doing just what the early settlers of
America did.

Education in the United States has an English heritage because
the first settlers in our country were English. Though the early
English influence was soon to be altered by persons from many other
lands—the Dutch, the Irish, the Scotch, French Huguenots, Swedes,
Germans (the Pennsylvania "Dutch"), Jews, and Negroes—still the
English pattern largely predominated. Both in England and in other
western European lands from which the settlers came, it was the
home and the church, not the state, that was primarily responsible
for education. Home and family responsibility for education is as
old as mankind. Church responsibility, too, is of ancient vintage, for
even among primitive peoples, the medicine men (the "clergy" of
the time and place) had certain educational functions and preroga-
tives. With the advent of Christianity, the church shared educational
responsibility with the home, the former assuming considerable
interest in religious and sacramental education and the home retaining responsibility for secular education. The Protestant heritage,
which was an important part of the tradition of many of the settlers,
particularly emphasized the responsibility of church and home for
formal education in literacy. This was especially true in the case of

1

those who brought the Calvinistic version of the Protestant tradition to New England.

People of the Book   These New England colonists were the people of a book, *The Book,* the Bible. Their life was centered around their Bible and the interpretation of it. One of the precepts of the *New England Primer* is

> Thy life to mend
> This Book attend,

meaning the King James version of the Bible. Children were further warned

> He who ne'er learns his A, B, C,
> Forever will a Blockhead be;
> But he who to his Book's inclin'd,
> Will soon a golden Treasure find.

Here, again, the Book was obviously the Bible—or perhaps the Primer, which was a hortatory and catechetical introduction to the Bible.

The New England Primer   The *New England Primer,* or other regional adaptations of it, was the very keystone to much of colonial schooling. The child was first introduced to his letters through a hornbook—a single printed page mounted on a small carved board with a wooden handle (somewhat like a modern decorative breadboard, but smaller), which was covered by a piece of cow's horn made transparent by boiling and scraping. (Glass could have been used, but it was too expensive and fragile; cellophane and plastics, which would have served ideally, were far over the inventors' horizon.) Instead of the hornbook, sometimes a battledore was used. This was a heavy cardboard or a few cardboards bound together. The content was much the same as the hornbook's.

Having progressed mechanically through the alphabet on the hornbook, the child then proceeded to the *New England Primer,* which was alleged to be "an easy and pleasant guide to the art of reading." This remarkable little book—one might almost say booklet—originally appeared in 1690 and ran through countless editions. It has been estimated that more than 3,000,000 copies were printed at a large number of printshops throughout the colonies. Since there

**A little girl of Colonial period
with her hornbook in hand.**

were no copyright laws, any printer was free to pirate any successful book. The content varied very little from one edition to another, though with time more secular influence was introduced. Still, even in the later editions, it reflected the ecclesiastical orientation of a Puritan society.

The child moved, in ordered sequence, through the "great capital letters"—*A, B, C*, etc.—and the "small letters"—*a, b, c* (including *&*) —to "easy syllables for children," thus:

Ab	eb	ib	ob	ub
ac	ec	ic	oc	uc
ad	ed	id	od	ud
af	ef	if	of	uf

ag	eg	ig	og	ug
al	el	il	ol	ul
am	em	im	om	um
an	en	in	on	un
ap	ep	ip	op	up
ar	er	ir	or	ur
as	es	is	os	us

Now, having exhausted the "grunt and groan" phonics which began with vowels, the child was directed to

Ba	be	bi	bo	bu
ca	ce	ci	co	cu
da	de	di	do	du
fa	fe	fi	fo	fu
ga	ge	gi	go	gu

—and so forth, through

wa	we	wi	wo	wu
ya	ye	yi	yo	yu
za	ze	zi	zo	zu[1]

A page from the New England Primer, which was published by Thomas Hall in Boston in 1795.

In *Adam's* Fall We Sinned all.

Thy Life to Mend This *Book* Attend.

The *Cat* doth play And after flay.

A *Dog* will bite A Thief at night.

An *Eagles* flight Is out of sight.

The Idle *Fool* Is whipt at School.

---

[1] Perhaps this may seem silly. But is it any more so than the "look, look, look, see, see, see, the plane goes up, up, up" of some contemporary primers?

Now, logically, he was ready for words—84 words of one syllable, filling one page; then words of two, three, four, five, and even six syllables, thus:

A	bo	mi	na	ti	on
Be	ne	fi	ci	al	ly
I	ma	gi	na	ti	on
Pu	ri	fi	ca	ti	on

Then came the Lord's prayer and creed, followed by the most noteworthy portion of the *Primer*: a series of couplets illustrating the alphabet, each with an accompanying woodcut:

> In Adam's Fall
> We sinnèd All.
>
> *and*
>
> As runs the Glass
> Man's life doth pass.
>
> *and*
>
> Young Obadias,
> David, Josias,
> All were pious.
>
> *and*
>
> Xerxes the Great did die
> And so must you and I.
>
> *ending with*
>
> Zaccheus he
> Did climb the Tree
> His Lord tó see.[2]

The Primer also presented some "Advice to His Children" by the Rev. John Rogers, a Protestant martyr burned at the stake by Queen Mary ("Bloody Mary") in 1554, as well as the Rev. John Cotton's "Spiritual Milk for American Babes, drawn out of the Breasts of both Testaments, for their Souls Nourishment." Another section reproduced the Shorter Catechism "agreed upon by the Reverend Assembly of Divines at Westminster."

[2] In the 1850's, a grandmother offered her grandchild ten cents to memorize these verses. When she had finished reciting the last one, she said she knew more and went on "The tree broke down and let him fall, and he did not get to see his Lord at all." The grandmother said this was very wicked and she hoped Anna would forget it. Mrs. C. C. Richards Clark, *Village Life in America* (Henry Holt, 1912).

One of the typical poems of the New England Puritan era was "The Day of Doom" by the Rev. Michael Wigglesworth. Whether or not the poem was extensively used in the colonial schools, it reflects a morbid preoccupation with eternal damnation which was characteristic of the clergy and schoolmen of the period. Children were looked upon as essentially evil and depraved, and usually in immediate danger of predestined damnation. The "Day of Doom" concerns itself, in part, with children who died before they had the chance to seek salvation. They plead that they themselves had not transgressed or disobeyed but were charged only with Adam's guilt:

> Not we, but he ate of the Tree,
> Whose fruit was interdicted:
> Yet on us all of his sad Fall,
> The punishment's inflicted.
> How could we sin that had not been
> Or how is his sin our
> Without consent, which to prevent,
> We never had a pow'r?

> Then answered the Judge most dread,
> God doth such doom forbid,
> That men should die eternally
> For what they never did.
> But what you call old Adam's fall,
> And only his Trespass,
> You call amiss to call it his,
> Both his and yours it was.

> You sinners are, and such a share
> As sinners may expect,
> Such you shall have; for I do save
> None but my own Elect.
> Yet to compare your sin with their
> Who liv'd a longer time,
> I do confess yours is much less,
> Though every sin's a crime.

> A crime it is, therefore in bliss
> You may not hope to dwell;
> But unto you I shall bestow
> The easiest room in Hell.

> The glorious King thus answering,·
> They cease and plead no longer:
> Their Consciences must needs confess
> His Reasons are the stronger.

To the Calvinist, the Devil was a very real person who lurked around every corner to snatch the souls of children who were by nature already predisposed to sin. Only by a rigorous education in a morbid theology could a few of them be saved from eternal hell-fire. Hence the strong emphasis on education for the soul's salvation.

The Primer was used either in the home or in a dame school—that is, a private venture school maintained by a literate or semiliterate widow or spinster in her own home, often in the kitchen while she did her household chores. For a few pennies this woman taught reading and the catechism and sometimes simple writing and the rudiments of arithmetic. The dame school concept was imported from England, where it had long served to introduce children to their letters. Undoubtedly, the quality of these schools varied greatly. One English school dame told a Parliamentary commission, "It's little they pays me, and it's little I teaches 'em." We must remember, of course, that reading (other than for one's soul's salvation) was not so important in the colonies as it has become in more recent times.

Apprenticeship   When she had
learned the bare essentials of reading and had perhaps made a sampler, the girl's formal education terminated. Now she awaited the availability of a husband. A boy either went to work in his own father's shop or farm or was placed out as an apprentice with someone else in the community. Formal articles of apprenticeship constituted a contract, setting forth the rights and privileges of the master and of the apprentice. A typical agreement provided that the child or youth would serve the master faithfully, "not absent himself from his or their service without leave and in all things behave himself as a good and faithful apprentice ought." The master, in turn, guaranteed to teach the boy his trade "or mystery," to feed, clothe and shelter him, teach him to read and write or have him so taught, and to provide him a new suit when the contract terminated.

There were two types of apprenticeship practiced in the American colonies. One was an apprenticeship for sustenance, for orphan children placed in foster homes by the local authorities. The other was an apprenticeship for craft training, wherein either an orphan or a child whose parents were living was placed out to learn a trade or "mystery," as it was often called. Since there were no vocational schools, one wanting to learn a craft such as printing or surveying found his way into the vocation through apprenticeship.

The following is an apprenticeship contract of the year 1783 which is similar in form and content to the articles of apprenticeship of the Colonial period. To make this reproduction as authentic as possible, grammar, spelling, and punctuation have been left as they appeared in the original contract.

An apprentice, Benjamin Franklin, learning to be a printer.

APPRENTICESHIP CONTRACT
Albany, New York 1783

This Indenture witnesseth that Jacob Stayley, son of Mary Stayley, hath put himself, and by these presents, by and with the Consent of his Mother doth voluntarily, and of his own free will and accord make himself Apprentice to Jacob Hochstrasser of the Hellenbergh in the County of Albany Weaver, to learn the Art, Trade and Mystery of Weaving and after the manner of an Apprentice, to serve from the day of the date,— hereof for and during the Term of Twelve Years and Three Months, next Insuing during all which time the said apprentice, his said Master faithfully shall serve, his Secrets keep, his lawfully commands everywhere readily obey, he shall do no damage to said master, nor see it to be dun by others, without letting or giving notice thereof, to his said Master. Shall not waste his Masters goods, nor lend them unlawfully to any. He shall not commit fornication nor Contract Matrimony within the said Term; at Cards, dice or any other Unlawful Games he shall not play, whereby his said Master may have damage, with his own goods or the goods of others: without lisence from his said Master he shall neither buy nor sell, he shall not absent himself day or Night from his Masters Service or Play in his leave, nor haunt Ale Houses . . . [several words illegible] . . . for him sufficient Meat, drink, Apparel, lodging and washing, fitting for an Apprentice during the said term of Twelve Years & three Months, and at the Expiration of said Term, shall give the said Apprentice, an Outfit of New Apparel and a young mare and for the true performance of all and singular, the Covenant and Agreements, afore said, the said partners by themselves, each unto the other, firmly by presents. In witness whereof the said partners interchangeably set their hands and seals here dated the Second of August in the seventh year of the Indipendence of this State Adommini, One Thousand and Seven Hundred and Eighty three—

Signed Seal'd and deliver'd
In the presence of us——

Anthony Turch

George Van Arnem

Jacob X Stayley
his
mark

Jacob Hochstrasser[3]

---

[3] The foregoing apprenticeship contract, so far as the author has been able to determine, has never before been printed. The original was in the family papers of Miss Leslie Brower, who was one of the author's students.

Laws provided the terms upon which articles of apprenticeship could be arranged. Colonial and town records show that frequently the selectmen were charged with overseeing the relations between the master and apprentice. Watertown, Massachusetts, in 1670 charged the selectmen to see that children received instruction in reading, in "knowledg of the capitall laws" of the colony, and in "some orthadox Catacise." Orphan girls were apprenticed to women who undertook to teach them "housewifery." Terms of the length of apprenticeship varied from place to place and from circumstance to circumstance.

The Latin Grammar Schools   For a small

number of boys there were opportunities to attend Latin grammar schools. These schools were not designed for all youth, but were specifically planned for an élite percentage of each generation. Never, between 1738 and 1789, did the enrollment in the two Latin schools of Boston exceed 202. In 1785 only 64 were enrolled in the two schools.

These Latin grammar schools were American adaptations of English schools which had been established during the Renaissance. In the England from which the colonists came, there were more than 300 such schools. Since the leaders of the New England colonies frequently were former students at these schools, it is only natural that Latin schools were early established here. Such a school had been projected for Jamestown, Virginia as early as 1621, but an Indian massacre effectively put an end to those plans. The Boston Latin Grammar School, said to be "the oldest, free, public, non-endowed, non-sectarian, secondary school with continuous existence in the United States" was established in 1635. Approximately 50 pounds was subscribed through voluntary contributions.

Latin schools were established in other towns, mostly in New England but also in New York, Virginia and elsewhere. It took little effort, really, to establish such a school; oftentimes the local minister conducted the school in his own home, using books which he himself had studied. A few of the larger schools had their own buildings and sometimes assistant teachers, called ushers, who were employed under the supervision of the minister. Few men made a lifetime career of teaching in Latin schools. Many were transients. Some were indentured servants. Others were young men who had prepared for the ministry and were awaiting a call. A notable exception was Ezekiel Cheever, who taught in the Latin schools of New England for seventy years, from 1638 to his death in 1708. So great was his fame as "a skilful, painful, faithful schoolmaster for seventy years" that the governor and other notables attended his funeral.

Cheever's *Accidence,* a grammar, was one of the most learned books produced in America. There is doubt that Cheever himself put it into final form, but it seems reasonable to assume that it was assembled shortly after his death from his lesson plans. This book was reprinted as late as 1838. One of Cheever's pupils was the renowned Reverend Cotton Mather, who chose the name of a noted French Huguenot Latin grammarian as Cheever's title of honor: "Corderius Americanus"—the American Corderius.

Reading and Writing Schools   There also existed reading and writing schools, especially in the larger towns. To these were sent both beginners and those who wished a higher degree of proficiency than they had been able to achieve at home or in a dame school. In addition to the two subjects implied in the name of these schools, some arithmetic and simple elements of accounting were taught. Sometimes all these subjects were taught in one school, and sometimes they were taught in separate schools. Emphasis on writing was less than on reading in many of the New England colonies, supposedly because reading was more important from the viewpoint of religious instruction. Until trade and industry became important, the religious motive for education was paramount.

Three Attitudes toward Schooling   Different attitudes toward schooling prevailed in the different colonies. Generally, in New England, the government was theocentric: at times it was difficult to draw a line between the civil government and church government. Religious tests existed for voting and for office holding. Civil enactments were often in the interest of the established religion. The same class of men exercised leadership and control in both church and state.

Compulsory Maintenance Attitudes   Generally in New England the state mandated the compulsory maintenance of schools and compulsory attendance. The precedent was early set in the Massachusetts laws of 1642 and 1647. The law of 1642 provided that committees of "prudential officers" should have charge of taking account, from time to time, of all parents and masters of apprentices and of their children concerning their "calling and implyment," especially of their ability to read and understand the principal tenets of their religious faith and the "capitall lawes of this country." It should be noted that this 1642 law did not compel towns to establish schools—that was to come later—but officers were charged with the responsibility of seeing that children were taught. Massachusetts was not yet ready to depart from the English tradition that education was a home and church responsibility. However, the government did concern itself with assuring that parents and masters did not neglect their responsibility. Where it appeared that a child's education had been neglected, the parents and master could be fined or children could be removed from their custody.

By 1647, a further step was made. The general court (i.e. legislature) enacted a law compelling every town of fifty householders to maintain a school in which reading and writing were taught in order to thwart "ye olde deluder Satan" who conspired "to keep men from the knowledge of the Scriptures." This was the famous "Old Deluder Satan" Act. The law further provided that all towns of a hundred householders were also to furnish instruction in Latin grammar so that youth might be "fitted for the university"—meaning Harvard College, established in 1636. It should not be assumed that the law of 1647 was universally popular. From time to time, authorities had difficulty enforcing it. Some towns found it more economical to pay the fine imposed than to maintain a school.

These two laws of 1642 and 1647 are commonly said to form the basis upon which the public school system of the American people has been founded. Some writers are inclined to discount this statement, charging that too much retrospective importance is given to these two acts in this interpretation. Surely the New England men who wrote the law could not foresee the development of a system of public education stretching from coast to coast; certainly they would have abhorred a nonsectarian or secular public school system. The folklore of American education nevertheless places great emphasis on these acts. Perhaps it is a case of the writers' having built better than they realized. Certainly additional school legislation was easier to enact after these basic principles had been settled, and certainly the role of Massachusetts in influencing education elsewhere in the country can not be gainsaid.

Martin, a historian of Massachusetts education, sets forth his interpretation of the significance of these two laws:[4]

1. The universal education of youth is essential to the well being of the state.

4 Martin, George H.: *The Evolution of the Massachusetts Public School System. A Historical Sketch.* New York: D. Appleton and Company, pp. 14–15.

2. The obligation to furnish this education rests primarily upon the parent.

3. The state has a right to enforce this obligation.

4. The state may fix a standard which shall determine the kind of education, and the minimum amount.

5. Public money raised by general tax may be used to provide such education as the state requires. The tax may be general though the school attendance is not.

6. Education higher than the rudiments may be supplied by the state. Opportunity must be provided at public expense for youths who wish to be fitted for the university.

Other New England states which adhered to the state-church affiliation enacted similar laws. The Connecticut law of 1650 is a verbatim reproduction of the Massachusetts law of 1647. Rhode Island, where religious freedom prevailed, did not feel inclined to legislate in this way.

The short-lived Netherlands colony which eventually became New York showed equal fervor in the cause of education. The 1629 charter of "freedoms and exemptions for the patroons, masters or private persons who shall plant any colony in, and send cattle to, New Netherlands" provided:

The patroons and colonists shall in particular endeavor as quickly as possible to find some means whereby they may support a minister and a school-master, that thus the service of God and zeal for religion may not grow cool and be neglected among them, and they shall from the first procure a comforter of the sick there.

The Dutch continued to control their colony only until 1664, but in this short period they had made the beginning of an educational system. During the first English occupancy (1664–1673) many of their educational rights were retained, but after a short return of the Dutch to control (1673–74), the colony again reverted to England and the Dutch educational influence was reduced. Restoration of English government resulted in disestablishment of the Dutch Reformed Church and the removal of schools from government control.

Under the English regime in New York, the dominant attitude was typically English, that education was a concern of the family and the church. The government might intervene to see that children were educated but it was not itself concerned with providing the means of education. A colonial law in New York provided:

> The constable and overseers are strictly required frequently to admonish the inhabitants to instruct their children and servants in matters of religion and the laws of the country.

The Parochial Attitude   A different attitude toward education prevailed in the middle colonies—New York, New Jersey and Pennsylvania. In these colonies there was no monopoly of orthodox religion. To each of them came persons from many Protestant backgrounds as well as some Catholics and Jews. Here Calvinism had no monopoly such as it early established and firmly maintained in Massachusetts and Connecticut. In New York were found English adherents of the established Church of England and of the various dissenting denominations, as well as Dutch people, mostly of the Reformed tradition. To the early Quaker settlers of Pennsylvania were soon added large numbers of German immigrants —Lutherans, Reformed, and several "plain people" sects, each jealously wanting to guard and preserve its own heritage. So great was the interest of German Lutherans in preserving their distinctive heritage among the immigrants that they sent missionary pastors to America. Soon after the Germans, there came many Scotch and Scotch-Irish Presbyterians. The sincere and intense desire of each of these denominations to preserve its own heritage made it impossible to establish one school system. The only satisfactory solution was to leave it to each denomination to establish its own schools in its own parishes. Unlike the established church in Massachusetts, these churches did not seek the arm of the civil government to assist in establishing and maintaining schools. Indeed, even when the time came when public schools were needed, these churches often resisted.

A greater degree of educational freedom therefore existed in these Middle Colonies. Churches served the educational needs of their parishes. Some private venture schools existed, especially in the larger towns. Yet many people had no schools whatsoever, and many children grew to adulthood unable to read or write. The laissez-faire attitude toward education existed in Pennsylvania until 1834 and was then overcome only because by that time many persons with a New England heritage had moved into the commonwealth. The enactment of the free school law of 1834 in Pennsylvania resulted from the agitation of Thaddeus Stevens, a Vermont migrant, and the solid support of Governor George Wolf, a Pennsylvania "Dutch-man." Even after the enactment of the 1834 law, resistance continued until well after the Civil War.

Laissez-Faire and Charity Attitude   Still a third attitude prevailed in the Southern colonies, from Maryland through Georgia. Except for the Catholics in Maryland, the policy-making settlers of the South were primarily loyal members of the established Church of England. They were content with the traditional English attitude that education was a commodity that those who could bought for their children, and that the church furnished schooling as a charity to the children of those who could not afford to purchase it. We see, then, the rise of private schools in Southern towns, the widespread use of tutors on isolated plantations, and the establishment of charity schools by various English religious and philanthropic societies, such as the Society for the Propagation of the Gospel in Foreign Parts. When a Virginian or a Carolinian—or even a New Yorker, for that matter—contributes money today to his church for educational missions in Africa or Asia, he is really only returning a portion of the investment made in the education of his ancestors by pious gentlemen and ladies in England who contributed funds to save their American colonies from heathenism.

The class structure in the Southern colonies also militated against the establishment of a system of education like either New England's or the Middle Colonies'. While there was a demarcation in all the colonies between the proprietary class and those who labored or held only small farms, this differentiation was more marked and more persistent from Virginia southward. One school system to serve these two classes was unthinkable, for they were miles apart on the social scale. Desegregation of the public schools apparently will serve to bring about more differentiation, for it now seems likely that families which had patronized the public schools will, in increasing numbers, turn to private, segregated institutions.

These differences in regional attitudes were reflected in the order in which these three sections achieved public schools. New England, with its tradition of church-state concern for education moved relatively easily into the founding of public schools, both elementary and secondary. In the Middle Colonies, there was more resistance, and the achievement of public schools was longer delayed. In the South, little was achieved in the founding of public schools until after the Civil War. An exception is North Carolina, which long has been a leader in Southern public education.

New England Attitude Prevailed The whole of
American education has been changed because the New England
attitude of compulsory school establishment and compulsory attendance prevailed. From the New England school the transition to the
public school as we have come to know it was relatively easy. Had
the parochial school attitude of the Middle Colonies prevailed, we
might eventually have evolved a system of state partnership in private and parochial education, much like that in England. There to
this day both government schools and "voluntary" schools maintained by religious bodies and private groups receive government
grants. Had the Southern attitude prevailed, American education
would possibly have been limited to parochial and purely private
schools. It is largely due to the New England colonial tradition that
a public school system for the education of all the children of all the
people, irrespective of class, color, or creed has become the American
ideal and—to a large extent—the American accomplishment.

The Colonial College One other type
of educational institution made an important contribution to the
development of the colonies. This was the college. By the time of
the Revolution, there were nine of these institutions in the colonies:
Harvard in Massachusetts, William and Mary in Virginia, Yale in
Connecticut, Princeton in New Jersey, Brown in Rhode Island,
Kings (now Columbia) in New York, Queens (now Rutgers, the
State University of New Jersey) in New Jersey, the University of
Pennsylvania in Pennsylvania, and Dartmouth in New Hamsphire.
More detailed attention will be devoted to these schools and their
contributions in Chapter 2. These nine colleges formed a third
level of colonial education for higher learning.

Three Levels Formed We see, then,
that the colonial period developed, in embryo form at least, the
three levels of education which we have come to classify as elementary, secondary, and higher. While each of these levels was to un-
dergo many changes between the colonial period and the present,
we can see, even then, the rough outline that education was destined
to follow in America. In each case, the colonists reproduced upon
these shores a counterpart or an adaptation of institutions they knew
in the homeland. We shall shortly see how additional adaptations
were made in the following decades, adaptations that would bring
these institutions into closer harmony with the emerging needs of
a new nation. We must not, however, over-simplify the English

heritage. In spite of strong traditions brought from England and, to a lesser degree, from the European continent, there were many colonial improvisations and adaptations. For one thing, the isolated settlements were free to go their own ways, informally making such adaptations of their inherited traditions as circumstances demanded. There were no standardizing agencies except the colonial governments. These governments made few enactments regarding education, and these few enactments were sometimes ignored. The exigencies of the frontier often caused the settlers to place priorities on other things than education. The French and Indian wars were cited by frontier settlements in Massachusetts as their reason for not complying with the acts of 1642 and 1647.

When we speak here of three levels of colonial education, we do not mean to imply that the colonial children and youth made an orderly progression through the dame school, the reading and writing school, the Latin grammar school and the college. Some did, it is true, but colonial education was not formally structured into our present ladder system. Many persons entered college without ever having attended institutions of a lower level, having been taught at home or privately tutored. Many stopped their formal education when they had achieved a minimum degree of literacy. Many who went to a Latin school never did matriculate at a colonial college. Nonetheless, the three levels of education—elementary, secondary and higher—were present in embryonic form, ready to be integrated or articulated or systematized by succeeding generations as circumstances warranted and the times required. Naturally, much water had to go over the dam before the present-day system evolved.

The only startlingly original contribution to education in the colonies was the conviction in Massachusetts and other New England colonies that education was a responsibility of the civil government and that it could compel the establishment and support of schools.

The colonial education pattern was based primarily upon two conceptions: first, that the school should be an instrument for the preservation of religious faith and denominational orthodoxy; second, that the school should properly be used to preserve the existing social and economic stratification that had been brought over from Europe. Both of these conceptions were destined to be challenged and upset in the development of the public school system, but they persisted, by and large, throughout the colonial period and well into the early history of the United States. As we shall see later, these two concepts fell because they were incompatible with the new spirit that arose from the forces behind the American Revolution. When the philosophical principles of the Declaration of Independence were translated into the daily lives of the American people, then the concepts of intolerant orthodoxy and socio-economic stratification were destined to retreat.

In any general textbook, there is a strong danger of over-simplification. Almost any statement made as a generalization must be followed by a footnote citing exceptions, qualifications, and deviations. What we have tried to do here is to follow the main currents in colonial education. The student is cautioned not to accept this chapter as an exposition of all education in all the colonies in all the years from 1607 to 1776. For regional adaptations and studies of the various periods, he will need to refer to specialized research works.

For Further Reading

The history of education would be rather dull and colorless if it were the mere recital of happenings. Historical events are meaningful only when they are interpreted and their significance is shown. But when we come to interpretation, a degree of subjectivity is introduced by the person making the interpretation. The student of history should be aware that different authors see the same events from many different perspectives. Whenever one confronts a historical situation, he sees it in the light of his own background—or as Herbart would say, he "brings to bear upon it his apperceptive mass."

The author has tried, principally, to be objective in his presentation of the educational development of the American people. He is aware, however, that his own background must inevitably color the interpretation. For this reason, the student is cautioned that he ought to read other authors. At the end of each chapter, a list of other standard readings will be furnished. In these, the same materials may be treated from a different viewpoint, and some additional materials will be presented. It then becomes the responsibility of the student to *think* and to form his own conclusions. To help the student select his readings, a brief statement about the references is supplied.

Bailyn, Bernhard. *Education in the Forming of American Society.* Vintage Books, Random House, 1963.

A fresh reappraisal of the role of education in colonial society. Rejects "distortions and short-circuiting of thought" in older histories of education in the colonial era. Contains an extended bibliographical essay and an exhaustive bibliography.

Boorstin, Daniel J. *The Americans: the Colonial Experience.* Random House, 1958.

Sections 28, 29, 30 deal with college education in the colonies.

Brown, Elmer Ellsworth. *The Making of Our Middle Schools.* Longmans, Green, 1921.

An earlier history of secondary schools. Good treatment of the Latin grammar schools.

Cubberley, Elwood P. *Public Education in the United States.* Revised. Houghton Mifflin, 1934.

For many years the most widely read history of American education. Almost encyclopedic in nature. Strong emphasis on the New England influence on education. The boldface numerical references refer to selections in an accompanying book of readings.

Cubberley, Elwood P. *Readings in the History of Education.* Houghton Mifflin, 1920.

Comparable to the same author's *Readings in Public Education in the United States,* but with fewer American citations. In this volume, selections 183 to 202, inclusive, are appropriate.

Cubberley, Elwood P. *Readings in Public Education in the United States.* Houghton Mifflin, 1934.

"A collection of sources and readings to illustrate the history of educational practice and progress in the United States." Here one finds excerpts from many original documents. For this chapter, selections 10 to 62 are appropriate. Included are pages of colonial textbooks, articles of apprenticeship, an analysis of the *New England Primer,* the widely quoted Dutch schoolmaster's contract, etc.

Curti, Merle. *The Social Ideas of American Educators.* Revised. Student Outline Series. Littlefield, Adams and Co., 1959.

An historical analysis of social thought. Chapter 1 deals with "Colonial Survivals and Revolutionary Promises."

Drake, William E. *The American School in Transition.* Prentice-Hall, 1955.

Chapter 2 develops the cultural background of colonial education. Chapter 3 deals with "Education for Salvation."

Elsbree, Willard S. *The American Teacher.* American Book Co., 1939.

An interesting account of teachers and their condition in the evolution of the profession. The first ten chapters deal with the colonial period, including qualifications, supervision, tenure, salaries, and status.

Fleming, Sanford. *Children and Puritanism.* Yale University Press, 1933.

The place of children in New England churches and schools: their books, their religious education, the repressive influence of Calvinism.

Ford, Paul L. *The New England Primer.* Dodd, Mead and Co., 1897.

A comprehensive analysis of the *Primer:* its origins, various printings, changing contents, and reproductions of portions of various editions.

French, William Marshall. *American Secondary Education*. Odyssey Press, 1957.

Chapter 3 deals with the Latin school in America, relying to a large extent upon Pauline Holmes' history of the Boston school.

Good, Harry S. *A History of American Education*. Second Edition. Macmillan, 1962.

One of the newer histories of education. The first three chapters describe developments in the colonial era.

Holmes, Pauline. *A Tercentenary History of the Boston Public Latin Grammar School*. Harvard University Press, 1935.

The standard history of America's first permanent secondary school.

Kilpatrick, William H. *Dutch Schools of New Netherland and Colonial New York*. Government Printing Office, 1912.

A detailed study of the early schools in New Netherland and New York. Emphasis on the church relationship to education.

Knight, Edgar W. *A Documentary History of Education in the South Before 1860*. University of North Carolina Press. 5 volumes. 1949 to 1955.

An exhaustive study of educational developments by the leading author on Southern education, who occupied the chair of educational history at the University of North Carolina.

Knight, Edgar W. *Public Education in the South*. Revised. Ginn and Company, 1941.

A sympathetic history of education in the South by one of the leading specialists in the field.

Martin, George H. *The Evolution of the Massachusetts Public School System. A Historical Sketch*. D. Appleton and Company, 1894.

A history of Massachusetts schools with considerable emphasis on the colonial period.

2

Colonial Latin Schools
and Colleges

Education for a Minority   The Latin grammar
school and the college were briefly identified in chapter one as part
of the colonial enterprise. In this chapter the character and importance of these institutions will be shown in more detail. Neither
institution should be regarded as "popular" in the sense of serving
large numbers of persons. By modern standards, all were very small.
Nevertheless, grammar schools and colleges were important, for they
served to keep learning alive in the colonies, and from them came a
high proportion of the leadership of the colonies and early national
government.

Four Types of Schools   In the history
of the American people from 1636 to the present, there have been,
at successive periods, four different types of secondary schools. The
first of these, an import from England, was the *Latin grammar
school,* which was the sole organized school of secondary character
throughout most of the colonial period. The second type was the
academy, which dominated secondary education from the Revolution to the Civil War-Reconstruction period. The third was the
high school, which we shall designate the *traditional high school.* The
fourth, which was also known as the high school, we shall call the
modern comprehensive high school. There are some indications that
a fifth type may be emerging, but we shall treat of that development
in Chapter 9.

The author acknowledges that many writers recognize only one
type of high school, but it is the contention of this book that the
early high school and the contemporary high school are so vastly
different in so many characteristics that they really represent two
quite distinct types.

A Colonial school master and his charges
holding their Primers.

When they were founded, each of the four types of secondary schools worked reasonably well in meeting the educational needs of the American people, as the American people first conceived these needs. But socio-economic and political conditions in the nation were dynamic, not static, and there came a time when each of these institutions no longer met America's needs. These early institutions for a while outlived their usefulness, sustained by our society's tendency to cultural and educational lag, but they eventually gave way to newer types of institutions more in harmony with the changing conditions in the country.

The Latin Grammar School   As indicated in
Chapter 1, the colonists transplanted to the colonies the Latin school which they had known in Europe. There were perhaps 300

of these in England at the time. With the Latin school, they brought the European philosophical outlook that secondary education was designed for a small, select class of persons who were destined for leadership in church and commonwealth. The influence of the Reformation and Renaissance was still a sufficiently potent factor to determine that these prospective leaders should receive a thorough grounding in those subjects which were commonly accepted as the equipment of any well educated person. According to the European tradition, these were the classical studies. Through these studies flowed the common heritage which had long set an educated man apart from the common herd. Such a school was proposed in Virginia as early as 1621 and some steps had been taken to collect gifts for its establishment, but an Indian massacre in 1622 turned the attention of the inhabitants to more immediate necessities.

The Boston Latin Grammar School   The institution claimed as "the oldest, 'free', public, non-endowed, non-sectarian, secondary school with continuous existence in the United States" was established as the Boston Latin Grammar School in 1635. The citizens of Boston "att a Generall meeting upon publique notice" voted that Philemon Pormont "be intreated to become scholemaster for the teaching and nourtering of children with us." Since no one else was so "intreated," it has been generally assumed that Pormont was the first teacher in the new Latin school for which public gifts were then being solicited. Various amounts, large and small, were collected to give the school a modest beginning of about fifty pounds.

Other Latin Schools   There is no complete record of all the Latin grammar schools established in the various colonies. Various historians, often working on local histories, have unearthed evidence of many from old town records, from newspaper advertisements, from correspondence, and from the biographies of famous and obscure men. Sometimes these Latin schools were not public, in the sense of being under the auspices of a governmental body. While the ones in Massachusetts were generally public in this sense, we find in other colonies that many were conducted as private venture schools. Several of the early "classical" schools in Pennsylvania, operated almost as an extra-curricular activity by clergymen, fall into this latter category. The most famous of these Pennsylvania classical schools was the institution founded in 1726 by the Rev. William Tennent near the Neshaminy Church in Bucks County. According to Whitefield, the Methodist missionary who visited there, "the place in contempt is called a college." For twenty years, Tennent taught young men for service in the state and church. His "Log College," as it came to be known, supplied the germ out of which Princeton College eventually developed.

Though Latin schools were not so common in the sparsely populated South as in the Northern colonies, there were such schools in the larger towns. One existed at the Virginian capital of Williamsburg, associated with the College of William and Mary. There was another at Charleston, South Carolina, and several existed in Pennsylvania and New York. One was even begun on New York's western frontier, at Schenectady.

Massachusetts Legislation   While Massachusetts had enacted a law in 1642 requiring town officals to see to it that children were taught to read, nothing at that time was included relating to secondary schools. In 1647, however, the colony passed a famous act charging that "ye ould deluder, Satan" was conspiring "to keepe men from the knowledge of ye Scriptures," having formerly under the Roman church kept the Latin Vulgate Bible "in an unknowne tongue" difficult for common men to understand, and having more recently kept men in ignorance "from ye use of tongues" that would allow them to read the Biblical texts for themselves. The legislature in an attempt to thwart Satan enacted that every town of fifty householders must maintain a teacher of reading and writing, and that every town with a hundred householders must provide a Latin grammar school to fit youths for the university.

This act was entirely unprecedented in English history. It reflected a strong Calvinistic influence in asserting for the first time that the state could require the establishment and maintenance of schools. This requirement was not intended to be paternalistic or socialistic. The welfare of the state, not of the individual, seems to have been paramount in the minds of the lawmakers. Following enactment of this law, Latin schools were established in several towns, but some towns found it cheaper to pay the fine assessed for failure to comply, and did not open Latin schools.

Latin School Students   When we speak of the Latin grammar school as a secondary school, we use terminology foreign to present-day American thinking and practice. Today, one goes to a secondary school after the completion of an elementary school curriculum of six or eight years. The secondary school today constitutes the middle section of the American educational ladder stretching from the kindergarten through the university. In colonial days in America and in many other countries there was a different concept behind secondary education. The elementary schools were for the common people and were terminal in character. The secondary school was a select school for a small portion of the population. After a child had learned to read from his hornbook and *New England Primer*, circumstances beyond his control determined for him which of three paths he would take: immediate employment, attendance at the reading and writing school, or attendance at a Latin grammar school. The circumstances which set his feet upon one of these paths were the socio-economic status of the family and the extent to which a tradition of education for the family was part of this status. Generally, it was the upper-class children from educated families that attended Latin schools as soon as they had learned sufficient rudiments from the dame schools.

The Curriculum   Now we can understand why pupils often attended a Latin school at the age of eight or nine. Within a few short years, they had sufficient exposure to the classical languages to meet the simple entrance requirements of the colleges. This accounts for the fact that it was not uncommon for boys of twelve to be enrolled at Harvard and Yale.

There were no sixteen standard Carnegie units, no standard college entrance examinations, none of the extensive processing required for college entrance today. The first entrance requirements of Harvard were stated thus:

> When any Schollar is able to understand Tully, or such like classicall Latine Author *extempore,* and make and speake true Latine in Verse and Prose, *suo ut aiunt marte;* and decline perfectly the Paradigms of *Nounes* and *Verbes* in the Greek tongue: let him then, and not before, be capable of admission into the college.[1]

Yale adhered to the Harvard standards for many years. In 1745, the Yale requirements for admission were stated thus:

> None may expect to be admitted into this College unless, upon Examination of the President and Tutors, They shall be found

---

[1] Translated into present-day terminology, this quotation from *New England's First Fruits,* published in 1643, says that one may enter Harvard when he can understand Cicero or a similar Latin author at once, can write and read Latin verse and prose, by his own efforts, and decline and conjugate Greek, and not before.

able Extempore to Read, Construe and Parce Tully, Vergil and the Greek Testament; and to write true Latin in Prose and to understand the Rules of Prosodia, and Common Arithmetic, and Shal bring Sufficient Testimony of his Blameless and inoffensive Life.

What the colleges demanded, of course, set the program of instruction in the Latin schools. Those who claim that the colleges of the nation, by their entrance requirements, have dominated the curriculum of the secondary schools, must acknowledge at least that such domination has had early precedent in American education.

Our best source for information on the curriculum of the Boston Latin School (and, presumably, of other New England schools) is the funeral oration preached by the Rev. Dr. Cotton Mather before the assembled notables when they came to pay their last respects to the venerable Ezekiel Cheever. He mentioned "all the Eight parts of Speech," "Prosodia," Ovid, Tully, Vergil, Homer, Livy's Latin Grammar, Cato, Corderius, "the Making of Themes," and the Testament, meaning the New Testament in Greek. The whole of the offering was apparently strongly laced with Calvinistic theology.

In its early years, the Latin school maintained a seven-year curriculum, but still graduated boys at thirteen or fourteen years of age. During the early period it was evidently common for an usher (assistant teacher) to teach the elementary subjects of reading, writing, and some "cyphering," as well as beginning Latin and perhaps Greek.

In 1789, the Boston school inaugurated a "new system," requiring that for entrance one must be ten years of age and "previously well instructed in English Grammar." This appears to have been the first appearance of the four-year secondary school program which came to be the dominant pattern in America. The four years curriculum was:

1st Class—Cheever's Accidence. Corderius's Colloquies—Latin and English. Nomenclature. Aesop's Fables—Latin and English. Ward's Latin Grammar, or Eutropius.

2nd Class—Clarke's Introduction—Latin and English. Ward's Latin Grammar, Eutropius, continued. *Selectae e Veteri Testamento Historiae* (Selected Stories From the Old Testament—in Latin) or, Castalio's Dialogues. The making of Latin, from Garretson's Exercises.

3rd Class—Caesar's Commentaries. Tully's Epistles, or Offices. Ovid's Metamorphoses. Virgil. Greek Grammar. The making of Latin from King's History of the Heathen Gods.

4th Class—Virgil, continued. Tully's Orations. Greek Testament. Horace. Homer. *Gradus ad Parnassum* (exercises in poetry). The making of Latin, continued.

When the academies began to exert an influence in education after the Revolution, further changes were made in the curriculum of the Boston Latin School. English was introduced gradually, to be followed by history, French, mathematics, and other "modern" subjects. Except for a continuing emphasis on Latin and Greek, the curriculum by 1900 was typical of the program of other good college preparatory high schools.

Method   While we are able to learn details about the curriculum of the Latin grammar schools from contemporary accounts, we find them notably silent when we search for information about methods used in teaching. Miss Pauline Holmes, the historian of the Boston school, found only two references to method in her study of more than a thousand documents. One of these related to the teaching of Latin in 1710 and one other spoke of Lancaster's system of mutual instruction.

Though John Locke had condemned the traditional method of rote learning in his *Thoughts Concerning Education,* published in England in 1693, there is no evidence that he exerted any significant influence on American practice. Though Locke condemned excessive attention to the composition of Latin themes and verses, the Latin school in America continued this emphasis.

It is safe to assume that strong reliance was placed upon the memoriter method whereby often students "learned by heart" many things which did not penetrate their understanding. The catechetical method, whereby the youth was conditioned to respond with a prescribed answer to a prescribed question, seems to have been universally used. Charles W. Eliot, president of Harvard, said about his student days in the Boston Latin Grammar School in 1844:

At ten years of age I committed to memory many rules of syntax, the meaning of which I had no notion of, although I could apply them in a mechanical way. The rule for the ablative absolute, for instance—"A noun and a participle are put in the ablative, called absolute, to denote the time, cause or concomitant of an action, or the condition on which it depends"—I could rattle off whenever I encountered a sample of that construction, but it was several years after I learnt the rule that I arrived at even the faintest conception of what it meant. The learning by heart of the grammar then preceded rather than accompanied as now exercises in translation and composition.

We should not be too critical of this formal method in the Latin schools, for one can still see many examples of it in present-day high schools, in spite of all that psychology and education have revealed to us regarding the learning process. All too many teachers still assume that if a youth can parrot a textbook statement, there is assurance that he has "learned."

Decline of Latin Schools   The Latin school performed the service for which it was designed. Considering its narrow aim of preparing some few of the best minds of each generation for service to church and state, it served its purpose effectively. But America was moving fast down a new path, and the Latin school could not show the way. To the East of the colonies lay a whole ocean to be used in international trade; to the west lay a whole continent to be explored, settled, and cultivated. An air of practicality and utilitarianism prevailed among Americans; they wanted to learn navigation, modern languages, accounting, surveying. These were not within the scope of the Latin school, so the Americans "invented" a new institution to meet these needs.

While some Latin schools remained to serve their limited purpose, many of them disappeared, either through failure to attract students, or through a gradual transformation into the new type of school, the academy. An example of a grammar school's conversion into an academy is the institution which the Rev. William Andrews opened as a grammar school in Schenectady; apparently it did not "take," and he transformed it into an academy. He wrote to Sir William Johnson:

> I lately took the Liberty of acquainting You, that I had opened a Grammar School in this Town, and since that, I have determined on forming it into an Academy, and propose giving Instruction in Reading, Writing, Arithmetic, Geography and History to those who may be designed to fill the Stations of active Life, exclusive of those who may be taught the Learned Languages—Bookkeeping and Merchants accounts to fit them for Business.

Certain of the other early academies in New York, notably the Washington Academy at Salem and Farmer's Hall at Goshen, were metamorphosed from Latin schools. In several instances, the academies merely absorbed the Latin schools and extended their curricula by offering "new" subjects.

The First Nine Colleges   At the time of the Revolution there were nine small colleges in the American colonies, stretching from Dartmouth in New Hampshire, to William and Mary in Virginia. In between were Harvard, Brown, Yale, Rutgers (originally Queens), Columbia (originally Kings), Princeton, and the University of Pennsylvania. Of these, Harvard, Yale, and William and Mary were already ancient, by American standards, but the others were still on the youngish side. Dartmouth had not granted its first degrees until 1771.

These institutions were the result of efforts by the colonial people and governments to transplant to America segments of the English universities. The two great English universities, founded in the middle ages, were institutions where scholars taught and learned. There, the teaching and degree-granting institution was the university. The word university, which now denotes an institution of higher learning, is derived from the Latin expression *universitas,* which originally could refer to any aggregation of persons recognized as a unit or corporation. In the medieval period, the term was sometimes applied to various sorts of guilds and associations, but in time the term came to be limited to associations of teaching masters and their scholars. The corporate existence of these persons was assured by charters from the popes (since learning was considered a prerogative of the church), from the emperors (who claimed authority over institutions in their realms), or from the kings of the rising national states (who were jealous of the authority of popes and emperors). Often, of course, the corporations antedated the charters issued by these various authorities.

In time, students at the universities began to live in special housing units. These were commonly called colleges, the word college signifying merely the association of persons with a common interest. (The term survives to our day in this special sense in "college of cardinals" and "electoral college." Neither is a place where one goes to educate oneself, either for the cardinalate or for the electoral function.) A university often included several colleges, and in time some of the teaching was transferred to the colleges, though the university retained the degree-granting privilege.

When our colonial ancestors ventured to bring higher learning to America, they modestly began with colleges, since the size of the prospective student body and the colonial resources did not warrant founding a more comprehensive university on an ambitious scale. In fact, there was considerable question whether even a modest college could survive.

Founding of Harvard   The founding of Harvard in 1636, destined to be the only fully operating college in English-speaking America for nearly 60 years, is succinctly described in a document known as *New England's First Fruits,* written in 1643:

> After God had carried us safe to New England, and wee had builded our houses, provided necessaries for our liveli-hood, rear'd convenient places for Gods worship, and setled the Civill Government; One of the next things we longed for, and looked after

Harvard College in 1770, an early engraving by Paul Revere.

was to advance Learning, and perpetuate it to Posterity; dreading to leave an illiterate Ministry to the Churches, when our present Ministers shall lie in the Dust. And as wee were thinking and consulting how to effect this great Work; it pleased God to stir up the heart of one Mr. Harvard (a godly Gentleman and a lover of Learning, there living amongst us) to give the one halfe of his Estate (it being in all about 1700£) towards the erecting of a College, and all his Library; after him another gave 300£, others after them cast in more, and the publique hand of the State added the rest: the Colledge was, by common consent, appointed to be at Cambridge, a place very pleasant and accommodate and is called (according to the name of the first founder) Harvard Colledge.

The college had been inaugurated by the general court (legislature), but historians question whether or not it would have survived except for the death and providential bequest of the Rev. Mr. Harvard. There are numerous other instances of colleges being named after benefactors (Doane, Baldwin-Wallace, George Pepperdine, Yale, for example), but the Rev. Mr. Harvard certainly got a bargain for his modest bequest in having named after him an institution destined to rise to so great a place in American education.

Purposes of Colleges It is a part of American folklore that all the colonial colleges were inaugurated to prepare ministers. Here the quotation from *New England's First Fruits* (about replacing the ministers lying in the dust) is overdone. Certainly preparing persons with sufficient education to become ministers was important, but it was by no means the exclusive function of the early colleges. The curriculum reproduced the rather dry, formal program of the English universities, which historians admit had fallen into an unfortunate decline after the first promise of the Renaissance had wilted. Such as it was, the colonial college curriculum was thought to embody the linguistic and classical education required of any gentleman.

Arid as it may have been, the curriculum introduced the rough colonial boys to the best thoughts of eminent men of antiquity. It should be remembered that the founding fathers of the republic were schooled in this curriculum. We say "boys," for students went to Harvard, Yale, William and Mary, and the other colleges at an age much younger than do present-day freshmen. Cotton Mather, who admittedly was a bit of a prodigy, entered Harvard at the age of twelve. Students of fourteen or fifteen were not at all unusual. Admonition was usually tried for the first breach of academic regulations, but beating was commonly practiced. The first president of Harvard was dismissed for beating an usher (an instructor, one would now say) for the space of two hours with a "cudgel big enough to have killed a horse, and a yard in length."

Student Life in Colonial Days   Despite the prescriptive regulations of early Harvard, its students had a gay time, drinking, playing cards ("very instruments of the devil"), and gambling. Hazing was a favorite sport. So much was Cotton Mather troubled by the lawlessness of his classmates that his father, the Rev. Increase Mather, rode out to Cambridge to register a complaint, first to the tormenters and then to the acting president. He threatened to remove Cotton from the school, but the masters "were loth that I should do it yet could not give satisfactory answers to my reasons." The biographers of Cotton Mather conclude that Harvard "wove one more heavy strand to a disposition already weighted with piety, filial duty, and the fear of sudden death."[2]

Even as now, students in college complained of their food. Students at Harvard told an investigating committee that the president's "lady" served them watered beer, mackerel "with the guts left in them," and hasty pudding that tasted like "goats' dung."

All Small Institutions   Yale, originally known as the Collegiate School, had a most unpromising beginning, despite a reasonably liberal endowment by Elihu Yale, a colonial who had amassed a fortune as a military governor in India. Like the tabernacle in the wilderness, the Collegiate School wandered from town to town in Connecticut until it was finally settled at New Haven because of "the amenity and salubrity of the air and the cheapness and abundance of victuals." As a part of the deal, it was agreed that Hartford could have the new state house if New Haven got the college.

All of the colonial colleges were small institutions. Harvard began with nine students, and the number remained small throughout the period before the Revolution. Kings College (Columbia) had ten students in its first class, of whom just half persisted to graduation in 1758. Of the five others, "one in his third year went to Philadelphia, one about the middle of his second year went into the army, a third after three years went into merchandise, a fourth after two years went to privateering, and a fifth after three years went to nothing." This

2 Boas, Ralph and Louise: *Cotton Mather*, Harper, 1929, pp. 27–38.

pattern of small beginnings was later to be repeated with the founding of other colleges on the ever-moving western frontier. Many a sophisticated college of the present day had most humble beginnings.

Deism The colleges were early accused of various forms of radicalism. Yale was founded because ultra-conservative New England clergymen were appalled by the liberalism of Harvard. Many of the colleges took up the contemporary European philosophy of Deism, a belief in a personal God combined with scepticism of Christian revelation; this leaning toward Deism brought down upon many colleges the antagonism of the conservatives. Obviously the modern style of complaint against college professors and students for their disconcerting and dangerous views is nothing new.

A Venture in Faith It must have taken a great deal of faith in the future for the colonists to open grammar schools and colleges, particularly in the earlier years of the settlements. When the whole of Old England had but two universities, the various colonies had established nine colleges, rather well distributed from Massachusetts to Virginia. It was touch-and-go with certain of these institutions for many years, but they did manage to survive even the rigors of the Revolutionary War. With their student bodies depleted, with their faculties scattered, and with their buildings used in some instances for the quartering of troops, these colleges had nevertheless so thoroughly demonstrated their worth that soon after the Revolution they were reorganized and again dedicated to serving the needs of their constituencies. They served, too, as the prototype of many other colleges planted on the western frontier, as we shall see.

For Further Reading

Brown, Elmer Ellsworth. *The Making of Our Middle Schools.* Longmans, Green, 1921.
A good account of the Latin grammar school.

Brubacher, John S. and Willis Rudy. *Higher Education in Transition.* Harper, 1958.
A history of higher education in the United States, with an extensive bibliography.

Butts, R. Freeman. *The College Charts Its Course*. McGraw-Hill, 1939.
Chapters 4 and 5 deal with the colonial college, especially from the point of view of curriculum.

Cubberley, Elwood P. *Public Education in the United States*. Revised. Houghton Mifflin, 1934.
This and the accompanying book of readings sketch the work of the Latin school and give a short account of the colonial colleges.

French, William Marshall. *American Secondary Education*. Odyssey, 1957.
A chapter on the Latin grammar school, more complete than in most textbooks.

Holmes, Pauline. *A Tercentenary History of the Boston Public Latin Grammar School*. Harvard University Press, 1935.
A detailed account of the Boston Latin School. The first few chapters deal with the colonial period.

Martin, George H. *The Evolution of the Massachusetts Public School System. A Historical Sketch*. D. Appleton and Company, 1894.
The Latin schools of Massachusetts.

Maurer, Charles L. *Early Lutheran Education in Pennsylvania*. Dorrance, 1932.
The story of German language schools in colonial Pennsylvania.

Meyer, Adolph E. *An Educational History of the American People*. McGraw-Hill, 1957.
The first six chapters discuss the European background, "the Bible State," Southern laissez-faire attitude, and early practices.

Mulhern, James. *A History of Secondary Education in Pennsylvania*. Science Press, 1933.
Development of Latin schools, academies, and high schools. The early portion deals with the Latin school in the colony of Pennsylvania.

The New England Primer.
Published in many editions from 1690 well into the 1800's. The most readily available copy is a facsimile reproduction published by Ginn and Company.

Noble, Stuart G. *A History of American Education*. Farrar and Rinehart, 1938.
Considerable stress upon environmental influences on the development of American education. The first five chapters deal with the colonial period.

Reisner, Edward H. *Historical Foundations of Modern Education*. Macmillan, 1927.
Chapter 17 gives a background on humanistic schools which influenced the Latin school in the colonies.

Rudolph, Frederick. *The American College and University*. Alfred A. Knopf, 1962.

Chapter 1 deals with the colleges of colonial America. Stresses that they were class institutions to prepare the leisured few for leadership.

Wickersham, James P. *History of Education in Pennsylvania*. Inquirer Publishing Co., Lancaster, 1886.

Woody, Thomas P. *Early Quaker Education in Pennsylvania*. Teachers College, Columbia University, 1920.

Detailed study of the schools established in the Philadelphia area by the Society of Friends.

3

Education in a New Nation

The Colonial Way Persists   With the Declaration
of Independence and the successful termination of the Revolution
with the Treaty of 1783, the United States became an independent
nation. It would be too much, however, to expect that a new system
of education would emerge immediately. The colonial concept of
education and colonial practices were destined to cast a long shadow
over the new republic for several decades. Merle Curti contends that
as late as a little over a hundred years ago "American schools still
bore the characteristic impress of the colonial era" in that they still
"reflected the class prejudices and the religious interests of colonial
society." He maintains that the colonial inheritance was so stubborn
that it "seriously interfered with the educational plans and democratic aspirations of Revolutionary patriots, idealistic humanitarians,
and educational reformers who desired to broaden the basis of the
public schools and endow them with new social and cultural functions."[1]

Indeed, from the viewpoint of many recent criticisms of our public
education,[2] and from the viewpoint of those seeking a democratic
education open to all children regardless of color, creed, nationality,
economic status, or any other limiting factor, it would still be very
justifiable for Mr. Curti to attribute many modern educational problems to the survival of some of our old colonial concepts.

We see, then, the persistence of the colonial pattern, particularly
into the national period. Small children went to dame schools or to
the simple reading and writing schools, if they went at all. Some
children were taught at home, either by tutors in the case of wealthy

[1] Curti, Merle: *The Social Ideas of American Educators*. Littlefield, Adams and Co.,
Paterson, N.J., New Student Outline Series, 1959, pp. 3–4. By permission of the
American Historical Association.

[2] See particularly such books as Bestor's *Educational Wastelands* and *Restoration
of Learning*, Lynd's *Quackery in the Public Schools*, Smith's *And Madly Teach* and
The Diminished Mind, Rickover's *Education for All Children*.

36

The interior of an early dame school.

families, or by parents in other families. And a large share of the children grew up illiterate or with only a bare minimum of formal education. Here we must caution the reader against too close an association between illiteracy and lack of intelligence; some illiterate people are very intelligent. Some literate people aren't very intelligent.

A small portion of the children had, as they grew older, an opportunity to attend academies, the secondary institutions which had succeeded the Latin grammar schools. A still smaller number attended the colleges which had survived the Revolution or had been reestablished soon after the war was over.

The characteristics of the schools on each of these three levels will be treated in detail in the subsequent chapters. Here we are concerned with an over-view of education in the early national period.

Education and the Democratic Ideal Success of the Revolution assured rejection of the idea that there should be an official aristocracy with special privileges. Very soon after our Constitution was adopted and put to use, the fate of the new nation was entrusted in principle to the wisdom of the people. In contrast with the European system, this was indeed a revolutionary situation. Privilege did its utmost to assert itself, through limitations on the ballot, through limitation of popular participation in public affairs, and through economic and social sanctions, but clearly the day of privilege was passing.

Having adopted the principle that government in America should be conducted by the verdict of the people, the founders of the republic turned to education, stressing its importance as the best insurance of the perpetuation of a democratic state. Benjamin Franklin had already foreshadowed this emphasis by establishing his academy in Philadelphia. Now several of the best minds turned to the formulation of comprehensive and visionary plans for a system of education in the infant republic.

What form of education is most compatible with a republican form of government? Can education be consciously employed to assure the perpetuation of a democratic society, organized as a republic? Can education be for all? What should schools teach in the new social order? These were among the questions which faced thinking men right after the Revolution.

The Essayists

Some of the founding fathers referred only briefly to education as an essential to the republican form of government, but a surprisingly large number went further with comprehensive essays. The leading essays were written by Benjamin Rush, surgeon general of Washington's army and a founder of Dickinson College; by Robert Coram, a Revolutionary pamphleteer; by James Sullivan, a pamphleteer and jurist who later became governor of Massachusetts; by Nathaniel Chipman, jurist and later United States senator; by Samuel Knox, physician, minister, and president of the Frederick Academy in Maryland; by Samuel H. Smith, who later established *The National Intelligencer,* an influential newspaper; by Amable-Louis-Rose de Lafitte du Courteil, a French emigré who taught at Bordentown Academy in Pennsylvania; by Pierre Samuel DuPont de Nemours, French political economist and statesman who founded the DuPont powder factory in America; and by Noah Webster, New England scholar and dictionary author.

Though each essay reflects the individuality of its author, certain central themes run through most of these essays. These men took it for granted that America's distinctive republicanism demanded a peculiarly American system of education. Almost all the writers projected education as a national opportunity, a national endeavor, and a national responsibility, with a highly centralized organization. All assumed that education should be public, free, universal, scientific, pragmatic, and utilitarian, aiming at social progress through conscious educational effort.

We cannot here present the details of each of these essays, but certain points from several will be mentioned briefly. The reader is cautioned that this is a selective summarization.[3] Rush advocated a uniform system of education for all, to prepare for citizenship. He anticipated Herbert Spencer, the English educational reformer, by championing the teaching of science, and by suggesting the replacement of Greek and Latin by more functional and utilitarian subjects. In his proposed eight-year curriculum he included reading, spelling, speaking, writing, arithmetic, natural history, geography and history —especially the history of republican institutions. All citizens, he said, should be taught a "supreme regard" for their country—not blindly through indoctrination but through a complete exposure to republican principles and duties. He went so far as to say that the schools should convert men into "republican machines." In what may have been a jocular vein, he advocated "schools of forgetting" which he said teachers, legislators, and divines should be encouraged to attend!

Writing of the "wretched state of the country schools," Coram advocated a general tax for the support of schools adapted to American needs. It should be the responsibility of government, he said, to secure a proper education to every child. Equal representation demanded equal educational opportunity, not only among classes, but also between town and country areas.

Sullivan looked upon schools as the best agency to free the American people from "slavish adherence" to European ways. Schools should provide a universal education, free from religious or political domination. Chipman, too, believed that principles of democratic government could best be assured by a national system of education.

Knox thought that elementary education should be terminal for some and preparatory for admission to higher schools for others. He wanted a national system of public education, including a national university. Smith wanted a national school system to stress the scientific attitude and to place emphasis upon invention, experimentation, discovery and resourcefulness.

Lafitte du Courteil and DuPont both advocated a national system, under democratic but central control. Webster wanted to use the

[3] The writings of Rush, Coram, Sullivan, Chipman, Knox, Smith, Lafitte de Courteil, DuPont de Nemours, and others may be examined in a more extensive summary by Allen O. Hansen in *Liberalism and American Education in the Nineteenth Century* (Macmillan, 1926).

schools consciously to develop an American patriotism and to set the stage for continuing human progress.

American Philosophical Society   The American Philosophical Society, the oldest scientific society in America, had been founded in Philadelphia in 1743 by Benjamin Franklin and his associates. It had early concerned itself with such practical phenomena as the uses of plants, improvement of cider and wines, new methods of preventing and curing disease, and various other utilitarian and philosophical experiments. After the success of the Revolution, the Society turned its attention to the role of education in a republic. The members viewed education as one of the most pressing problems facing the new nation. The society accordingly offered a prize "for the best system of liberal education and literary instruction, adapted to the genius of the government of the United States; comprehending also a plan for instituting and conducting public schools in this country, on principles of the most extensive utility."

Several essays were submitted, but all have been lost except the two submitted by Knox and Smith, previously referred to. They divided the prize. Essays by the other writers cited above, though not formally entered in this essay contest, probably gained more attentive readers by appearing in the favorable climate of educational discussion encouraged by the Philosophical Society.

Philosophical Basis of Essays   All these essay writers had been deeply influenced by the dominant ideas of the late eighteenth century, commonly called the period of the "Enlightenment." It can be clearly demonstrated that these ideas came to America from the contacts of Americans with the French revolutionary philosophers and with liberal Englishmen. Among those who gave birth to these enlightened ideas we may mention Marie Jean Antoine Nicolas Caritat, Marquise de Condorcet, commonly called Condorcet; Jean Jacques Rousseau; Helvetius; and John Locke. Many Frenchmen and liberal English thinkers had been elected to membership in the American Philosophical Society, as certain Americans had been elected to French and British societies. (Among Frenchmen elected, the student of history will recognize such names as Lavoisier, LaFayette, Barbe de Marbois, Vergennes, Talleyrand, and DuPont de Nemours.)

Allen Hansen summarizes these revolutionary ideas which influenced the American education plans:[4]

---

[4] Hansen, Allen O.: *Liberalism and American Education in the Eighteenth Century,* New York: Macmillan. 1926.

1. Mankind and human institutions are infinitely perfectible; there is no limit on possibilities for human progress.

2. Man can determine and regulate the lines of his progress.

3. Flexible, not static, institutions are necessary for human progress.

4. Institutions exist only to further man's progress.

5. Education is the principal means of progress.

Education and the Constitution   The United States is one of the few nations of major importance in which the national government does not control education. With us, the theory is that the regional State government is educationally sovereign, and that the state in practice delegates a degree of this power to local instrumentalities known as school boards. We shall see fluctuations in this theory as we survey our educational history, but it still remains the orthodox American answer to the question: Who shall control education?

At the time the federal constitution was written, education could have been declared a function of the federal government, along with defense, regulation of commerce, etc. The point remains, however, that there is no mention of any relation of the federal government to education. It should be remembered that the British view of education as a function of the home and church was still dominant in most of the states. Further, the constitution was a conservative document put together by essentially conservative men. Some of them shared the Jeffersonian belief that that government governed best which governed least. Neither in Britain nor in France, then the leading powers in the world, was there a precedent for national control and support of education. In England, all was laissez-faire; in France, still a monarchy, the church dominated schooling. It is true that some mention of education was made in the constitutional convention, with a particular suggestion that Congress be empowered to establish a university and seminaries for the promotion of the arts and sciences, but the convention seems to have agreed with Gouverneur Morris that such specifics were unnecessary, since "the exclusive power at the seat of government will reach the object." It could be that Morris and others could not anticipate the tenth amendment to the constitution which stated that "the powers not delegated to the United States by the Constitution, nor prohibited by it to the States, are reserved to the States respectively, or to the People."

There is a point of view that the Supreme Court, which finally decides what the constitution means, could in a grave emergency find that federal control of education would not necessarily be unconstitutional.[5] The point remains, however, that no congress has ever attempted to assert control over the national school system, so the court has never had to decide. As will develop later, the federal government has extended itself into various enterprises and aspects of education, but no substantial challenge has ever been made to the principle that State governments are responsible for educational control. Yet from the earliest period, the federal government was forced into involvement in education wherever the states had no jurisdiction. This was the case with the Northwest Ordinance, which granted federal lands for schools in territories where future states would be newly organized. Not even Thomas Jefferson, who favored strict construction of the Constitution in favor of states' rights, felt justified in challenging this federal activity in the area of education.

Views of Founding Fathers   From Washington to the present, presidents and important statesmen have expressed an interest in the promotion of education. Such expressions were common in the early days of the republic. Washington recommended establishment of a national university and even left a part of his estate for that purpose.

Jefferson, of all the founding fathers, took the most active interest in education. In 1779 he had proposed a bill for the establishment of public schools in Virginia. He would have divided the state into school districts and would have required each district to maintain a school for teaching boys and girls at public expense for three years and "much longer at their private expense" if parents or guardians chose to continue their attendance. At the end of the three years, each district was to select the most promising boy of poor parents for additional instruction at a grammar school, where tuition and maintenance would be free. After this grammar school education, the most promising were to be sent, again at public expense, to the College of William and Mary.

Though Jefferson's plan might be criticized today because it assumes an intellectual elite, limits free education of girls to primary grades and condescendingly grants education to the poor with the heavy hand of charity, still it was so visionary in its day that it could not be adopted. Land-holding legislators who could purchase

5 See pp. 380–381.

education for their children were not prone to furnish education free to the less fortunate citizens, with the funds coming from taxes. Still, there is in Jefferson's proposal the embryonic form of a free, modern system of education. It took a long time for the embryo to emerge, and when it did, it came to a great extent through the New England tradition.

The Decline of Schools However much we may admire the post-Revolutionary proposals made concerning the extension of schools and educational opportunities, the times were unfortunately not propitious for their achievement. The sparse distribution of America's 3,000,000 inhabitants over thirteen states and the western territories militated against any well-organized achievement of nationwide social objectives. Transportation and communications were crude. The Revolutionary War had exhausted the nation. Debt and threatened repudiation of government obligations plagued the economy. Many other matters engrossed the people—most of whom, after all, weren't sure they really needed schools anyway. Though the states undoubtedly had legal authority over schools, they let this authority decline through disuse. What energy went into concern for schools was usually directed toward academies and colleges, not toward a system of common or public elementary schools. And yet how could secondary schools and colleges be developed without a widely developed base of fundamental education in the common school subjects?

The Decline in New England As a result of the tendencies cited above, the schools declined to their lowest point since they had first been founded by the colonies. Nowhere was this more true than in New England and New York. So much emphasis is placed upon the leadership of these two states in later educational reforms that the student is sometimes unaware of the fact that education was at a low ebb there from the Revolution to the period of the so-called common school "revival" in the 1830's.

The Town System One of the reasons for the low status of education was the district system, which had divided states into microscopic districts, each almost sovereign in the conduct of its schools. Originally, the town in Massachusetts had been the unit of local administration. (By "town" was meant

a geographical division of the state which would be called a township in other parts of the country.) These towns were irregular in
area, following the rivers, creeks, and hills which abound in New
England. The nicely geometrical-patterned townships of the West
were highly impracticable.

At first, all citizens were required to live at the "center," of
the organized community, within a half mile of the meeting house.
This assured their greater protection from marauding Indians, their
attendance at the church service, and the enrollment of their children in the town school. With the decline of the extreme emphasis
on orthodoxy early in the 1700's, and with the constant American
impetus to push on to independent farming on unsettled land, the
restrictions regarding residence gradually broke down. Someone
would move to a more remote portion of the town (i.e. township)
to carve a farm out of the wilderness, to set up a mill or a forge near
a fast-running stream, or just to get away from prying neighbors.[6]

Thus the town as a unit disintegrated. People still came to the
center to attend church and to participate in the civic affairs at
the town meeting, but they found it difficult and often impossible
to send their small children long distances through mud and snow
to the town school. Whether or not their children went to school
the parents were still compelled to pay taxes for the school's support.
Nothing could be done until the number of people living away from
the center in the various small communities outnumbered those
living at the center. Then they could marshal their forces and go
into a town meeting and demand a redress of grievances. At this,
the people in the rough-and-tumble town meetings were very adept.
These town meetings were a democracy at its grass-roots level.

The Moving School   The first compromise
effected was the moving school. The master now moved from community to community, holding short sessions at separate schools in
each area. The proportion of instructional time depended upon the
amount of school taxes each settlement paid into the town funds. In
theory, the children were free to migrate with the teacher; however,
in practice, they usually attended only when the school was "kept"
near their own homes. Sometimes it took as long as three and a half

6 On many a wooded New England hillside one can still find stone fences among
the trees, giving evidence that once a sturdy yeoman and his family tried to eke an
existence out of its rocky soil. After a generation or two, the family abandoned the
homestead, either to move to a New England mill town or to move "west" to the
fertile valleys of New York, Pennsylvania, the Ohio country—and even to Oregon.

years for the teacher to "go around the town." Obviously, this was an unsatisfactory solution.[7]

The District School   Localism was rampant in early America. There was pressure not only for the division of the town for school purposes, but also for towns to be broken up into smaller units for road maintenance, for recruiting militia, and for collecting taxes. Formation of small school districts, several to a town, was a logical step. Such authority was granted late in the eighteenth century. Power to elect school trustees, levy school taxes, and elect a teacher was granted by Connecticut in 1766 and by Massachusetts in 1789. This is the origin of the one-room country school district which was carried by New England people into states as far as the west coast. At the time, these small districts served a useful purpose, but by the 1830's it had become apparent to Horace Mann that the law authorizing them was "the most unfortunate law on the subject of education ever enacted in Massachusetts." In our own time we have seen serious efforts to reduce the number of school districts in the United States. These efforts, with their success and their failure, will be discussed in Chapter 20. Suffice it here to say that once Humpty Dumpty had been shattered into many pieces, it took valiant effort by all the king's horses and all the king's men to put him together again. For a long time the little red schoolhouse (which more often than not was white) continued as the only school of the people.

The First State Superintendent   New York enacted a law in 1795 to distribute $100,000 of state funds to the counties for the maintenance of common schools. Yet this early experiment excited so little enthusiasm that it was allowed to expire after only five years of life. Soon afterward, however, immigration of many New England people into the state strengthened those natives who wanted state support. By 1812 the first permanent school act in New York was adopted. Through this act the district system was instituted, local taxation was required, and provisions were made to distribute state funds. Futhermore, in one of its most significant sections, the 1812 act provided for the appointment of a state superintendent of common schools.

---

[7] In remote areas of Canada a school train operates to this day. A school car is switched off on a siding, school is held for some days or weeks and then the car is moved to another location. This, too, is a moving school, but the whole school (except pupils) moves, not just the master. And he does not have to "board around."

The man named to the state superintendent's position was a young attorney named Gideon Hawley. Portraits made later in Hawley's life always show him as an elderly man of stern visage and with ample white sideburns, although he was actually only 27 at the time he became superintendent. Other than for the reproduction of a portrait and brief mention, most educational histories have badly neglected Hawley's reputation. It is not generally acknowledged that he performed "one of the finest pieces of constructive and administrative work for the public interest in New York's history."[8] Few persons have had a longer or more fruitful association with the development of a state's educational system. Except for one nine-month period, he served the cause of education in New York from 1813 to his death in 1870. Hawley served as superintendent of common schools from 1813 to 1821, and concurrently as secretary of the Regents of the University of the State of New York from 1814 to 1841, and as a regent from 1847 until 1870. Had it not been for the vicissitudes of New York politics, he would undoubtedly have remained longer in the state superintendency.

Hawley adhered to the party of DeWitt Clinton. When the Van Buren forces triumphed in an election, they began a systematic housecleaning in the state offices. While it is true that they were merely carrying out a tradition of spoilsmanship, they went too far in removing Hawley. The legislature refused to sanction this "gross outrage," and passed a law constituting the Secretary of State as an ex officio superintendent of common schools. Hawley continued as secretary to the Regents, but was removed from the common school arena, for the Regents were concerned only with secondary education and the colleges and universities.

Hawley's Achievements   Hawley was an efficient administrator, for he assiduously collected statistics, recommended changes in the education laws, and perfected a system for the careful management of the permanent school funds. He extended compliance with the school law into the most remote areas of the state. In an age when the common school curriculum consisted almost exclusively of the three R's, and these scantily taught, Hawley advocated requiring the schools "to embrace a more extended course of study," since these schools were "the only channels for the general diffusion of useful knowledge." Each school was urged to pursue a course of instruction "as liberal and comprehensive as its circumstances warrant." Hawley wanted these added to the curriculum:

8 Smith, Ray B.: *History of the State of New York*, pp. 342–343.

English grammar, "beauties of the Bible," geography, surveying, history and Constitution of the United States, with sections of the criminal code.

He also wrote on methodology. Two passages in particular are striking:

> In the instruction of youth, the first object of a teacher should be to make study a voluntary and agreeable employment. . . . Unwilling study is always languid, and the impression received from it, necessarily feeble and transient. . . . To effect this important end, the study of the pupil should be adapted to his capacity; a given task, limited to what he can easily perform, should always be assigned to him; he should be assisted in his progress by the kindness and attention of the teacher.
>
> To exercise the reasoning faculties of youth, by giving them clear and distinct ideas of what they should study, and accustoming them to a practical application of their knowledge, is not of less importance than making study voluntary and agreeable. Knowledge is lasting, in proportion as it is the result of thought and reflection. . . . [Students] are not made to study understandingly, and to apply what they learn to practice; their knowledge is too apt to be mechanical, a mere matter of rote, lodged only in the memory.

In his eight years, Hawley had laid "the foundations of a permanent and noble system of education." The number of schools had more than doubled, and attendance had greatly increased. In 1821 it was reported that 96% of the children of school age had attended at some time during the school year.

Lack of Concern   While the schools of the New England states, of New York, and of Ohio remained in a relatively favorable position in the early part of the nineteenth century, not so much can be said for the schools in the other states. In the case of Indiana and Illinois, early school progress was hamstrung by conflict of the two educational philosophies brought into the states by settlers from other sections. Migrants from New England and New York found that their school plans were resisted by migrants from states accustomed to the laissez-faire and parochial-school concepts of education. Many other states, from Pennsylvania south, were reluctant to make any fundamental changes in the educational structures they had developed from colonial traditions.

Northwest Territory   After the Revolution,
settlers from other regions began to move in large numbers into
the territory west of the Appalachian mountains and north of the
Ohio River. With the completion of the Erie Canal in 1825, the
migration went on at a more rapid pace. In some instances, whole
congregations moved west with their minister and with their traditions. Since a large share of these migrants came from New England,
new territories as a whole were strongly interested in education.

The states along the Atlantic seaboard renounced their claim to
lands west of the Appalachians. Until the time these new lands were
formally admitted as states, the regulation of them fell to the lot of
the national government. Even before the adoption of the Constitution, Congress had enacted the Ordinance of 1785, which provided
for a land survey of the Northwest Territory and for the reservation
of the sixteenth section of each township for the maintenance of
schools. This did not require that schools be built upon this sixteenth section. The land was to be rented or sold by the state and
the proceeds devoted to education. The Northwest Ordinance of
1787 contains the oft-quoted statement: "Religion, morality, and
knowledge being necessary to good government and the happiness of
mankind, schools and the means of education shall forever be encouraged." This was a pious pronouncement that doubtless had a
great moral value, but it did nothing toward the support of schools
beyond what the earlier ordinance had prescribed. Possibly, the
resolution may have made migration more attractive to Eastern people who read in it an assurance that their children would not need
to grow up in ignorance.

The precedent of the land grant was followed in the admission
of Ohio, first, and then in the admission of all the other states with
the exception of Texas (which had been an independent nation),
Maine, and West Virginia, which had been formed from older states
already in the Union. After 1850, more than one section was allotted
for school purposes. Because their lands were of low value, four sections were allotted in Utah, Arizona, and New Mexico.

In recent years the advocates of federal aid to education have read
into these land grants an indication that the national government
intended them primarily to encourage education. Those who oppose
federal aid, on the other hand, declare that Congress was not com-
mitting itself to a permanent program of aid but was merely offering
inducements to fill up the wilderness with settlers.

These land grants appear to have suggested to older states that
they, too, should establish permanent school funds to subsidize
schools in an age when a general tax for that purpose would not

have been found acceptable. After 1787, several states did establish such funds. When Connecticut sold its "Western Reserve" in Northern Ohio in 1795, it appropriated the price of $1,200,000 to a permanent school fund. Other states built their school funds from other sources, including annual appropriations and state lotteries. These permanent funds did serve to get public schools started in some of the states, but it soon became evident that they would be woefully inadequate to support the number of schools needed.

Philanthropy in New York   The cities along the Atlantic Seaboard were naturally more conscious of needs for schools than were the rural regions. Since the state governments were not disposed to establish these schools, a number of philanthropic individuals organized societies to accomplish this purpose. These philanthropists were working out of a spirit of brotherly love, it is true, but they were also striving to protect their property and the social order from the consequences of allowing indigent children in the cities to grow up illiterate and without moral training. In England, philanthropists met a similar problem in the same way. If a public agency would not act, then a philanthropic and quasi-public one would.

In 1785, the Manumission Society was organized to "mitigate the evils of slavery, to defend the rights of the blacks, and especially to give them the elements of an education." It opened a school for Negro children in 1787. The "Association of Women Friends for the Relief of the Poor" engaged a widow and opened a school for indigent white children.

These schools paved the way for and ultimately merged with the New York Free School Society, which later changed its name to The Public School Society of New York. It should be noted that while the society did include "public" in its title, it was not public in our sense of the word. DeWitt Clinton, then mayor and later governor of New York, was the guiding light of this society. Since its aim was "to provide schooling for all children who are proper objects of a gratuitous education," the society was nonsectarian. Both the city and state granted it financial assistance. Eventually, when free public schools were established, the society went out of existence, having served its purpose. Its buildings and equipment were given to the New York school district.

In many other Eastern cities, similar societies were formed—in Philadelphia, Washington, Albany, Providence, Savannah, Baltimore, and others.

Monitorial Schools   Operating schools designed
to offer a free education to all the indigent children of a city was
a relatively expensive proposition, even if a teacher could be obtained at a very low expense. No wonder then that these societies
clasped to their bosoms a man named Joseph Lancaster, who had
just arrived from England with a novel procedure. Lancaster, an
English Quaker, and Dr. Andrew Bell, a Church of England minister, apparently hit upon the same idea at about the same time, and,
as is so often the case, spent considerable energy in trying to out-do
one another.

The idea was simple. The teacher would teach certain older,
abler pupils. They would be monitors and would teach the other
children. Ordinarily, a monitor was responsible for ten pupils. The
scheme worked, after a fashion, in the teaching of reading and religion. It was better than nothing, and it was cheap. One master could
be responsible for a student body of 200 or more—even a thousand,
it was claimed.

A master supervising while his monitors
teach in an early Lancasterian school.

Lancaster was all the rage in America. He was invited to address the Congress of the United States. He was honored wherever he went. Monitorial schools sprang up quickly—in Albany, Schenectady, Philadelphia, Lancaster, Pittsburgh, Erie, Baltimore, Norfolk, Richmond, Louisville, Hartford, and many other places. The large and influential Public School Society of New York adopted the plan and even prepared people to become Lancasterian teachers. So many communities wrote to DeWitt Clinton for advice that he even established a teacher's placement agency. Some monitorial high schools were established.

Though the monitorial schools were too mechanical and relied almost exclusively upon memoriter learning and repetition, they did serve three purposes. They did give an education of sorts to thousands of boys and girls who might otherwise have been neglected. They served, too, to awaken the public to the need for public schools. Then, finally, they focused attention on group instruction in the place of individual tutoring.

Toward a New Idea   Though the Lancasterian schools pointed out the need for a better system of education, it took a long time to achieve the free public school. By 1830, however, there were definite signs that a better way would be found. How this was accomplished and how much effort was involved will be the theme of Chapter 7.

For Further Reading

Beck, Walter H. *Lutheran Elementary Schools in the United States.* Concordia Publishing House, 1939.

Chapter 1 gives a summary of Lutheran schools (Dutch, Swedish, German) in the colonies and in the early national period.

Burns, Rev. J. A. and Bernard J. Kohlbrenner. *A History of Catholic Education in the United States.* Benziger Brothers, 1937.

Chapter 4 presents the problems of educating Catholics in the early days of that faith's organization in the United States.

Conant, James B. *Thomas Jefferson and the Development of American Public Education.* University of California Press, 1962.

Conant's analysis of Jefferson's persisting influence upon education.

Cubberley, Elwood P. *Public Education in the United States.* Revised. Houghton Mifflin, 1934.

Chapter 4 deals with "early national and state attitudes."

Cubberley, Elwood P. *Readings in Public Education in the United States.* Houghton Mifflin, 1934.

Several sources regarding early national attitudes and problems in education are given in selections 63 to 79.

Curti, Merle. *The Social Ideas of American Educators.* Revised. Student Outline Series. Littlefield, Adams and Co., 1959.

Chapters 1 and 2 deal with the social aspects of the schools in the early national period.

Drake, William E. *The American School in Transition.* Prentice-Hall, 1955.

Chapter 4 gives emphasis to the realistic movement. Brief summary of plans for reform of American education.

Elsbree, Willard S. *The American Teacher.* American Book Co., 1939.

The educational developments during the early days of the republic are summarized in Chapter 11.

French, William Marshall. "The First State Superintendent of Schools." *School and Society.* Vol. 47, No. 1222 (May 28, 1938).

Contributions of Gideon Hawley to development of education in New York.

Good, Harry S. *A History of American Education.* Second Edition. Macmillan, 1962.

Chapter 3 discusses education in the new republic.

Hansen, A. O. *Liberalism and American Education in the Eighteenth Century.* Macmillan, 1926.

Plans presented to the American Philosophical Society for a system of education in accord with republican ideals.

Knight, Edgar W. *Education in the United States.* Ginn, 1941.

Chapter 6 discusses "the promise of a new period."

Knight, Edgar W. *Public Education in the South.* Ginn, 1922.

Chapter 5 describes Jefferson's plan of education for Virginia and the work of lesser Southern leaders.

Noble, Stuart G. *A History of American Education.* Farrar and Rinehart, 1938.

Chapter 6 on "Liberalism in Education, 1775–1800" and Chapter 7 on "Education During the First Forty Years of the Republic, 1790–1830."

4

The Basis for Educational Reform

An Age of "Great Movements"   Burgeoning American democracy could not permanently be content with educational procedures and institutions which had been inherited with only slight modifications from the colonial era. Great changes could be attempted and achieved when the time was ripe, but such a time did not come until the 1830's and 1840's.

Agitation for the establishment of free public schools was not an isolated movement of reform. It was closely interrelated with other reform movements and the changing social and economic conditions of the time. The interest in the achievement of a policy of state-supported, universal, common-school education was interwoven with other progressive trends. These included such movements as: the spread and implementation of democracy, improvement in the social order, urbanization, growing nationalism, religious upheaval, immigration, the rise of the labor movement, humanitarian crusades, communistic experimentation, the industrial revolution, and the increase in national wealth.

Having burst the straitjackets of Puritanism and rigid traditionalism, nineteenth-century men found themselves free to act in a number of new fields. The decade of the 1830's in particular was, as William Ellery Channing said, "an age of great movements." The age, he said, showed a unique "tendency and power to exalt a people" through the progress of the whole human race.

The interest in education in the early decades of the nineteenth century was to a large extent an outgrowth of a sociological theory that education could be a means of attaining greater moral strength and material prosperity, and a means of relieving the sad lot of much of humanity. William Russell, principal of an academy in New Haven, expressed his faith in education thus: "The information,

53

the intelligence, and the refinement which might be diffused among the body of people would increase the prosperity, elevate the character, and promote the happiness of the nation to a degree perhaps unequalled in the world." From the writings of this period, one could compile hundreds of similar statements.

Arguments that education promoted prosperity and served to diminish crime were used forcefully and effectually by early propagandists for free schools. Addresses and state papers manifested the faith of speakers and writers in the efficacy of education—even in the formal memoriter style of education then current. With one exception, all the governors of New York from George Clinton, the first, to the governors of the Civil War period referred to education in their messages to the legislature. While some of these messages may be written off as the platitudinous generalities to which public officers are addicted, too many of them were backed up by earnest work to be discarded lightly.

E. C. Wines, a Philadelphia schoolmaster, declared that through education of all the people, the nation could reduce crime and pauperism as well as lessen the influence of "theatres, circuses, gaming, horse racing, licentiousness and intemperance." S. S. Randall cited prison statistics in New York: from 1840 to 1848, he said, 27,949 persons were convicted of crime; of these, 1132 had received a common school education; 414 had a "tolerably good education"; only 128 were well educated. Of the remaining 26,225, only about half could read and write; the "residue were destitute of any education whatsoever."

Horace Mann, in a classic address in 1839, set forth society's right and obligation to educate the child even in the face of parental objection. In a western state, the argument took this more flowery form: "Far better to pay taxes which will rise like vapors to descend in refreshing showers, than to build jails, penitentiaries and almshouses."

The Growth of Democracy   The growth of democracy, especially as manifested in extension of the franchise, operated in such a way as to show the necessity for at least a minimum degree of schooling. The early part of the century saw the fall of the Federalist party with its Hamiltonian, aristocratic tendencies, and the "rise of the common man." Such a rise brought forth two reactions: first, it enabled the common man to vote himself schools; second, it made the remaining conservatives more willing to help provide a minimum of public schooling for the people, whom Hamilton had characterized as "a great beast," in order to protect conservative property from an ignorant electorate.

Education for Citizenship

The theory of education for citizenship was current in political and educational literature. In the former field, such men as Thomas Jefferson, De-Witt Clinton, Levi Lincoln, and Edward Everett were stressing the value of education in a democracy. In the field of education, the same message was broadcast by Carter, Mann, Barnard, Gallaudet, Lindsley, Woodbridge, and others.

In England, increasing democratization of education closely followed a series of extensions of the suffrage. With the possible exception of the amendments regarding Negro and woman suffrage, the United States has had no national legislation comparable to the English extensions of suffrage. Here the extension has come in individual states at various times. But here, too, such legislation was followed by extensions of educational opportunity. The clearest-cut case is in Rhode Island. For years, there had been a struggle for enfranchisement and for the substitution of a new constitution for the colonial charter under which the state still operated. Eventually, the Dorr rebellion resulted. Shortly thereafter, there were extensions of suffrage and of education. Henry Barnard was called from Connecticut to be secretary of the state board of education.

In the rest of the country, general manhood suffrage had become almost universal by 1828. To a far greater extent than before, it was now realized that the right of more people to vote demanded more education. Now, as James Truslow Adams said, the people had their opportunity to express themselves at the polls. And it became the function of education to raise up a generation that would not rock the boat of the republic by making wrong choices.

The necessity of a degree of education for all voters was shown by Thomas Cooper in 1829. He said there were then abroad "notions that tend strongly toward an equal division of property, and the right of the poor to plunder the rich. The mistaken and ignorant people who entertain these fallacies as truths, will learn, when they have the opportunity of learning, that the institutions of political society originated in the protection of property." There were many similar expressions to the effect that education was a conservative force, essential to the preservation of the then existing social order. There was then as much concern with education against agrarianism as there has been in recent years against communism and "creeping socialism."

Another reason for the extension of education was the fact that "common men" were now being elected to office. Thus, additional doors of education and opportunity needed to be opened to poor youth so that they might be better prepared for public office.

Urbanization   Urbanization, too, contributed to the demand for better schools for a greater proportion of the children of the land. As long as the great majority of persons remained in agricultural pursuits in rural areas, following the folkways of their ancestors, no great demand was heard for any considerable improvement in educational opportunities or standards. Until recent times, the American farmer has been a very conservative person. Only when later decades brought good roads, easy communication, modern appliances and conveniences, and such social organizations as the Grange did the farmer make any marked advance over the folkways of his ancestors. Hamlin Garland's books well describe the circumscribed life on the farm even after the Civil War.

But when the people began to crowd into the cities in ever-increasing numbers to carry on the factory work made possible by the industrial revolution, they created social and economic problems of vast proportion. Both the laborers themselves and humanitarians saw that education was the most promising source of solution to these problems. Humanitarianism and trade unionism coincided in time with urbanization and the industrial revolution.

It was, therefore, primarily in the cities that the new industrial, political, and social relationships had to be worked out. Small children were unmercifully exploited in the factories. Some persons held that child labor was a positive good. Alexander Hamilton contended poor children were better off in a factory than in a school, but humanitarians saw the danger of an uneducated proletariat arising unless education were made available. This was the genesis of the Sunday School movement in America: children who worked in mines and factories for 10 to 16 hours a day, six days a week, were to be taught the fundamentals and some religion on Sunday.

The need for education was very great in the congested cities, but there was usually sufficient concentrated wealth there to supply a sound base for philanthropic contributions and for school taxation. Consequently, the urban areas forged ahead of the rural communities in educational progress. It was the most rural areas which resisted longest the Pennsylvania and New York free school acts. Only after the urban areas had fully developed the provisions of these laws, and the more progressive rural areas had begun to see their importance, did it gradually become possible to enforce compliance in the more remote areas.

Nationalism   Increased nationalism engendered by the war of 1812 was another, though minor, factor contributing to the demand for schools. A struggle with an enemy, particularly if it be long and of uncertain outcome, seems to result in demands for educational reform and expansion. To cite but a few examples, this was true in Germany during the Napoleonic wars, in England in World Wars I and II, and in the United States during our wars of long duration. Certainly we are aware of the cold-war motivation for educational reforms and extensions in recent times. Indeed, we have contemporary legislation significantly called the National Defense Education Act.

The contribution of education to national unification was not unrecognized in America. One of Noah Webster's aims in writing his "speller," readers, and dictionary was avowedly patriotic.

When Calvin E. Stowe reported to the Ohio legislature in 1837 on his inspection of European schools, he pointed out that the Prussian schools attempted to awaken a strong national spirit. Other visitors abroad also began to sound more clearly the note of nationalism in American education. They began to portray the school as the bulwark of a republican form of government and as an essential to the defense of the nation.

The Religious Factor   When extreme Calvinism became embattled with Unitarianism, and when all the Protestant denominations became concerned about the immigration of large numbers of Roman Catholics, there arose a demand for a non-sectarian public school as a means of compromising and escaping these religious controversies in education. Thus the Massachusetts board of education and Horace Mann advocated teaching the commonly agreed-upon parts of the Bible as a generally inoffensive religious compromise. They were opposed by orthodox Calvinists, who claimed such a common denominator would necessarily be "the lowest and least religious form of Unitarianism," but the public schools weathered the controversy because they had the only practicable solution. Methodists, who were not in favor of parochial schools, showed a great growth in numbers and in influence in the first half of the nineteenth century.

In New York, the fear that the Roman Catholics would ask for state-aid for their parochial schools (as the non-denominational but

Protestant-oriented Public School Society had done successfully) resulted in a demand for truly public schools. No one seemed to care that this would not be a satisfactory answer for the Roman Catholics. In many speeches, Catholicism was portrayed as a "traditional enemy of free institutions," although a few men, such as Governor William H. Seward of New York, did espouse the cause of parochial and foreign language schools.

The many sects of urban areas could not afford to maintain separate schools. Even less could the churches in sparsely settled rural areas. The logical answer seemed to be the expansion of a system of public education under lay control. After an acrimonious controversy in New York, which saw Hebrews and Scotch Presbyterians allied with Roman Catholics against Methodists, Episcopalians, Baptists, Dutch Reformed, and Reformed Presbyterians, the legislature created a city board of education to establish real public schools, and forbade the awarding of any portion of public funds to any school in which "any religious sectarian doctrine or tenet should be taught, inculcated or practiced."

Immigration   The United States
has traditionally had the reputation of welcoming to its shores and to its citizenship the oppressed and the economically disadvantaged

A cartoon of the late Nineteenth Century depicting
the welcome hand extended to immigrants.

from all over the world. No lists were kept of the early immigrants, but it has been estimated that 200,000 came from the inauguration of the national government until 1819. In the next decade, the number was 140,000. In 1830–1840, the figure was 600,000, and in 1840–1850, the number was 1,700,000. By 1850, it was estimated that 2,800,000 of the population was foreign-born, constituting 12% of the total inhabitants of the United States. Political revolutions on the European continent and the Irish potato famine of 1845 sent tens of thousands to our shores. Before the American people was a whole continent waiting to be tamed, and we relied upon foreign labor to do much of the work. It was primarily Irish laborers who dug the Erie Canal—not with huge earthmovers, but with pick and shovel and wheelbarrow. Factories needed more laborers than the native population could supply. Railroads required a huge reservoir of construction workers.[1]

But many people thought our republican institutions were imperiled by the dilution of our citizenry by so many people who came from lands where monarchy and despotism still prevailed. Ardent hostility was demonstrated by riots and the development of the Know-Nothing political party. More sober voices pointed out that the immigration was inevitable and that it strengthened the country economically. Many were convinced that even if they could not Americanize the first-generation immigrants, they could make good citizens of the second generation through the agency of education.

The work of Edward Austin Sheldon in Oswego, New York, (like that of Pestalozzi, with whom he has often been compared) began as a purely humanitarian enterprise. Appalled by the condition of poor French Canadian and Irish children in that community, he organized his "ragged school," and thus became interested in public education. It was from this ragged school that the public schools of Oswego developed. Sheldon became the superintendent of schools, and when his unofficial teacher-training classes became the nucleus of New York's second normal school, he became principal of that school.

Conditions of squalor, congestion, and disease were frightening in the hovels into which many of the immigrants were crowded. In 1849, for instance, 39 Irish immigrants were found living in one small cellar. In Lowell, 120 families inhabited one building. Often six to eight lived in one room and slept in one bed. In New York, owners of slum property had a yearly 100% return on their investment.

The first attempt at improving such conditions through education was the establishment of charity schools, such as Sheldon's in Oswego

---

[1] It is said that the word "paddy" for railway track laborer comes from "Patrick," indicating that the Irish dominated this work.

and the Public School Society's in the metropolis. These, as we have seen, were transformed into public schools.

Attitude of Organized Labor

By 1836, it is estimated, there were 300,000 men enrolled in the labor union movement, principally in the manufacturing states of southern New England, New York, and Pennsylvania. Philadelphia and New York were in the vanguard of union organization.

The writings of union leaders strongly emphasize the importance they placed upon education. The Philadelphia workers in 1829 demanded reform in education to provide for an open ladder from the infant school to the higher grades, free and open to all. They demanded competent teachers and a state system of education under the direction of responsible, popularly elected officials.

Stephen Simpson, one of the outstanding leaders of labor in the early part of the nineteenth century, advocated free public schools for the self-improvement of the worker. In his volume *The Working Man's Manual,* he declared it was "the ignorance, not the occupation of the working people, that degrades them on the one hand, and impoverishes them on the other." He demanded public education—"not, however as a bounty, or a charity, but as a right; that all contribute their share of labour to the expense and support of government, so all are equally entitled to the great benefits of popular instruction." This is the voice of labor, conscious of its strength and demanding action.

A labor resolution in 1830 declared that "next to life and liberty, we consider education the greatest blessing bestowed upon mankind." The *Farmer's and Mechanic's Journal* in 1838 recognized that relatively few out of the many could receive more than a common school education, but insisted that every child in the republic should at least receive this basic schooling.

The historian of the labor movement, Richard Ely, concluded that the efforts of the early friends of labor were directed largely to the public school as the necessary educational agency in our democracy, and that the present public school is in part the result of labor agitation.[2] The whole educational system, he said, was more largely due to the movement to benefit the working masses than to any other single cause.

When general trades unions coalesced in 1834 to form the National Trades Union, the interest in education continued. The new union

2 Ely, Richard T.: *The Labor Movement in America.* Crowell, 1890.

agitated for public education and the democratization of the schools. In 1835 the associated unions were called upon to name committees to examine the systems of education in their respective states and communities. The national union made it clear that it would not approve subsidizing private secondary institutions from public funds, since such a distribution of funds was held to be contrary to "republican principles."

Although the direct and immediate initiative for public schools may have come from humanitarians, educators, and students of social questions, labor soon took over this agitation and made it its very own.

Humanitarianism   The preceding part of this chapter has mentioned the role of the great humanitarians in helping to create a conscious need for the free public school, common to all the children of the community. The humanitarians looked upon education as the most important agency for the amelioration of many social problems. Was a man an alcoholic? Education could have saved him. A criminal? That was because he had not been taught the right, or how to make an honest living. A spendthrift, a wastrel or anything else? Still education was the panacea, the antidote for the present generation and a preventative for the next.

Many of the greatest names in the humanitarian crusades were also associated with education. Dorothea Dix, whose work improved the lot of the inmates of prisons and asylums, began her career as a teacher. Her interest in the education of the lower classes continued throughout her life.

Thaddeus Stevens exemplifies the identity of leadership in education with that in other humanitarian endeavors—in his case, in the cause of abolition. In fact, history has chosen to remember Stevens for his work in abolitionism and in the vindictive punishment of the South during reconstruction, and has pretty well neglected his nobler efforts to bring a system of public education to Pennsylvania. It was largely through his efforts that the free school law of 1834 was passed in that state.

Horace Mann chose to devote his life to a variety of great causes. In the field of education, he was for many years secretary of the board of education in Massachusetts, editor of a school journal, and writer of reports that were influential with educators abroad as well as throughout the United States. In addition, Mann was a pioneer in higher education in the West (that is to say, in Ohio), and a U.S. Congressman (successor to John Quincy Adams) active in the ranks of the abolitionists. The Rev. Samuel May, one of Mann's normal school principals, was even better known for his role in abolition than in education.

Thus many of the leading reformers in the first half of the nineteenth century were reformers in education as well as in other causes such as abolition, temperance, labor organization, feminism, the care of the insane, and the education of the handicapped.

The Industrial Revolution   The phenomenon we call the industrial revolution is not something embalmed in history. While the typical student may think of it as something that happened in the United States and in other great nations, particularly in Great Britain, in the first half of the nineteenth century, we now know that we are still in the period of this industrial revolution. Automation is only a new aspect of this same historic movement that is very much with us today.

There were two important conditions that stemmed from this industrial revolution: the tremendous increase it produced in the national wealth, and the problem it created in the inhumane exploitation of children in the first half of the last century.

The early machines, such as power looms, created a tremendous demand for cheap, ordinary labor. Only the ability to perform a few simple operations with great dexterity was required. One did not need to know how to read or write, multiply, or diagram a sentence. Since children from time immemorial had worked around the house and later the farm or shop, it was natural that they be moved into the factory. Here they participated in repetitive work rather than in the numerous activities of a simpler age. Their opportunity to learn was greatly reduced. Further, they were worked for unreasonably long hours—hours so long that they went from bed and breakfast to work and from this work to supper and bed. Though Rousseau had forcefully pointed out some fifty years earlier that children were entitled to a childhood, the factory now entirely absorbed their time and energy.

Here the humanitarians took over and insisted that children should be in school, for their own welfare and for the well-being of the nation. Needless to say, those who waxed fat and rich from the cheap labor of children were horrified at proposals to limit their labor and to compel children to attend school. They insisted a child of seven or eleven had a constitutional right to work twelve or more hours a day. It was not until 1840 and 1842 that Connecticut and Massachusetts, respectively, passed mild acts to place some restriction on the labor of children in factories. Charles and Mary

Beard, the historians, commented that the early child labor laws, as enacted by legislatures, had loopholes through which a camel could pass. The New Hampshire law of 1847 is typical: no child of less than 15 years of age could work more than ten hours a day without the written consent of parents or guardian. Unfortunately, many parents were willing or desperate enough to write the consent. There were instances of a father's taking his children to a factory early in the morning, then adjourning to a tavern to while away the day until he could pick them up after dark and escort them home.

As late as 1900, the federal census revealed that 2,000,000 children were gainfully employed. Among their jobs were shucking oysters, manning spindles in cotton and silk mills, dipping chocolates, plucking chickens, and separating slate from anthracite coal. But such labor was held to be their constitutional right. Men and women who wanted to regulate child labor, to protect children from exploitation, were termed "radicals" and "socialists." Even as late as 1915, Scott Nearing was unceremoniously dismissed from a position as assistant professor of economics at the University of Pennsylvania because his agitation against child labor earned him the enmity of powerful local manufacturing and financial interests.

A coal miner but still a child.

The child labor situation shows a bit of the seamy side of the Industrial Revolution in its relation to education. Fortunately, we can also observe a brighter influence related to the revolution.

Rise in National Wealth   When a machine takes over work formerly done by the hands and muscles of man, it can produce a uniform product more easily, more quickly, and much more economically. And the machine can release man from much hard toil.

How many women would need to be employed to mix, roll, and bake without mechanical contrivances the crackers eaten each day in the United States? How few men and women do make them by the aid of automatic machinery which carries through the whole process from mixing the ingredients to wrapping the finished carton? How much stooping and lifting is saved by machinery on an automobile assembly line? Machines create both wealth and leisure and both of these are prime essentials for education.

While the first impact of the machine age was to crush many children under the heavy press of long labor, in the final analysis it was humane use of machinery which produced the wealth that could be taxed for school purposes.

The word *school* is derived, interestingly enough, from the Greek word *scholay*, which originally meant leisure. The present relevance of this is clear: unless one can be spared the leisure from the work of the world, he can't go to school. When the machine age advanced far enough, we could dispense with the labor of children and send them to school. Certainly, there would be consternation in our present society if children, 2,000,000 or more strong, stormed into industry for work. Yet that number was employed only a few decades ago. In proportion to the population then and now, the number would be closer to 5,000,000.

In the first half of the nineteenth century, the wealth of the nation multiplied decade by decade. Shipping interests made fortunes in international trade, especially after the development of the clipper ship, which virtually gave the United States mercantile command of the seas for many years. Manufacturing and merchandizing progressed by leaps and bounds. The National Road and the Erie Canal increased a mutually profitable trade with the West. The growth of cities added to land values and to taxable wealth.

By 1836, the treasury of the United States was so full of surplus revenue that it constituted an embarrassment to the federal government, despite huge expenditures in Clay's "American System" of internal improvements and pork-barrel legislation. A bill was introduced to distribute the money among the states. The bill was amended to deposit the money with the states, subject to the demands of the treasury. The bill became law, and the so-called surplus revenue was distributed the next year. Though the money "deposited" was not ear-marked for any purpose, some states devoted all or a part of it to education. Some states just wasted their share. Maine and Pennsylvania used some of the principal for schools. New York distributed income from investments to the schools, both elementary and secondary. Twenty-three of the twenty-six states then in the union used at least some of the fund or its interest to aid schools.

America was, by mid-century, reaching that stage in her exuberant growth when she could afford education for a greater proportion of her children. All the factors mentioned in this chapter served to show the need. Now America needed only to be aroused to action.

The early decades of the nineteenth century, particularly the 1830's, appear to have been the years in which the pattern of American life was being worked out in the great social laboratory of the nation. While the detailed pattern of the great sociological movements was not yet complete, the pattern was emerging. Such was the case in the development of the common school system. While many years were still needed to bring the schools to their present form, there were many indications to show the shape these developments would take. We now turn to these developments in elementary, secondary, and higher education.

For Further Reading

Bourne, E. G. *History of the Surplus Revenue of 1837*. Putnam's, 1885.

The origin and the disposition of the funds deposited with the states by act of Congress in 1837.

Brubacher, John S. *Henry Barnard on Education*. McGraw-Hill, 1931.

The educational influence of Henry Barnard, with quotations from his writings.

Carleton, Frank T. *Economic Influences upon Educational Progress*. University of Wisconsin, 1908.

Stress on the influence of economic factors in determining educational developments. Rise of national wealth as an important factor.

Cubberley, Elwood P. *Public Education in the United States.* Revised. Houghton Mifflin, 1934.

Chapter 5 deals with "influences tending to awaken an educational consciousness," including philanthropy; social, political, and economic factors, including labor movements.

Fish, Carl R. *The Rise of the Common Man.* Macmillan, 1927.

The changes brought about by increased democracy. Chapter 10 refers to education.

Martin, George H. *The Evolution of the Massachusetts Public School System. A Historical Sketch.* D. Appleton, 1894.

The schools of Massachusetts before and after the humanitarian movement.

Reisner, Edward H. *Evolution of the Common School.* Macmillan, 1930.

Gradual changes in the schools, their methods and curricula.

Tiffany, Francis. *Life of Dorothea Lynde Dix.* Houghton Mifflin, 1890.

Life of a teacher who became one of the very great humanitarians, especially in awakening America to the reform of its prisons and asylums.

Williams, E. I. F. *Horace Mann.* Macmillan, 1937.

A standard biography of the great humanitarian-educator.

5

Early Elementary Schools

The Colonial Heritage   The United States
entered upon nationhood with a great amount of colonial baggage
encumbering it. This was particularly true in the realm of education.
In New England, the district school system was continued without
change, and there also existed a large number of private and proprietary schools for persons who did not care to patronize the public
institutions. Edward Everett Hale, author of *The Man Without a
Country,* recounted in later years that his parents would as soon
have sent him to jail as to a public school in Boston.

In New York, Pennsylvania, and Maryland, the parochial-school
concept prevailed, with additional charity schools such as the ones
the Public School Society soon established for children of the poorer
classes. In the South, education was largely a matter for home and
church, with some "missionary" schools being maintained by the
Society for the Propagation of the Gospel in Foreign Parts.

All these schools, of whatever nature, were simple institutions to
promote reading and writing and the simplest elements of arithmetic. In both the public schools of New England and in the parochial
schools and mission schools elsewhere, there was a distinctly religious
flavor.

Well into the national period, there were no special institutions
to prepare teachers for these schools. Anyone with only a modicum
of knowledge and ability to discipline unruly children was held fit
to be a schoolmaster. There were no state certification standards, so
each district or each governing board could hire whomever it chose
to direct the destinies of a school. With teachers generally lacking
even minimum skill in pedagogy, the schools concentrated upon
memoriter learning and blind repetition of the basic text. The
teacher dared permit no deviation, for his knowledge did not extend
farther.

New Texts by American Authors   Up to the
Revolution, most of the few textbooks in American schools were
imported from England. Exceptions to this generalization were the
New England Primer, two spelling books of decidedly limited cir-
culation, and foreign-language texts used in schools of the Germans
("Pennsylvania Dutch") in Pennsylvania.

Almost at once after the close of the war, school textbooks by
American authors began to appear. To the natural zeal of persons
to write a book, another motive was involved in their publication.
The United States was undergoing a nationalistic movement characteristic of any colonial people who have recently cast off the shackles
of the mother country. We now witness much this same reaction in
the large part of Africa which has recently attained its independence
from Britain and from France.

A new republican state, operating under a republican constitution,
wanted to assert its educational independence, and there was a ready
supply of authors to help it do so.

Webster's Spellers and Readers   We can not,
in a general text, make a detailed study of all those textbooks which
poured from the American presses, but we can touch upon the more
prominent ones which had a profound influence upon the education
of the American people. The one text most esteemed by successive
generations of Americans was *A Grammatical Institute of the English
Language* by Noah Webster.[1]

This text was divided into three volumes or parts, a speller published in 1783, a grammar the next year, and a reader in 1790. These
were commonly known as part one, part two, and part three; the first
part was most frequently referred to as the "Blue-back Speller" from
the color of the paper covering the cardboard binding.

While he modeled the speller on English books, particularly Dilworth's *Guide to the English Tongue,* Webster had in mind to
produce a distinctively American book. Webster saw the possibility
of using school books to form the American mind, American language usage, and American patriotism. This he did, unashamedly
and without equivocation. "The spelling book," he said, "does more
to form the language of a nation than all other books." Webster's
biographer points out that he did not propose to restrict his first
textbook merely to the teaching of correct spelling, but had the

---

1 The full title is *A Grammatical Institute of the English Language, Comprising
an Easy, Concise, and Systematic Method of Education, Designed for Use of English
Schools in America.*

wider objective of moulding the national thinking and national manners. The preface to the speller states his objectives:

> To diffuse an uniformity and purity of language in America, to destroy the provincial prejudices that originate in the trifling differences of dialect and produce reciprocal ridicule, to promote the interests of literature and the harmony of the United States, is the most earnest wish of the author, and it is his highest ambition to deserve the approbation and encouragement of his countrymen.

The speller warned Americans of vulgarisms, which had crept into the language in the colonies. He told them to say "chimney" instead of "chimbley"; "resin," not "rozum"; "confiscate," not "confisticate." Fables and little moral tales were included, as well as a "federal catechism" and a considerable amount of American geographical knowledge.

The second part of the *Institute* was "a plain and comprehensive grammar founded on the true principles and idioms of the language," prepared especially for American schools. Wherever he felt justified in doing so, he accepted current American usage instead of the rules of the preceding grammarians. Still, there were 29 pages of a grammatical catechism, several pages of false syntax and 58 more pages of finer points in grammar and punctuation.

The third part of the *Institute* contained reading and speaking selections ("pieces," they were commonly called), carefully chosen to develop a patriotic American and nationalistic spirit. Instead of "pieces" selected from classical authors, he emphasized the speeches and the writings of the Revolutionary fathers. On the title page was this quotation from Mirabeau: "Begin with the infant in his cradle; let the first word he lisps be Washington."

Of the three parts, the speller was the most successful—so successful indeed that the royalties supported the Webster family while the author was working on his famous *Dictionary of the English Language*. In one year, 1828, the sale was 350,000 copies; by 1843, it had reached a million copies per year. A study of early school texts points out that Webster's was the only common school book that saw the opening of the nineteenth century and was still in use by thousands of children when the century drew to its close. Near the end of the century, it had been removed from urban and more progressive schools, but it was still extensively used in the more remote rural areas.

The reader never achieved so great a circulation, for it had formidable competitors in *The American Preceptor* by Caleb Bingham and in *The English Reader* by Lindley Murray. These, and other lesser known books, followed Webster in the inclusion of many patriotic selections and in the attempt to cultivate manners and the fundamental virtues of truth, honesty, and thrift.

Morse's Geography

The Rev. Jedediah Morse in 1784 published an *American Universal Geography,* emphasizing the geography of the United States. The next year, a revised and abbreviated edition was published under the title of *Elements of Geography.* This was very different from present-day geographies, for it was a small, 144-page book with but two maps in black and white, and no illustrations. Like Webster in his speller and grammar, Morse sounded a patriotic appeal.

> Till within a few years we have seldom pretended to write and hardly to think for ourselves. We have humbly received from Great Britain our laws, our manners, our books, and our modes of thinking, and our youth have been educated rather as the subjects of a British king than as citizens of a free and independent republic. But the scene is now changed. The revolution has been favorable to science in general; particularly to that of the geography of our own country. In the following sheets the author has endeavored to bring this valuable branch of knowledge home to the common schools. . . .

Two competing geographies soon appeared, *A Short but Comprehensive System of the Geography of the World* by Nathaniel Dwight, and *Rudiments of Geography* by William C. Woodbridge. The availability of these books served to introduce the study of geography into the common and secondary schools of many districts, as well as into academies and even into Harvard College.

Grammars

Throughout the colonial era, when one spoke of grammar, he commonly meant Latin grammar. English grammar was not commonly taught, it being assumed that one would learn basic grammar from usage. Some private-venture schools advertised the subject, but it was introduced into very few district schools or academies. Franklin, however, included it in the curriculum of his Academy in Philadelphia. The text most commonly used was Dilworth's *New Guide to the English Tongue,* published in England in 1740. After the Revolution, the most popular for some years was *Webster's Grammatical Institute of the English Language,* but the one destined to be most widely used for the longest period of time was *English Grammar* by Lindley Murray, a Pennsylvania Quaker residing in England. So extensive was the circulation of various editions and abridgments of his book that he has frequently been called "the father of English grammar." These texts commonly dealt with orthography, etymology, syntax, and prosody.

Arithmetics   Several English arithmetics had been reprinted ("pirated" might be a better word) in the colonial period. The most popular of these was Thomas Dilworth's *The Schoolmaster's Assistant, Being a Compendium of Arithmetic both Practical and Theoretical.* This book contained all the commonly taught phases of the subject in a single volume; separately graded arithmetics did not appear until about 1830. The book had subdivisions devoted to whole numbers, vulgar fractions, decimal fractions, questions, and duodecimals. Under decimal fractions, the author treated square root, cube root, sursolid root, second sursolid root, square biquadrate root, and squared square cube root. Some of the problems under "questions" were posed in poetic form, while many other items were presented in catechetical form.

The first native American arithmetic was produced by Nicholas Pike in 1788. It was said to be "composed for the use of the citizens of the United States." His *A New and Complete System of Arithmetic* carried testimonials of President Stiles of Yale College, the governor of Massachusetts, and other prominent men. It was a profound volume which contained not only the fundamentals of simple arithmetic but also algebra, geometry, trigonometry, mensuration, and conic sections. Among items treated were cross multiplication, tare and tret, barter, alligation, calculation of Easter until the year 4199, and many other topics which have long since disappeared from arithmetics. It included a treatment of the new coinage system of the United States, but the problems were still concerned with English money. An *Abridgment* was published when it was found that the original was far beyond the capacity of pupils and teachers alike. Numerous other arithmetics followed Pike's in rapid succession. The most noted of these were Warren Coburn's *First Lessons in Arithmetic on the Plan of Pestalozzi,* soon to be renamed *Intellectual Arithmetic upon the Inductive Method of Instruction,* and Joseph Ray's *Eclectic Arithmetic,* later to be revised and printed in three separate graded volumes known as *The Child's Arithmetic, Mental Arithmetic,* and *Practical Arithmetic.* By the time Ray wrote his books in 1834, textbooks were being published in Cincinnati as well as in Boston and Philadelphia, which had had an early monopoly in their production.

Histories

For some years after the Revolution, the teaching of history as a separate subject was not common. The first elements of historical information were conveyed in readers, spellers, and geographies. As early as 1785, a book entitled *Introduction to the History of America* was compiled by liberal use of scissors and paste by a Philadelphia printer, John M'Culloch. In 1802, Noah Webster, a prolific writer, published his *Elements of Useful Knowledge,* volume 1 of which was called *Historical and Geographical Account of the U.S. for the Use in Schools.* Webster's son-in-law, C. A. Goodrich, in 1822 published a more popular work, *A History of the United States,* which brought history down through the administration of President Monroe. A widely-read series was prepared by S. C. Goodrich, who wrote under the *nom de plume* of Peter Parley.

McGuffey's Readers

The series of books outselling all others for use in the common schools were the famous McGuffey *Readers* compiled by the Rev. William Holmes McGuffey, a frontier clergyman and college president. These readers were a graded series of six books. Some authors speak of them as six graded readers; the present author hesitates to use this terminology, for he has found by experience that casual students read this to mean a sixth-grade reader. There were six readers, graded in difficulty from the primer stage to an anthology for students in the highest grades of the common schools.

Since McGuffeyism has become somewhat of a cult in American life, a more extended treatment will be given to these readers than to any other textbooks used in the common schools. It is interesting to note that McGuffey was solicited to write the *Readers* by an enterprising publisher in Cincinnati. McGuffey, indeed, was the publisher's second choice for authorship, the first and unsuccessful offer having been made to Catherine Beecher of the famous Beecher family which also produced Harriet Beecher Stowe. Though the books attained a high circulation, McGuffey's contract called for royalties up to only $1000 for the first four readers. His brother,

Alexander, wrote the *Fifth Reader* for another small fee, and William compiled the *Sixth Reader*. In 1920, it was estimated that more than 122,000,000 copies of these books had been sold since 1836. They were standard texts in almost all the states, particularly west of the Appalachians and in the South.

The McGuffey *Readers* were termed eclectic, apparently a favorite word with the publisher, who had already published Ray's *Eclectic Arithmetic*. The word signified a selection from many sources, and this was characteristic of these readers. Choice selections were made from American folklore, and from "The Best American and English Writers." It was emphasized that these were "Elegant Extracts" in both prose and poetry.

To a child in rural America in the nineteenth century, the McGuffeys furnished his first contact with the elegant society of

A page from the first reader of the McGuffey Reader series.

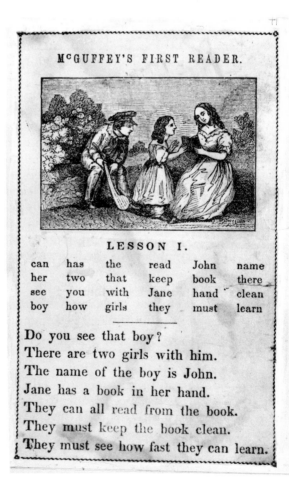

MᶜGUFFEY'S FIRST READER.

LESSON I.

can	has	the	read	John	name
her	two	that	keep	book	there
see	you	with	Jane	hand	clean
boy	how	girls	they	must	learn

Do you see that boy?
There are two girls with him.
The name of the boy is John.
Jane has a book in her hand.
They can all read from the book.
They must keep the book clean.
They must see how fast they can learn.

cultured people. Coming from homes which often had no reading material or such scanty material as a few free patent-medicine almanacs distributed by firms which made liniment and remedies "good for man or beast," the children of the frontier found in the McGuffeys real guides into some of the better thinking of men worthy of emulation. This, it would appear, explains the hold of the McGuffeys upon the affection and veneration of successive generations of self-made men. Titans of industry would reminisce about the McGuffeys' part in their character formation and would, on the least provocation, quote *verbatim* long passages from the texts.

Henry Ford had so high a regard for William Holmes McGuffey that he reprinted the *Readers* and had his birthplace near Washington, Pennsylvania, dismantled and moved to his museum of Americana at Greenfield Village, Michigan. A speaker, representing Henry Ford at the centennial observation of McGuffey's readers, declared that "Abraham Lincoln, William Holmes McGuffey, and Thomas Edison are the three Americans Henry Ford reveres most." More than 3000 members of the Federated McGuffey Societies of America attended the centennial observance at Miami University, Oxford, Ohio.

The McGuffey selections were, in the parlance of the day, called "pieces." In school, children read pieces, spoke pieces, played pieces. Every selection was a piece. Most of these pieces were chosen because they pointed a good moral lesson or condemned bad behavior: kind boys freed birds from their cages and bad boys pulled legs from live flies. There were many short homilies such as "Modesty is one of the chief ornaments of youth," and "Our best friends are those who tell us our faults and teach us how to correct them."

As Webster had done, McGuffey substituted a morality built upon secular experience for the gloomy moralizing of the Puritan texts. The texts emphasized the folk virtues of charity, honesty, temperance, truth, obedience, kindness, frankness, and reliability. They fitted perfectly into the psychology of the period and in turn served as the moral preceptor of many a youth whose formal education would terminate in the rural school. In a day when a school had few or no supplementary readers, a class might read and reread the same stories many times in a year. Further, in the one-room school, one would hear the younger children reading the same selections one had read and reread in years before, and at the same time one would also hear the more advanced students reading what one would meet in years to come. Thus, the difficult materials were not entirely unfamiliar, for one had heard them many times before one ever saw them.

Many of the McGuffey titles and "pieces" passed into the common language of America. When President Theodore Roosevelt told William Howard Taft in 1910 that "I don't propose to be a Meddlesome Mattie, but——," the American people knew at once just what he meant, even as an earlier generation recognized Lincoln's adaptations of the King James version of the Bible.

Not only did the *Readers* contain material to be read; they were liberally sprinkled with rules for reading and declaiming, beginning with the *Third Reader* and continuing through the sixth. One finds such rules as:

Be careful and give a full sound to the vowels. Regard to this rule will correct the common flat, clipping, and uninteresting way in which many read.

Following the "pieces," there were questions designed to show the reader what to look for in the selections and to provide the teacher with ready-made queries with which to test the reading.

Many persons who in later life achieved fame spoke in glowing terms of the McGuffey contribution to their character foundation and to their developing interest in reading and elocution.[2]

Other Subjects   The general scope of common school subjects has been covered in our discussion of spellers, readers, grammars, arithmetics, geographies, and histories. Practically no science was included in the early elementary-school curriculum. Such little science as was included was usually physiology. The first introduction of this subject in a school text seems to have been in Comenius' *Orbis Pictus,* a popular European text in Latin, published in 1658. But physiology came late into the district school in America. The earliest American physiologies, usually written by doctors of medicine, were technical in nature, dealing largely with the parts of the human body and their functions. Apparently no text before 1900 dealt in any way with reproduction. After 1850, the emphasis on the learning of names of bones decreased, balanced by a larger presentation of topics dealing with hygiene and the prevention of disease. Texas uniformly cautioned farmers not to drill wells where drainage from barns and outhouses could contaminate them.

[2] See in particular Hamlin Garland's testimony in his *Son of the Middle Border,* Macmillan Company, and Herbert Quick's observations in his *One Man's Life,* Bobbs-Merrill.

Penmanship did not call for textbooks, but copy books were a well-accepted means of teaching writing. After some practice on a slate, the pupil was advanced to copying pages of material, reproducing as neatly as possible a sentence beautifully engraved on the top line of the copy book. The author well remembers from early in this century a sentence, "white strawberries grow in Chile."

The Teachers
It was to the textbook that America looked for the education of her children. Written by learned, if frequently self-taught, men, the text brought a compendium of knowledge into the district school. The function of the teacher was not so much to enrich the presentation (for many teachers themselves had never passed beyond the confines of the text), but rather to hear lessons recited and to keep order.

Teaching was, as Ambrose Suhrie[3] pointed out, the "noblest of professions in theory and the sorriest of trades in practice." Frankly, teaching was not regarded as a promising calling. It was a vocation a young man might adopt while studying in a college, pursuing the independent study of law, or waiting for "something to turn up." It was also a discreet calling for a young woman who wanted to support herself until an eligible prospective husband came along. If one never did, then teaching assured the maiden lady a degree of independence she could not claim while living on the bounty of male relatives.

Typical of the student earning his way through college by teaching a winter term of district school was the schoolmaster in Whittier's *Snowbound:*

> Brisk wielder of the birch and rule,
> The master of the district school.
>
> *who*
> Sang songs, and told us what befalls
> In classic Dartmouth's college halls.
>
> *He was a man who*
> Could doff with ease his scholar's gown
> To peddle wares from town to town;
> Or through the long vacation's reach
> In lonely lowland districts teach

3 Suhrie's book *Teacher of Teachers* (Richard R. Smith Publisher, Inc.) is a goldmine of information on the changing status of teaching in the nineteenth and early twentieth centuries.

> Where all the droll experience found
> At stranger hearths in boarding round.

and

> Great Olympus at his will
> Became a huckleberry hill.[4]

Frequently, these masters were transients, moving from school to school and from teaching to some other vocation. Dr. Frank E. Spaulding recalled that in the latter part of the nineteenth century in Dublin, New Hampshire, during 21 terms of school he had twenty different personalities as teachers. Only one taught two terms, and these terms were separated by a few years. Most of these teachers were young, in their teens or early twenties. "Those twenty-one teachers were possessed of personalities so unimpressive that I remember them chiefly en masse, not as individuals," he wrote.[5]

Among itinerant schoolmasters were men who later achieved high places in American life in other callings. President James A. Garfield, while a student at Williams College in Massachusetts, crossed the state line and taught a rural school near Poestenkill, New York. Walt Whitman kept school at Smithtown Branch, Long Island. Thaddeus Stevens taught for a short time in Pennsylvania.

Most of the teachers were themselves products of the one-room district school. Some had attended an academy or even a college for a short time, but many had not. After 1839 there was a sprinkling of normal school students in the district schools, but these formed only a small percentage of the total number. Teachers' institutes and reading circles brought to some of these teachers a small introduction to methodology and a review of elementary-school subjects.[6]

The Schoolhouses   Schoolhouses were simple, box-like structures made of wood or of other native materials. Stone or brick might be used if they were plentiful and cheap. If of wood, the structure might be unpainted or it might be white or red. The little red schoolhouse of nostalgic memory and sentimental ballad was often white or a dingy gray where once-white paint had suffered the ravages of the elements. In the more progressive districts, two outhouses were located unobtrusively behind the schoolhouse. In many districts, there were no such facilities.

[4] Whittier, James Greenleaf: *Snowbound.* Copyright 1894, Houghton Mifflin Co.
[5] Spaulding, Frank E.: *One School Administrator's Philosophy: Its Development.* New York: Exposition Press, 1952, p. 103. (Dr. Spaulding later was superintendent of schools at Ware and Newton, Mass.; Passaic, N.J.; Minneapolis, Minn.; Cleveland, Ohio; and chairman of the department of education, graduate school, Yale University.)
[6] See Chapter 13.

The interiors of the schoolhouses were at first equipped with crude desks built in a continuous line next to the interior walls on three sides of the room. Against these were backless benches. When more pupils appeared than could be comfortably housed, they were just crowded closer together. At the fourth end of the room was placed a high desk, often on a platform, for the master. Small children, called abecedarians, often congregated at the base of this platform or in the open space at the center of the room when it was not used for recitations. Heat frequently was supplied by an open fireplace near the master's desk. Thus, he could keep warm, and if he needed to cool off, he could move about the room.

At a later period, double desks in rows were used, in turn to be succeeded by individual desks. Well into the present century, desks and seats were screwed to the floor. At first they were home-made locally, but in time a uniform product from school supply houses was used. In time, a stove (sometimes surrounded by sheet steel) replaced the fireplace. Sometimes, it was located in the center of the room, and sometimes along one side or end. In choosing seats on the "first day" in September, students had the choice of being too hot or too cold all winter.

The rough simplicity of an early schoolhouse.

In most cases, there was no further equipment, other than a plentiful supply of hickory switches for discipline. Some schools had blackboards—first wooden plaques painted black, and then later slate, but the trustees of many districts thought blackboards were a new-fangled idea that would only be a passing fashion. On rare occasions, a school might have a globe, a small collection of rocks, an unabridged dictionary and, rarer still, a small collection of books to supplement the texts. Rarely was there any artificial illumination, though occasionally one would find a "coal oil" lamp for use on stormy days. Drinking water came from a pail with a common dipper. This assured that all would democratically share in the measles, mumps, or chicken pox brought to school by any youngster. Frequently the school bore out the testimony of S. L. Pressey:

> The little red schoolhouse of sentimental memory in the crooner's ballad had inadequate lighting, no decent ventilation, unadjustable desks, and sanitation that was nothing to boast of. It was, in fact, an almost perfect environment for all children to contract every disease or disorder picked up by any member of the group.[7]

Attendance   Potter and Emerson, writing in the *School and the Schoolmaster,* reported that schools were vexed by frequent absences. They said that in Massachusetts more than a third of the registered "scholars"[8] were absent on an average day, and that absences in New York formed "a still greater proportion." Until such time as states saw fit to enact compulsory attendance laws, the teacher had no way of compelling pupils to come to school with any degree of regularity. Massachusetts was the first state to enact a compulsory attendance law, in 1852, but it was weak in nature and more marked by violation than by observance. Michigan's first attendance law was passed in 1871, New York's in 1874, Minnesota's in 1885, West Virginia's in 1897, Virginia's in 1908, and Texas' in 1915. When Mississippi finally enacted a law in 1918, all the forty-eight states then in the union had attendance laws, though they varied greatly in their requirements and enforcement. All the states upheld attendance laws until 1959, when the right to abstain from schooling was restored in those few Southern states that repealed their attendance laws as a means of resisting the Supreme Court's ruling on desegregation of schools.

[7] S. L. Pressey: *Psychology and the New Education.* Harper, 1937, p. 25.
[8] Those attending school in the 1800's were frequently called "scholars." Later, the term "student" came into greater use, to be followed by "pupil." Some teachers have suggested, in despair, that even "pupil" is too euphemistic and think "registrant" might be more appropriate.

The student who wants to obtain the vicarious experience of participating in the daily life of the country school will find two books of great value in recapturing the flavor of a by-gone age in rural America. One of these is a factual account, Burton's *The District School As It Was,* and the other a work of fiction, Edward Eggleston's *The Hoosier Schoolmaster.*[9]

The opening scene of the novel shows a young man, an applicant for the position of teacher in a rural school in Indiana, interviewing a seasoned school trustee, who begins

"Want to be a school-master, do you? You? Well, what would *you* do in Flat Crick deestrick, *I'd* like to know? Why, the boys have driv off the last two, and licked the one afore them like blazes. . . . They'd pitch you out of doors, sonny, neck and heels, afore Christmas."

When the prospective teacher persists, the trustee warns

"Ef you think you kin trust your hide in Flat Crick schoolhouse I ha'n't got no 'bjection. But ef you get licked don't come on us. . . . Any other trustees? Wal, yes. But as I pay the most taxes, t'others jist let me run the thing. You can begin right off a Monday. There a'n't been no other applications. You see, it takes grit to apply for this school. The last master had a black eye for a month. . . ."

Supervision   When all schools in New England were town schools, they were under control of the town meeting and of "prudential officers" appointed at the meeting. When districts were established, supervision fell to the lot of special lay officers, known in New England as the school committee, in Pennsylvania as the school directors, and generally elsewhere as the board of education, or even more commonly as the school board. Sometimes, the whole board inspected the school, usually after having given the teacher a few weeks' notice; sometimes, one member was deputized to be the official visitor.

New York in the early 1840's enacted a law providing for one or two persons in each county, known as deputy superintendents of schools, to inspect the schools in their respective areas. These superintendents, Horace Mann enviously said, were "men of superior

---

9 *The Hoosier Schoolmaster* is an American rural, folk classic. Hundreds of thousands of copies were sold from 1871 until comparatively recently. It was translated into French, German, Danish and was published in a "pirated" edition in England.

intelligence, practically acquainted with the business of school-keeping, and enthusiastically devoted to the duties of their office."

Urbanization of the American people resulted in a considerable growth in schools and in school business. Board members in large districts found that supervisory duties were too onerous, and at first solved the problem by having a hired secretary carry on school business in the name and subject to general supervision of the board. In time, this came to be a professional office rather than a professional duty of a lay officer. Buffalo, New York, was one of the first cities to have a superintendent of schools. By 1861, twenty-six cities had superintendents, although by 1870, there were still only 29. Statistics for 1962 indicate that there are now 155,650 chief administrators and staff associates in the public schools of America. Generally, the chief administrator is known as the superintendent of schools, but in some states certain districts have a supervising principal or an associate superintendent instead.

State Superintendent   New York had the
first state superintendent of common schools, Gideon Hawley, under provisions of an act of 1812. He continued in office until 1821, when the superintendency was assigned as an ex officio duty to the secretary of state. The separate superintendency was restored in 1854, this time under the title of superintendent of public instruction. This office was continued until 1904, when the state combined its elementary education and secondary education departments into one agency headed by a commissioner of education.

To all intents and purposes, Horace Mann was state superintendent in Massachusetts, though his legal title was secretary to the state board of education. Henry Barnard's title in Connecticut was secretary to the state board of commissioners for common schools. Michigan and the new states of the West generally adopted the title, superintendent of public instruction. Whatever their exact title, the state chief school officers are chosen in various ways. Certain ones, as in New York, are chosen by a state board of education; others, as in Pennsylvania, are chosen by the governor; still others, particularly in states which strongly came under the Jacksonian concept of the direct election of public officers, are elected by the people of the state along with other state officers. Professional opinion has it that selection by a strong, long-term, non-partisan state board is the best system.

The "One-Room" District School System   Throughout the
eighteenth and nineteenth centuries, the district school was typically

a one-room affair, though in larger villages and cities there were larger schools, often with several rooms. In the former, one teacher taught all the children at the various grade levels, working on a close schedule of recitations throughout the day. In the larger schools, pupils were graded, with one teacher commonly responsible for only one or two grades.

Completion of the program of the district school ended the formal education of most of the pupils. Indeed, many did not stay to complete the higher grades, there being no legal compulsion for them to do so. If a boy found school distasteful or if he "had a run-in with the teacher," he just quit. Often, a work opportunity seemed an attractive alternative to school attendance.

For those who did persist, the school offered an introduction to the literature of a polite society, mastery of the fundamentals of arithmetic, an introduction to the world through geography and history, a great deal of drill in English grammar, and thorough practice in reading and spelling. An older generation is prone to romanticize this little school, treasuring up moments of pleasure and forgetting or lightly passing over the tribulations and shortcomings. Ideally, a well equipped one-room school conducted by a well qualified teacher did offer a splendid learning environment where the older pupils helped the younger and the teacher got to know everyone's strengths and weaknesses. The difficulty was that these district schools were often poorly equipped and unsanitary, while the teachers frequently lacked both professional techniques and any knowledge beyond the textbook.

Nonetheless, the district common school did bring literacy to the masses and did promote a degree of homogeneity among people from many different social, political, and economic backgrounds. It taught common ideals to almost all the children of almost all of the people, the rich and the poor, the descendants of first settlers and the children of the latest immigrants from foreign lands. Were it not for the common school, the destiny of our nation might well have been different. The school opened doors for the poor but able boy to "get ahead" in the American social order. Thus were obviated the violent revolutions which upset many other nations.

The Leaders of the Common School   We have seen the contribution made to the advancement of the common elementary school by the textbook writers and by certain public-spirited leaders. There were many other persons who made contributions to the development of the school, and some of their efforts have already been partially described. At this point it would be well to note that there were many other pioneers in the early common-school movement. In addition to Horace Mann in Massachusetts, Henry Barnard in Connecticut and Rhode Island, and Gideon Hawley in New York, there were such other important educators as Thaddeus Stevens, "father of the common school in Pennsylvania," and Calvin H. Wiley, first state superintendent in North Carolina. There were John Griscom of New York, William C. Woodbridge of Massachusetts, and Calvin Stowe of Ohio, each of whom travelled in Europe, studying schools and reporting home to their fellow Americans on what they found. There was Lowell T. Mason, who first introduced music into the common school. There were Joseph Lancaster, who brought the monitorial system of instruction to America, and DeWitt Clinton, who promoted it. And there were thousands of people of modest circumstances who organized schools and encouraged them all over the country.

The Elementary School   Throughout the nineteenth century, many names were applied to the institution we now call the elementary school. While each of these names was acceptable in its time and place, and while they are still used in layman's language, they are no longer appropriate, from a strictly professional point of view. We shall mention each of these names, suggest its significance, and indicate why it is no longer appropriate for professionals or professionals-in-preparation to use it.

District School. This was the school maintained by a local school district after the New England town had been subdivided. It was this pattern that New England people carried into most of the other states. It was an appropriate term when the only school maintained by a public school district was an elementary school. Now that school districts also maintain secondary schools (and, in some cases, junior colleges), the term "district school" is obsolete.

Common School. When most of the boys or girls dropped out of school during the elementary school years or when they had completed its program, and when the few who persisted to secondary education were acknowledged to be receiving a special privilege, then "common school" was an acceptable term. We can properly speak of Horace Mann and the "common school revival." When the high school became a part of the American heritage of most youths, it also became common; so no longer is the term acceptable, unless one refers to both elementary and secondary schools as common—in the sense of readily available to most people of school age.

Public School. One still sees, in some cities, older brownstone school buildings labelled "Public School 63" or, more simply, "P.S. 84." At the time they were built, the term was suitable, for they were the only public schools in fact, or at least in the consciousness of the general public. With the high school now as public as these elementary schools, the term is too general. Many districts have solved this semantic problem by giving a proper name to all schools, both elementary and secondary, and discontinuing the use of a number preceded by "P.S." One is more likely to find an Alcott School, or a Horace Mann School, or even a Walt Disney School today than to find a "P.S. 84" or any other number.

Primary School. Some of the early elementary schools concentrated only on the first few years of schooling. Then the "primary" name was appropriate. Today, most elementary schools include six grades, and some still have eight. "Primary" is now commonly limited to schools offering instruction in kindergarten and grades 1, 2, 3. The French may still speak of an *école primaire,* but here we refer to the elementary school.

Grammar School. The Latin grammar schools were the first to bear this name. One did not need to prefix the word "Latin," for everyone knew the grammar schools were Latin schools. Later, there were English grammar schools, and somehow, the name was applied to the "district" school. One can still hear older citizens say, "When I was in grammar school. . . ." But today, the curriculum has been so expanded that the term does not adequately describe what goes on in the school. Critics of modern education would also claim that the graduates know no grammar! This term is about as appropriate for the elementary school as "horseless carriage" is for a modern automobile.

By the process of elimination, we then come to the conclusion that there is only one name left for the school which embraces the kindergarten and grades 1 through 6 or 1 through 8. That is *elementary* school. One could, with reasonable accuracy, call it a school of the fundamental processes, which it really is, but we have enough pedagogical gobbledygook as it is! We need not inflict this on the American public.

For Further Reading

Burton, Warren. *The District School as It Was.* (By one who went to it.) Lee and Shepard, 1897.

First published in 1833 and reprinted many times, this is an authentic account of the district school in the early nineteenth century.

Cubberley, Elwood P. *Public Education in the United States.* Revised. Houghton Mifflin, 1934.

Chapter 9 deals with the character of the schools established in the early part of the nineteenth century, the textbooks used, the evolution of the graded school, the rise of the district system, and the methods employed.

Cubberley, Elwood P. *Readings in Public Education in the United States.* Houghton Mifflin, 1934.

Readings 172 to 193 cover teacher contracts, Webster's textbooks, McGuffey's Readers, Morse's geographies, description of schools before the Civil War, teachers' institutes, and the district system.

Culver, Raymond B. *Horace Mann and Religion in the Massachusetts Public Schools.* Yale University Press, 1929.

Detailed study of Mann's attempts to solve the problem of retaining a religious emphasis in the schools in the face of denominational rivalries.

Eggleston, Edward. *The Hoosier Schoolmaster.* Grosset and Dunlap, 1913.

First written and published in 1871, this fictional work accurately portrays the district school of the nineteenth century and life in rural America at that time.

Martin, George H. *The Evolution of the Massachusetts Public School System. A Historical Sketch.* D. Appleton and Co., 1894.

Changes effected by the reformers, especially Mann.

Minnich, Harvey C. *Old Favorites from the McGuffey Readers.* American Book Co., 1936.

Selection of the most popular stories from the six graded McGuffey Readers.

Minnich, Harvey C. *William Holmes McGuffey and His Readers.* American Book Co., 1936.

Biography of McGuffey related to the educational problems of his times. To be read along with Minnich's selections from the Readers, cited above.

Nietz, John A. *Old Textbooks.* University of Pittsburgh Press, 1961.
Information regarding many old textbooks used in American schools by a professor who made a hobby of collecting them.

Reisner, Edward H. *Evolution of the Common School.* Macmillan, 1930.
Considerable detail about changing conditions in this period of reform.

Spaulding, Frank E. *One School Administrator's Philosophy: Its Development.* Exposition Press, 1952.
Autobiography of a famous superintendent of schools who later became chairman of the department of education at Yale University. Born in 1866, Dr. Spaulding's education and career encompassed the period from then until the late 1930's. The first five chapters relate his schooling in New Hampshire.

Suhrie, Ambrose L. *Teacher of Teachers.* Richard R. Smith, Inc., 1955.
Autobiography of a country boy who taught in a district school, a high school, normal school, and university college of education. The first few chapters give an excellent portrayal of the district school.

Warfel, H. R. *Noah Webster: Schoolmaster to America.* Macmillan, 1936.
Webster's influence on the schools through his textbooks and dictionaries.

Winship, A. E. *Great American Educators.* Werner School Book Co., 1900.
Biographical sketches of Horace Mann, Mary Lyon, David Perkins Page, and others, prepared for use in normal schools and teachers' reading circles.

6

Early Secondary Schools

New Type of Needs While the Latin
grammar school was undoubtedly a valuable institution, and while
it well served the function it was established to perform, the changing
times soon showed that this was not destined to be the secondary
school to meet the new needs of the American people. A Latin education was necessary (or so it was then thought) for a minister, and
it was undoubtedly ornamental for a gentleman. It seemed, however,
to have little relevance for the increasing number of young men
who were eager to "get ahead" in practical occupations. For them,
some more pragmatic education was necessary.

Americans were taking to the sea to engage in commerce—particularly in the two types of triangular trade.[1] Navigation skills and
mathematics were needed by an increasing number of adventurous
young men who wanted to go to sea. Westward expansion demanded
the services of surveyors. Acceleration of trade demanded bookkeeping and correspondence skills. Developing complexities of national
life made law an attractive vocation. For all these vocations there was
a need of young men who had what came to be called an "English"
education—that is, an education in English rather than in Latin, and
directed to immediate vocational needs rather than to the acquisition
of a "liberal" education.

The rise of a middle class that could afford to purchase an education and could dispense with the immediate labor of its sons made the
establishment of a new type of school feasible. It was manifest that
a study of classical authors, heavily laced with Calvinistic theology,
would not appeal to these youths, but that a school which unlocked
the doors to vocational efficiency and financial success would be

---

[1] The first involved shipping rum from New England to West Africa, where it
was bartered for Negro slaves, who were then transported to the West Indies, where
they were sold for molasses, which was taken to New England to be processed into
more rum. The second type involved carrying trinkets and tools from New England
to the Oregon coast to be bartered for furs, which were taken to China to be traded
for silks and spices, which were brought back to our Atlantic coast ports for sale.

tremendously well-received by practical-minded young men from the middle classes.

Private Venture Schools   The need for
schooling in practical matters was, for a time, met by private schools where the master taught his "mystery" in his own house. Colonial newspapers frequently carried advertisements that some person had opened such a school to teach mathematics, accounting, navigation, surveying, or some other subject needed by young men in the expanding economy. One such advertisement reads:

> Over against the Post-Office in Second-street, Philadelphia, is taught Writing, Arithmetick in whole numbers and Fractions, Vulgar and Decimal, Merchants Accompts, Algebra, Geometry, Surveying, Gauging, Trigonometry, Plain and Spherical, Navigation in all kinds of Sailing, Astronomy, and all other Parts of the Mathematicks by THEOPHILUS GREW. His Hours are this Winter from 9 to 12 in the Morning; from 2 to 5 in the Afternoon; and (for the Conveniency of those who cannot come in the Day time) from 6 to 9 in the Evening. He teaches Writing and Arithmetick at the usual Rate of 10s. per Quarter. Merchants Accompts, Navigation &c. for 30s. per Quarter. And will undertake to furnish anyone with sufficient Knowledge in any of the foregoing Branches, in three Months time, provided the Person have a tolerable Genius and observes a constant Application.

These private venture schools served, in their time, much the same purpose as private music, dancing, and speed-reading schools do at the present, offering subjects not given in regularly organized schools to pupils who were willing to pay.

Franklin's Academy   In the forefront
of practical Americans stood Benjamin Franklin, one of the nation's best-known self-made men. Though he had for a time attended the Boston Latin Grammar School, he ran away from his home and settled in Philadelphia, where he rose to eminence by dint of hard work and an insatiable curiosity. Constantly on the lookout for better ways of meeting common needs, whether the needs be heating a room or educating a people, Franklin proposed to his fellow citizens that a new type of school be established in Philadelphia. He had seen the success of certain of the private venture schools. Further, as a deist, he wanted to have education divorced from the direction of orthodox clergy.

Benjamin Franklin

Franklin's *Proposals for the Education of Youth in Pennsylvania*, published in 1749, was a landmark in the development of secondary education, for it was the first advocacy of a realistic approach to America's growing need. Franklin did not claim any originality for his ideas; indeed, it was a part of his strategy in this, as in other proposals, to convince his readers that he was merely assembling the best of ideas from many sources. He advocated a new secondary school which would teach physical development, handwriting, drawing with perspective, arithmetic, accounting, geometry and astronomy, English (both grammar and literature), history (of England, and of the ancient and modern world), geography (with maps), oratory and debate, logic, morality, natural history (including gardening and agriculture), and, according to individual needs and preference, ancient and modern languages.

This proposal, it will be seen, shifted the emphasis from classical studies to the practical. As such, it was in tune with a new European realistic movement which was destined soon to produce the *realschule* in Germany as a competitor of the classical *gymnasium*.

Franklin and his associates, in petitioning the Philadelphia authorities for financial assistance in their new venture, set these as reasons for the academy:

1. That the Youth of Pensilvania may have an opportunity of receiving a good Education at home, and be under no necessity of going abroad for it; Whereby not only considerable Expense may be saved to the Country, but a stricter Eye may be had over their morals by their Friends and Relations.

2. That a number of our Natives will be hereby qualified to bear Magistracies, and execute other public offices of Trust, with Reputation to themselves & Country; There being at present great Want of Persons so qualified in the several Counties of this Province. And this is the more necessary now to be provided for by the English here, as vast Numbers of Foreigners are yearly imported among us, totally ignorant of our Laws, Customs, and Language.

3. That a number of the poorer Sort will be hereby qualified to act as Schoolmasters in the Country, to teach Children Reading, Writing, Arithmetic, and the Grammar of their Mother Tongue, and being of good morals and known character, may be recommended from the Academy to Country Schools for that purpose; the Country suffering at present very much for want of good Schoolmasters, and obliged frequently to employ in their Schools, vicious, imported Servants, or concealed Papists, who by their bad Examples and Instructions often deprave the Morals or corrupt the Principles of the Children under their Care.

4. It is thought that a good Academy erected in Philadelphia, a healthy place where Provisions are plenty, situated in the Center of the Colonies, may draw a number of Students from the neighboring Provinces, who must spend Considerable Sums yearly among us, in Payment for their Lodging, Diet, Apparel, &c., which will be an Advantage to our Traders, Artisans, and Owners of Houses and Lands.

These reasons were calculated to appeal to the pride and prejudices of the Philadelphians: their dislike of the "vast number of foreigners" who were now speaking German in Philadelphia, their hostility to "concealed Papists," their need for teachers in their schools, and their desire to attract people who would "spend considerable sums."

When the academy was established, Franklin's plan had been modified to provide for two schools, one providing for the realistic studies, to be known as the English school; the other, a classical institution. The master of the classical division was to direct the whole institution at a salary three times the amount paid to the English master. Apparently from the beginning, the fate of the realistic division was determined, for it soon withered away and the academy became, to all intents and purposes, the classical preparatory school for the new university founded in 1784.

When Franklin returned from service to his colony and nation abroad, he was greatly disappointed with what he found in the academy. He studied the minutes of the board of trustees and wrote them a scathing letter:

> From the beginning, the contempt of your employes for the new, the English course has been allowed to damage it. They get you to give the Latin master a title. You gave none to the English principal. To the Latin head you gave 200 pounds; to the English, one half as much money and twice as many boys. You voted 100 pounds to buy Greek and Latin books, nothing for English. I flatter myself, gentlemen, that from the board minutes it appears that the original plan has been departed from; that the subscribers have been deceived and disappointed; that good masters have been driven out of the school, and that the trustees have not kept faith.

Other Academies Even though the Philadelphia academy never made the contribution to education that Franklin had so fondly hoped, the idea of the academy had a far better fate. Starting with the Phillips Academy at Andover in 1780 and the Dummer Academy in 1782, Massachusetts had twenty such schools by 1800. While certain short-lived schools which might meet the criteria for being called academies had been earlier established, the Regents of the University of the State of New York incorporated the Erasmus Hall Academy at Flatbush (now a part of

An early engraving of the English Commons, Phillips Academy, Andover, Massachusetts.

New York City) and the Clinton Academy at West Hampton, both in 1787. By 1800, New York also had twenty incorporated academies. Two of the New York academies, Washington Academy at Salem and Farmer's Hall at Goshen, had previously been Latin schools. Miller, the historian of the New York academy movement, declared that "there was no conflict resulting in the extermination of the old and the rise of the new, but simply an absorption of the old by the new."

Other historians, while conceding Miller's point about the transformation of some Latin grammar schools, contend that the genesis of the academy more truly lay in the private venture school. Perhaps there is merit to both points of view. One might even hazard a guess that the academy would have developed to meet a pressing need, even if the Latin school and the private venture school had not preceded it.

Academies in New York   While academies were general throughout all the states and in many of the territories during their heydey from the Revolution through the Civil War, we know most about the ones in New York. This is because New York academies found it advantageous to incorporate or charter themselves under the state and report on their condition annually to the Regents in order to receive state grants from a so-called "literature fund." ("Literature" was then used in the sense that we would say "education" fund.) In no other state do there appear to have been so many academies established; in no other were they so generously supported for so long a time from state funds; and nowhere else did they so long dominate secondary education.

The academies in New York received legal recognition at the first session of the legislature in 1784, when a general act provided for their establishment as quasi-public institutions. The law of 1787 made the Regents "an imperial rather than a federative body" and allowed them to charter academies and colleges on conditions they might prescribe. This act has been called the "Magna Charta of academies." It specified the terms under which an academy might request a charter: (1) those petitioning for the charter must have contributed more than half the funds for its support, (2) there were to be not less than twelve or more than twenty-four trustees, (3) the name of the intended corporation must be stated, and (4) the annual revenue should not exceed "4000 bushels of wheat." The law further specified that when "the State of Literature in any Academy is so far advanced," it might be elevated to the status of a college.

The Regents were assigned the supervision of academies through visitation, examination, and reports. Over the years, requirements for establishing academies were revised from time to time.

In Other States   As the American people moved westward, they took the academy with them. These institutions were set up in new territories and states soon after the establishment of common schools and churches. Many a young pioneer terminated his formal education with a year or so in a village academy. Often, the western colleges found it necessary to maintain preparatory departments, which were often called academies, to qualify common school graduates for meeting their relatively low entrance standards. In many states, academies were operated by individuals or associations without ever being formally incorporated. Even in New York, apparently, some operated without charters.

Curriculum   Since the academy was a new venture, the trustees authorized a wide range of courses to meet popular demands. There was considerable experimentation in such offerings. The reports to the Regents show that New York academies offered 114 different subjects at some time or other between 1787 and 1900. Naturally, not all these subjects were offered in any one academy, and certain subjects were offered only in one or in a few schools. There is also some overlapping in the listing, but still the offering appears formidable.[2]

In addition to such courses as English (literature, grammar, spelling, punctuation, declamation and elocution), history (of England, France, Greece, New York, the United States), mathematics (arithmetic, algebra, geometry, calculus, mensuration, surveying, etc.), and science (botany, zoology, chemistry, hydrostatics, optics, mineralogy, meteorology), the academies also offered these more unusual subjects: carpentry, conchology, domestic economy, dialing, embroidery, mapping, mythology, phreno-mnemotechny, nautical astronomy, waxwork—and many others.[3]

[2] The list is reported on pages 176–178 of George F. Miller's *The Academy System of the State of New York*, published in volume 2 of the fifteenth annual report of the New York State Education Department for the year ending July 31, 1918. It is reproduced in the present writer's *American Secondary Education* (Odyssey Press, 1957) pp. 71–73.

[3] Explanation of some of these subjects is necessary. Conchology was the study of sea shells. Domestic economy was home economics or homemaking. Dialing was a study of ways of measuring time by dials or of measuring distances, especially in mines. Phreno-mnemotechny was then highly regarded as a "science." It claimed to be able to tell a person's mental abilities by measurement of the bumps on his head. Horace Mann was one of the great advocates of this "science," but let's not be too hard on him, for future histories may scoff at our preoccupation with the I.Q.!

As the academies matured, there was a tendency toward the elimination of some of these "free wheeling" subjects and a growing emphasis upon the "standard" subjects more frequently acceptable toward college entrance. Even so, each institution set its own curricular pattern without interference by state authority.

Other Names

Most of the institutions were called academies. There were, however, other names adopted by certain institutions which obviously belonged to the generic class of academies. Among these other names were: institute, collegiate institute, seminary, and even college. After the civil war, when certain academies were transferred by their trustees to the public school authorities, they came to be known as "free academies." To this day, certain secondary schools in New York, now public high schools, are still known as free academies. Academies for girls were commonly called "female academies," until that term seemed to be insufficiently genteel.

Method of Teaching

The great reliance of masters in the nineteenth century was upon mental discipline. Since the mind was to be trained, emphasis was upon memoriter learning and drill—and more drill. Lectures sought to repeat what was in the textbook. Recitations were designed to ascertain how well one had memorized pages from the textbook. Some schools advertised that they had globes, collections of rocks, and "philosophical apparatus," but these were few. One outstanding co-curricular activity was debate and declamation, fostered by rival literary societies. Occasionally an understanding master developed methods more in harmony with newer concepts in pedagogy.

Influence of the Academies

To a poor farm boy in rural America, going to the county seat to an academy was a greater adventure than it is today for a youth to go halfway across the United States to attend a college. Often, it meant his first experience with a celluloid collar and a "store-bought" suit. Too, it meant coming under the tutelage of a cultured master who knew and exacted etiquette as well as the formal subjects. It meant meeting a wide range of experience not encompassed in the home circle.

A serious boy, determined to succeed, found in the academy a key to success in life. Anyone who had a few years at an academy was relatively better prepared in his time to make his mark than is even a college graduate today. For one thing, the proportion of academy students was much less in the nineteenth century.

Studies of two academies in particular, the Belleville Academy in New York and the Verona Academy in Mississippi reveal that an astonishing number of people were sent forth from these two institutions to lead highly successful and profitable lives. Presumably, similar studies of other—but not all—academies might produce similar results.

Academies served to send forth the young men who designed and built America's railroads and factories, who became leaders in the professions, in banking, and in commerce. These schools served very successfully as a transitional institution between the class-conscious Latin school and the free public high school. Their very success was their undoing, for they demonstrated to America the worth of a secondary school education. This success led to a demand for free public high schools.

Female Academies—Coeducation   The first academies, in keeping with tradition, were for young men. Their success and the growing prosperity of the country led to the founding of female academies. In less populous areas, two academies could not be supported, so experiments with coeducation were begun. By the time

A water-color class, typifying the courses taught in early female academies.

of the Civil War, many academies, except boarding schools and schools in the larger urban areas, were entirely coeducational.

Academies Today   A certain number of academies in larger cities and suburbs continue to exist today, either as boarding schools or as country day schools. They are more common in the East and in the South than west of the Appalachians. In the East in particular, they serve primarily as preparatory institutions for the "Ivy League" colleges. In the South, they frequently are military schools for boys or finishing schools for girls. Many hold very high standards and are accredited by the regional accrediting associations. Some others are weak institutions which seem mainly to serve as institutions designed to promote snob-appeal. Still others offer remedial education to children with special difficulties. Some of these modern academies have taken the lead in promoting educational innovations.

For Further Reading

Brown, Elmer Ellsworth. *The Making of Our Middle Schools*. Longmans, Green, 1921.
    Contains good historical development of the Latin schools and academies.

Butts, R. Freeman. *A Cultural History of Education*. McGraw-Hill, 1947.
    Relates the development of secondary schools to life in America at the time. See especially Chapter 16.

Cubberley, Elwood P. *Public Education in the United States*. Revised. Houghton Mifflin, 1934.
    Chapters 3, 4, and 5 describe the periods in which Latin schools and academies arose. Not much detail about either type of school, however.

Cubberley, Elwood P. *Readings in Public Education in the United States*. Houghton Mifflin, 1934.
    See particularly selections 142 to 152.

French, William Marshall. *American Secondary Education*. Odyssey Press, 1957.
    Chapter 3 deals with the Latin grammar school and Chapter 4 with the academies, mainly from Holmes, Gifford and Miller, cited in this bibliography.

Garland, Hamlin. *Son of the Middle Border. Macmillan,* 1923.
    Autobiography of a boy who attended an academy on the frontier. See Chapters 17, 18, 19.

Gifford, Walter J. *Historical Development of the New York State High School System.* Sixteenth Annual Report of the New York State Education Department. Vol. 2. University of the State of New York, 1922.

Chapter 1 covers much the same material as in Miller's *Academy System of the State of New York* (see below) but in more concise manner.

Holmes, Pauline. *A Tercentenary History of the Boston Public Latin Grammar School, 1635–1935.* Harvard University Press, 1935.

Origin and development of America's pioneer secondary school. An exhaustive study.

Kilpatrick, William H. *The Dutch Schools of New Netherland and Colonial New York.* U.S. Bureau of Education Bulletin, No. 12, Government Printing Office, 1912.

Best account of the Dutch Latin school in New York.

Miller, George F. *The Academy System of the State of New York.* Fifteenth Annual Report of the New York State Education Department, Vol. 2. University of the State of New York, 1922.

The most comprehensive study of the academies ever made. While limited to the academies of New York, it illustrates the general development of these schools.

Woody, Thomas. *The Educational Views of Benjamin Franklin.* McGraw-Hill, 1931.

Includes Franklin's Academy in Philadelphia—its founding, its development, Franklin's disappointment.

7

Development of the Common School

The Promise Incomplete   In Chapter 5, we gave a treatment of the early elementary schools. A conclusion reached from studying their history in the first half century of our nationhood is that they had made a contribution to the education of the American people but that they needed to be extended and reformed if they were to fulfill their early promise. The movement to extend and to reform the common school is the theme of this chapter.

Earlier historians of education spoke of this movement as "the common school revival." This interpretation seemed to imply that education had been at a high peak and then had gone into either a precipitous or gradual decline, and thus was ready for a revival. In those colonies where there had been some system of education before the Revolution, there was doubtless some deterioration because of the exigencies of the war. In some states, the decline came after the Revolution because of sheer neglect. In many areas, there was no decline, for there was no particular educational eminence to decline from! To be accurate, then, we might more properly think of the developments chronicled in this chapter as a beginning rather than a rebirth—a *naissance* rather than a renaissance.

Aspects of the Reform   The problem of making the public school an effective agent for the education of children in American democracy took on many aspects. Among the major problems were these:

1. To demonstrate to the people the need for universal education.

2. To improve existing schools through obtaining new buildings and equipment.

98

3. To extend the length of the school term.

4. To prepare better teachers.

5. To improve the curriculum.

6. To establish control and supervision.

7. To make the school free and available to all children.

8. To compel attendance.

9. To extend educational opportunity beyond the rudiments of learning for an ever-increasing proportion of children and youths.

Efforts along these nine avenues were implicit within the schools in the early national period, but they became explicit in the period from the 1830's to the end of the century. To rebuild the early school system into one suitable for a modern industrial nation was not an easy task. It took decades of long, hard effort. Nor can we yet claim that the goal has been completely reached, as we shall see.

Demonstrating the Need From the earliest times, when essayists for the American Philosophical Society urged a republican system of education for a republican form of government, there have always been torchbearers in every generation who kept before Americans the goal of improving their schools and making them a part of the common heritage. Some of these torchbearers were men of national reputation whose endeavors in the cause of public education have won them a permanent place in the esteem and affection of the American people. Many others were people of more modest claims who carried out reforms on a smaller scale— perhaps only in one small school district.

James G. Carter One of the great propagandists for public schools was James G. Carter of Massachusetts. It was he who first called the attention of his state to the failure of its schools to fulfill their early promise. He pointed to the extent of the schools' decadence, to the cause of it, and to proposals to remedy it. Shortly after graduation from Harvard, he launched a campaign to improve the schools of Massachusetts. He wrote voluminous articles and letters to the newspapers in behalf of improved public education. His agitation led to the state legislation of 1824 and 1826, which provided that each town should choose a school committee to have superintendence over all town schools, including the selection of textbooks and the appointment of the teachers.

Carter also stimulated the establishment of a permanent state school fund from monies received from the sale of state lands in Maine and from state claims against the federal government. This permanent fund was to be distributed to the districts only if they taxed themselves, and if they made statistical reports required by state law. Here is an early example of the present practice of using state school funds on the matching basis as an inducement for improvements.

Carter had long advocated state concern with the schools. As chairman of the house of representatives committee on education, he reported out a bill to establish a state board of education which had been endorsed by Governor Edward Everett.[1] Through skillful parliamentary tactics, Carter got a reluctant legislature to adopt the measure. The new law was mild. The state board of education had some duties to report annually on the status of the schools, but it had no authority to compel reform. Localism was so strongly in the saddle that a bill for any significant measure of state control could not have been adopted.

Horace Mann   Many persons expected
the Massachusetts Board of Education to elect Carter its secretary, in recognition of his labor for seventeen years in behalf of education. The board, however, selected Horace Mann, about whom the historian of Massachusetts education says, "If Mr. Mann's qualifications for the position were not peculiar nor pre-eminent, they were neither few nor inferior."[2]

Thus was Horace Mann embarked on a career that was destined to make his name a household word in America, and to place that name on public schools in nearly every state of the union. At the time, Mann was president of the state senate. When his friends chided him for relinquishing a promising political career to become secretary of an untried board of education with only tenuous existence, and for a salary of only $1500 a year (out of which he had to pay his own expenses), he exclaimed, "I will be revenged upon them; I will do them more than $1500 worth of good!"

There is some humor in Mann's speeches and essays, but it is of this wry sort, not a hilarious humor. He was never able to escape

[1] The world little notes nor long remembers that Everett was the principal speaker at the dedication of the Gettysburg battlefield where President Lincoln was asked to make the few remarks which we know as *the* Gettysburg Address.
[2] Martin, George H. *The Evolution of the Massachusetts Public School System, A Historical Sketch* (D. Appleton and Company, 1894), pp. 157–158.

Horace Mann, who gave up
a political career for
one in education.

his strict Calvinistic upbringing, which at times made him tedious
and pompous, though in time he was to reject Calvinism and turn
to Unitarianism. Still, he never could tolerate fiction, for to read it,
he said, was to waste valuable time.

Although the board provided only that its secretary should "collect
information of the actual condition and efficiency of the common
schools and other means of popular education, and to diffuse as
widely as possible, throughout every part of the Commonwealth,
information of the most approved and successful modes of instruction," yet he attacked what could have been a perfunctory challenge with all the zeal of a missionary. He toured the state in behalf
of public schools, calling conventions of the populace even in obscure hamlets. On one occasion, he and Governor Everett arrived
at a schoolhouse early and found the housekeeping deplorable, so
the two of them swept and tidied up the room before the audience
arrived. He exhorted wherever he could corral a group to listen to
him, from Cape Cod to the New York state line. Often, he met
complete apathy, for he recorded that "to make an impression in
the Berkshires in regard to the schools is like attempting to batter
down Gibraltar with one's fist." When the few state funds were
exhausted, he held meetings at his own expense. He published annual reports, and a widely read *Common School Journal* at his own
expense. "It was born, not because it was wanted, but because it was
needed." Its object was to make known throughout the state the
need for an educational awakening, and to introduce to teachers
the newer concepts of teaching then known to only a few.

In the face of discouragement after discouragement, he labored
valiantly in the cause of education. It is to their eternal credit that

there were several men in Massachusetts who gave their encouragement to his endeavors. One of these was Edmund Dwight of Boston. Knowing Mann's feeling that a reform in education rested not upon propaganda alone, but upon a well-prepared teaching corps, Dwight authorized Mann to announce to the Legislature that he would give $10,000 for the establishment of normal schools if the state would contribute a similar sum. Here was real educational pioneering, for there were then no normal schools in the United States.

Nor did Mann limit his evangelical mission to the state which employed him. He recommended David Perkins Page for the principalship of New York's first normal school. In 1842, he addressed the deputy superintendents in New York in behalf of establishing normal schools. In 1846, he went to Albany to address a convention called by advocates of a statewide system of free public schools.

The New York state convention to revise the constitution was to meet that year, and the friends of the free-schools movement conceived the idea of conducting a demonstration to stir up opinion against the "rate bill" system and to petition the constitutional convention to provide for free public schools. Mann spoke "with an ability and eloquence which cannot fail to carry conviction to every mind," as a contemporary described it. His speech, though he modestly declared that "I had not been expected, however, to be called upon, either at this time or in this manner," is a masterly presentation of the argument for entirely free schools.[3] He pointed out that "the subject of free schools, and of the right of a state to maintain them, is never agitated in Massachusetts," and declared that a Massachusetts parent would be as much surprised at having a rate bill presented to him as he would be "if called upon to pay for enjoying the free light of the sun, or common air of heaven." (The "rate bill" system is discussed later in this chapter.) He then launched a vigorous attack against the narrow viewpoint of entrenched wealth which, he held, kept New York from free schools. Seeking to convince these substantial citizens that they should approve free schools, Mann pointed out that education was a balance-wheel and a conservative force in society. But wealth, he continued, had no right to deprive all youth of an education. In the oratorical style of the day, he made this point thus:

Generation after generation comes from the creative energy of God. Each one stops for a brief period upon the earth, resting

[3] It is reprinted in Finegan's *"Free Schools."* Annual Report, New York State Education Department, 1919, Vol. 1, pp. 102–111.

only as for a night, like a migratory bird upon its passage, and then leaves it forever to others, whose existence is as transitory as their own; and the flock of water fowl which annually sweep across our latitudes in their passage to another clime, have as good a right to make a perpetual appropriation to their own use of the lands over which they fly, as any one generation has to arrogate perpetual dominion and sovereignty for their own purposes, of that portion of the earth which it is their fortune to occupy during their brief temporal existence.—By the great and irrepealable law of nature, every child succeeds to so much more of the property of the community, as is necessary for his education. He is to receive this, not in the form of property, but in the form of education.[4]

He urged the forceful argument that free public education is necessary to society in a republic:

Now what is the fundamental, the paramount, indispensible need and necessity of a people? I say it is education . . . education will give strength, competency and order . . . take away education and all things will rush to ruin as quickly as the solar system would return to chaos if gravitation and cohesion were destroyed.

The convention, Mann recorded in a letter to May, "treated me very civilly." It is to be regretted that his arguments and those of the friends of free education had so little effect upon the constitutional convention. It so happened that the state had to wait till 1867 to see the rate bill finally abolished.

Another of Mann's great contributions was an improvement in methodology. On a trip abroad, he became familiar with many school procedures in Europe, especially in Prussia, and he wrote his *Seventh Report* advocating the introduction of certain of these foreign reforms into our schools. This report aroused the anger of the Boston schoolmasters, for it seriously reflected on their school-keeping. There followed a long and tedious exchange of arguments in the press, ending with a victory for Mann's reforms.

Another of his great reforms was the introduction into Massachusetts of the New York state system of district school libraries. No one knew more than Horace Mann the value of a collection of books within ready reach of the youth of the state. In his boyhood home,

[4] This argument is sheer agrarianism, of course, and would be suspect as un-American in many quarters today. But then we must admit that the American public school is the best example of socialism in practice in America.

Mann had had the advantage of using the library of books given to the community of Franklin, Massachusetts, by Benjamin Franklin. Incidentally, in naming the town for Poor Richard, Mann's townspeople asked the philosopher to contribute a bell for the meeting-house. Plain-spoken Ben told them to spare the expense of a steeple in which to hang a bell, and instead sent them a gift of books, saying that from what he had learned of their character, they would prefer sense to sound. Though Mann said these books were more suited to the "conscript fathers" of the Revolutionary era than to the "postscript" children of his own generation, they formed the basis of his education.

Not forgetting what these few eighteenth-century books had meant to him, Mann urged the legislature of Massachusetts to copy the New York plan of 1838, which matched state with local funds in supplying libraries to the common school districts. This act, which supplied 1,600,000 books in New York within 15 years, Mann held to be "one of the greatest moral enterprises of the age." In 1842, Massachusetts provided a similar bounty.

In visiting schools, Mann found that many teachers had far less learning than was necessary to teach even the fundamental subjects, so he brought the teachers' institute to the state. He and the normal school faculties often served as teachers of these institutes. "Conductors," they were quaintly called.

Mann had never played; he had been a serious youth. As a nephew said, "There was a great vacuum in the place where my uncle's sense of humor might have been." Though serious in nature, Mr. Mann did not believe in slave-driving. Upon one occasion, he wrote to Cyrus Peirce, the principal of one of the normal schools,

> I heard you were going to add another hour to study-time this term. I protest against this. Your love of approbation for the fame of the school must not be a Moloch, before which young virgins are sacrificed.

Though his educational work was not completed, in 1848 he was prevailed upon to take the seat in Congress vacated by the death of that stalwart old abolitionist and presenter of anti-slavery petitions, John Quincy Adams. For the humanitarianism of abolition, he put aside temporarily the humanitarianism of education. For five years, he served in Congress, first as a Whig and then as a Free Soiler. His chief work was an attack upon slavery and upon Daniel Webster after that Senator's Seventh of March Speech. In a famous statement, he called Webster a "fallen star . . . Lucifer descended

Antioch College as it appeared in the Antioch College Catalogue in 1866.

from heaven." These two men, once friends, became political enemies; it is the irony of fate that their statues stand side by side now on the steps of the capitol in Boston, as Massachusetts' two foremost citizens.

In 1852, on the same day in September, Mann was nominated for governor of his state and elected to the presidency of Antioch College in Ohio. He accepted the latter offer. Antioch was a new venture in American higher education. Founded by the so-called Christian Church, a liberal Protestant sect who believed in each person's interpreting the Bible for himself, it was founded upon the cornerstones of co-education, non-sectarianism, no proselytizing of students, no honors or prizes or other extrinsic means to motivate work. To inaugurate these reforms, the Christians departed from the then time-honored custom of choosing a clergyman for president, and elected Mann. This was the first instance in which a layman was elected to the presidency of a western college.

The nobility of Antioch's purposes called forth Mann's highest ideals, but the practical affairs inherent in starting a new college on an unsound financial basis in territory hostile to its ideals were most discouraging and disillusioning. The college was located on land recently robbed of its magnificent forest. Mud was all about. The buildings were half ready. There was no president's house. Pigs insisted upon entering the dining room and wallowing where the doorsteps should have been. On one occasion, a "lady professor" had to vault over a pig to get into her residence. As Mrs. Mann tells it,

> One day a professor (a lady) was arrested, on the entrance to the hall, by a hog of unusual dimensions, which had made his watery bed where a doorstep should have been. She looked at it in dismay a moment, and then, being light of foot, tripped over it as if it had been a bridge, and sprang over a board which had been inserted where the door should have been hung, the board having been placed there by some friendly hand to prevent the intrusion of living bridges.

Students at Antioch caused considerable trouble. Their preparation was so poor that of 75 who entered only eight qualified as freshmen, the others being persuaded to enroll in the preparatory department. The young men smoked and drank and chewed—all of which habits Mann frowned upon. Students who failed circulated untruths about the college.

Though the Antioch adventure was most disappointing, Horace Mann stayed on in face of financial difficulties and slanderous libels. He continued to stand for a high idealism. To his last graduating class, he could throw the challenge

> I beseech you to treasure up these my parting words: Be ashamed to die before you have won some victory for humanity.

There has been considerable recognition of Mann's services to American education. Cubberley says in his *Public Education in the United States:*

> No one did more than he to establish in the minds of the American people the conception that education should be universal, non-sectarian, and free, and that its aim should be social efficiency, civic virtue, and character, rather than mere learning or the advancement of sectarian ends.[5]

His statue stands in front of the State House in Boston; a replica is in the foyer of the headquarters of the National Education Asso-

5 Cubberley, Elwood P.: *Public Education in the United States,* Revised and Enlarged, p. 226, Houghton Mifflin, 1934.

ciation in Washington. His bust was the first placed in the Hall of Fame. Schools are named in his honor. Antioch named its library for him. In 1939 the profession made much of the Mann centennial. Tributes to him are numerous in current literature. A Mann bibliography contains thousands of items.[6]

But the least Horace Mann would wish is to be embalmed in oratory. He would far rather have had his successors devote themselves to the active improvement of education. As John Dewey puts it:

> If we are content to glorify his work without applying his passionate ardor of thought and action to the problem to which he was devoted, in the forms that problem has now assumed, we shall be traitors to his memory. Our commemoration will be honest only as we employ it to rededicating ourselves to the cause to which he sacrificially devoted his life.[7]

Some of the flavor of Mann's evangelistic efforts in behalf of public education is conveyed by these quotations from his speeches and publications:

> As are the parents, so are both the teacher and the school.

> The best thoughts are those that spring from a clear brain warmed by a large heart.

> Education is our only political safeguard; outside of this ark there is no salvation.

> Public schools were my first love; they will be my last.

> Education must be universal. It is well when the wise and learned discover new truths; but how much better to diffuse the truths already discovered, amongst the multitude.

> If it were in my power, I would scatter books broadcast over the land, as the sower scatters grain in the furrows of the field.

Mann was the first American educator to attain an international reputation in pedagogical circles. The *Seventh Report* was translated into German and French and "read with admiration in the highest circles abroad"; copies were printed by German and English govern-

[6] Clyde S. King, librarian of the Horace Mann School, New York City, estimates that his forthcoming bibliography on Mann will have from 3000 to 5000 references, including newspaper items.

[7] *Social Frontier,* November, 1936, pp. 41–42.

ments; and the London *Athenaeum,* usually hostile to things American, had a complimentary review.

Mann's *Seventh Report* and his visit to European leaders, together with his other reports and his *Common School Journal,* enhanced his international prestige. Particularly in France did he draw his admirers, for his political, anti-clerical, and social philosophy accorded well with the rising republicanism of that land, particularly after the fall of Napoleon III. Felix Pecaut, writing in 1888, commended Mann's system of moral teachings: "We must all watch over this precious germ, which contains a part of our national destiny; it will produce what public spirit (by which I mean the religious spirit as well as the philosophical spirit and the practical sense of the nation) shall make it produce; if it perishes, both churches and philosophers will have their share of the responsibility." One acquainted with French developments in the educational program of the Third Republic would undoubtedly find that Mann, after his death, continued to exert an influence upon the development of the civic-morality curriculum of the French schools.[8]

Gabriel Compayré, in *Horace Mann and the Public School in the United States,* pays the following tribute:

> Mann's countrymen have not forgotten what they owe him. They have raised statues to him, and in 1897 they celebrated the anniversary of his birth; but what is better still is that they remain faithful to his inspiration, and he may be said to be still present in their midst. It may be said also that his spirit has penetrated into Europe and particularly into France. It will not be detracting from the honor due to the organizers of elementary instruction in France under the Third Republic to say that they were in great measure inspired by the thought and example of the great American educator. To mention but one, our Pecaut, above all, appears to us as a French Horace Mann, more impressive, of a deeper and more intense inner life, more reserved and discreet; a Horace Mann without the gift of oratory, but with greater moderation and delicacy of mental quality, worthy in any case to figure, like him, in the front rank in the golden book of great modern educators.

The rising democracies in Latin America had educational growing pains similar to those in the republic to the north, and Mann's ideas about the close correlation between public education and democracy had considerable potential relevance throughout South Amer-

---

[8] After 1888, to guide them in the development of their republican system of education, the French had available *The Work and Writings of Horace Mann,* by M. J. Gaufres, published for the Musée Pédagogique in its "Educational Memoirs and Documents."

ica. Someone was needed to introduce Mann's ideas into that continent. In 1845, an Argentine named Domingo Faustino Sarmiento was appointed to survey the European educational scene, in the expectation that the traditionally cultured nations could supply valuable inspiration for Argentina, Chile, and other new Latin republics. But when in London Sarmiento found and read a copy of Mann's *Seventh Report,* he directed his major efforts to investigating education in the North American nation. "After this important work fell into my hands," wrote Sarmiento, "I had a fixed point to which to direct myself in the United States."

Sarmiento arranged an introduction to Mann, and was soon entirely absorbed in the American's philosophies and projects. After extensive visiting of American educators and school facilities under Mann's auspices, Sarmiento returned to Chile, convinced that Mann's work could be a central influence in promoting the cause of popular education for literacy in the Latin American countries. Starting with the publication in 1849 of his book *De la Educacion Popular,* Sarmiento wrote tremendously influential works interpreting and developing Mann's ideas for application to education in the Spanish-speaking world in South America. Throughout his life he continued to battle for public education, especially during a term as president of his homeland. At one time he was instrumental, through Mann's widow, in persuading several American normal school graduates to teach in the Argentine.

Today, in any treatment of American educational history, the name of Horace Mann still looms large, partly because of his educational reforms which led to the universality of the free public school in our country, and partly because of his inspiration in the development of education abroad, notably in France and South America. Truly, the words of Reuben R. Stetson on the teacher are appropriate: "Not for the present only do you work, for generations yet unborn shall feel the weight of your impress upon plastic mind."[9]

Other Massachusetts Leaders   Mann, of course, was not able to bring about the Massachusetts awakening by his own efforts alone. In addition to Carter, who paved the way, there were many others who stood by his side in the campaign. Particular mention should be made of Robert Rantoul, William Ellery Channing, and Edmund Dwight. Rantoul was a humanitarian and promoter of the lyceum movement, who wrote frequently on any cause designed to better the condition of man. Channing saw education

[9] Several of the preceding paragraphs were originally published in the author's article, "Horace Mann and Education Abroad," in *School and Society,* Vol. 88, No. 2172, April 6, 1960. Used here by permission of *School and Society.*

as an important instrument to assure the progress he believed inherent in the race. Dwight, one of the state's most prominent manufacturers, had considerable influence with the legislature and contact with other leading families. He annually supplemented from his own resources the state salary for the secretary of the board of education.

Gideon Hawley   The first state officer charged with the responsibility of the common schools was Gideon Hawley, appointed state superintendent in New York in 1813. While he appears to have lacked the evangelical fervor of Mann, he did perform a valuable service in supervising the state "literature" fund, in collecting statistics, in helping to establish the state's first normal school, and in exhorting the state to improve its schools and the teachers to upgrade their methods.

Hawley was acutely aware of his duty "to advise and direct the mode of instruction and course of studies to be pursued in common schools," and he reported to the legislature that he would cheerfully prepare a manual for this purpose if the funds were provided for publication. The preparation of such a manual was authorized in 1819, and the first New York state "syllabus" was the result.

In an age when the common-school curriculum consisted almost exclusively of the three R's, and these were scantily taught, Hawley's *Instructions for the Better Government and Organization of Common Schools* made a noteworthy contribution. Stressing the fact that reading, writing, and arithmetic were "the first rudiment of education, and to instruct in them is the peculiar province of a common school," he pointed out that still "there is an obvious propriety in requiring common schools to embrace a more extended course of study," since they were "the only channels for the general diffusion of useful knowledge." It would provide "a good common education to every child in the state." Each school should, therefore,

> as a duty growing out of its acceptance of the public bounty, . . . adopt and practically pursue a course of instruction as liberal and comprehensive as its circumstances warrant.

The curriculum should embrace English grammar, "beauties of the Bible," geography, principles of surveying, the history and Constitution of the United States,

> the crimes and punishments which form our criminal code, and such parts of our civil jurisprudence as every man, in his daily intercourse with the world, is concerned to know.

In this day when any educational theory of more than three years' standing is held to be outmoded, it is interesting to remind ourselves again that Hawley's *Instructions* emphasized such "modern" ideas as motivation and maturation.

> In the instruction of youth, the first object of a teacher should be to make study a voluntary and agreeable employment. . . . Unwilling study is always languid, and the impression received from it, necessarily feeble and transient. . . . To effect this important end, the study of the pupil should be adapted to his capacity; a given task, limited to what he can easily perform, should always be assigned to him; he should be assisted in his progress by the kindness and attention of his teacher.

The more advanced phases of education, such as grammar and "the combination of rules in arithmetic," were held to be unsuited to the ordinary capacity of young children, since they required exercise of considerable judgment and analysis. These "should be reserved for them, in after years, when their judgments shall have become more mature."

Teaching for thinking was advocated in a strong passage:

> To exercise the reasoning faculties of youth, by giving them clear and distinct ideas of what they study, and accustoming them to a practical application of their knowledge is . . . not of less importance than of making study voluntary and agreeable. Knowledge is lasting, in proportion as it is the result of thought and reflection . . . they are not made to study understandingly, and to apply what they learn to practice; their knowledge is too apt to be mechanical, a mere matter of rote, lodged only in the memory.

The *Instructions* are concluded with expositions of the Pestalozzian method of object teaching and of the Lancastrian system of instruction, both of which are commended to teachers who are urged to steer a middle course between practice and theory in the development of an eclectic plan which would produce, "doubtless, the perfection of education."

Henry Barnard   While Mann was
the evangelist of the common school revival, Henry Barnard was its scholar. His *American Journal of Education,* begun in 1855 and continued through thirty-one volumes, is a great storehouse of educational information about schools in the United States and

abroad. Through its column, American educators were speedily introduced to new problems and theories. William T. Harris once called the *Journal* "an educational course of reading of 24,000 pages and 12 million words."

Barnard was a member of the Connecticut legislature in 1838, when he sent circulars to that body in behalf of reforming the deplorable schools of the state. When Thomas H. Gallaudet refused the secretaryship of the new Connecticut board of education in 1839, Barnard was appointed. He served until 1842, when a hostile governor who objected to "dangerous innovation" and "needless expense" prevailed upon the legislature to abolish the board and the secretaryship. Refusing a Massachusetts normal-school principalship, Barnard went to Rhode Island, where he served as state commissioner of public schools until his recall to Connecticut in 1849 to serve as principal of the state normal school and ex officio secretary of a new state board of education. From 1858 to 1860, he was president of the University of Wisconsin, and from 1867 to 1870, he was the first United States commissioner of education. In his periods as state secretary, he met much the same types of problems as Mann had in Massachusetts.

Thaddeus Stevens   Although the state of Pennsylvania had some legislation for "educating the poor gratis," in keeping with its parochial-charity concept of education, there was no real system of public schools in the state until 1834. Friends and foes were locked in battle over whether or not schools should be established. The workingmen in urban areas wanted free schools. The German-speaking farmers were adamant in opposition, for they saw free schools as a threat to their language and their parochial schools.

Governor George Wolf and Thaddeus Stevens may have been deeply divided on some contemporary hot political issues (such as Anti-Masonry), but they were allied on the public school issue, both strongly in favor of it. After placating his Lutheran constituents by helping to get a charter and state aid for their local college (Pennsylvania College, now known as Gettysburg College), Stevens went on to push for public schools. When opponents in the legislature objected to state funds for the college, Stevens exclaimed, "If a bill had been brought into this house to improve the breed of hogs," there would be no opposition, but when a bill was proposed to "improve the breed of men," dollars came before anything else.

A bill establishing free schools was passed in 1834, but it aroused so much hostility that its enemies tried to achieve repeal in 1835. Stevens now threw his energies into the effort to save the schools. In a long and impassioned speech he rallied the friends of education, and repeal was soundly defeated.[10]

The issue was then carried to the people in the next gubernatorial election. So strong was the opposition to Governor Wolf, because of his advocacy of free schools, that his party split, one faction nominating the Rev. H. A. Muhlenberg, a Lutheran clergyman whose church wanted parochial, not public, schools. Commenting on this development, Stevens said, "Let those who would govern through ignorance, who would make the poor man's children vassals and servants to do homage to the rich, join the sooty ranks of the Cimmerian tribe whose chieftain's black banner bears the dark inscription, 'Muhlenberg and no free schools.' "

Stevens' Anti-Masonic party then put forth Joseph Ritter for governor, who won the election. In 1836, the school laws were amended and consolidated into a system which was destined to govern the education of the commonwealth for many years. The consolidation provided for the formation of school districts, the levying of taxes for school purposes, and the appointment of a state superintendent of common schools. A considerable degree of local option was maintained, however, for districts could still, at a public election, decide whether or not to maintain free schools. Further, school directors were authorized to grant public money to non-public schools rather than maintain a public school. This was designed, of course, to placate the proponents of parochial schools. The exercise of local option was not rescinded until 1848. When schools were established, they were entirely free. Pennsylvania never had the rate bill system which was common in other Eastern states.

Governor Ritter courageously asked that the state educational appropriation be raised from $75,000 to $800,000, and the legislature did vote $700,000. Much of the fund was used for construction of schoolhouses.

At the time in 1848 that free schools were mandated throughout the state, there were still nearly 200 "non-accepting" districts which had refused to establish free schools. Many of these had been permanently opposed to free schools. Some had given the system a short trial and rejected it. Others had voted "yes" one year and "no" another year with unaccountable caprice. Even as late as 1868 there were 23 districts with about 6,000 children that had not yet put free common schools into operation.

[10] Liberal extracts of Stevens' speech, reconstructed from his notes, appear in Wickersham's *History of Education in Pennsylvania*, pp. 333–338.

Calvin Stowe   Calvin Stowe had
great influence in Ohio in the cause of public education. A professor at the Lane Theological Seminary in Cincinnati, he was
appointed to go to Europe to purchase books for that institution.
The Ohio legislature delegated him to study the schools abroad and
to report to it. In this report, he contrasted the state of education in
Ohio and Germany, much to the disadvantage of the former. His report was printed to the extent of 10,000 copies in Ohio, and was
later reprinted by the legislature of five other states.

Murphey and Wiley   Archibald D. Murphey,
who came to be known as the "father of common schools" in North
Carolina, presented a report in 1817 in which he advocated a plan
of education somewhat similar to the one proposed by Thomas
Jefferson for Virginia. There was to be a state board of education
to manage the permanent school fund and to gather school statistics.
Preference in public education was to be given to poor children who
were to be provided a free schooling for three years without any
expense for tuition, books, or other materials. Those "most distinguished for genius" were to be continued beyond the three
years of schooling, again without cost. Murphey's proposal, like
Jefferson's, was in advance of the community sentiment and was not
enacted into law. However, a public school endowment was established in 1825. By 1839, there was a successful system of public education supported from the state fund and from county taxes. In
1853, Calvin Wiley became state superintendent and served until
1866. Like Mann, he campaigned for education in all parts of his
state; he compared educational progress in North Carolina with
advancement elsewhere; he edited an educational journal; published
a *North Carolina Reader;* and constantly tried to advance educational standards even during the Civil War. In 1860, he could report
that 150,000 of North Carolina's 221,000 children were in schools
taught by 2700 teachers, for an average of four months.

Other Leaders   Nearly every state
produced a local leader of the public school movement. In Kentucky,
it was Robert J. Breckinridge; in California, John Swett; in Illinois,
Ninian Edwards; in Louisiana, Alexander Dimitry; in Michigan,
John D. Pierce and Isaac E. Crary. It would be most enlightening
to the student to dip into the educational history of his own state to
see how a few individuals there were able to awaken the consciousness of the people in the cause of public schools. It should be re-

membered, of course, that states which entered the Union after the "common school revival" usually provided in their constitutions and basic laws for the establishment and maintenance of a system of free schools.

The "Rate Bill" System

Today when one speaks of a public school, one naturally assumes that it is also a free school. It comes, then, as somewhat of a surprise to learn that at one time in the United States parents had to pay in order to send their children to the public school. This was the so-called "rate bill" system. The "rate" was a charge assessed against the parent or guardian, usually on a per diem basis, for the attendance of children at a public school. Its origin goes far back in English history. In America, the "rate" system was used in certain colonies, notably Massachusetts and Connecticut. From there, it spread to other colonies, but nowhere did it so long persist as in the state of New York. It is therefore to the history of that state that we shall turn for a closer examination of the system and for a study of the campaign to abolish it.

How the "Rate Bill" Worked

Let us assume that it cost a school district sixty dollars to operate a school for a school year. This is not much money, we know, for the cost of maintaining a school was relatively small. Land for the school, usually the most worthless land in the township, was often given to the school committee free, or at such a token charge as one grain of corn per year, forever, to the donor and his heirs. The equipment was homemade. A building would be erected, and infrequently maintained, by volunteers participating in a "bee." Custodial work was done by the teacher. Firewood might be furnished by some parents in payment of their assessment. A teacher cost very little— perhaps four to twelve dollars a month. Pupils brought their own books from home, often in an astonishing variety. Sixty dollars, under these circumstances, might represent a sufficient annual budget for a district school.

Let us assume further that state grants from permanent school funds might amount to twenty dollars for this particular district. This left forty dollars to be raised by other means. Since local taxation was not authorized (or, if authorized, it may have been so unpopular as not to be exercised), to raise this deficit, custom provided that the trustees or school committee add up the total number of days attended by all pupils, divide this amount into the deficit (in our example, $40.00) to find out the cost of instruction per day, per child.

To make our example easy, we shall assume that children attended for a total of 2000 school days in the given school year. This would make the cost of instruction two cents per day, per child. His attendance in days was then multiplied by this amount to arrive at the "rate" for each child. Then the "rates" of all children in one family were added and a duly certified claim was given to the local tax collector for collection before a designated date. A small collection fee was added. If the amount was not paid by a certain date, a penalty was attached; if not paid in a certain length of time, attachment of the delinquent's personal or real property was authorized.

In the case of indigent parents who were willing to take a pauper's oath, there was ordinarily no "rate" applied. In some cases, the education then was free, the total number of days on which the "rate" was calculated being omitted. In other cases, indigent parents were required to furnish a certain number of cords of wood of specified size and quality.

It should be noted that the "rate" was applied only if a child attended school. To avoid paying this tax, some parents kept their children out of school. To keep their payments down, others did not at all discourage absences. Every time a child missed a day, the parent saved a few cents—in our example, two cents. If one had eight children enrolled, and they all stayed home, the saving amounted to sixteen cents per day, a not inconsiderable item in an economy where a man worked ten hours to earn a dollar.

Not only was the "rate" system used in the district school. The records of the Public School Society (a non-government philanthropic agency operating schools for the poorer class in New York City) show that this Society, too, assessed rates when enrollment figures rose faster than charitable contributions. For "the alphabet, spelling, and writing on slates, as far as the 3rd. class, inclusive" the rate was 25 cents per quarter; for advanced classes, it went as high as $2.00 per quarter. When rates were first announced by the Public School Society in 1826, attendance immediately fell to a marked degree.

A Typical "Rate Bill"   We quote portions from a typical "rate bill" in one of the district schools in the state of New York in the year 1848:

Rate bill containing the name of each person liable for teachers wages in district No. 14 in the Town of Tioga for the term ending the third Day of October 1848 and the amount for which each is liable with the fees for the collector thereon

Names of inhabitants sending to school	No. days sent	Bill of school	Collectors fees	Whole amount to be raised
Elston Holmes	102	.37	.02	.39
Charles Holmes	65½	.24	.01	.25
Fremire	84½	.30	.02	.32
David Taylor	311½	1.14	.06	1.20
Norman Goodrich	61	.22	.01	.23
Alanson Goodrich	26	.09	.01	.10
Silas Goodrich	212½	.77	.04	.81
James Wheat	232	.85	.04	.89
Hamilton Lamont	213	.77	.04	.81
Wesley Saxton	241	.88	.04	.92
John Cortright	76	.27	.01	.28
Gideon Cortright	121	.44	.02	.46
Moses Cortright	60	.22	.01	.23
Washington L. Burnes	266	.97	.05	1.02
Mary Griffing	9	.03		.03
Lorin Brink	159	.58	.03	.61
John Heacock	223	.91	.05	.96
Hibbard Preston	159	.58	.03	.66
Wm. C. Foot	8	.03		.03
Asher Tappan	37	.13	.01	.14
James Hinyon	8	.03		.03
		$10.48		$11.01

The above excerpt obviously gives the names of parents, not of the children attending, for it would have been impossible for any single child to have attended for 311½ days. The only conclusion is that David Taylor had several children attending the school. One would conclude, too, that the tax collector got very little for his efforts, the difference between the amount payable to the district and the total amount certified for collection being only 53 cents.

On the back of the rate bill appears this notation: "School Bill. Please to collect this as quick (*stricken out*) Soon as possible for I am in want of it. W.J.H."

Rate bill containing the name of each person liable for teacher wages in district No 14 in the Town of Tioga for the term ending on the third Day of October 1848 and the amount for which each person is liable with the fees of the Collector thereon

names of Inhabitants sending to school	Whole no days of school	amount	Collector's fees	amount to be raised	
Elston Holmes	102	37	0,02	39	39
Charles Holmes	65½	24	1	25	25
Fremire	84½	30	2	32	32
David Taylor	311½	1.14	6	1.20	23
Norman Goodrich	61	22	1	23	10
Alanson Goodrich	26	9	1	10	22
Silas Goodrich	212½	77	4	81	44
James Wheat	232	85	4	89	43
Hamilton Lamont	213	77	4	81	
Wesley Saxton	241	88	4	92	61
John Cortright	76	27	1	28	14
Gideon Cortright	121	44	2	46	69 2
Moses Cortright	60	22	1	23	5
Washington L Barnes	266	97	5	102	82
Mary Griffing	7	3		3	
Lorin Brink	159	58	3	61	
John Heacock	223	91	5	96	
Solomon	182	66	3	69	
Hibbard Preston	159	58	3	61	
Wm E Foot	8	3		3	
Asher Tappan	37	13	1	14	
James Kinyon	8	3		3	
		10.48		1101	

A Rate Bill of the 1800's.

A rate bill in the same district for the year 1849 contains this statement:

To the Collector of School District No. 14 in the Town of Tioga in the County of Tioga State of N.Y.

You are hereby commanded to collect from each of the persons in the annexed rate bill named the several sums mentioned in the last column thereof with five per cent for your fees excepting such sums as may have been collected by the teacher or paid to the trustees and within thirty days after receiving this warrant to pay the amount so collected by you into the hands of the trustees of said district or one of them and in case any one person therein named shall neglect or refuse to pay the amount set opposite his name as aforesaid, you are to levy the same by distress and sale of the goods and chattles of such person.

Given under our hands this eighteenth day of April in the year of our Lord one thousand eight hundred and forty nine April 18th 1849

Silas Goodrich   *Trustees of School*
E H Holmes   *District No 14th Tioga*

The Cities Abolish "Rates"   Rural America has traditionally been more conservative than urban areas. While the "rate bill" persisted until 1867 in the country and in small towns, as we shall see, the cities moved earlier to eliminate it. The cities were confronted with the practical problem of getting the children into school. Since many of them were kept away because of the "rates," the only solution was to abolish this tax. Accordingly, the friends of free schools obtained from the state legislature special acts permitting specified districts to set up systems of free schools without any rates assessed against parents for the attendance of children. New York City, the largest urban area, received such legislative permission in 1832. The Public School Society struggled along for a few years, but in 1853 it surrendered its charter and turned its assets over to the city's public school department. In its history, it had provided at least some education for 600,000 pupils.

Other cities, both in New York and elsewhere, also sought special legislative acts for the establishment of free schools. All the larger New York municipalities except Albany had established free school systems by 1853. Elsewhere in the nation, free school districts were established in such cities as Baltimore, Charleston, Cincinnati, Chicago, Louisville, and New Orleans.

Steps in Social Change   Generally, social and
educational progress passes through four distinct stages:

1. A few far-sighted individuals recognize a need, and they seek
   to enlighten the general public through constant agitation and
   propaganda. They do this both as individuals and as voluntary
   associations.

2. These individuals convince a majority (either a numerical majority or perhaps only a majority of the power element) in a few
   communities. The state is then asked to enact special legislation
   permitting a specifically named community to embark on a new
   path.

3. When several communities are won to the new proposal, the
   legislature enacts general, permissive legislation which enables
   any community choosing to do so to provide the agency desired.

4. When enough communities have availed themselves of this general, permissive legislation, then a demand is heard that the
   social benefits shall be extended to all the areas of the state
   through mandatory legislation, and even in opposition to local
   indifference or objection.

Such was the history of the establishment of free schools in the
state of New York. In the period preceding 1826, a state-wide system
of free public schools does not seem to have been widely advocated
in New York. By 1826, however, the subject of free schools was
in the air in America. For a time, the state saw fit to delegate to
charitable and philanthropic societies and even to organized religious congregations the responsibility for maintaining schools, but
this was only a social palliative that was found to be inadequate.

By 1846, free public schools had been established in New York
City, Brooklyn, Rochester, Poughkeepsie, Buffalo, Williamsburgh,
and certain small districts. In Albany, the rate bill was less than $200,
and the schools of Utica and Troy were almost free. The state
superintendent estimated in 1848 that a fourth of the schools in the
state were free.

Free School Campaign   New York's State
Superintendent Christopher Morgan in 1848 carried on a campaign
to make all the schools entirely free. In denunciation of the "rate"

system, he presented several arguments, which may be briefly summarized thus:

1. It was difficult to collect the "rates" assessed in local districts. In one instance, a bed was seized for non-payment of the school "rates."

2. It was difficult to collect taxes in local districts to pay for the free education of indigent children. He cited several lawsuits, some of them involving only a few cents.

3. Trustees found it difficult to exercise their power of exempting indigent parents from the tax.

4. Since parents paid their "rates" in proportion to the attendance of their children, they winked at truancy and absence, refusing to support the teachers in demands for punctuality and regularity of attendance. To the presence of the "rate bill" he attributed the principal cause of "irregular attendance of scholars."

Superintendent Morgan went on to say that it was not true that the people were unready for free schools. He showed that in eleven places where referenda had been held, the people had indeed voted for free schools.

Propaganda Campaign   Samuel Young, superintendent of common schools in 1842, had said that if "the cold and apathetic indifference, the stagnant tranquility of the community," could be aroused, the evil of the "rate bill" system could be abolished. Others were of a like mind, for a strong propaganda campaign was launched to influence the public before the state constitutional convention of 1846. At four annual state conventions of county superintendents, much time was given to agitation for free public schools. County and local teachers' institutes added their voices. Petitions to the legislature in behalf of free schools were widely circulated, signed, and forwarded to Albany. *The District School Journal,* published in Albany, devoted much space to the issue. Both Whig and Democratic political conventions, in various parts of the state, endorsed free schools.

Persons who were opposed to free schools set forth their views with equal vehemence. "One of the people," writing in the *Newburgh Telegraph,* charged that a system of free schools would be "in direct conflict with the inherent and constitutional rights of every citizen," for it would tax the whole community "for the education of children of those who are rich and able to educate their own children" as well as for the education of the indigent. To educate the rich gratis would be to violate the property rights of all.

When the state constitutional convention failed to propose a system of free schools, the propaganda effort was intensified by both sides. During 1850, more than 200 petitions were submitted to the legislature. One petition portrayed the free-school advocates as highwaymen:

> "You, sir have been industrious, frugal and painstaking, and hence you are able to educate your children; while I have been idle, careless and profligate. Now, sir, the power is mine; surrender to me your purse or your life, that my children may be well educated as yours."

In rebuttal, another writer pointed out that throughout the state children in the district schools were

> singled out from their more fortunate neighbors and branded as paupers, to be educated at public expense, and jeered at by their associates as the dependents of charity. Where is the child who would not feel the shame, whose cheek would not burn with blushes at being thus exposed a victim of cruel fate?[11]

Free School Act of 1849   By 1848, the propaganda effort of the New York humanitarians and the pioneering special legislation had brought the issue of free schools clearly before the people of the state. Numerous petitions and resolutions were addressed to the legislature. One of them read, "Resolved, that the taxable property of the state ought to educate the children of the state." In 1849, the legislature passed "an act establishing free schools throughout the state," which would provide free schools for all persons from five to twenty-one years of age. A curious provision for referendum was included in this law. Note these two sections:

> Section 10. The electors shall determine by ballot at the annual election to be held in November next, whether this act shall or shall not become a law.

> Section 14. In case a majority of all the votes in the state shall be cast against the new school law, this act shall be null and void;

---

11 Many more propaganda statements like these two are to be found in Dr. E. R. Van Kleeck's *The Development of the Free Common Schools in New York State,* an unpublished Ph.D. dissertation, Yale University, 1937.

and in case a majority of all the votes in the state shall be cast for the new school law, this act shall become a law, and shall take effect on the first day of January, 1850.

The Fatal Defect The effect of these sections was to pass on to the people the responsibility of deciding whether or not the law should take effect. This was a fatal defect. In the November elections of 1849, the people voted 249,872 to 91,571 for free schools. In spite of this verdict, much opposition remained, and the legislature in 1850 voted to submit the question of repeal of the law to the people that November.

A violent campaign erupted throughout the state of New York. Special free school and anti-free school newspapers were established. Special conventions were called by friends and foes of free schools, with railroads offering special rates to those who attended. Repeal was defeated by a majority of only 25,000 votes. It temporarily appeared that New York would have a state-wide system of free schools.

Now the opponents of free schools took their case to the courts, and in 1853 the state court of appeals held in *Barto* v. *Himrod* that the law of 1849 was unconstitutional, on the grounds that the state constitution conferred upon the legislature power to enact laws, and that the legislature could not divest itself of this responsibility by delegating its powers to the people in a referendum. Consequently, the "rate bill" continued legal, except in those districts which had received special legislation allowing them to establish entirely free schools.

Final Victory in 1867 While the "rate bill" still continued, the state did increase the amount of its special grants to school districts to reduce the amount of the "rate." Still, this was not enough for many districts, so again the legislature was flooded with petitions for special legislation of a permissive character. In 1853, the union free school act granted general permission for the unification of school districts and tax support. Finally, in 1867, the rate bill was abolished throughout the state, and New York joined her sister states in promoting a system of free, public, common schools for all her children.

The Victory Not Complete Achievement of a system of free public schools in the various states at various times, culminating in the free school victory in New York, marked a significant stage in the educational opportunity of the American people.

The mere achievement of the schools was only an incomplete victory for this education, however. It would not be complete until these schools were brought under the control and supervision of an agency higher than the local district, until compulsory attendance was established, and until the program of the school was extended and enriched beyond the six or eight years of the usual district school.

Establishing Control   The establishment of effective control on the state or intermediate level progressed at an uneven rate from state to state. The mere establishment of a state superintendency or a state board of education was insufficient. What was needed was a state certification system for teachers, legislation on the length of the school term and school day, supervision by competent administrators with a professional background, standards of health and sanitation, and district consolidation. Not all of these have yet been achieved to a maximum degree.

Compulsory Attendance   Even after the free school had become universal, many children did not attend, either because they chose not to or because their parents kept them away, either to work at home or to be employed elsewhere. The first compulsory attendance law became effective in 1852 in Massachusetts. Though it met with opposition, it was a weak law, for it required attendance between the ages of eight and fourteen for only twelve weeks a year, with only six of these weeks required to be consecutive. Nor were twelve weeks required if the school did not "keep" that long in the child's home district, if the child were ill, if other provisions were made for his education, or if the parents were paupers. A later law in Massachusetts gave to local school committees the responsibility of enforcement, but it was some time before public attitudes were such as to bring about general compliance.

In general, the New England states and states formed under the influence of New England migrants were most zealous in enacting attendance laws. Up to 1900, thirty-two states had enacted at least mild attendance laws. In the states of the Old South, hampered as they were by the devastation of the Civil War and the problems of Reconstruction, it was not easy to pass such laws until the earlier decades of the twentieth century.

Extension of Program Upward   With the increasing complexity of American life during the latter part of the nineteenth century, it soon became apparent that the simple literacy provided by the old common school was insufficient. There arose a demand that the curriculum be enriched and extended. This involved introducing new subjects into the elementary school and also the greater provision for attendance at schools on the secondary level. The broader extension of free public schools to the secondary level will be explored shortly, but first it is necessary to describe the fuller development of the elementary school.

For Further Reading

Barnard, Henry (editor). *The American Journal of Education.* 31 volumes.
    Barnard's monumental professional magazine. There is a separate Analytical Index to the American Journal of Education, published by the United States Bureau of Education, 1892. Articles on contemporary educational problems as well as historical and comparative materials.

Brubacher, John S. *Henry Barnard on Education.* McGraw-Hill, 1931.
    The work of "the scholar of the Awakening." Extracts from his more important writings. A scholarly appraisal.

Cubberley, Elwood P. *Public Education in the United States.* Revised. Houghton Mifflin, 1934.
    Cubberley devotes a chapter to "The Battle for Free Schools". His categories of friends and enemies of free schools will bear further analysis, but the arguments for and against free schools are well stated.

Cubberley, Elwood P. *Readings in Public Education in the United States.* Houghton Mifflin, 1934.
    Especially selections 98–123.

Curoe, Philip R. V. *Educational Attitudes and Policies of Organized Labor in the United States.* Teachers College, Columbia University, 1926.
    Shows organized labor as a strong factor in the campaign for free common schools.

Finegan, Thomas E. *Free Schools, A Documentary History of the Free School Movement in New York State.* University of the State of New York, 1921.
    A comprehensive collection of documents.

Fitzpatrick, E. A. *The Educational Views and Influence of DeWitt Clinton.* Teachers College, Columbia University, 1911.
    The governor of New York as an ardent friend of public education.

French, William Marshall. "Horace Mann and Education Abroad" *School and Society*. Vol. 88, No. 2172 (April 6, 1960).

Mann's influence in other lands, especially in South America and in France.

Randall, S. S. *The Common School System of the State of New York*. Privately printed, Troy, N.Y., 1851.

A contemporary account of the struggle to establish free schools and to eliminate the rate bill.

Stewart, Watt and William Marshall French. "The Influence of Horace Mann on the Educational Ideas of Domingo Faustino Sarmiento". *Hispanic American Historical Review*. Vol. 20, No. 1 (February, 1940).

An example of Horace Mann's international influence. Sarmiento, inspired by Mann, reformed the schools of the Argentine.

Van Kleeck, Edwin R. *The Development of Free Common Schools in New York State*.

An unpublished (1937) dissertation at Yale University.
Thorough presentation of the campaigns for free schools in the state of New York. Numerous specific reference to leaders, opponents, newspapers. Available through inter-library loan service.

Wickersham, J. P. *A History of Education in Pennsylvania*. Inquirer Publishing Co., 1886.

Wickersham, state superintendent of public instruction in Pennsylvania, wrote this monumental history shortly after free schools had been achieved there.

Williams, Edward I. F. *Horace Mann*. Macmillan, 1937.

A centennial biography of Mann, written by a professor of education who devoted years of study to the project. Relates Mann's life and works to the broad advance in American education.

8

The Changing Elementary School

The Traditional School   Though the middle
third of the nineteenth century had witnessed the development of
the free common school in most of the states, and though much
progress had been made in the externals, not much change took
effect regarding what went on in the school itself. It is, of course,
true that some new subjects, such as geography, history, and physiology had been introduced, and some teachers had even studied a
bit about methods of teaching. The district school, however, was
merely a reproduction of the school of an earlier age with but very
few modifications in its content or in its methodology. It was still
the "little red schoolhouse" which came to be sanctified in American folk literature.

The teaching material was still found in the textbooks almost
exclusively, and it was the teacher's responsibility to drill this content into the minds of the pupils, primarily through the process of
rote learning and memorization. The mark of a good "scholar" was
the repetition of the textbook with as little variation as possible. The
books even included at the end of each chapter certain catechetical
questions for the teacher to ask. A later generation was to say that
this was a book-centered, a curriculum-centered, a teacher-dominated
school. For those who could endure its rigors, particularly those with
minds like sponges, this school did a good job. Those with poor
memories, those interested in the why of things, and those to whom
the regimen of the school did not appeal left at an early age.

Ideas from Abroad   While the American
people were content with this type of school, never having known
anything different, and while the majority of teachers were also
satisfied, some persons thought there must be better procedures. On
trips abroad, or through correspondence, some leaders in the profession became aware of newer methods. Through the teachers'

127

institutes, through the normal schools, and through the columns of the journals for teachers, they sought to call these newer ideas to the attention of the teachers. Horace Mann's *Seventh Report* dealt largely with his observations on the methods used in European schools. Calvin Stowe reported on the systems of elementary education there. Publication in this country of Victor Cousin's report on education in Prussia resulted in considerable discussion—even in the wilds of Michigan.

We have already noted the adoption of the English monitorial system of instruction earlier in the nineteenth century by a number of school societies and school districts, particularly in the urban areas of the East, where the demand for schooling kept far ahead of the number of teachers or the funds requisite to maintaining schools.

The influences that made themselves felt in the middle and later parts of the nineteenth century came primarily from the continent of Europe, not from England, as had the monitorial school. In fact, it would not be too much to say that Victorian England had very little interest for American educators. The three great names associated with the European influence on American schools are Pestalozzi, Froebel, and Herbart.

Pestalozzian Influence   Johann Pestalozzi, an earnest but unsuccessful Swiss, had early come under the influence of Jean-Jacques Rousseau's *Émile,* a revolutionary scheme for the education of a child according to what Rousseau called "the plan of nature." The *Émile* opens with the startling declaration that all is good as it comes from nature, but that all degenerates under the hand of man. In an age of extreme artificiality and superficiality, Rousseau was trying to get people to see that children should be treated as children, not as miniature adults. His book is full of sentimentality, exaggeration, faulty reasoning, and error of fact, but it caught the imagination of a Europe trying to cast off the encrusted weight of centuries. Though placed on the papal index and ordered to be burned in Paris, the book became a "best-seller" and was read extensively throughout Europe.

Inspired by Rousseau's thesis, Pestalozzi tried his best to ameliorate the lot of the poor. He tried the ministry, but failed. He studied law, but got no clients. At last he opened a school on his farm at Neuhof and took in fifty abandoned children, hoping to show that society could be regenerated through a work-and-morals type of schooling. Whether or not this could have been achieved, we do not know, for Pestalozzi used up all his resources within two years and the school closed.

The French were so enamoured of the principles of their Revolution that they insisted upon sharing them with the rest of Europe, even at the point of a bayonet. They invaded Switzerland and orphaned many children. Put in charge of these, without books or other teaching apparatus, Pestalozzi developed his own methods. There, and in other schools he later established, he evolved what we may call the *child-centered approach*. He sought to have all education center on the child, his needs, his interests, and his abilities. He rejected memorization and sought understanding. He regarded sense-impression as "the absolute foundation of all knowledge." He tried to "organize and psychologize the educational process" by relating school experiences to the natural development of the learner. Self-activity, intuition, and development of the senses were the keys to education. Real things needed to be brought into the school instead of verbalisms about things. The teacher should organize and correlate these materials, not be a drillmaster. Love, not punishment, should be the motivating factor.

Pestalozzi amid the children of his school.

Here was something very new in education at the time, though many of these reforms had indeed been anticipated by great educators before, especially by Comenius. But here was an actual school where children crawled over the teacher like puppies. Here they learned by doing. And the world beat a path to Pestalozzi's door, even Alexander II, czar of all the Russias, stopping in on his way to Vienna to help carve up the map of Europe. The Prussians, eager to reform their system of primary education, studied Pestalozzi's procedures, and adopted many of them in 1804. Several Prussian teachers were sent at government expense to study under Pestalozzi, being cautioned not to concentrate only on his techniques but also to "warm yourselves at the sacred fire which burns in the heart of this man." So great was the Pestalozzian influence in Prussia that a German educator, Diesterweg, said that applications of his principles were responsible for much of the success of the German common schools.

Unfortunately, not all who visited Pestalozzi warmed themselves at his heart. Some took isolated ideas home and formalized them. This was particularly the case with the Rev. Charles Mayo and his sister Elizabeth, who developed formal lessons *on* objects rather than lessons *from* objects. Instead of having children study salt, their manual defined salt as crystalline, saline, soluble, etc. It was this extreme reliance upon verbalism without understanding that Charles Dickens held up to ridicule in his novel *Hard Times*. Sissy Jupe is the daughter of a circus actor whose knowledge of horses extends as far back as her memory reaches. Mr. Gradgrind, the teacher, asks her to define one, but the prescribed words from the textbook do not come to her. Then,

"Girl No. 20 unable to define a horse," said Mr. Gradgrind.

"Bitzer," said Thomas Gradgrind, "your definition of a horse!"

"Quadruped, Graminivorous. Forty teeth, namely, twenty-four grinders, four eye-teeth, and twelve incisive. Sheds coat in the Spring; in marshy countries sheds hoof too. Hoofs hard, but requiring to be shod with iron. Age known by marks in mouth." Thus (and much more) Bitzer.

"Now, Girl No. 20," said Mr. Gradgrind, "you know what a horse is."

This may sound like an author's exaggeration, but it is borne out by the facts in the Mayos' manual. Lesson XVI, for instance, describes an oyster as "an animal, opaque, marine, natural. The valves are circular, stiff, pulverable; the outside is rough, scaly or laminated, irregular, dull, dingy, brown, uneven. The inside is pearly, bright, smooth, slightly concave, iridescent, cold. The mollusc is soft, eatable, nutritious, cold, smooth, lubricious." The manual then goes on, at some length, to define laminated as "derived from lamina, a plate," etc. etc. Poor Papa Pestalozzi must have rotated in his grave to have this travesty on education carried on in his name.

The Prussian schools had already absorbed much of the Pestalozzian philosophy by the time Mann visited them and pronounced them the best in the world. Mann and other visitors introduced the Prussian version of Pestalozzianism into the United States. A Pestalozzian disciple, Joseph Neef, came to America and taught for a short time in Philadelphia before moving to the utopian colony at New Harmony, Indiana. Neither he nor his two books on Pestalozzian principles seem to have had any great influence on American schools, which were scarcely ready in the early 1800's for reform. By the time the schools were ready, the books were forgotten.

When Pestalozzianism came to the United States as a major factor in school reform, it came by a round-about route and in impure form. Edward Austin Sheldon, who came to be known as "the American Pestalozzi," founded a school for the ragged children of Oswego, New York, in 1848. Soon this evolved into the Oswego public schools, with Sheldon as superintendent. Sheldon organized his schools and prepared his untrained teachers according to his own empiric concepts of what education should be. Finally, he had them so well organized that he was dissatisfied with the results, for he was perceptive enough to note that children were memorizing, not understanding. In 1859, in a museum in Toronto, he saw materials sent out by the Home and Colonial Infant Society of England. Though these were the formalized perversions of Pestalozzianism that the Mayos had developed, they fascinated Sheldon. He imported books and apparatus from England and persuaded Margaret E. M. Jones, an English teacher, to come to Oswego. Later she was replaced by Hermann Krusi, who was born at Yverdun, Switzerland, while his father was teaching with Pestalozzi.

"Object teaching" became the byword in the Oswego schools and in the normal school Sheldon opened there. From Oswego, the American adaptation of the Mayos' English adaptation of Pestalozzianism was carried over the United States, particularly after a commission from the National Education Association visited Oswego and pronounced its work good. It appears that some of the Oswego Pestalozzianism was verbalistic, while some teachers were having students study biology by dissecting dogs, stewing flesh off cats to prepare skeletons, and taking botanical field trips. At Oswego, too, Henry Straight worked out some influential principles of correlation that were later endorsed by Francis Parker.

Herbartian Influence

Pestalozzi was a warm-hearted, undisciplined reformer of education who held that "the essential principle of education is not teaching, it is love." His was a great spirit, but the world wanted system and organization, not spirit. We have already noted the killing hand of the Mayos' attempt to systematize Pestalozzianism.

It was a German philosopher, Johann Friedrich Herbart, who supplied the necessary system and its psychological rationale. He was a product of the University of Jena, a scholar and an organizer. Like John Dewey, the American philosopher who was destined later to affect educational theory and practice, Herbart had little contact with children in a classroom situation. His approach was theoretical and logical. His writings dealt primarily with the aim, the content, and the method of instruction. It was primarily his concept of method that was imported into the United States by eager young men who studied under Herbart or his disciples in the German universities. To them, education was a science: all one had to do to produce results was to manipulate the intellectual apparatus according to prescribed formulas.

Herbartianism, as introduced into American education by Charles A. McMurry, Frank McMurry, and Charles DeGarmo (all of whom had studied in Germany), placed education upon a theoretical level and introduced an awesome new vocabulary that profoundly described phenomena which had not been noted or deemed worthy of consideration: apperception, correlation, culture-epoch theory, role of interest, social function, etc.

So far as the mass of American teachers were concerned, it was the Herbartian methodology that was of immediate interest to teaching. If introduced under proper auspices and at the right time, the Herbartian methodology of the "five formal steps" was a psychologically sound way to structure a lesson plan. These five formal steps were (1) preparation, (2) presentation, (3) association, (4) generalization, and (5) application.

In *preparation,* the object was to manipulate the student's mind to put him into a receptive mood. This might today be called motivation. In *presentation,* the new material was presented and analyzed. In *association,* the new material was compared with what the student already knew, with likenesses and differences being noted. In *gen-*

eralization, the new facts were formulated into a general principle or rule. In *application,* the general principle was tested with appropriate problems.

For prospective teachers who did not know much subject matter beyond what they themselves were teaching to their pupils, and who did not know much about child nature, this was a wonderful framework upon which to hang their teaching. In normal schools, the daily Herbartian lesson plan was sacred. Regarding any subject, even a daffodil or poetry appreciation, one had to formulate a five-part lesson plan with an appropriate amount of time and emphasis on each of the five steps. The only trouble was that often children in school did not respond the way the teacher, in making out the plan, thought they would! The Herbartian plan, administered by unimaginative teachers fearful of critical supervisors, was very much responsible for the extreme formalism that was fastened upon the elementary school. In a period of standardization, a rigid plan was considered good pedagogy, and unimaginative standardization was about all one could expect with inadequately prepared teachers, formal textbooks, and crowded classes.

Froebelian Influence   The third foreign educator to affect American theory and practice profoundly was Friedrich Froebel, an introspective mystic who had studied with Pestalozzi. From Pestalozzi's procedures, he chose play, the self-activity principle, and music as being most important in relation to the education of younger children. His school he called a Kindergarten—i.e., garden of children. To Froebel, the teacher was the good gardener who planted young plants in good soil, supplied water and fertilizer, kept the bugs away, and let them develop according to nature's plan. Unsuccessful for many years, Froebel finally met the Baroness Bertha von Marenholtz Bulow-Wendhausen, who became convinced that the man described to her as an "old fool" really could transform education. She devoted the rest of her life to propagating Froebel's ideas. When the Prussian government forbade kindergartens as possibly revolutionary, she went abroad to propagandize for them.

The first kindergarten in the United States was conducted in German at Watertown, Wisconsin, by Mrs. Carl Schurz, a former pupil of Froebel's. The first English language kindergarten was conducted in Boston by Elizabeth Peabody, a sister-in-law of Horace Mann and of Nathaniel Hawthorne. Several German emigrées opened training schools for kindergarten teachers as private ventures, and in 1873, a public-school kindergarten was opened in St. Louis by Miss Susan Blow. From there, it spread rapidly to many American cities.

The kindergarten, with its emphasis upon self-activity and play, has been generally used as a transition agency between the home and the school. Here the child learns to socialize with his peers, working out stories and playing. The American kindergarten movement was a battle scene for some years between the traditionalists who wanted to keep "the gifts" and other elaborate Froebelian dogma intact and the reformers who wanted to keep the spirit of the kindergarten without Froebel's methodological paraphernalia. In the end, the reformers won the battle, but not before many acrimonious words had been said and written. The Froebelian "gifts" were toys such as balls and blocks, from which the child was expected to derive mystical concepts embodied in such terms as thesis, antithesis, and synthesis. The unity of all God's creation was to be absorbed from sitting on a circle painted on the kindergarten floor.

The kindergarten has served to bring children to school a year earlier than they otherwise would attend, to promote a degree of socialization, to provide some readiness for first grade experiences. Perhaps more important, the kindergarten concept of play as an educative experience has been absorbed by much of the rest of the school system through a sort of pedagogical osmosis, and has colored methodology up through the junior high school years.

Manual Training   Traditionally, the district school was a place for learning out of books. This learning was almost exclusively intellectual and verbal. It came as a great shock to American educators to see, in a Russian educational exhibit at the Philadelphia Centennial Exposition in 1876, a display of woodwork and ironwork done by Russian pupils. Though Cornell University, a land-grant college, had an exhibit of models of machinery, it was the Russian exhibit which captured the imagination of American educators. Soon various types of manual training high schools were developed in the larger cities, and gradually the use of simpler tools and apparatus came to be taught in some elementary schools. While the boys made footstools in a make-shift shop, girls were instructed in sewing or elements of cooking. Strangely enough, when criticized, this type of activity was defended on the grounds of formal discipline, for it was said that it trained the observation, strengthened the will, and exercised reasoning power. No one thought it justified because it was fun, because it provided a respite from verbalism, or because it taught the use of tools and apparatus.

Science Instruction   Science came into
the elementary school as a formal course in physiology, with great
emphasis upon naming all the parts of the body, tracing the circulation of the blood, memorizing the digestive process, and otherwise
treating the human body as a subject for "human geography."
-Gradually, there was a shift to hygiene. Through the pressure of
humanitarian societies, some nature study was incorporated with
"kindness to animals" as the desired product.

Since most elementary teachers had never studied science, except
perhaps biology in high school, the schools had largely neglected any
systematic study of science. After Sputnik, considerable effort was
made to introduce science into the elementary grades through in-
service training workshops, summer science institutes for teachers,
and other "crash-programs." To the present writing, much effort
remains to be made before a completely satisfactory program is
achieved.

The Transformation   In a book
entitled "The Transformation of the School," Professor Lawrence
A. Cremin has traced the influence of progressivism in American
elementary education since 1876. When we compare the extremely
formal schools of the 1870's with the modern elementary school, his
descriptive title seems most appropriate, for a marked change has
been effected in these intervening years. Cremin portrays the schools
of the 1890's:

> Whatever the high-minded philosophies that justified them, the
> schools of the 1890's were a depressing study in contrast. Every-
> where, mundane problems of students, teachers, classrooms, and
> dollars had become overwhelming. Rural schools, built during the
> educational renaissance of the forties and fifties, had been allowed
> to fall into disrepair and disrepute. Cut off from the pedagogical
> mainstream and frequently beset by problems of rural decline,
> they remained ungraded and poorly taught. Recitations averaged
> ten minutes per subject per class, and untrained teachers con-
> tinued to concentrate on "the same old drill in the same old
> readers." McGuffey had been good enough for mother and dad;
> he would certainly do for the youngsters.
>
> In the cities problems of skyrocketing enrollments were com-
> pounded by a host of other issues. In school buildings badly
> lighted, poorly heated, frequently unsanitary, and bursting at the
> seams, young immigrants from a dozen different countries swelled

the tide of newly arrived farm children. Superintendents spoke hopefully of reducing class size to sixty per teacher, but the hope was most often a pious one. Little wonder that rote efficiency reigned supreme. It needed none of Harris's elaborate Hegelian justifications; it was simply the basis of survival.

As school budgets mounted, politicians were quick to recognize one more lucrative source of extra income. In the continuing consolidation of hamlets into villages, villages into towns, and towns into cities, school boards grew to fifty, seventy, or indeed, more than a hundred members. Responsibility being difficult to define, corruption reared its ugly—if familiar—head. Teaching and administrative posts were bought and sold; school buildings— like city halls and public bathhouses—suddenly became incredibly expensive to build; and politics pervaded everything from the assignment of textbook contracts to the appointment of school superintendents. In short, the school system, like every other organ of the urban body politic, was having its growing pains.[1]

A schoolroom on the Lower East Side of New York City, about 1886. Note the open gas jet for illumination.

[1] Cremin, Lawrence A.: *The Transformation of the School*. New York: Alfred A. Knopf, 1961, pp. 20–21. Quoted by permission.

The "Quincy System" was one of the first noteworthy attempts to give America better elementary schools. Francis W. Parker, the superintendent, brought the spirit of reform into schools which had been conducted in a spiritless memoriter fashion. He started children reading simple words in place of drilling the alphabet by rote. Arithmetic was developed inductively, with a plentiful use of actual objects to manipulate. Geography started with field trips rather than with the universe. Supplementary books and magazines replaced stodgy textbooks. Parker maintained that he had invented nothing new, but had merely applied sound principles of learning that were "used everywhere except in school!"

Later, as principal of the Cook County Normal School in Chicago, Parker was to develop his educational philosophy around two principles: to center education around the child, and to correlate the subjects of the curriculum in such a way as to make them meaningful to the learner. For his innovations, he has been called the father of progressive education in America. Holding that Parker "began the emancipation of the American Child," Curti declares that "he threw dynamite into self-satisfied educational circles."[2]

Dewey's Experiment

Soon the attention of the country was directed to an experimental school conducted by Dr. and Mrs. John Dewey at the University of Chicago from 1896 to 1904. Known as the "Laboratory School," this institution was used to test Dewey's pedagogical theories. With 140 children, twenty-three teachers and ten assistants, it offered a type of education that was unattainable in the conventional school, but it blazed the way for many educational innovations. Its primary emphasis was on pupil activity rather than passivity. Children were to learn of the world through participation in miniature editions of the world's activity. Unfortunately, the school closed in 1904 because of a quarrel between Dewey and William Rainey Harper, president of the university. Dewey took himself off to Columbia University. As professor of philosophy there until 1952, he continued to write voluminously on education, but never again conducted a school. His principal works on education, particularly *School and Society* and *Democracy in Education* became the bibles of the progressive movement.

Other Experiments

Numerous other experimental schools flourished for a brief period at the turn of the century. At

---

[2] Curti, Merle: *The Social Ideas of American Educators.* Littlefield Adams and Co., 1959, pp. 394–395. By permission of the American Historical Association.

the University of Missouri, Junius L. Meriam conducted such a
school which divided a day's work into four activities—plays, stories,
observation, and handwork. At Fairhope, Alabama, Mrs. Marietta
Johnson conducted a school designed to "minister to the health of
the body, develop the finest mental grasp, and preserve the sincerity
and unself-consciousness of the emotional life." All formal studies
were delayed—reading and writing to the age of eight, for example.
Arithmetic books were not used until the junior high school years.
This, and several other schools of experimental nature, are described
in John Dewey's *Schools of Tomorrow*. Mrs. Johnson later became a
leader in the Progressive Education Association, and her ideas filtered
into general educational theory, but the tomorrow has come and the
schools have not adopted her ideas.

At Gary, Indiana, William Wirt experimented with twelve-month
public elementary schools on a "platoon plan" with a miniature
community organization. (The "platoon" idea appealed because of
its alleged economy, for students were in a room only half the day,
the rest being spent in shops and other work centers. Thus few rooms
were needed, theoretically. This idea cropped up again, many years
later, in the Trump plan for secondary schools.) After several years,
an independent survey indicated that many of the alleged claims for
this type of school had been inflated. More than two hundred cities
had adopted some modification of the Gary plan, but it no longer
attracts attention.

A Play School, renamed City and Country School, was conducted
in Greenwich Village, New York City, on the principle that first-
hand experiences such as field trips and construction were more
educative than formal lessons. The release of the child's native
capacity was the keyword.

The argument for the unconventional school was set forth in a
book entitled *The Child-Centered School* by Rugg and Shumaker.
It carried the banner of the progressives far to the left of conventional education practice, almost making a fetish of allowing the
child to choose his own methods and curriculum. It even surpassed
Rousseau in its progressivism.

Influence on Schools   Many of these
experimental schools had little influence on the practices of the general run of elementary schools. Gradually, some of the more promising concepts found their way into classroom practices of teachers who
had been exposed to the theories in their normal school preparation
or in summer session classes. Schools and teachers, though, are of

conservative stuff, and resistance was great. Occasionally, a teacher would say "I don't teach subject matter. I teach children," but generally teachers still taught subject matter to children. They might be more humane to children, they might even consider the child's interests and abilities, but they were unwilling to throw a whole century of tradition out the window.

Kilpatrick's Progressivism					At Teachers College, Columbia University, William Heard Kilpatrick assumed the mantle of interpreter of John Dewey's philosophy to American teachers. After he had written his article, "The Project Method," and later expanded it into a volume, *Foundations of Method,* his classroom became the Mecca of progressive teachers. From the plains of Kansas, from the snows of Alaska, and from the banks of the Ganges, teachers beat a path to his door. Many went back home with a zeal to get students to participate in planning their own work, setting their own goals and achieving their own education. Others, with the shadow but not the substance, went home and taught Latin by having students carve busts of Roman statesmen out of huge bars of Ivory soap!

Evaluation							The moral of the progressive movement seems to be that an inspired, dedicated teacher with enthusiasm and a new idea can make it work. Conversely, a teacher without the same zeal and inspiration can put in an equal amount of time without having the idea work. Teaching is an individual art. Methods cannot be prescribed. A teacher needs to know about many methods, but from these he must learn to adapt and improvise until he finds one that fits his particular personality, is compatible to the subject, and is adaptable to his students.

Progressive Education Association				A group of friends of experimental schools organized the Progressive Education Association at Washington, D.C. in 1919, with Charles W. Eliot as honorary president. The aim, according to an organizer, was "reforming the entire school system of America." Its journal, *Progressive Education,* sought to acquaint the public and professional educators with the ideals and the proposed reforms of the association. During the depression of the 1930's, many of the members sought, with some success, to turn the association in the direction of advocating social reform of a politically liberal nature. This resulted in a large measure of criticism from conservative forces. By 1944, the association changed its name to American Education Fellowship, but began a decline which resulted in its dissolution in 1955. Its friends claimed that it had achieved its objective, the reform of the schools. Its enemies rejoiced that it had expired before it had wreaked more damage than it had.

The Critics Attack   During the depression, George S. Counts' pamphlet "Dare the Schools Build A New Social Order?" brought attacks from conservative and reactionary elements who claimed to fear that the profession would use the school as an instrument to sovietize America. Although the attacks died down during World War II, they increased in number and in harshness in the postwar period. The political climate of the Senator McCarthy period, coupled with the unrest that followed the war, made such attacks acceptable to many people. In this period, numerous magazine articles held many aspects of American education up to ridicule, particularly progressive education, the work of the teachers colleges, and particularly Teachers College of Columbia University. Book after book by Albert Lynd, Alfred E. Bestor, and Mortimer Smith appeared. Admiral Hyman G. Rickover later joined in with a series of magazine articles and books. These attacks were levelled at all stages of American education, from the kindergarten to the graduate school, but the public elementary and secondary schools bore the brunt of the attacks. The pace was stepped up when the Russians succeeded in getting devices into outer space before the United States, as if the schools were solely or principally responsible for our shortcomings. Invidious comparisons were made between American and Russian, Dutch and English education, often by persons who had only a superficial knowledge of what American education has accomplished. Various motives lay behind these attacks: many reflected genuine alarm and concern; others seemed to be the disguised manipulations of persons who wanted to discredit the American educational system because it was claimed to be the best example of socialism in action; others seemed very much an appeal to return to the aristocratic ideal of education solely for an élite.

Growth in the Schools   In the 1930's, influenced by the depression and its accompanying postponement of marriages and reduction in the birth rate, it was estimated that the population of the United States would level off at about 130,000,000 and that we would no longer need a large number of new teachers each year. There were proposals in Pennsylvania to close several of the normal schools and to turn their campuses into hospitals for the mentally ill. Less than half the candidates for positions were employed in teaching. Survey committees advised urban school districts to close and sell elementary schools in areas of declining population.

Suddenly, all this changed. The upsurge of the birth rate during and after World War II brought an ever-increasing flood of pupils into the elementary schools, then into the secondary schools and colleges. Schoolrooms were crowded. Desks were put closer and closer together. Library corners and work tables were taken away. By the time a new school was opened, it was already crowded. Teachers in sufficient quantity could not be found. School boards which had discharged married women teachers during the depression, to provide vacancies for men and single women, now tried to tempt them back at higher salaries. Many persons with sub-standard preparation were hired on temporary certification. One superintendent remarked, "If she can get into my office under her own power, I'll hire her." When told by a college placement officer that even the teachers "at the bottom of the barrel" had been placed, a superintendent replied, "Turn it over and thump it a few times, maybe someone else will fall out for our school."

Neither in dollars nor in real earning power did teachers' salaries keep pace with economic trends. Many teachers left the profession. After some years, readjustments were made. Of these, we shall speak further in Chapter 20.

For Further Reading

Brickman, William W. and Stanley Lehrer (editors). *John Dewey, Master Educator*. Society for the Advancement of Education, 1961.
A thorough analysis of Dewey's philosophy and its relation to educational theory and practice.

Cremin, Lawrence A. *The Transformation of the School*. Knopf, 1961.
Most complete history of the progressive education movement in the United States from 1876 to 1957. Relates the changing educational procedures to the contemporary changes in American life. This book was on several lists as one of the most significant books on education published in 1961. Has an extensive bibliography.

Eby, Frederick and Charles F. Arrowood. *The Development of Modern Education*. Prentice-Hall, 1934.
Chapter 17 discusses Pestalozzi and the common school movement; chapter 20, Herbart and the Herbartians; chapter 21, Froebel and the kindergarten movement; chapter 22, G. Stanley Hall and John Dewey.

Elsbree, Willard. *The American Teacher*. American Book Co., 1939.
Chapter 28 deals with changing methods in American education.

Good, Harry G. *A History of American Education*. Revised Edition.
Macmillan, 1962.
"Practice versus Theory" in chapter 13.

Knight, Edgar W. *Fifty Years of American Education*. Ronald, 1954.
Fifty years of educational change, 1900 to 1950.

Meyer, Adolphe E. *An Educational History of the American People*.
McGraw-Hill, 1957.
Chapter 13 presents "The Rise of a Native Pedagogy"—i.e., the Quincy
Method, John Dewey's contributions, the Progressives. Chapter 14
describes the psychological movement in education. Chapter 16 dis-
cusses the "new" education.

National Society for the Study of Education. *Modern Philosophies of
Education*. Part 1 of the Fifty-fourth Yearbook, University of Chicago
Press, 1955.
Edited by John S. Brubacher, this yearbook presents the realistic,
Thomistic, idealistic, experimental, and empiric philosophies.

Ratner, Joseph. *Intelligence in the Modern World: John Dewey's Philosophy*. Modern Library, 1939.
An analysis of Dewey's philosophy. The lengthy introduction, pp. 3–241,
is a critical essay. The remainder of the book is an anthology of Dewey's
most significant writings.

Wiggin, Gladys A. *Education and Nationalism. An Historical Interpretation of American Education*. McGraw-Hill, 1962.
Chapter 5 gives extended treatment to the search abroad by John
Griscom, Alexander D. Bache, Calvin E. Stowe, and Horace Mann for
educational patterns adaptable to the United States.

9

The American High School

An Extensive Institution Thirty thousand-odd secondary schools dot the map of America at the present time. They exist in all the fifty American states and are available to almost all American youth. They are located in downtown areas of our largest cities—and at remote crossroads in the wildest stretches of the country. In size, they vary in enrollment from less than ten students each to large institutions of more than 5000 students. The number of schools could be greatly reduced by judicious centralization or consolidation.

High schools are now so much a part of America that they are often taken for granted by the pupils who attend them and by the general public. It comes, then, as a bit of a surprise to the average student to learn that the high school is a relatively new institution. While the first high school was established in 1821, and others followed soon thereafter, the number of high schools was not great before the Civil War. Most of the Americans who received a secondary education before that war did so in academies, not in public high schools.

The First High School The economic opportunities opened by the industrial revolution in Boston, as elsewhere, produced a large middle class of people who wanted a better education for their children than the common schools offered, yet had no aspiration to send them to the Latin school en route to Harvard. These were middle-class people with middle-class aspirations for their boys. They wanted their boys to have sufficient education to carry on mechanical and mercantile responsibilities, and they did not want to send them out of Boston to attend the academies, which might have met their needs.

A special committee was organized to propose some local solution to the problem. Out of the report of this committee developed an institution at first known as the English Classical School, opened in

1821, with George B. Emerson as the principal. Students, boys only, were admitted at the age of twelve, upon examination, to pursue a three-year terminal course. The high school course included English, mathematics, science, and history. There were no offerings in foreign language or in any narrowly vocational subjects. Navigation was, however, included in mathematics.

The name "high school" does not appear in the official records of the school at first, but it soon came to be known as the English high school. Each class in the school was a unit, taught in one room all day by one teacher, except that the lower two grades were divided into two sections each, taught as units, by one teacher for each section. Mr. Emerson himself took the seniors in the principal's room. The school began with 100 boys.

Girls' High School

The success of the first high school for boys aroused an interest in a similar school for girls in Boston. One was opened on the monitorial plan of Joseph Lancaster, in 1826. It opened with 130 girls selected from the 286

Classroom scene in a girl's high school in the 1850's.

candidates who had been examined. So popular did the school become by 1828 that the authorities abolished it to escape dealing with the dilemma of increasing taxes to enlarge it, or facing the wrath of parents whose daughters were rejected. As an alternative, the elementary school course for girls was lengthened and enriched.

Massachusetts Law of 1827   When a few other towns also established high schools for boys in the next few years, it became apparent that here was a new institution that would meet a great need to prepare the non-college-going abler boys "for active life or qualify them for eminence in private or public station," as the mayor of Boston put it. James G. Carter proposed and the legislature enacted a law requiring every town of 500 or more families to establish a high school and to provide for the teaching therein of United States history, bookkeeping, algebra, geometry, and surveying. In towns of more than 4000 inhabitants, these other subjects were also required: Latin, Greek, history, rhetoric, and logic. Penalties were prescribed for failure to provide the school. Subsequently, smaller towns which chose to operate high schools were legally empowered to do so. By 1840, approximately twenty-five high schools had been established in Massachusetts.

Pennsylvania High Schools   A section of Pennsylvania's revised school act of 1836 authorized Philadelphia to establish a Central High School "for the full education of such pupils of the public schools of the First School District as may possess the requisite qualifications." This high school for boys was opened in 1838 under the temporary principalship of Dr. Alexander Dallas Bache, the president of the new Girard College. Funds from Pennsylvania's share of surplus federal revenue distributed to the states in 1837 were used toward the $72,000 cost of erecting a high school building. The equipment included even an astronomical observatory, one of only four in the United States. Bache, a great grandson of Benjamin Franklin, was a West Point graduate, and he fastened some of the West Point military discipline upon the school. Having travelled extensively in Europe and having visited 278 schools of all types there, he wrote an influential *Report on Education in Europe*. His interest in the German *gymnasium* fitted him to direct a high school of high scholastic standing in Philadelphia. The Central High School was given authority to grant the degree of bachelor of arts to its graduates. It may be conjectured that the founders had in mind that the school would be an American counterpart of a *gymnasium* whose graduates would be educated at the level of leading secondary schools abroad. This appears to be the only high school in the United States authorized to grant the A.B. degree.

Bache organized three courses: a "realistic" one and a "classical" one, both of four years in duration, and a shorter English course occupying two years. Most of the students were enrolled in the realistic course, but those aspiring to enter college took the classical course. Both courses were identical, except that the former required more mathematics than the latter, and the former required modern languages while the latter required Latin. Admission to the school was by examination, as was the usual practice in early high schools.

Other high schools were organized in the larger cities of Pennsylvania in the next few years. Pittsburgh had a high school in 1849, and the borough of Easton had one in 1850. Other early high schools were at Honesdale, Carlisle, Norristown, Harrisburg, Lancaster, and York.

Success of the Central High School for boys in Philadelphia led to the establishment of a Girls' High and Normal School in 1848. This evolved into a municipal normal school.

New York Developments   The academies of New York were so numerous, so wide-spread and so firmly entrenched that we find this state slow in the development of high schools. When they were organized, they followed the usual pattern: first, a few communities obtained special permissive legislation; then, in time, a general permissive act was passed; finally, some years later, mandatory legislation required either establishment of secondary schools in districts without them, or else tuition-paid enrollment of local youths in neighboring district high schools.

The first schools in New York which met the usual criteria for a public high school were authorized by special legislation in 1847, and were established in 1848 and 1849. These were the Lockport Union School and the New York Free Academy. Two high schools, one for boys and one for girls, had been conducted by the High School Society of New York City from 1825–1826 to 1831, but these were not public high schools, since they were operated by a philanthropic society on the monitorial plan. Several other monitorial high schools in various parts of the state were authorized by special acts in between 1825 and 1856, most of them being operated by stock companies. Some that were authorized were never organized.

When public high schools were established they were usually admitted to the University of the State of New York on the same basis as the academies.

Origins of High Schools   There was no
one common origin of high schools in the United States. Generally,
they had one of three origins. In certain instances, they were founded
as the result of a state law, as in Massachusetts, or of special legislation, as in New York and Pennsylvania. In many other cases, academies previously operated by individuals or by stock companies
transferred their assets to a public board of education and were
incorporated into the public school system. In still other instances,
the high school was merely a gradual extension of the district school
into the secondary field.

The first two of these origins are self-explanatory, but the third
may require some further explanation. When local educational opportunities were limited to the offering of the district school, a
teacher who had had experience in an academy, in a state normal
school, or even in a college would sometimes find opportunity to
introduce a few of his older and abler pupils to secondary school
subjects. Indeed, this went so far in certain districts that Henry
Barnard warned district school teachers not to neglect teaching the
fundamentals to the beginners in their eagerness to provide advanced
courses for the more mature.

Union Free School Act   The states had
been divided and subdivided into small, fragmentary districts, each
with its own small district school. Some men of vision saw, as Horace
Mann did, that this was unfortunate. Without precedent, these men
undertook halting efforts to remedy the situation. By 1838, the state
superintendent in New York declared that the continual subdivision
of districts was "one of the greatest evils of the common school system." It became apparent that small districts could operate only
small, one-room, one-teacher schools, offering only a curriculum of
limited scope. At Geneva, New York, districts decided to unite rather
than subdivide, thus setting an example for other areas. The *District
School Journal* in 1841 advocated union schools. From 1840 to 1853,
more than twenty-five union or consolidated districts were formed
and extended their programs to include secondary school subjects.
Pittsford Union School claimed to have prepared students for admission to Harvard College.

Success of the Lockport Union School and the New York Free
Academy blazed a new trail, and numerous other districts sought
special legislation. Several existing academies were authorized to
consolidate with the common school systems. In some instances, petitions were denied, apparently because of irreconcilable differences

in the regulations of the state department of common schools and of the Regents of the University. (The former had charge of common, district schools, but the latter had jurisdiction over the academies. Naturally, there was some friction between these two departments of the state government.)

The need was now apparent for general, permissive legislation. This resulted in the Union Free School Act of 1853. This act, which greatly accelerated the development of public high schools, made these provisions:

1. Legal voters of contiguous districts could create a board of education, which would be a corporate body with power to prepare a budget.

2. These boards of education, in addition to other defined powers, could establish in a union school "an academical department" with full power for its control.

3. These boards could arrange with trustees of the local academy, with their unanimous consent, to absorb the academy into the union school district as its "academical department."

4. Such "academical departments" were to "enjoy all the immunities and privileges now enjoyed by academies," including a share in the Regents' grant to academies.

While these "academical departments" were not officially called high schools, they covered the same materials and served the same purpose as institutions which were called high schools in other states. Now the way was open for any area of the state to combine small districts into one large enough to operate a public high school efficiently, if the local voters saw fit to establish one. Some friction between the two state departments could, of course, be expected, but high schools were established in increasing numbers. Finally, the two departments were consolidated in 1904 into the University of the State of New York—The State Education Department, charged with general supervision of all the educational institutions of the state.

Western High Schools

The newer states of the old Northwest Territory also adopted the high school. In Ohio, both Cleveland and Columbus opened modest high schools in 1846. Chicago opened one in 1856. Apparently some of them offered subjects which would now be classed as elementary, as well as secondary.

Southern High Schools   Because the South
followed a different educational tradition, it was slow in establishing
public secondary schools. Too, the exhaustion of resources in the
Civil War and Reconstruction periods slowed the development of all
public schools. It was not until late in the nineteenth century that
high schools were begun, and for some years many of these offered
only incomplete programs. Preparation for college remained a function of academies and military schools, in most cases. When public
high schools did develop there, they were often oriented toward agricultural and vocational objectives.

Legality of High Schools   Since the early
high schools were in effect upper- and middle-class institutions, not
designed for all the children in a school district, there were many
people who questioned their legality. Was it legal to support, by
taxes levied on all the property of a district, a school which served
only some of the people of the district? Should even the poor be
taxed to support a school they could not afford to attend? Where, in
the state constitutions or in the basic law, was there any authority
for tax support of public high schools?

The first lawsuit involved in this question was in Pennsylvania in
1851, when the state supreme court decided that the local districts
might constitutionally offer a program more extensive than that
mandated by state law as a minimum.

In the state of Iowa, the state supreme court held in 1859 that the
Clayton County High School must be regarded as a part of the common school system authorized in the state constitution. In Indiana,
the supreme court upheld taxation for the support of public high
schools.

In Illinois an act had provided for local option regarding the
establishment of public high schools "for the education of the more
advanced pupils." The constitutionality of this act was attacked on
the grounds that the state constitution merely provided for "a thorough and efficient system of free schools, whereby all children in this
state might receive a good common school education," and that a
high school was not properly necessary for a "good common school
education." In this case, the court declared:

At the time of the adoption of the constitution there was a wide
difference of opinion in different parts of the state as to what constituted a common school education, and we apprehend that a
constitution which would have impaired in any degree the free

high school system in existence in many parts of the state, would not have received the approval of the voters of the state. But, however that may be, while the constitution has not defined what a common school education is and has failed to prescribe a limit, it is no part of the duty of the courts of the state to declare by judicial construction what particular branches of study shall constitute a common school education. That may be, and doubtless is, a proper question for the determination of the legislature, and as a law has been enacted by it which does not appear to violate the constitution, it is not the province of the courts to interfere.

The Kalamazoo Case   For some unknown reason most educational historians have neglected the above-cited decisions, in their preoccupation with the most famous case of all, the celebrated Kalamazoo case. This case is one of the most frequently studied cases in American educational history, ranking in importance with the Dartmouth College case, *Plessy* v. *Ferguson, Brown* v. *Board of Education,* and a few others.

The constitution of Michigan had provided for a system of common schools and for a state university, but made no provision for intermediate schools. When the constitution was adopted, secondary education fell to the lot of private academies which were often regarded as quasi-public in nature. Not satisfied with this type of secondary education, the citizens of the village of Kalamazoo in 1872 voted to establish a public high school and to employ a superintendent of schools. Taxes were levied upon real estate to raise the necessary funds. To test the legality of these proceedings a citizen by the name of Stuart entered a friendly suit challenging the right of the board of education to collect that portion of the tax which would provide for the high school and the superintendent's salary. The case was carried to the state supreme court which eventually decided that such action by a school district was legal and constitutional, when duly authorized by a majority of the voters at an election.

Justice Thomas C. Cooley, in writing the decision of the state supreme court, reviewed the arguments and then declared that in his judgment the people of the state when adopting the constitution had clearly intended to have a complete system of public education. The inference seemed irresistible, he said, that the people expected the common schools to expand to comprehend the secondary school subjects. The decision then continues:

> If these facts do not demonstrate clearly and conclusively a general state policy, beginning in 1817 and continuing until after the

adoption of the present state constitution, in the direction of free schools in which education, and at their option the elements of classical education, might be brought within the reach of all the children of the State, then, as it seems to us, nothing can demonstrate it. We might follow the subject further and show that the subsequent legislation has all concurred with this policy, but it would be a waste of time and labor. We content ourselves with the statement that neither in our state policy, in our constitution, nor in our laws, do we find the primary school districts restricted in the branches of knowledge which their officers may cause to be taught, or the grade of instruction that may be given, if their voters consent in regular form to bear the expense and raise the taxes for the purpose.

Having reached this conclusion, we shall spend no time upon the objection that the district in question had no authority to appoint a superintendent of schools, and that the duties of the superintendency should be performed by the district board. We think the power to make the appointment was incident to the full control which by law the board had over the schools of the district, and that the board and the people of the district have been wisely left by the legislature to follow their own judgment in the premises.

Since Justice Cooley's decision was cited as a precedent in other western states whose legal establishment and authority for education

Kalamazoo Union High School, one result of the Kalamazoo Case.

were similar to Michigan's, the case did have a wider application than in Michigan alone. From this fact, some writers have concluded that the case was of great national significance. However, it had no influence on many of the major test cases, for the free high schools of New England, New York, and Pennsylvania were not challenged *after* the Kalamazoo case, and the only Pennsylvania challenge, as we have seen, was earlier. We have also noted that other cases in the Northwest had been settled in the same way as the Kalamazoo case before it came to trial. The conclusion, then, is that the case came as something of a climax to earlier testing efforts, but that it was not in itself quite so influential as has commonly been assumed. Nonetheless, in all justice, it must be pointed out that Justice Cooley gave a thorough and well-reasoned decision.

As a result of court decisions and in accord with what was manifestly the spirit of the American people, the high school thus came to be accepted as an integral part of the common public school system. While decades would still pass before it attracted a large proportion of youth of high school age, the high school now was available for such as chose to attend.

Attendance Data   At first, relatively few persons attended the high schools. Among many reasons for this, the following were most important:

1. The high schools were selective institutions, entrance being by examination. Unless one scored high on the examination, he was not encouraged to attend; unless he passed the examination, he was denied admittance.

2. In many families and in many communities, there was not a sufficient educational tradition to encourage attendance.

3. Many school districts did not maintain high schools. For a resident of one of these districts to attend high school, he would have to travel many miles and would often have to pay tuition.

4. Many families could not or would not spare their children from employment.

5. Since the curricular offerings were largely theoretical and academic, high school just did not appeal to many adolescents.

6. Normally, one had passed the age of compulsory attendance before completing the district school, so there was no legal compulsion to attend high school. In several states, especially in the South, there were no compulsory attendance laws.

7. Child labor was encouraged. Some held it to be a positive good, a better education than a school could provide.

8. Maintenance of preparatory departments by many western colleges discouraged the organization of local high schools.

9. In some areas, free high schools smacked of charity education. Many families preferred to patronize private academies.

10. Going to high school over muddy and snow-blocked roads was often not practical.

11. In some areas, public high schools were too weak and insignificant to warrant patronage.

12. Even when the education was free, "hidden costs" of books, lunches, transportation, school clothing, etc. operated to discourage attendance.

13. The high school, in philosophy and procedure, was essentially a middle-class institution, taught by middle-class people, for middle-class ends. As such, it often did not appeal to the poorer people.

Nonetheless, attendance at the high schools increased significantly, decade by decade. National statistics tell the story:

Year	Census of persons 13–18	Enrollment, grades 9–12
1880	6,144,083	110,277
1890	8,095,962	297,894
1900	9,233,341	630,048
1910	10,926,305	1,032,461
1920	11,681,024	2,383,542
1930	14,020,910	4,427,000
1940	14,694,291	7,132,009
1950	12,839,415	6,392,000
1960	17,243,860	9,619,000

It will be noted in the above tabulation that the enrollment in high schools approximately doubled in each decade from 1880 to 1940. (The lower population and lower enrollment in 1950 is attributable to the lower birth rate in the 1930's, a period of economic depression.)

Lack of Uniformity   Since high schools were created in a large number of local areas throughout the United

States, and since there were almost no effective state or national controls over them, a rather large variety of schools evolved. The only generalization we can make about them is that they were public and that they offered post-elementary programs. A high school might offer a full four-year curriculum, or it might be an incomplete school offering two or three years only. It might concentrate on college preparatory subjects or it might emphasize terminal courses not geared to college admission. Obviously most of the high school seniors did not go to college, even if they did take a college preparatory course, for there was a great disparity between the number of graduates and the freshmen enrolled in the colleges. Until far more evidence is available, it is not safe to conclude that the primary emphasis of the early high school was college entrance. The New York high schools offered many subjects which were not acceptable to the colleges as subjects for admission. If this were true in New York, which maintained a considerable degree of state control over high schools, it would apparently be more so in other states.

New York moved to bring about a degree of uniformity by prescribing examinations for entrance into high school and examinations for a Regent's diploma at the conclusion of the high school course. In 1877, the Regents were authorized to institute academic examinations to "furnish a suitable standard of graduation from the said academies and academical departments of union schools, and of admission to the several colleges of the State." The Regents were authorized to discriminate in the distribution of state funds on the basis of results from their examinations. Since the Regents were the examining authority, it was logical that they should have furnished schools the "first complete curriculum" in 1878, indicating the subjects to be taught and their scope. This is the origin of the New York state secondary school syllabus.

No other state applied the New York system, so standards in other states varied more than in New York. Regional accrediting associations, inspections of high schools by the state university, and the College Entrance Examination Board tests had to be established before any reasonable degree of uniformity could be achieved. Some well publicized reports by certain national committees also contributed to standardization, as we shall see.

University Inspection   When graduates of a large number of high schools of doubtful quality applied for admission to a college or a university, the question would arise "Is this person prepared to do college work successfully?" On paper, the student might have met all the prescribed subjects, but what were the standards of the local school? Did it have a library? Were the teachers college graduates? If one had had Cicero and Vergil, how many books? If physics had been studied, for how many weeks—six or thirty? Each college was forced to give its own entrance examinations. Going some distance to take these examinations was a hardship to prospective students. The University of Michigan in 1871 hit upon a happy solution. It announced that it would send an inspector to any high school in the state that requested his visit. If the school passed inspection, the university would admit as a freshman any graduate of the school certified by the principal. The inspector was able, of course, to motivate the schools to improve their standards. And approval by the university of one school would put pressure on other schools to obtain this benefit for their graduates. In time, several western states employed the system of university inspection. In others, the state department of education evaluated schools and issued approved lists.

College Entrance Examination Board   The complexity of the problem of admission from high school to the colleges and universities was compounded as much by the disparity among the requirements of the colleges as by the lack of uniformity in high schools. A tabulation of college entrance requirements of 500 institutions in 1898 showed that great differences existed and that no two had the same prescribed pattern. As Nicholas Murray Butler put it, "If Cicero was prescribed, it meant in one place four orations and another six, and not always the same four or six." The principal of Philips Andover complained that "out of over forty boys preparing for college next year we have more than twenty senior classes." It appeared that the only cure for this anomalous situation was for the schools and the colleges to agree upon a uniform system of examinations. A commission of teachers of English in New England colleges were able to agree upon uniform requirements for intensive study in literature. Other disciplines soon followed. Nicholas Murray Butler urged the organization of a board to set uniform examinations. President Eliot of Harvard tried to persuade the New England Association of Colleges and Secondary Schools to organize such a board, without success. Butler and Eliot then assailed the Middle States Association and precipitated a debate.[1] Finally the Middle

[1] President Warfield of Lafayette College declared Lafayette would not be bound by any board; if it wanted to admit the son of a benefactor or of a trustee or of a faculty member, Lafayette would do so. Eliot replied that the purpose of the examinations was not to admit students, but merely to administer examinations and to issue certificates to those who passed; "President Warfield, it will be perfectly practicable under this plan for Lafayette College to say, if it chooses, that it will admit only such students as can not pass these examinations. No one proposes to deprive Lafayette College of that privilege." Great laughter followed, and the opposition was silenced.

States Association agreed to sponsor such an agency. It was established in 1899 by representatives of colleges and secondary schools, who held that a series of uniform examinations, uniformly administered and held. at many places, would be beneficial to schools and colleges alike.

Examinations were set in nine subjects (chemistry, English, French, German, Greek, history, Latin, mathematics and physics) according to standards prescribed by learned societies in these various disciplines. The first examinations were given in 1901, with 973 candidates taking 7889 examinations. At first, there were thirty-nine readers, all sitting around a table at Columbia University. Since that time, the examinations have been given every year in centers throughout the United States and elsewhere in the world. Now, of course, many of the examinations are objective and machine-scored. In the spring of 1962, a total of 716,246 examinations was taken by 419,997 candidates.

National Committees: Committee of Ten   The National Education Association, which had been organized in 1857 but which had been relatively inactive for several years, began in the last part of the nineteenth century to take a vigorous interest in the quality of education. Turning to the chaos in secondary school-college relations, it appointed in 1892 a Committee of Ten to study the problems and to suggest solutions. The membership of the committee was heavily weighted with college representatives: Harvard's President Charles W. Eliot was chairman, and there were five other college and university representatives. Only one public high school principal and two private school headmasters were included. The tenth member was Dr. William T. Harris, United States commissioner of education and formerly superintendent of schools at St. Louis. It was the first of a long series of committees and commissions to consider phases of education as a national problem, from a nation-wide viewpoint.

The Committee of Ten found that high schools were teaching nearly forty subjects for varying lengths of time with varying emphases. Such disparities appeared to the committee to be unsound. (It should be remembered that this was an age when the leaders in education were striving for uniformity and standardization, as we have seen in reference to the College Entrance Examination Board; when a high degree of uniformity had eventually been achieved, many leaders then saw fit to encourage individuality!) There were corollary movements toward standardization elsewhere, both within and without the field of education: in the elementary school, for example, attempts were made to set grade norms and to provide identical copies of the same textbook for each pupil; in methodology, stress was upon uniform lesson plans according to the standardized Herbartian technique; in the world of transportation, a standard gauge rail had been adopted for the railroads; we had even adopted five standard time zones in the United States.

With the aid of a large number of sub-committees of subject specialists, the Committee of Ten attempted to develop a standard secondary school curriculum. The sub-committees were asked to make specific recommendations regarding these problems:

1. In the school course of study extending approximately from the age of six years to eighteen years—a course including the periods of both elementary and secondary instruction—at what age should the study which is the subject of the Conference be introduced?

2. After it is introduced, how many hours a week for how many years should be devoted to it?

3. How many hours a week for how many years should be devoted to it during the last four years of the complete course?

4. What topics, or parts, of the subject may be reasonably covered during the whole course?

5. What topics, or parts, of the subject may best be reserved for the last four years?

6. In what form and to what extent should the subject enter into college requirements for admission?

7. Should the subject be treated differently for pupils who are going to college, for those who are going to a scientific school, and for those who, presumably, are going to neither?

8. At what stage should this differentiation begin if any be recommended?

9. Can any description be given of the best method of teaching this subject throughout the school course?

10. Can any description be given of the best mode of testing attainments in this subject at college-admission examinations?

11. For those cases in which colleges and universities permit a division of the admission examination into a preliminary and a final examination, separated by at least a year, can the best limit between the preliminary and final examinations be approximately defined?

The outcome of the work of the Committee of Ten was a conclusion that every subject in the high school should be taught in the same way and to the same extent to "every pupil so long as he pursues it, no matter what the probable destination of the pupil may be or at what point his education may cease." Apparently the learned professors on the committee had not heard about individual differences! Their report tended to cast the concept of secondary education into the uniform mold of college-entrance requirements. It is true that the committee did recommend four separate courses of study (classical, Latin-scientific, modern language, English), but these courses were as alike as Siamese twins, except for a few options. The committee further subscribed to the mental-discipline theory of education by suggesting "four years of strong and effective mental training," in the classic languages, and in confessing that the modern language and English programs "must in practice be distinctly inferior to the other two." No attention was paid to vocational subjects, except for a condescending mention of bookkeeping, commercial arithmetic, and instruction in "trade or the useful arts."

Though the report carried considerable prestige because of the personnel of the committee, not all school men approved. Oscar D. Robinson, principal of the high school at Albany, New York, dissented strongly, charging that the committee was in error in assuming that preparation for college necessarily constituted the best preparation for life. He said there was an over-emphasis on Latin and mathematics and an inadequate appreciation of such subjects as drawing, music, political economy, and manual training.

It has been customary in the last quarter century for writers of texts in education to excoriate the Committee of Ten for fastening a rigid curriculum upon the secondary school. Now, with secondary schools "tightening up" in their curricular requirements and rejecting the life-adjustment curricular philosophy, the Committee of Ten may gain a more respectable place in society. We must bear in mind, of course, that neither the Committee of Ten nor any other early committee ever contemplated that all the youth of America, with their diverse abilities and inabilities, would enroll in high school. To these committeemen, the school was still a selective institution for abler students.

Committee on College Entrance Requirements   John Dewey built a philosophy based upon the premise that education is the constant reconstruction of experience. Whether or not that is a good definition of the educative process, we can be sure that the last sixty years has been a period in which secondary education was characterized by the constant reconstruction of its aims, objectives, and content by experienced committees. The second great committee of national scope was appointed in 1895 by the National Education Association. This was the Committee on College Entrance Requirements. This committee recommended several innovations: a six-year secondary school of grades seven through twelve, a limited number of free electives, sequential courses, acceleration of gifted students, and the famous Carnegie Unit for the evaluation of high school work. (One unit was to be assigned for study of one subject four or five times a week for a school year.) While the committee held that absolute uniformity might be undesirable and certainly was unattainable, it did suggest that a standard study unit would be helpful in measuring all high school courses.

Economy of Time   A third committee, working from 1905 to 1911, attempted to shorten the educational course by two years. It labored for six years, but was unable to make any time-saving alteration in the eight-year elementary school and the four-year high school. Although the American time-plan had evolved slowly and haphazardly, as we shall see, it had apparently reached the status of an embedded tradition by the turn of the century.

Articulation of High School and College   A committee of nine addressed itself to the problem of articulating the secondary schools and the colleges. It defined a sound high school education as one of fifteen units of work, with at least eleven of these units in English, foreign language, mathematics, social science, and natural science.

Commission on Reorganization   In 1918, the fifth of the series of national studies of secondary education was published as the report of the Commission on the Reorganization of Secondary Education. The committee faced up to the fact that persons in high school would be living in a changed postwar world. The committee tried to assess what this world would be like and to suggest emphases for education in that world. The report shows the philosophical influence of Herbert Spencer, the English sociologist-philosopher, who had written *What Knowledge Is of Most Worth?* fifty-eight years earlier. Spencer's five categories for the selection of educational experience were certainly the intellectual parents of the commission's famous *Seven Cardinal Principles,* which were set forth as the objectives of American secondary education. These objectives were:

1. Health.
2. Command of the fundamental processes.
3. Worthy home membership.
4. Vocation.
5. Citizenship.
6. Worthy use of leisure time.
7. Ethical character.

This report came at a strategic time. Since we had just won a war to "make the world safe for democracy," it now seemed appropriate for Americans to direct education to social and civic ends. Optimism abounded; people were prosperous; prospects for the development of industry and culture seemed unlimited. Many people who could not or would not master the conventional subjects in the conventional way were now beginning to enter high schools. The Spencerian Cardinal Principles seemed to be a wonderful package of new educational objectives.

Changing High School Population   With few exceptions, pupils who went to high school before World War I (and even for some years thereafter) had been rather carefully selected through a series of elimination processes. By and large, elementary teachers had firm standards of achievement to be attained in each grade. If one did not meet this standard, he did not pass. Admission to high school was still by examination. Retention in high school was dependent upon one's scholastic record.

After World War I an accelerating change in the high school constituency took place. People who had formerly dropped out of school early were now retained. An increasing percentage of youth continued in school—not just the academically able, but the less academic as well. Psychologists preached that one would sear a pupil's soul for life by "flunking him." Teachers, exposed to this psychology and to community pressures, often gave way and passed less than able pupils. Child labor laws were enacted or strengthened, and by 1918 children and youth were nearly all forced to remain in school.

Society sent these people to school and the school felt obliged to modify its program to give them something they could learn and (it was hoped) use. Numerous non-academic courses were added to the curriculum, and often academic courses were modified or watered down to meet the needs of this new pupil population, whom Commissioner Butterfield of Connecticut called "The New Fifty Per Cent."

The high schools made many mistakes in adjusting to these new pupils, no doubt. At times the schools seemed even to have developed a cult of anti-intellectuality. The great wonder is that more serious errors were not made in attempting to adjust an established, traditional institution to nearly 2,000,000 new students in one short decade, when there were not enough skilled teachers or buildings to cope with the flood. The great wonder is that the schools did not break down entirely. If any institution of society—a church, for example—suddenly had its membership doubled by the influx of people without any traditional attachment to that institution, many of them not wanting to be there, its problem would then be comparable to that which the schools faced after 1918.

Reasons for Increased Enrollment   There were many sociological reasons for this tremendous increase in the secondary school population. They could be elaborated at great length, but we shall state them here briefly:

1. Child attendance laws set a higher school-leaving age. Enforcement was more stringent.

2. Child labor laws were made more severe and were more stringently enforced.

3. There were more high schools available.

4. Transportation to school at a distance was now being provided.

5. Better economic circumstances were permitting families to encourage youths to stay in school longer.

6. Stay-in-school campaigns were inaugurated. Articles and advertisements stressed that one increased his lifetime earning power significantly for each additional year of schooling.

7. Curricular revision and a new methodology made the school more attractive to an increasing number of·boys and girls.

8. An extensive program of extra-curricular activities attracted and retained many youths.

9. Mechanization in industry closed many jobs which these youths might otherwise have been tempted to take.

10. Attending high school became a socially accepted "thing to do" —a social norm—especially as more schools stressed education for citizenship.

National Survey of Secondary Education   The extraordinary growth of population in the high schools seemed to indicate the need for a thorough study of the schools, their curricula, and their philosophy of education. Such a study was proposed by the North Central Association of Colleges and Secondary Schools in 1929 and was undertaken by the United States Office of Education. The findings were published in twenty-seven monographs. Fortunately, there was a one-volume summary. The chief outcome was the motivation of curricular reform on the local level throughout the country.

Issues of Secondary Education   The Department of Secondary School Principals of the National Education Association[2] undertook to lay the groundwork for a national program of secondary education by instituting another study of the issues facing secondary schools. Under the direction of Dr. Thomas H. Briggs, the committee asked ten pertinent questions about the secondary schools, their pupils, their programs, their methods, and their philosophies. The report, called "The Issues of Secondary Education" (cited in the bibliography of this chapter, as are also the other reports), gives a good view of the secondary school in the early 1930's.

The Depression of the 30's   The great financial depression of the 1930's had a decided impact on the secondary schools, as well as on schools at other levels, and upon all facets of American life. Girls, in general, tended to remain in school, but large numbers of boys and youths left as soon as they could, either to find jobs to help with family financial problems, or to join the ranks of the disillusioned unemployed. Eventually the federal government created the Civilian Conservation Corps to provide employment in conservation activities and the National Youth Administration to subsidize students to remain in school and college. To save teachers' salaries, several subjects were dropped from many high schools. Classes grew larger and teachers (often with their pay

---

[2] Now known as the National Association of Secondary School Principals, an affiliate of the NEA.

months in arrears and reduced drastically) became more harried and defeatist. Some teachers turned to radical ideas. One educator, George S. Counts, wrote a book whose title was typical of the spirit of the times during the depression: *"Dare the Schools Build a New Social Order?"*

American Youth Commission   The American Youth Commission, sponsored by the American Council on Education (a non-government agency), made an exhaustive study of youth's reaction to the secondary school. Published under the title *Youth Tell Their Story*, this study reflected the anxieties of the times:

> Four out of every ten youths assert that they leave school because their parents cannot continue to send them. For them, the solution is primarily a matter of providing opportunities that don't exist. For a large proportion of the remainder, the solution is more definitely a matter of so adjusting our school programs as to make them sufficiently attractive to compete with other things. Our data reveal that, with several groups of youth, unsatisfactory school adjustment—by which is meant a combination of lack of interest, disciplinary difficulties, and too difficult subjects—is a more general reason for leaving school than a lack of family funds. So far as the youth's own statements of why he left school can be accepted as the real reasons, all of this indicates that, for large groups of youth, *the schools simply have failed to function as a genuine force.* The fact that relatively high percentages of youth giving lack of interest as their reason for dropping out were found among those who left school at the upper high school level, as well as among those who left at the elementary level, indicates that all along the line the schools, as they are now set up, are adapted to neither the needs nor the interests of large numbers of our young people.

Other publications of the commission stressed the need for reforming the curriculum. The report was studied thoroughly, but it made little impact on the schools, possibly because of the inherent lag in curricular reform that we have seen before.

The Regents' Inquiry   Another study of secondary schools in the depression years formed a part of the Regents' Inquiry into the Cost and Character of the Schools in the state of New York. Two volumes of this inquiry, *When Youth Leave School* and *High School and Life* concluded that there were "challenging discrepancies between a democratic theory of education and current school practices." It was reported that many left school early because they were not satisfied with what the school gave them, and ones who stayed till graduation did not later use in any effective way what they had been taught. While the secondary school was "reasonably successful" in fitting its better students for continued learning, it failed in most other regards.

Changes in Accrediting   From their founding, the regional accrediting agencies had stressed standardization, often through mechanical ways. Now, in a time of ferment, it came to be recognized that perhaps qualitative factors should be more important than quantitative and that individuality should be encouraged. The six accrediting associations set up a Cooperative Study of Secondary School Standards to work out new criteria for accrediting secondary schools. The conclusion was that a school should be judged in terms of its own educational philosophy and how effectively it achieved its own objectives. Two manuals, *Evaluative Criteria* and *How to Evaluate a Secondary School,* were published to help establish principles for a sound and helpful evaluation.

Common Learnings   Even during national emergencies, nations look to their school systems and try to improve them. During the trying days of World War I, the British were debating how to make England a fit land for heroes to return to, and several proposals were made for educational reform. During World War II, American educators formulated plans and projections for postwar education. The Educational Policies Commission, sponsored by the American Association of School Administrators and the National Education Association, published a liberal, and indeed visionary, prospectus called *Education for All American Youth* which described secondary education in two hypothetical communities—"Farmville" and "American City." The emphasis was on "common learnings" taught in a core program.

Some headway had been made to implement these suggestions in a few districts, but a decided change in the educational climate put a stop to these experiments. The report had apparently assumed that the postwar era would be tension-less with no one challenging American democracy.

Life Adjustment Curriculum   Simultaneously, Professor Charles A. Prosser had proposed his "life adjustment curriculum" for the sixty per cent of secondary school students who were not headed for college or for skilled occupations. (This was Butterfield's "New Fifty Per Cent," enlarged.) A national conference engendered enthusiasm, and Professor Harl A. Douglas even proclaimed what was good in "life adjustment" for this sixty per cent would also be good for all secondary school pupils. A Commission on Life Adjustment Education propagandized for this new departure.

Reaction after Sputnik   Conservatives had sharply criticized the direction American education was taking. Among the educational conservatives within the profession were Professors William C. Bagley and Isaac Kandel of Teachers College, Columbia University. Many non-educationists, laymen, and college professors in other disciplines, were more critical. The writings of Arthur Bestor, an advocate of basic education, are typical.

These criticisms did little to stem the tide toward life adjustment until the Russians orbited Sputnik. Then suddenly, the schools became the whipping boy of all that was wrong in the slowness of our space program. No one stopped to wonder if a ponderous bureaucracy or inter-service rivalries had anything to do with our slow strides. People who knew about schools and people who didn't made journalistic hay in interstellar space. The student can readily locate these articles in the *Reader's Guide to Periodical Literature* under a special classification, "Education, criticisms of," for the years 1958 through 1962.

The Conant Reports   In its history, Harvard has had two presidents who took a keen interest in secondary education. These were Charles W. Eliot, already mentioned, and Dr. James B. Conant. Having served as United States high commissioner and then ambassador to the West German Republic after his retirement from Harvard, Dr. Conant returned to the United States resolved to make a study of the American high school, for he regarded public education essential to the preservation of democracy. With a background of experience as a scholar in science, as head of a great university, and as a diplomat, Conant studied American high schools under a Foundation grant and made several constructive recommendations for improving school programs. His three most important works were *The American High School Today*, a briefer report on the junior high school, and *Slums and Suburbs*.

Sub-titled "a report to interested citizens," *The American High School Today* treated the comprehensive high school as a unique feature of education and made recommendations for improving public secondary education. These recommendations were:

1. Better and more adequate counseling, with one counselor for each 250 or 300 students.

2. Individualized programs. Elimination of such classifications as "college preparatory," "commercial," etc.

3. Certain required programs for all, including English, history, American problems, and at least one year of mathematics and science.

4. Ability grouping, subject by subject.

5. Each student to be given a durable record of courses and grades, to supplement the diploma.

6. Increased emphasis on English composition, with reduction in the load of teachers of English.

7. A diversified program of "marketable skills" such as typing, office machines, vocational agriculture, industrial arts.

8. Special consideration for slow learners.

9. A "tougher" program for the academically talented.

10. Use of the advanced placement program and tutoring for the highly gifted.

11. Institution of an annual academic inventory.

12. A flexible schedule with at least six periods in addition to physical education and driver training.

13. Prerequisites for advanced academic courses.

14. Elimination of ranking all students. "I have found that in many schools the desire to rank high has led bright students to elect easy courses."

15. An academic honors list.

16. Institution of a developmental reading program.

17. Tuition-free summer schools.

18. Offering of a third and fourth year in foreign language.

19. Enriched and differentiated science courses.

20. Making the homeroom into a significant social unit.

21. A required twelfth-grade course in American problems, with student discussion of current and controversial topics.

22. Reduction in the number of high schools from 21,000 to 9,000 to permit each larger resulting school to offer an adequate program. School district reorganization on a statewide basis.

23. Comprehensive high schools rather than specialized ones.

Being relatively mild, the recommendations did not create a furor in education. Conservative lay critics were not pacified, and within the profession there were some reservations. Generally, it was thought that Conant's services were largely in arresting the vituperative condemnation of the schools.

Slums and Suburbs is a more important volume from the sociological point of view, for it forcefully called to the nation's attention the wide disparity in the quality of instruction in the slums and in the suburbs.

Junior High Schools The American system of an eight year elementary school and a four year high school seems to have just happened, without being rationally planned. Indeed, there were variations of this 8–4 system in various parts of the country. In some areas, there were 7- or 9-year elementary schools, and high schools with 2, 3, and 4 year programs. The generally accepted practice, however, was 8–4. At the turn of the century, this apportionment of time began to be questioned. The pioneer work of G. Stanley Hall in the field of adolescent psychology demonstrated that the children in the upper elementary grades deserved to be taught differently from those in the first six grades.

To promote retention of students in school longer, some leaders advocated elimination of the eighth grade graduation, which many had come to regard as the end of a "common school" education. If persons were moved from a six-year elementary school into another unit, they might be persuaded to remain in school longer—particularly if they were offered a more diversified and challenging set of experiences.

In many instances, the concept of the junior high school was brought down from the clouds of academic theory to the level of reality by the school district's building problems. With more and more students remaining in school longer, and with the natural increase in the pupil population, both elementary and secondary schools bulged at the seams. Rather than add wings to several elementary schools and to the high school as well, boards of education saw fit to pull the seventh and eighth grades out of the elementary schools, and often to shift the ninth grade out of the high school, combining them into a new school, the junior high school. In certain states, it was advantageous for a district to do this, for now the seventh and eighth grade pupils could be counted in statistics in secondary education; commonly, state grants per capita were higher for secondary than for elementary average daily attendance.

The junior high school movement was, then, a resultant of the combination of idealistic philosophical concepts and matter-of-fact practicality. In some cases, theory led to junior high schools; in others, the schools were established, and then theory made a virtue of necessity. Professors of education proclaimed the junior high school a great innovation and constructed special courses in its rationale. The two most significant books on the junior high school were by L. V. Koos and by Thomas H. Briggs. Each called his book *The Junior High School.*

While these junior schools ordinarily included grades of 7, 8, and 9, there were variants. In 1952, 74.2% of the schools followed this pattern, but others were organized around grades 7 and 8 only, or grades 7 to 10. In urban areas, the junior high school was usually a separate administrative unit, but in the rural areas it often was a division of the combined junior-senior high school on the 6–6 plan.

No one is certain which was the first junior high school. Many district schools had early extended their programs to cover at least a part of the junior high school years, but these were hardly real junior highs. The departmentalized seventh and eighth grade school organized at Richmond, Indiana in 1896 was perhaps the first junior high, though it was not called that. Schools begun in Columbus, Ohio and in Berkeley and Los Angeles, California early in this century seem to have been junior highs. By 1916, thirty-six states reported having 54 such institutions; in 1917, there were 272; in 1952, 3227.

Vocational and Agricultural Education   Land-grant colleges had been authorized in Lincoln's administration to promote education in agriculture and the mechanical arts, but as time went on it became apparent that these institutions alone could not bring to all the people the useful knowledge being accumulated. Establishment of county agricultural agents helped, but not enough. When the United States saw the approaching shadows of World War I, it became apparent that we might become the breadbasket of the world and would need to increase our agricultural production. Further, the war would cut off the importation of hundreds of thousands of immigrants, among whom were many skilled workers. Obviously, we needed to improve and disseminate skills in agriculture and in mechanical areas.

The Smith-Hughes Act of 1917 provided for creation of a federal board of vocational administration to apportion United States funds to the states to subsidize instruction in agriculture, vocational subjects of a mechanical kind, and home economics in the high schools of the states. Each state was to create a similar board or to assign the responsibility to an existing board. Federal funds were to be used to pay for the teaching of these subjects and for necessary administrative and supervisory services, including the preparation of teachers.

This federal subsidy greatly increased the availability of these courses to the youth of the country. These courses, in turn, served to retain youth in school for specific vocational preparation. No one can estimate the financial and social return on the investment made by the federal government.

The success of this program, with a relatively restrained amount of federal interference with local schools, is cited as a favorable case by those who advocate federal aid to education.

The Drop-outs

The implied ideal of American education is to have every child and every youth in school from the age of five to eighteen or more (unless he has previously attained a high school diploma) successfully meeting educational challenges and growing in ability to serve himself and the commonwealth. We have not attained this goal. Whether or not we ever will is still debatable. But one thing is evident: decade by decade, we have come closer and closer to the ideal.

The first struggle was to provide the schools; the next to compel attendance. The struggle now is to retain in school for a longer period of years those who have enrolled. While the holding power of the school has increased, decade by decade, the drop-out still constitutes a great problem. The problem is complex, for human motives are seldom simple. Matters of home tradition, environment, the desire to earn money, disillusionment with the school and its curriculum, the turbulence of growing up, and many other factors are involved. Current educational periodicals discuss the problem at length. In many schools, campaigns are conducted to persuade youth to remain.

The Trump Plan

The move toward well-graded schools containing twenty-five to thirty-five pupils in a room, with each room a standardized duplicate of its neighbor, has long been a part of the American educational goal. When this goal had been nearly achieved, some educators came to the conclusion this wasn't what we wanted, after all. Under the sponsorship of the National Association of Secondary School Principals, Dr. J. Lloyd Trump evolved a procedure in which teachers and pupils would be involved in large group instruction, small group discussions, independent study, and team teaching. This is commonly called "The Trump Plan." It is now being tried in a number of secondary schools. To what extent it will make an impact upon the schools remains, at this writing, still to be seen. The pages of history of education texts are littered with the corpses of other proposals to reform the secondary school—the platoon system of Gary, Indiana, the Batavia plan, the Dalton plan, the Lancasterian monitorial system, etc. The fact remains that the school is a conservative institution, staffed by conservative administrators and conservative teachers, and has an antipathy toward radical departures.

New Materials and Techniques   From the days of Comenius and Pestalozzi, good teachers have sought to substitute real experience for the usual verbalisms of the classroom. Good teachers have always tried to use whatever was available in their environment to suffuse their teaching with rich meanings. With teachers better educated than ever before, both in subject matter and in teaching methodology, we expect more realistic teaching. Fortunately, the industrial revolution and man's inventive genius have placed a host of servants at the disposal of the teacher. Books are lavishly illustrated. Pictures are universally available. Reference books are of a high order. Thousands of titles are available in film strips and educational motion pictures, enabling the teacher to bring the world into the classroom. Radio has brought events to classes as they happened. A growing number of educational television stations bring skilled specialists to the child in the classroom. A television teacher can spend far more time in planning a lesson than can the classroom teacher. To relieve the teacher of much routine instruction in basic concepts, there are now teaching programs which may be used in "machines" and "machine-technique" books of programmed learnings.[3] New developments in instructional materials will be further discussed in Chapter 20, which deals with schools as they may be in years to come.

[3] In one education class where the teacher was speaking of teaching machines, a student interrupted with the query, "What's new about that? I've had *teaching machines* all my life."

For Further Reading

Benjamin, Harold. *The Saber-Tooth Curriculum*. McGraw-Hill, 1939.
Satire on educational conservatism in the curriculum.

Bestor, Arthur. *Restoration of Learning*. Knopf, 1955.
Violent criticism of progressivism in American education. Plea for "basic education."

Briggs, Thomas H. *The Great Investment*. Harvard University Press, 1930.
The thesis that secondary education is the best investment that society can make in its youth.

Brown, Elmer Ellsworth. *The Making of Our Middle Schools*. Longmans, Green, 1921.
Much material on the traditional high school.

Butterfield, E. W. "The New Fifty Per Cent". *Junior-Senior High School Clearing House*. January, 1934.
A plea for a suitable curriculum for non-academic students.

Case, Gilbert. " 'Quackery in the Public Schools'—An Answer." *Atlantic Monthly*. June, 1950.
Reply to Lynd, below.

Commission on the Reorganization of Secondary Education. *Cardinal Principles of Secondary Education*. Bureau of Education Bulletin No. 35, 1918.
The Seven Cardinal Principles, which redirected American secondary education.

Cubberley, Elwood P. *Public Education in the United States*. Revised. Houghton Mifflin, 1934.
Cubberley, in Chapter 7, describes "The Battle to Extend the System Upward" through the high school.

Cubberley, Elwood P. *Readings in Public Education in the United States*. Houghton Mifflin, 1934.
Chapter 8 presents portions of many documents, including the Kalamazoo case decision.

Douglas, Harl R. *Secondary Education for Life Adjustment of American Youth*. Ronald, 1952.
The cause of life adjustment advocated. Contrasts "old" and "new" high schools on pages 26 and 27.

Eckert, Ruth and Thomas O. Marshall. *When Youth Leave School: Report of the Regents' Inquiry.* McGraw-Hill, 1938.
The schools of New York allegedly were not meeting the needs of youth in the depression years of the 1930's.

Franzen, Carl G. F. *Foundations of Secondary Education.* Harper, 1955.
Chapter 8 on "Early School Leavers."

French, William Marshall. *American Secondary Education.* Odyssey Press, 1957.
Chapter 5 presents "The Battle for Free High Schools".
Chapter 6 describes the early high schools.
Chapter 7 shows the influence of Herbert Spencer.
Chapter 8 discusses the non-academic student and
Chapter 9 discusses "the curriculum crisis".

Gifford, Walter J. *Historical Development of the New York State High School System.* University of the State of New York. Bulletin No. 753, 1922.
The best account of the growth of high schools in the state of New York.

Good, Harry G. *A History of American Education.* Second edition. Macmillan, 1962.
Chapter 8 deals with the rise of the high school.

Lynd, Albert. *Quackery in the Public Schools.* Little, Brown, 1953.
Strong criticism of progressive education.

Prosser, Charles. *Secondary Education and Life.* Inglis Lecture. Harvard University Press, 1939.
Plea for life adjustment curriculum.

Scott, C. Winfield and Clyde M. Hill. *Public Education Under Criticism.* Prentice-Hall, 1934.
Anthology of criticisms and attacks upon education, both elementary and secondary. Analysis of these criticisms.

Spencer, Herbert. *Education.* Appleton, 1860.
Four essays on education, including the famous "What Knowledge Is of Most Worth?"

Thomas, Harrison C. "The High School as a Common School". *School Review,* April 1, 1955.
The changed pupil population in secondary schools, now a cross-section of the whole population.

Tompkins, Ellsworth and Walter H. Gaumnitz. *The Carnegie Unit: Its Origin, Status and Trends.* U.S. Office of Education, Bulletin, 1954, No.7.
The Carnegie unit and alternate proposals.

10

The Growth of Colleges

Westward Movement   Even during the
Revolution, pioneers were migrating westward. At the close of the
war, the trickle turned into a tide. The same fear of illiteracy that
had been evident to the writer of *New England's First Fruits* was
shared by these migrants. They established common schools and
academies and then erected colleges as capstones of their educational
systems. By 1800, these pioneers had started colleges on the frontier,
from Maine to Georgia. Eighteen new colleges were established—
double the number that existed at the time of the Revolution. Many
of these were as modest and weak as the colonial colleges had been.

It was, of course, frightfully easy to found a college. A few zealous
and ambitious people would petition a territorial or state legislature
and the legislature would readily grant a charter. In some states,
filing papers in the local court house was legally sufficient. These
charters were frequently very generous, allowing the incorporators
and their successors forever to grant degrees "commonly granted by
the leading universities of the United States and Europe" to any
persons who met whatever standards they saw fit to prescribe.

This is still the basis of the "diploma mill" college in the United
States. A group of men might obtain a charter, motivated by the
best intentions. Finding the road rough in operating a bona fide
college, their successors might operate a shoddy diploma mill, conferring high sounding but bogus degrees. In spite of pressure by state
departments of education, the United States Office of Education, and
the accrediting associations, they still operate. The author can tell
the reader where he can get a shiny doctorate (in philosophy, or if
one prefers, in metaphysics) for $300 and few questions asked. Of
course, the degree is bogus, but that mere fact apparently does not
discourage "students" from enrolling.

Many colleges were founded on the frontier with high hopes and
nothing else. Some soon succumbed. Others, with better luck or

173

tougher character, survived to become useful and creditable institutions. As an illustration, one might take the founding of Hastings College in Nebraska. Hastings was only a crude frontier village of seven houses when a local store owner said to his friends "Why not have a Presbyterian College in Hastings?" They interested the synod which was long on encouragement and prayer but notably short on financial aid. The college opened in 1882 with the local pastor as first president, in a room in the postoffice building. Frank E. Weyer, who served the college as dean from 1918 to 1960, has told the story of the college, its trials and its triumphs, in highly readable fashion.[1]

Motives for Frontier Colleges   Mixed motives entered into the founding of these frontier colleges, some of them noble and some decidedly less so. In many cases, the pioneers in the West

The pioneer settlement of Hastings, Nebraska in the 1870's when proposal was first made to establish a college.

[1] Weyer, Frank E.: *Hastings College, Seventy-five Years in Retrospect*. Published by the college, 1957. Dean Weyer's daughter, Dorothy Weyer Creigh, has told the story of Bellevue College, another Presbyterian College in Nebraska, which was one of the many pioneer colleges that did not survive.

wanted educational advantages for their children without sending them back to "the effete East." In some cases, the founding of the college was a blatantly commercial venture to attract settlers and to sell real estate. Dr. Janet Carpenter, professor of English at Hastings College from 1906 to 1947, said that her family, migrants from Massachusetts, chose Hastings as their residence because of the modest college there. (Grand Island, where they left the railway, had none!) In other instances, colleges were founded with spendthrift prodigality as a byproduct of the intense denominational rivalry on the frontier. If the Methodists or Baptists had a college in a new state, then the Presbyterians and Congregationalists had to have colleges also, lest their young people be won from the faith of their fathers. So keen was this rivalry that one Baptist father said he would rather see his daughter in hell than enrolled in a Methodist college.

"Union" Colleges In some instances, to forestall ruinous denominational rivalry, colleges were incorporated by several denominations acting in cooperation. Union College at Schenectady, New York, owes its name to this fact. Muskingum College in Ohio was also founded by a union of denominations, but the old United Presbyterian Church soon maneuvered to gain control.

Petty Restrictions Though many of the more famous Eastern colleges had thrown off the shackles of Puritanism, piety and pseudo-piety reigned in many of the denominational colleges until very recent times. In the 1930's, college catalogs contained such statements as these:

Students are expected to dress simply and modestly.

The necks of dresses should not be low and the skirts should be long, covering the knee in any posture, while the sleeves should extend to the elbow.

A display of jewelry or the wearing of beads and necklaces is not permitted.

Young men are expected to attire themselves in conformity to public dress conventionalities, such as suitable neckwear and coat at all classes, in the dining hall, and at all public occasions.

Students arriving in town in time for the official opening of college in September are met, on request, by a representative of the college, without charge. At other times, a chaperone's fee will be charged for meeting trains.

Students addicted to the use of either tobacco or alcoholic liquors are requested not to register.

It has been well said that the devil's triangle is the card table, the dance hall, and the theatre.

The playing of cards is forbidden.

We are firmly convinced that dancing is a great evil, and that it has caused the loss of character of many.

All women are required to be in their own rooms in the evening after 7:00 o'clock.

Students who are not home students may go to the depot only on special permission from the dean of women.

Young men and women may meet together in the reception room on Sunday from 3:30 to 5:30 p.m. and on Friday evenings from 7:00 until 9:30 p.m.

This school is not a church, nor a prayer meeting, yet we are careful that a healthy religious atmosphere shall, as far as possible, pervade the entire institution.

Parents will furnish the counselor of women with the names of young men from whom their daughters may receive visits.

Faculty members faced similar restrictions. A professor at one, walking home past the president's house, found it expedient to conceal a Sunday newspaper under his coat. Faculty were censured for smoking away from the campus. Generally, the word "Sabbath" was used instead of "Sunday."

Who Should Control the Colleges?   The early colleges represented a mixture of control by private persons and by government officials. They frequently received government support of various kinds. After the Revolution, serious questions arose as to whether the colleges should be allowed to remain in the control of their trustees or whether they should be taken over by the state governments. The state of New York reopened Kings College, which had been closed during the Revolution, and renamed it Columbia College. It was placed under the control of a state board, the Regents of the University of the State of New York, in 1784. Three years later it was remanded to a separate board of trustees, but under the general supervision of the Regents, who were also authorized to charter and to supervise academies and other colleges which might be established.

Pennsylvania, for a short time, seized and controlled the institution known as the University of Pennsylvania. The trustees and faculty were dismissed, and new ones installed. In 1789, the college and its assets were returned to the old board, voluntarily.

A more notable case was the Dartmouth College case. Dartmouth's original charter had been issued by George III, and the college operated under it until 1816. The college trustees were conservative and Federalist in politics. The new Democratic-Republican party controlled the legislature and was irritated by the Federalist control of the college in the state. The legislature tried to alter the charter materially and to replace the name of the institution with "University of New Hampshire."

The charter trustees refused to surrender, and for a time two institutions existed side by side. The charter trustees brought suit to retain the college and engaged Daniel Webster, a swarthy young man who had attended Dartmouth, as attorney. The case eventually reached the United States Supreme Court, which held that the charter granted by the British king was a contract and that it therefore came under the protection of Article 1, section 10, of the Constitution of the United States. This section provides that "no state shall . . . pass any bill of attainder, ex post facto law, or law *impairing the obligation of contracts.*"

This case, which involved control of one small college, occupies a notable place in American history, for it was construed as a precedent in all cases involving charters of all kinds of institutions. This decision seemed to decrease the police power of the state by placing chartered industrial, financial, educational, and other corporations under the protection of the federal judiciary in any dispute with the state which had granted the charter. The states soon hit upon the expedient of limitations upon the charters of corporations.

Historians disagree as to the effect of Justice Marshall's decision in the Dartmouth College case upon higher education. Some contend that the decision delayed the establishment of state universities. This does not seem entirely credible, since some state universities were already operating before the decision was handed down. It seems safer to say that the effect was the delay of the establishment of state universities in the more conservative states of the eastern seaboard, but there is little evidence that many of them would have seen fit to found state universities at that time, at any rate. Private colleges have not been notoriously anxious to invite state competition, and these private eastern colleges had their friends in influential places.

Two modern historians, the Beards, contend that the decision had a two-pronged effect: it promoted the growth of independent colleges by guaranteeing that they were safe from state expropriation, and it served notice on the states that if they wanted universities under state control they would have to make a fresh start with new foundations. It is interesting to note that one of the nine original colleges, Rutgers, has become the State University of New Jersey, in recent years. This was achieved by a mutually satisfactory agreement, not by such seizure as New Hampshire unsuccessfully attempted.

University of Virginia   The University of Georgia was the first state university to be chartered, but the state provided small financial aid, and the institution was hardly a credit to a sovereign state until well after the Civil War. The University of North Carolina, now a leading university in the South, had an equally inauspicious early career. It, too, had a state charter and no state funds.

Virginia fared somewhat better. Founded through the interest of Thomas Jefferson (who despaired of reforming the College of William and Mary to his taste), it opened in 1825. While Jefferson found fault with some of the faculty's qualifications, it seems to have offered a higher grade of instruction than any of the other early state universities. Its architecture, designed by Jefferson, set the pattern of Georgian colonial as the ideal for the American campus. This ideal, in time, was superseded by Victorian gingerbread, and then by pseudo-Gothic, but seems coming into its own again, except where "modern" architecture has been adopted.

Western Universities   Ohio established two universities under the land-grant provisions of the Ordinance of 1787. These were Ohio University at Athens and Miami University at Oxford, in 1804 and 1809, respectively. (The Ohio State University at Columbus was founded much later as an agricultural and mechanical college under the Morrill Act.) Ohio University was the first state institution of learning chartered in the old northwest

University of Virginia—Buildings designed in detail by
Thomas Jefferson and constructed under his supervision.

territory. Unfortunately, many of the state universities differed but little from the denominational colleges which surrounded them. Often the universities even had clergymen as presidents.

There was a parallel in political ideals, educational philosophy, and curriculum between Thomas Jefferson, who was instrumental in founding the University of Virginia, and Judge Woodward, who projected the grandiose Catholepistemiad or University of Michigania in 1817. This university, which soon gave up its jaw-breaking name, had two faculty members in its early years: The Rev. John Monteith, a Presbyterian minister, president and occupant of seven of the professorial chairs, and Pére Gabriel Richard, a Catholic priest, vice president, and occupant of six chairs.

The Teachers College   The early agitation
for and development of state-supported teacher training institutions was closely associated with the need for preparing teachers for the common schools. Practically no one gave attention to the idea that these normal schools should prepare teachers for the academies and for the new high schools which were developing. The academies and high schools, still small in number and in size, looked rather to the liberal arts colleges for their teachers. This is not to say, however,

that they there found a sufficient supply. Often non-college graduates taught in the high schools. Ambrose L. Subrie records that when
he went to a high school principalship in northern Pennsylvania in
1895, there were only two college graduates teaching in all the high
schools of the county. (He was not one of them; at the time, he was
a graduate of a rural elementary school who had taken summer
courses at a normal school.)

The larger high schools, which paid better salaries and offered
the amenities of living in a town or city, could often command the
services of college graduates, particularly of women college graduates, to whom few other vocations were open. The smaller and
poorer schools often took normal school graduates as teachers, even if
they had themselves never attended high school! The normal schools
did not require high school graduation for admission until late in
the nineteenth century or early in this century. The schools, then,
had a choice of teachers: liberal arts graduates who had taken no
professional courses in education but who had, it is supposed, a
reasonable command of the subjects they would teach, or normal
school graduates who had been steeped in methodology but were
woefully lacking in study of the subjects they would teach.

As early as 1871, the Buffalo Normal School hoped to offer collegiate and scientific courses which it hoped would be "as thorough
and extended" as pursued in the liberal arts colleges, but this plan
was too ambitious and was not carried out. Other normal schools
did sometimes offer courses designed to cover high school subjects,
but with indifferent success.

The rapid growth of high schools made teacher recruitment an
increasingly vexing problem. It was at this juncture that two institutions in particular directed their attention to meeting the
growing need for high school teachers. They were the normal schools
at Ypsilanti, Michigan, and at Albany, New York. They limited admission to high school graduates, and attempted to concentrate on
preparing teachers for secondary schools.

The decision at Albany was to limit instruction to the professional
subjects, such as history of education, philosophy of education,
methods, practice teaching, and "such other matters as bear directly
and immediately upon the work of the teacher." The aim was to save
high school students "from the gross empiricism to which they had
hitherto been subjected" by teachers lacking in professional skills.
The name of the normal school was changed to State Normal College,
and authority was granted to confer the degree of bachelor, master,
and doctor of pedagogy. Despite these high hopes, however, most of
the students at Albany took the shorter English course, and rela-

tively few became candidates for the bachelor's degree. It was for a time expected that persons with baccalaureate degrees from other colleges would enroll for a year of instruction in pedagogy—a "fifth year," in current terminology. While some did enroll, the number never was significant. Two advanced degrees were conferred purely upon an honorary basis for many years. In 1906, the State Normal College at Albany again reorganized its program to provide for a four-year course in "liberal arts and pedagogics," with a major emphasis on the liberal studies, and with only 18 semester hours of courses in education. Authority to grant the A.B., B.S. and Pd.B. degrees was granted. The first two degrees were for persons who took the four year course; the Pd.B. (bachelor of pedagogy) degree was for college graduates taking a one-year professional course. Albany's first four-year class was graduated in 1908. From that time to the present, the college has interpreted its duty as the complete, rounded education of prospective secondary school teachers in both "liberal arts and pedagogics." It may be significant that Albany State College was the first so-called teachers college to be accorded the privilege of having its women graduates enrolled in the American Association of University Women—an organization that is avowedly not an official accrediting agency, though its recognition of various schools serves substantially as an accrediting function. Under the presidencies of William J. Milne, a prolific writer of textbooks in mathematics, and A. R. Brubacher, the college attained high standards under the name of New York State College for Teachers. Through its doors have passed thousands of students who became high school teachers and administrators, not only in New York, but also in many other states.

The practice in most states was not to designate one normal school for the preparation of high school teachers, but rather, to let several normal schools share this responsibility in addition to their existing function of preparing teachers for the elementary school. As these normal schools lengthened their courses to four years of study built upon high school graduation, they were renamed state teachers colleges. Many have gone through further metamorphoses and are now known as state colleges or, in some states, as state universities. In the process, some have lost or minimized their primary objectives of preparing teachers.

Unfortunately, some of these institutions and their students suffered under inferiority complexes as long as the name "normal" or "teachers" was in their official title. The poor quality of some normal schools seemed, in their eyes, to "tar all with the same brush." By a like token, of course, some liberal arts colleges are very mediocre in quality, but that seems not to rub off on the reputation of better institutions. The author has always felt that teaching is a noble profession, and that one need not feel inferior in association with an education which proclaims in its title that it is carrying on this great work. But we Americans, whose undertakers prefer to be called "morticians," and whose plumbers or waste collectors prefer to be "sanitary engineers," have seen fit to change the names of institutions which should proudly have vaunted their mission.

Generally, the traditional liberal arts college paid no attention to providing professional preparation for teachers. In many cases, they were downright hostile to the idea that any pedagogical studies were required. Indeed, in a campaign to destroy the Massachusetts normal schools in 1840, a Dartmouth professor said he had taught for 42 years, yet he believed he "should be able to communicate in an hour and a half all that could profitably be communicated by way of precept to aid one in acquiring the art of teaching." The present burst of criticism of courses in education is not new; Bestor, Lynd, Smith, and Rickover are merely playing over again the 1840 Dartmouth record! Some few liberal arts colleges which were founded, as Haverford was, at least in part to prepare teachers were quick to disavow this purpose as soon as it lost prestige.

The new state universities, on the other hand, were more receptive to the idea of establishing education departments. The first professor appointed at the newly founded State University of Iowa was a professor of pedagogy. Especially did these new universities, after the Morrill Act, emphasize the preparation of teachers of agriculture and the mechanical arts. When high schools continued to grow in size and number, many state universities began to prepare teachers in all the secondary school subjects. Beginning as modest departments associated with the liberal arts college, many of these have now burgeoned into full-fledged schools of education, offering both undergraduate and graduate degrees.

When states began to require courses in pedagogy for certification to teach in high schools, the liberal-arts colleges faced a dilemma. Should they offer the courses, or should they tell prospective teachers to go elsewhere? In the case of women's colleges and coeducational institutions, this might remove a considerable share of the potential student body. Most colleges responded by opening departments of education, not always enthusiastically. In some cases, the courses were assigned to broken-down ministers or to professors whom a department wanted to get rid of. Only when graduate schools began offering advanced degrees in education was this situation generally remedied.

One other institution which was destined to have a national and international influence on education must be mentioned. The teacher-training division of the Industrial Education Association of New York City, known as the New York College for the Training of Teachers, with the ardent promotion of Nicholas Murray Butler, became the Teachers College of Columbia University. It soon developed into a Mecca to which flocked teachers from all over the United States and from many foreign lands. While it had conservatives and essentialists such as Isaac L. Kandel and William C. Bagley on its faculty, it gained the reputation of being the center for the promotion of progressive education. There William Heard Kilpatrick translated and made explicit the democratic philosophy of John Dewey. Dewey was not a professor in Teachers College; he was a professor of philosophy in Columbia University. Nonetheless, his philosophy was able to cross 120th Street, sometimes jocularly called "the widest street in the world" because it separates Teachers College from the not-always-friendly university of which it is a part. Present critics of progressivism who want "more work and less play" in school imply that there was a plot on the part of the Teachers College faculty to soften up the American people for a communist take-over by ruining their educational system. Teachers College is accused of fashioning "social studies" out of traditional history courses, and of promoting "life adjustment" education.

Correspondence Study   Correspondence study, whereby a student could take college or university courses without ever appearing on the campus or personally meeting his professor, began as a university-extension program in England. Its success there attracted the attention of Americans and a group of 32 professors at Johns Hopkins, Harvard, Wisconsin, and other institutions in the 1880's organized a Correspondence University in America. It was not chartered, however, nor was it authorized to grant degrees. Perhaps for this reason, or perhaps because it was loosely organized, the program was soon abandoned.

In 1873, Illinois Wesleyan University began a program of non-resident instruction leading to academic degrees. Even the doctorate in philosophy could be received by mail. A 5000-word thesis was required for the Ph.D. degree. Candidates for any degree were required to be more than 24 years of age. When criticism came from the University Senate of the Methodist Church, and from the North Central Association of Colleges and Secondary Schools, the regional accrediting agency, the college abandoned its extension program in 1906.

The Chautaqua College of Liberal Arts, chartered by the legislature of New York, inaugurated a correspondence school program leading to degrees, in 1883. William Rainey Harper, later president of the University of Chicago, served as president while teaching as a professor of Biblical literature at Yale. Harper himself taught Hebrew to more than 1000 correspondence students. When he became president at Chicago, he determined to have a correspondence division incorporated as an integral part of the university. Instruction was by both "formal and informal correspondence." At first, examinations were conducted at the university, but later "acceptable supervision by competent educators at a distance" was approved. One might take by mail half the number of courses required for a bachelor's degree. In 1893, there were 82 correspondence students; in 1906, there were 1587 students and 113 instructors; in 1930, there were 6100 students taking 459 different courses from 145 instructors. President Harper pointed out that "whatever a *dead* professor can accomplish in the classroom, he can do nothing by correspondence." He also emphasized that dead students would accomplish nothing by correspondence, since this type of study placed more responsibility on the student than did the usual classroom sitting.

In 1919, it was reported that 73 institutions were engaged in correspondence teaching. In 1928, the number offering courses was 154, ranging from Shurtleff College in Illinois (with only 178 resident students) to Columbia University. Some universities, particularly the Pennsylvania State University and the University of Wisconsin, still engage in correspondence study. A number of proprietary schools also advertise home study courses over a vast range of subjects from algebra through plumbing to zoology. Some colleges will accept correspondence study credits from an accredited university and some will not. States frequently will accept correspondence study credits toward teacher certification, in a limited quantity.

Extension Study   Many colleges and universities such as the Portland State College (Oregon) and Pennsylvania State University have extended their teaching far beyond their own campuses. In some instances, this may mean sending a professor a few miles to give instruction in the evening or on Saturday morning to a group of teachers at a convenient central spot. In another instance, it may mean the world-wide extension of the University of Maryland, which holds a contract with the Department of Defense to offer an extensive range of courses in extension centers at military bases around the world. During World War II similar courses were offered by the Armed Forces Institute—USAFI, to many servicemen.

The College Curriculum Within the scope of a one volume history of education, we can not go into an exhaustive treatment of the changing conception of the responsibility of the college and university in the intellectual fare it serves its students. Still, any history of education that merely treats of the founding and expansion of colleges without a hint of curricular developments treats of the husk and not of the kernel. Admittedly with a broad sweep, we shall now turn our attention to the major changes in the curricular structure of American higher education.

Persistence of Classics As has been indicated earlier, the colonial college reproduced in America, as well as it could, the curriculum of the colleges in the universities at Oxford and Cambridge. Admittedly, this was not too stimulating an affair, for the English universities were then at a rather low level of performance. In America, the colleges concentrated upon the classics, flavored with the tradition of disputation which had come down from the medieval university. All this was heavily seasoned with religion, especially at Harvard, Yale, and Princeton.

Professor Butts points out that Harvard's first curriculum was a combination of three traditions: the seven liberal arts from the medieval university tradition, the classics from the Renaissance ideal of the education of the gentleman, and sectarian religion from the Reformation. Included in the curriculum were most of the seven arts (music was omitted), the classical languages, philosophy, and divinity. History was taught for only an hour on Saturday afternoons in the winter, but of course much ancient history was also covered in the classical studies. Students had so little knowledge in mathematics that it has been reported some of them had difficulty in finding the proper pages in their texts.

The Enlightenment Restrictive Puritanism in time gave way to a more liberal spirit which is known as the Enlightenment. Its heyday was from the middle of the seventeenth century to the latter part of the eighteenth century. Its principal characteristic was a de-emphasis upon divine providence and heavenly intervention in the affairs of men and a corresponding emphasis upon natural law and human reason. This is tantamount to saying that secularism and science were now arising to challenge theology.

The universities in England were little changed by the new emphasis, continuing in the tradition of logic, the classics, and philosophy. In Scotland and in Germany, the "new" learning was more popular.

In America, the realistic studies found a more hospitable home in the academies than in the traditional colleges. We have seen the scope of new subjects in these academies, particularly the studies which seemed to have a practical, utilitarian application to the problems of American life. By 1700, however, some new science found its way into Harvard, with Cartesian logic competing with Aristotelean; Copernican and Galilean astronomy replaced the Ptolemaic; and geometry and Newtonian physics were introduced. Even French was introduced as a sort of extracurricular subject for those who had permission of their parents to study it. Yale remained much more traditional in its curriculum, for the president proclaimed that "colleges are religious societies . . . for training up persons for the Work of the Ministry."

Both Kings College and the University of Pennsylvania emphasized the realistic learning and a broader concept of the liberal arts. A general statement from Kings spoke of such matters as

> the arts of reasoning exactly, of writing correctly and speaking eloquently; and in the Arts of numbering and measuring; of Surveying and Navigation, of Geography and History, of Husbandry, Commerce and Government; and in the Knowledge of all Nature in the Heavens above us, and in the Air, Water, and Earth around us, and the various kinds of Meteors, Stones, Mines and Minerals, Plants and Animals, and of every Thing useful in the Comfort, the Convenience and Elegance of Life, in the chief Manufactures relating to any of these Things: And, finally, to lead them from the Study of Nature to the Knowledge of themselves, and of the God of Nature . . .

Kings College fell short of these objectives, but the proposal was there for later years to achieve.

Method in Colleges   Textbook recitation was the prevailing procedure in the colleges, and the professors were content to have it that way. Commonly, one professor taught everything to a class throughout its college career. George Ticknor, a Harvard graduate who had studied at Göttingen, where he was greatly impressed by German scholarship, tried to reform Harvard's program after he returned there to teach, but met disheartening resistance from the faculty. His denunciation of the American program reads:

> The attempt to force together sixty or eighty young men, many of whom have nothing, or almost nothing, in common; who are of

very unequal ages, talents, attainments, habits, and characters; and to compel them to advance *pari passu* during four of the most active and valuable years of life, giving to the most industrious and intelligent no more and no other lessons, than to the most dull and idle, is a thing that is unknown to the practical arrangements for education in other countries; that is not attempted in ours either before or after the period of college life; and that has been practiced at college only from adherence to an ancient arrangement, long after the motives for that arrangement had ceased to exist. For though it might be inevitable in the earliest periods of the establishment at Cambridge, when there were fewer tutors than classes, and was, probably, less injurious in its operation, while the classes were quite small, and the instruction of their members by a general average not so likely of course to be an injustice to the best of them; yet, after the whole of this state of things was reversed, after the number of instructors was increased, till it amounted to four or five for each class, and the number of students to be taught together had risen to sixty or eighty, and a general average was necessarily become a great neglect and injustice to the most active and able, all ground for continuing the system of instruction on the old alphabetical and arbitrary arrangement of the classes failed. This arrangement, however, exists, in nearly all our colleges, and was continued at Cambridge, from one period to another, partly from ancient usage and habit, and partly because it was not thought easy to alter what had been so long established.

For a time, the elective system was practiced at Harvard, but conservative presidents got rid of it. It remained for President Charles William Eliot to restore it in the 1860's.

Meanwhile, the traditional point of view that there was an essential body of knowledge that every graduate should have largely prevailed in most of the colleges. This could largely be conveyed through textbook recitation, without recognition of the individual backgrounds, interests, and abilities of the students.[3]

Realistic Studies   A fast-growing

America, moving from an agrarian society to an industrial civilization, greatly needed leaders in various engineering and manufacturing fields, yet few colleges even bowed respectfully in the direction of such learning. Consequently, much of the advance in this learning

[3] For detailed information on this conflict in curriculum and methods, see *The College Charts Its Course,* by R. Freeman Butts (McGraw-Hill, 1939), especially chapters 4, 5, 6, 7, 8.

was empirical, trial-by-error, without theoretical foundation. Whenever a need developed, men with the tradition of tinkering tried various solutions in the hope that one of them would work. This situation may account for the fact that the Mohawk and Hudson railway located its first Albany station on a hill too steep for its locomotives to climb.

Stephen Van Rensselaer established a school at Troy, New York, in 1824 for "affording an opportunity to the farmer, the mechanic, the clergyman, the lawyer, the physician, the merchant, and in short, to the man of business or of leisure, of any calling whatever, to become practically scientific." The student was to become familiar with practical applications as well as with theoretical presentations. His school was, for a time, operated on less than college standards. Its early existence was so precarious that Van Rensselaer suggested that it be offered to the state for the purpose of preparing teachers "in the application of the experimental sciences to agriculture and the other useful arts." He was willing to have it moved to any neighboring county. The governor approved, but the legislature did not act, so the school continued its independent existence. It did not develop into a true college of engineering until 1850. Some Harvard scholars, in protest against the neglect to science there, left and went to the Rensselaer school soon after it was founded. For some years this school and the United States Military Academy were the only two in the United States offering applied science. In 1847, Harvard opened the Lawrence Scientific School and Yale followed, a few years later, with its Sheffield Scientific School. In response to a growing demand, several more independent schools opened in the 1860's. Among these were the now-famous Massachusetts Institute of Technology (1861), Worcester Polytechnic Institute (1865), and Lehigh University (1866). Several other independent scientific schools were established later.

Morrill Act   This interest in
scientific education led to the demand for the founding of public institutions to emphasize the realistic studies. In 1850 and in 1858, Michigan petitioned Congress for a grant of 350,000 acres of public land to endow an agricultural college. Jonathan Turner of Illinois had advocated a national policy of land grants to states for developing colleges of agriculture and the mechanical arts. Illinois legislators endorsed his plan in 1853 and forwarded it to Congress.

Justin P. Morrill, a congressman from Vermont, adopted the idea and introduced a bill into Congress. It provided that each state be granted 20,000 acres of public land for each senator and each representative in the national congress, in order to establish colleges which would teach agriculture and mechanical arts "without excluding other scientific and classical studies." Military tactics would be a required subject. The bill passed both houses, against much Southern opposition, but was vetoed by President Buchanan. It is said he was fearful of the new idea, and also thought the act would imperil existing colleges.

President Lincoln signed a revised bill in 1862, passed after the Southern congressmen had withdrawn to join the Confederacy. This bill allowed 30,000 acres of public land for each senator and representative. Time for accepting the grant was extended to 1874. States which were yet to be admitted to the Union and the states in rebellion were included in the provisions.

Under this Morrill Act, a total of 11,367,832 acres of land was given to the states. Students sometimes assume this land was within the states to which it was given, and that the colleges were erected thereon. Such was not necessarily true. The land was part of the public domain in western states. The states were to sell the land and apply the proceeds to the program of education.

Farm labor, 1859, at Farmers' High School, the A. and M. College which later became the Land Grant college, Pennsylvania State College

Eighteen states added this endowment to their state universities, which were then charged with setting up appropriate departments; five made grants to already existing private colleges (in New York, it was Cornell), and the others organized separate agricultural and mechanical colleges. In some states, two such A. and M. colleges were established, one for whites and one for Negroes.

The cash yield of the land, to 1910, was $13,736,178, with almost $15,000,000 yet unsold. The influence was greater than this sum would indicate. Some new and vigorous colleges were started, new life was infused into existing ones, and significant influence was felt upon the educational programs in engineering and scientific agriculture. Subsequently, federal financial grants were made to these land-grant colleges.

The first two colleges established under the Morrill Act were the Michigan Agricultural College (now Michigan State University—not to be confused with the older University of Michigan) and the Pennsylvania State College (which had originally been founded as the Farmers' High School in 1855). For some years, these were exceedingly modest institutions, leading a precarious existence.

The Farmers' High School, like other institutions, had to struggle against adversaries who sought designation as the A. and M. college. This does not signify that the competitors were suddenly interested in agricultural and mechanical education; rather, they were interested in the largesse of the federal government.

Pennsylvania failed to attract the anticipated number of students. A five-story dormitory designed for 400 students was often less than half filled, and at one time it housed only 30 students. Perhaps the military strictness had something to do with its lack of appeal. Students had to rise at 5 A.M., attend all classes, and put in three hours a day of labor on the college farm. The college limped along without much success until the late 1880's, when new vigor was infused into it as the Pennsylvania State College. Later, it was renamed Pennsylvania State University.

Education of Women   So far, in speaking of college education in the United States we have referred to education of men. Although the education of women will be fully treated in Chapter Twelve, we must here briefly survey opportunities in higher education for women. The way into higher education for them, as we shall see, was paved by the academies, many of which were coeducational, and by the normal schools which were opened to men and women on equal terms at the beginning. College education for "females," as they were often called, was a somewhat different matter.

Even before 1830, Catherine Beecher and Emma Willard had campaigned for better educational opportunities for women in the East, and in 1834 Mary Lyon opened her Mount Holyoke Seminary, which was at first on the level of an academy. Eventually, it was raised to collegiate stature.

The West was more hospitable to coeducation than the more traditional East. When the Oberlin Collegiate Institute (now Oberlin College) announced in 1833 that it would admit women and Negroes as candidates for degrees, the academic world was horrified—more at the admission of the former than of the latter, it would appear. Antioch College, under the presidency of Horace Mann, was coeducational from its opening day in 1853.

Elmira College, the first Eastern institution of collegiate rank for women, opened in 1855 with the provision that "no degree shall be conferred without a course of study equivalent to a full ordinary course of college study as pursued in the colleges of this state"— meaning, of course—the colleges for men. Vassar College for women was opened in 1861, well endowed by a Poughkeepsie brewer. Wellesley Female Seminary became Wellesley College with the power to confer degrees, in 1877. Smith College opened in 1875 with a dozen students—three more than Harvard had at its opening. Bryn Mawr opened in 1885. Other colleges for women continued to be founded.

Certain conservative colleges for men established coordinate institutions for women. Among these were Harvard, Tulane, Western Reserve, and Columbia.

In 1870, the University of Michigan admitted women students, followed by the universities of California, Missouri, Illinois, and Wisconsin. Certain later state universities were coeducational from their founding. All state universities now admit women.

Accreditation   Once a college
had been chartered, it was relatively free to go its own way, constrained only by its charter provisions. These in many cases were very generous. For a time, a common tradition of the prescribed classical studies caused the colleges to be quite similar in admission standards, in scope of work covered, and in graduation requirements. While the quality might differ from place to place, still there was a certain common element.

As the colleges were multiplied after the Revolution, greater differences appeared. Some colleges appeared to maintain no standards at all, while standards in others were flexible, to say the least. Rather than have degrees debased generally, some central agency of control was necessary. In other nations, the solution would be inspection and regulation by a national ministry of education, but there was no governmental control on the national level in the United States. True, the University of the State of New York did inspect and require annual reports from academies and colleges within the state, but New York was the only state making this provision. Even if every state exercised this supervision, there would still be a large number of varying standards—at present, fifty such sets of criteria for evaluation. With students and graduates often crossing state lines, chaos could result, for more than 200 colleges had been chartered between 1860 and 1890.

Many of these colleges were weak and unable to maintain reasonable standards of performance. They might, on paper, offer extensive courses and advanced degrees which they were not equipped to execute in common decency. There was manifestly a need for an agency to separate the collegiate sheep from the collegiate goats. Fortunately, the University of Michigan stumbled upon a solution. It was having difficulty in assessing the high school preparation of its applicants, for there was as much diversity of standards in the high schools as in the colleges. The university offered to admit, on certificate by the high school principal and without entrance examination, graduates of schools inspected and approved by the university. Thus began the system known as accreditation. At first, however, it was applied only to secondary schools.

Faced with the problem of preparing students for widely differing college entrance examinations, the Massachusetts high school authorities in 1884 conferred with President Eliot of Harvard about their problem. Out of the discussions grew the New England Association of Colleges and Secondary Schools, the first regional attempt to bring together college and secondary school representatives. The North Central Association of Colleges and Secondary Schools was organized the next year, followed by the Middle States Association in 1889 and the Southern Association about the same time. Later, the Northwestern Association and the Western Association were organized, thus covering the whole United States and its territories.[4]

4 Areas served by each of the associations are: New England Association, the 6 New England states; Middle States Association, New York, New Jersey, Pennsylvania, Delaware, Maryland, District of Columbia and Puerto Rico; North Central Association, Arizona, Arkansas, Colorado, Illinois, Indiana, Iowa, Kansas, Michigan, Minnesota, Missouri, Nebraska, New Mexico, the Dakotas, Ohio, Oklahoma, West Virginia, Wisconsin and Wyoming; the Northwest Association, Alaska, Hawaii (secondary schools only), Idaho, Montana, Nevada, Oregon, Utah and Washington; the Western Association, California, Guam and Hawaii (higher education); Southern Association, Alabama, Florida, Georgia, Kentucky, Louisiana, Mississippi, the Carolinas, Tennessee, Texas and Virginia.

The accrediting associations set standards which institutions had to meet to obtain and retain membership. For a time, these standards were administered in a rather inflexible and arbitrary way, but within recent years there has been noted a tendency to judge an institution in reference to how well it is fulfilling its stated objectives rather than in an objective reference to certain standard norms. Associations have primarily been interested in entrance and graduation requirements, faculty preparation and effectiveness, financial support, library, records of graduates in advanced institutions, academic freedom, and in buildings and equipment. They have frequently found athletic policies too hot to handle, other than by occasional pious resolutions.

All these associations stress that they are voluntary, but naturally a college is under strong internal and external pressure to obtain accreditation. Such pressure comes from alumni, prospective students, donors, and others. In addition to these six regional accrediting associations which accredit an institution as a whole, there are many agencies accrediting parts of an institution. These are commonly called professional accrediting associations. They cover such fields as medicine, law, dentistry, nursing, chemistry, education, music, journalism, etc. There is even a voluntary National Commission on Accrediting to attempt to bring order among the various agencies and to restrain the too ambitious ones.

Many colleges remain unaccredited. This does not imply that they do not do good work, any more than accreditation implies the absence of all shoddy work from the institution so accredited. Several non-accredited colleges in 1956 formed a Council for the Advancement of Small Colleges to attempt to improve their financial status so that they might individually meet accreditation standards.

Here, in a voluntary and rather democratic way, the colleges and universities have brought reasonable order out of a rather chaotic condition.

For Further Reading

Brubacher, John S. and Willis Rudy. *Higher Education in Transition.* Harper, 1938.
Problems of the colleges and universities in a changing America.

Butts, R. Freeman. *The College Charts Its Course.* McGraw-Hill, 1939.
Chapter 2 deals with roots of classical education in American colleges; Chapter 3 deals with the inroads of science; Chapter 4 the enlightenment; Chapter 5, the early nineteenth century; Chapter 6, the mental discipline approach at Yale.

Hofstadter, Richard and Wilson Smith (editors). *American Higher Education, A Documentary History*. 2 volumes. University of Chicago Press, 1961.

Selected documents about American colleges and universities.

Hofstadter, Richard and Walter P. Metzger. *The Development of Academic Freedom in the United States*. Columbia University Press, 1955.

A study prepared by the American Academic Freedom Project. Chapters 4, 5, 6 and 7 apply to this chapter. The authors speak of a "great regression" in freedom prior to the Civil War. Chapter 7 deals with Darwinism in the colleges and the attempts to repress it.

Rudolph, Frederick. *The American College and University*. Knopf, 1962.

Chapter 2 presents "The Legacy of the Revolution"; Chapter 3, the development of college movement; Chapter 4, the religious life in the era of "petty sectarian colleges"; Chapter 5, student life in the early colleges.

11

Development of the Universities

What Is a University?   Until a few
decades after the Civil War, higher education in America was carried
on in the colleges. True, some of them might have been officially
named "universities" in their charters, but they were not yet of
this stature, in the present sense of the word. There are various
levels in distinguishing between colleges and universities. The layman thinks of a college as an undergraduate institution conferring
only the bachelor's degree, and the university as an undergraduate
college with affiliated graduate and professional schools which confer master's and doctor's degrees. In medieval Europe the word
"universitas" at first merely signified an association or corporation;
in time, it came to mean an association of masters and scholars. At
that time, a college was a residence hall for university students, "college" merely signifying a group of persons with a common objective.
The definition of a university by Daniel Coit Gilman, first president
of the Johns Hopkins University, is "the most comprehensive term
that can be employed to indicate a foundation for the promotion
and diffusion of knowledge—a group of agencies organized to advance the arts and sciences of every sort, and train young men as
scholars for all the intellectual callings of life." The best definition
of a university today includes all these features. It further implies
a largeness of spirit, academic freedom, and a willingness to treat
its students as adults. It is not a custodial institution primarily
engaged in didactic teaching of what is already known or believed.

The First American University   Though certain institutions
had awarded higher degrees (Harvard and Yale early gave the M.A.,
as a matter of course to graduates of three years' alumni-hood who
had kept out of jail and who paid a small fee, and Yale conferred
the Ph.D. degree first in 1861), there was no institution of university
stature in America until Johns Hopkins University was founded in
Baltimore in 1867 by a wealthy railroad magnate. His objective

was the establishment of a graduate institution which would emphasize pure scholarship and the advancement of knowledge. Research, the characteristic attitude of the German universities, was to be the prime objective.

In their search for a president to develop this new concept of higher education, the Johns Hopkins trustees asked the presidents of Harvard, Yale, Cornell, and Michigan to suggest candidates. They all submitted the name of Daniel Coit Gilman, who had reorganized the Sheffield Scientific School at Yale and was then president of the University of California. He raided other colleges for able faculty who had German doctorates or were sympathetic with his vision of a university.

Hopkins did maintain an undergraduate school, too, but that was merely to serve as a feeder for the university, and to meet the needs of a college in Baltimore.

The contrast between Hopkins and the existing colleges was this: Hopkins searched for new truth, whereas the colleges already had the truth in their Renaissance and Reformation traditions and sought only to pass it on. The Hopkins professor of chemistry came from Williams College where, when he asked for a small room to use as a laboratory, he was told that Williams was a college, not a technical school. Apparently at Williams, chemistry was to be taught, not discovered.

The Spirit Spreads   Under the competition of Hopkins, other institutions came to develop graduate schools. Gilman spoke and wrote widely about research. Harvard and Yale began to take a more serious interest in graduate study. Hopkins-trained G. Stanley Hall carried the spirit to Clark University at Worcester, Massachusetts. Soon John D. Rockefeller was to give William Rainey Harper carte blanche at a new institution, the University of Chicago. The state institutions, especially in the North Mississippi Valley, took up the issue and greatly expanded their interests and activities. In New York, the first great university, Cornell, proclaimed that it would be a place where "any person can find instruction in any study." While neither Cornell nor any other university has reached this ideal, the expansion of the scope of studies in American universities has been phenomenal.

Role of Philanthropy   Starting with the Rev. John Harvard's bequest to the infant institution which adopted his name, and still continuing in the present, American colleges and universities have been the beneficiaries of philanthropy. The social, political, and economic conditions which permitted the amassing of many huge fortunes after the Civil War, often at excessive cost to the rest of society, eventually were a great benefit to the advancement of higher education. We have already noted the Johns Hopkins and John D. Rockefeller philanthropies. Ezra Cornell endowed the university which bears his name with $500,000 gained mainly in the Western Union telegraph enterprise. In California, the railroad entrepreneur Leland Stanford endowed an institution in memory of his deceased son. He called it "My University," and was active in its management. After his death, Mrs. Stanford ran it as "her" university, so much so that the president even suggested to faculty members that they move to other positions. One professor who offended Mrs. Stanford was dismissed for opposing the exploitation of such coolie labor as had helped build the Stanfords' railroads. In the post-bellum South, the largest university philanthropy was the founding of Vanderbilt University, an institution which claimed "an open-minded hospitality to all truth."

There are numerous other instances of significant philanthropies to higher education. Every college or university had its angel, small or large, and some of them had many. The Duke family used a part of its tobacco fortune to develop Trinity College in North Carolina into one of the South's great institutions, Duke University—complete with harmonious architecture, and a statue of Duke smoking a cigar. John M. Morehead, an alumnus, gave the University of North Carolina nearly twenty million dollars in his lifetime.

Fund Raising Projects   Nor were all
the philanthropists men and women of great fortunes. Often when large contributors gave money to institutions, either individually or through foundations they established, it was upon the basis of their gifts being matched by an equal amount of money garnered by the college from other sources. Many a college president spent much of his time on the road soliciting such contributions to match a conditional grant. In time, a number of professional fund-raising firms were established to conduct financial campaigns for colleges. They would conduct surveys of an institution's constituency, estimate the amount that could be set as a goal, and then proceed to direct volunteer campaign workers in the drive.

A Social Protest   The pouring of
huge sums of money into the colleges and universities by American

tycoons did not pass unnoticed by the social reformers. In a book critical of the domination of American higher education by the captains of industry, Upton Sinclair wrote:

> Slaves in Boston's great department store, in which Harvard University owns twenty-five hundred shares of stock, be reconciled to your long hours and low wages and sentence to die of tuberculosis—because upon the wealth which you produce some learned person has prepared for mankind full data on "The strong Verb in Chaucer." . . . Men who slave twelve hours a day in front of blazing white furnaces of Bethlehem, Midvale, and Illinois Steel, cheer up and take a fresh grip on your shovels—you are making it possible for mankind to acquire exact knowledge concerning "The beginnings of the Epistolary Novel in the Romance Languages."[1]

The Elective Principle   Throughout the colonial and early national period, the college curriculum had been relatively static. True, new subjects were gradually introduced. But when history, English literature, and science (in the guise of *natural philosophy*) were added, they were fitted into the existing classical curriculum with a minimum of friction. The curriculum remained relatively static. Since the colleges were committed to the cultivation of the mind, with emphasis on training the senses, memory, judgment, and the will, it was held that certain prescribed courses could do this better and more economically than a wide range of subjects. The colleges were committed to a prescribed curriculum to be pursued by all students, to compulsory class attendance, recitation from textbooks, strict supervision, custodial discipline, and a high degree of compulsion.

A break in this tradition came in the regime of Charles W. Eliot as president of Harvard. After serving in the Lawrence Scientific School at Harvard and failing of permanent appointment, he had moved to the new Massachusetts Institute of Technology as a professor of chemistry, and was then called to the Harvard presidency, where he served for forty years.

Attacking the then universal doctrines of faculty psychology—the "training of the mental faculties" through a prescribed curriculum— Eliot declared that there were individual differences in the minds of college students, and that the college should cater to these differences. Further, he said, a young man of twenty ought to know what

---

[1] Sinclair, Upton: *The Goose-Step, A Study of American Education*, pp. 90–91.

Dr. Charles W. Eliot, for forty years president of Harvard University (1869–1909).

he liked and what he was suited for. By giving free play to the natural preferences and inborn aptitudes of the student, the free election of college studies would cause enthusiasm for one's chosen work to enhance one's devotion to scholarship. Rigid prescription of courses was dropped, first in the junior and senior years, and then eventually throughout the college program, until only prescribed courses in English and a foreign language remained in 1894. Even the foreign-language requirement disappeared in 1897.

Dropping of the prescribed courses did not free Harvard men to earn degrees by taking "snap" courses in basket-weaving, circus acrobatics, or ping-pong. That was a refined twist of the elective system to be developed by other institutions in search of athletic prowess or other nonacademic objectives. At Harvard, the election had to be made from substantial college courses—though conservative President James McCosh of Princeton would charge that Harvard had twenty courses for the dilettante eager to escape an education.

For a time, other colleges resisted the educational heresy emanating from Harvard, but one by one all but the most tradition-bound gave way to the impetus for election. Cornell, which required only physical education, strengthened the case of the electives. By 1901, many colleges were allowing from fifty to seventy per cent election in courses toward a degree.

Development of Science   One of the
great contributions of the university movement was the development of the study of science, not only in the universities, but also, in time, even in the most remote and isolated colleges. While there had been

some tinkering with science in the colleges before the Civil War, what little that was offered was a descriptive science taught from textbooks. One exception was at the Rensselaer Polytechnic Institute, to which faculty and students alike fled from the more traditional schools. Gifts to Harvard and Yale established the Lawrence and Sheffield Scientific Schools, respectively, at those universities.

Neither Harvard nor Yale received this new departure with any enthusiasm among the traditional faculty. In both cases, the science professors and students for a long time were regarded as poor relations, not quite fit to sit at the proper academic table. At Yale, the Sheffield students were segregated in the college chapel. Entrance requirements were lower for the science students, and the course was shorter. Obviously, they couldn't have the A.B. degree. Harvard conferred the degree of bachelor of science and Yale compromised with the bachelor of philosophy degree. Soon a Harvard president was to say that the Harvard B.S. degree did not signify any knowledge of science; it merely attested to a lack of knowledge of foreign languages!

The adoption of the principle of election opened the gateway to more extensive demands for courses in science. Over the hill but fast approaching was the idea that even an A.B. student might be required to take a course in science before he could be called a liberally educated individual.

Was Eliot Inconsistent?   It would at
first appear that President Eliot was fundamentally inconsistent in abolishing required courses on the college level in favor of free election at the same time as he was trying to fasten a prescribed, standard college entrance program upon the developing high schools. The only logical way to explain this apparent ambivalence is to say that Eliot must have felt that the student must complete his general education in the high school, as the German student did in the gymnasium, and that he would then be free to specialize at Harvard as one did in a German university.

Because many high schools throughout the country, particularly the new high schools in more remote areas, did not provide the same high type of education as the schools customarily preparing students for Harvard, most colleges were unwilling to abandon prescribing courses in at least the freshman and sophomore years. Only now, when high schools are offering more thorough work of a higher caliber to their college preparatory students, are a few colleges considering a revision of their requirements. Some colleges are now beginning to relax their rigidly minute prescriptions for the freshman and sophomore years. True, the student still needs to distribute his classes over several academic fields, but he is not so strongly limited now to a few prescribed courses. In some instances, however, he may choose only between Tweedledum and Tweedledee—as for instance, between British literature or world literature courses taught on identical patterns.

Proliferation of Courses Once the elective principle was established, and as soon as college faculties were largely composed of persons who had received advanced training in research at the graduate schools of universities at home or abroad, there developed a great proliferation of courses in the colleges. Under the wide-open elective system, one course was considered as good as another. Young Ph.D.'s were eager to teach the particular branch of a subject in which they had done their research, with the result that courses subdivided and multiplied almost indefinitely. An additional consideration was, of course, the tremendous expansion of knowledge that exploded during the nineteenth century. One has only to look at the catalogs of his own college for the years 1900, 1910, 1920, 1930, 1940, 1950, and 1960 to see how the courses multiplied in number and in depth. Sometimes a single course offering in 1900 had expanded into courses totalling 50 or 60 semester hours by 1960. By 1962, the University of Southern California was offering 3500 courses, but decided to cut this number to approximately 2000. Even a relatively small school like Franklin and Marshall College, in a curriculum revision, found 80 courses to drop.

Some Checks on Election While President Eliot of Harvard reported that the elective principle was seldom abused there, many colleges found that unrestricted election did permit persons to achieve degree status by a discriminate selection of unrelated "snap" courses. Since a haphazard selection of courses did not give the student an integrated view of man and his problems, progressive educators tried to devise new programs which would do so. For a time, in the 1930's, general education seemed to be the answer. Students were required to take general education courses or survey courses in the social studies, communication, the arts, the humanities, and the sciences. There were two major defects in many of these programs, however: first, some of the courses were so general that they represented only a superficial mish-mash of subject matter; second, professors schooled in particular disciplines and specializations were sometimes unable or unwilling to work out general education courses that were intellectually respectable.

Colleges often prescribed distribution of courses into certain areas. In other words, to meet graduation requirements, one had to have had so many semester hours of English, history, science, etc. To these were added the required courses in one's major. Beyond that, perhaps one-fourth to one-third of the work was left to free election, but even here major departments strongly advised their students to take related courses in related fields.

Growth in Enrollments   There had been a slow but rather steady growth of enrollment until the 1850's. Then, suddenly, the enrollment began to drop, and many colleges even closed. In 1846, there were only 247 students enrolled in the two colleges of New York City. Some small colleges had more trustees than students! The reason for this scholastic retreat was the fact that the common man just was not interested in what the colleges had to offer. The American economy was booming, and one didn't need much education to make a fortune. What the colleges taught seemed to have no relationship to what President Tappan of Michigan called "the commercial spirit of our country."

The beginnings of curriculum reform, allowing study in the sciences, in the A. and M. colleges, and in some elective courses, helped to bring more students back to the colleges. But enrollment fell off during the Civil War, when many Southern colleges ceased operating entirely. In Northern Colleges, many of the students joined a military company *en masse*, and were mustered into national service under the command of a favorite professor.

With the development of several high schools after the war, many more students were encouraged to continue on to college. From the post-Civil War period, college enrollments were destined to grow much faster than the increase in the population of the country. While enrollment statistics are doubtless not completely accurate, the figures for colleges and universities show the tremendous increase in numbers enrolled, by decades, from 1870 to the present:[2]

1870	52,286	1930	1,100,737
1880	115,817	1940	1,494,203
1890	156,756	1950	2,659,021
1900	237,592	1960	3,610,007
1910	355,213	1962	4,206,672
1920	597,880		

[2] Table reproduced from *Progress of Public Education in the United States of America, 1961–62,* U.S. Department of Health, Education and Welfare Report OE–10005–62–B. (Through 1957–58, the statistics are for contiguous United States; for 1959–62, Alaska and Hawaii included; for 1961–62, an estimate.)

Likewise, the numbers of persons graduated from the colleges and universities showed astonishing expansion from 1869–70 to 1961–62:

Academic year	All degrees	Bachelor's degrees (and first professional)	Master's degrees (except first professional)	Doctor's degrees
1869-70	9,372	9,371	0	1
1879-80	13,829	12,896	879	54
1889-90	16,703	15,539	1,015	149
1899-1900	29,375	27,410	1,583	382
1909-10	39,755	37,199	2,113	443
1919-20	53,516	48,622	4,279	615
1929-30	139,752	122,484	14,969	2,299
1939-40	216,521	186,500	26,731	3,290
1949-50	496,874	432,058	58,183	6,633
1951-52	401,203	329,986	63,534	7,683
1953-54	356,608	290,825	56,788	8,995
1955-56	376,973	308,812	59,258	8,903
1957-58	436,979	362,554	65,487	8,938
1959-60	476,704	392,440	74,435	9,829
1961-62	515,200	425,000	78,800	11,400

The reader will note that the total number of degrees granted in 1962 was more than fifty times the number in 1870.

"The Tidal Wave"   At the close of World War II, the United States government passed legislation whereby veterans could attend college at government expense. This legislation was enacted partly to compensate these men and women for their interrupted educational careers. Too, it was obvious that the nation would need a larger supply of more highly educated manpower. One other justification for the legislation was to take these millions off the labor market at a time of readjustment from a war to a peace economy, for it was widely feared that there would be a postwar economic recession or depression. This was the time, too, that a federal agency advised colleges to discourage young men from preparing for engineering because the country had too many engineers! The number of veterans attending institutions of higher education under the various acts was more than 3,520,000.

"Well, Here We Are Back In School, Sort-Of"

The American Association of Collegiate Registrars in 1955 published a pamphlet entitled "The Impending Tide" which projected the number of persons who would attend college if $33\frac{1}{3}\%$, 40%, and 50% of the eligible age groups went on to college, from 1954 to 1971. By years, these projections were:

	$33\frac{1}{3}\%$	40%	50%
1954–55	2,649,942	2,629,293	2,629,293
1955–56	2,505,206	2,747,645	2,747,645
1956–57	2,539,762	2,867,474	2,867,474
1957–58	2,571,684	2,986.473	2,986,473
1958–59	2,633,968	3,143,769	3,143,769
1959–60	2,723,638	3,338,656	3,338,656
1960–61	2,874,678	3,616,531	3,616,531
1961–62	3,068,117	3,959,141	3,959,141
1962–63	3,193,389	4,120,502	4,223,515
1963–64	3,267,530	4,216,168	4,426,976

1964–65	3,396,114	4,382,082	4,710,739
1965–66	3,617,684	4,667,979	5,134,778
1966–67	3,831,145	4,943,810	5,561,787
1967–68	4,069,037	5,250,370	6,037,926
1968–69	4,145,538	5,349,082	6,285,172
1969–70	4,130,957	5,330,267	6,396,321
1970–71	4,219,047	5,443,932	6,668,817

Almost all these projections turned out to be underestimates. It is now estimated that 7,000,000 or more will be enrolled in higher education by 1970.

The Changing College What this unprecedented demand for higher education may mean will be discussed in Chapter 20, at greater length. Here we may mention only that it will necessitate a reorganization of the college day, the college year, the curriculum, methodology, and almost every feature of the universities.

Growth in Research The United States spent in 1962 more than $12,000,000,000 for research. Of all the scientists who ever lived, more than half are now alive. A computer today can do more calculation in ten minutes than a man can do with an adding machine in fifty years. The knowledge explosion of our times is evidenced by the fact that the volume of all chemical-research abstracts now doubles every two years.

For good or ill, we live in a time when research has become a matter of grave national concern. Both in undergraduate colleges and in the graduate schools of universities, the pace will continue to be accelerated. Today, the universities rely heavily upon federal grants for research. In 1960, a hundred institutions received 94% of all funds earmarked for higher education and twenty-five of them got 68% of the share. It was reported that a sudden withdrawal of federal funds from research projects in medicine, public health, engineering, and natural science would be as traumatic to the universities as cancellation of defense and other federal contracts would be to the nation's major industries.

Through its participation in research in all lines of human activity, but primarily in the sciences, the university today is a major instrument of the national defense and economic well-being of the United States.

Junior College Movement   Parallel with the
continued growth of colleges and universities, many sections of the
United States witnessed the development and expansion of a new
institution which came variously to be known as the junior college
or the community institute. In opening the University of Chicago
in 1891, William Rainey Harper proposed to divide the traditional
four-year collegiate program into two equal parts: the first two years,
to be known as the junior college, to complete the general education
of the students; the last two years to be an upper division for the
pursuit of the more advanced subjects in a more scholarly manner,
oriented toward the university concept. He even proposed that many
of the four-year colleges of the Midwest, including Muskingum (his
alma mater), might be induced to transform themselves into junior
college satellites of Chicago. This might have resulted in better
higher education, but Harper did not take into consideration the
tough desire of even small colleges to preserve their independent
existence.

As college attendance spread to a greater proportion of the American people, the matter of the great expense of going to college away
from home motivated many communities to establish institutions
which would offer the first two years of college locally, where the
student could save much of the cost of room and board by living at
home. In many instances, these junior colleges were upward extensions of the public high school, operated by the local school district.
Others were independent institutions which were created anew or
developed from remaining academies or seminaries. Still others were
existing four year colleges which, for reasons of economy, amputated
their junior and senior years.

Many of the junior colleges offered the liberal-arts work of the
freshman and sophomore years of the usual college. Others developed
curricula in technical and business specialties for which there was a
growing local demand. There are now approximately 600 junior
colleges. The majority of these are in the Mississippi River basin
and in the states west of that area. Of the students currently in California colleges and universities, more than half attend local junior
or community colleges.

Need for Further Expansion   The expansion of
all types of higher-education institutions has been so rapid and so
extensive that one might think we have reached or will soon reach
the saturation point. The present facts in our increasingly techno-

logical, automated civilization seem to indicate that such is not the case. The rapid replacement of cheap, unskilled labor by automated machinery means there is decreasing demand in our society for persons of little education, but persons with greater educational preparation and technical training will be in increasing demand. The elimination of 40,000 elevator operators in New York City alone indicates the trend. In the United States in the early 1960's, approximately 5,000 positions a day are eliminated by automatic machines and computers, and the 1200 computers in operation are just the beginning of expanding automation. At the same time, the demand for persons with technical and professional skills is increasing—not only for persons with full preparation, but also for those who can serve as assistants. Many persons who would be capable technical assistants, secretaries, and clerks can be adequately prepared in junior colleges. Yet these need not be terminal institutions for those people who wish to continue on as candidates for the bachelor's degree.

Education in the Professions   By modern standards, education in the professions of medicine, law, and theology was rather shoddy in the United States until the present century. There was scarcely any preparation in other fields which have later come to regard themselves as professions.

Even at reputable universities, the work in professional studies was weak, short, and of poor quality. While six months was required to qualify for the M.D. degree prior to 1800, the term had been shortened to sixteen weeks at Harvard in 1869. By 1850, there were forty medical schools, graduating more than 1000 persons a year. Most of these schools were proprietary and private, with the constant temptation to maintain slack requirements to attract more students. Even at Harvard and at other universities, the tuition fees went direct to the teachers, most of whom were also practicing physicians. Commonly, it was empirical medicine, rather than theory, that was taught. Eliot, at Harvard, turned the system over "like a flapjack," as Dr. Oliver Wendell Holmes said. He set higher admission standards, put the faculty on salaries, required a three-year course of study and written examinations. At the same time, he built up the school's endowment.

Attempts by the American Medical Association to set higher standards were generally unsuccessful until the famous Flexner report was published in 1910. It suggested that candidates must have had at least a high school education, that state boards should set higher standards for their examinations and should refuse to examine graduates of disreputable schools, and that the number of schools should be reduced by the elimination of the poorer ones. These reforms did greatly improve the quality of the practitioners of medicine, but at the same time they led to the reduction of the number of doctors per 1000 of population.

Medical education has become very expensive—so expensive that many able young people cannot afford it. An attempt to get federal aid for such education was blocked by the American Medical Association in 1950, according to Oscar Ewing, the Federal Security Administrator.

It was a part of American tradition that one did not need the formal education of a school to become a lawyer. Although there were both university and proprietary law schools in the United States, most lawyers were men who had studied on their own, as was the case with Abraham Lincoln, Thaddeus Stevens, and many others. Even as late as 1928, standards for admission to the bar were still low in many states. Since that time, they have gradually been raised.

There are no state or national standards of entrance into the ministry, since the state hesitates to trespass on the province of the church. While some denominations have long held the tradition of a college education and special training in religion as requirements for admission to ordination, others have been extremely lax and have ordained persons without adequate education who could persuade the church they had been "called." Part of the controversy which split the Presbyterian Church in the eighteenth century centered around the education of the clergy, the conservative branch holding out for full educational qualifications, and the Cumberland branch, anxious to fill pulpits in the West, willing to relax the standards. Except in certain denominations which are still apprehensive about higher education, the trend has been to require college graduation and a theological course.

University Regalia   Antiquity is one of the polite fictions of American higher education. Colleges often claim as their founding date the year in which they were first chartered, even if they did not begin operations for some years. In other instances, the date used is the year in which someone founded an academy which, often somewhat later, became a chartered college.

One of the trappings of antiquity—or, to be more correct, of the medieval period—is the use of academic regalia. In the medieval university, gowns were of warm and heavy stuff, to protect the masters and scholars from the intense cold of unheated lecture halls. The hoods were worn over the heads for the same reason. (The lecture halls also often had several inches of straw spread on the floors, into which feet were tucked, to keep them warm.)

Each American college and university prescribed its own academic regalia, and some of the productions were wonderful to behold: an A.B. from Squeedunk College might be far more resplendent than an LL.D. from Harvard. When the colleges were standardizing their admission requirements through the College Board examinations and were setting standards for accreditation, one would expect that they would also standardize the academic regalia they used.

Two "dandies" from Columbia College, New York typify the college dress of the Nineteenth Century.

Gardner Cotrell Leonard of Albany, New York, became interested in standardizing caps and gowns in 1887 and began servicing various New England colleges. At his suggestion, an intercollegiate commission was organized in 1894, under the chairmanship of Seth Low, president of Columbia. Mr. Leonard submitted sketches, models, and materials. The commission framed an intercollegiate code, covering the types of caps, gowns, and hoods for various degrees. Almost all American colleges adhered to this code.

The gown for the bachelor's degree is made of worsted, with a semi-stiff yoke, and is primarily distinguished by its long, pointed sleeves. The master's gown is worn open at the front and has long square sleeves, with the arm coming through a slit at the elbow. Doctoral gowns are of silk or synthetic and are worn open. They have broad velvet panels down the front and three velvet bars on the full sleeves. For many years, all gowns were black, except that the velvet on the doctor's gowns could be in the color designating the degree. In recent years, certain university boards, particularly Harvard and Yale, have approved doctoral gowns in the colors of the university as an alternative.

Hoods vary in size according to the degree, the bachelor's being the smallest and the doctor's the fullest. The hood lining carries the color of the institution granting the degree and the velvet border is in the color of the degree itself. The standardized colors for degrees are:

Arts and Letters	White
Theology and Divinity	Scarlet
Laws	Purple
Philosophy	Blue
Science	Golden Yellow
Medicine	Green
Pharmacy	Olive
Dentistry	Lilac
Veterinary Science	Gray
Fine Arts	Brown
Music	Pink
Library Science	Lemon
Pedagogy	Light Blue
Forestry	Russet
Commerce and Accountancy	Drab

Engineering	Orange
Physical Education	Sage Green
Humanics	Crimson
Oratory	Silver Gray
Public Health	Salmon
Agriculture	Maize
Economics	Copper

The square mortarboard is the commonly approved cap. For the doctor's degree, the tassel is gold; for other degrees, black. Contrary to local custom in some institutions, both candidates for degrees and degree holders always wear the tassel over the left front quarter of the cap. There is no authorization in the intercollegiate code for "switching" the tassel from right to left when the degree is conferred.

For Further Reading

Bittner, Walton S. and Hervey F. Malloy. *University Teaching By Mail.* Macmillan, 1933.
History and status of correspondence study to 1933.

Boas, Louise S. *Women's Education Begins.* Wheaton (Mass.) College Press, 1935.
Early developments in education of women.

Carmichael, Oliver C. *Graduate Education.* Harper, 1961.
Sharp criticism of the graduate schools in our universities.

Cole, A. C. *A Hundred Years of Mt. Holyoke College.* Yale University Press, 1940.
A centennial history of one of the pioneer colleges for women.

Conant, James B. *Citadel of Learning.* Yale University Press, 1956.
Three essays on the function of the modern university, the land grant colleges, and basic problems in American higher education.

Dodds, Harold W. *The Academic President—Educator or Caretaker?* McGraw-Hill, 1961.
Should the chief administrators of colleges and universities be educators or fund-raisers and public relations "fronts"?

Draper, Andrew Sloan. *American Education.* Houghton Mifflin, 1909.
Section III (pages 187 to 271) deals with university education early in this century. Draper was president of the University of Illinois before becoming the first commissioner of education in New York.

Earnest, Ernest. *Academic Procession, An Informal History of the American College.* Bobbs-Merrill, 1953.

A relatively light history of higher education.

Flexner, Abraham. *Universities, American, English, German.* Oxford University Press, 1930.

Criticism of American institutions and comparison with universities in England and Germany.

Gates, Charles M. *The First Century at the University of Washington.* University of Washington Press, 1961.

A well illustrated centennial history. Traces Washington from a most modest "academy" into a great university.

National Society for the Study of Education. *Education for the Professions.* University of Chicago Press, 1962.

Part II of the Sixty-first Year Book of the Society. Scholarly articles on the development of the professions and education for them. Includes law, medicine, teaching, engineering, business.

National Society for the Study of Education. *The Public Junior College.* Part I of the Fifty-fifth Year Book. University of Chicago Press, 1956.

Development, purposes, improvement and present status of the junior college by several different authors.

Rudolph, Frederick. *The American College and University. A History.* Knopf, 1962.

A new, easy-to-read, informal history with the marks of sound scholarship.

Selden, William K. *Accreditation, A Struggle over Standards in Higher Education.* Harper, 1960.

The attempts made to assure standardization of quality in education.

Sanford, Nevitt. *The American College.* Wiley, 1961.

Research reports and interpretative essays about colleges, their students and faculty.

12

The Education of Women

Few Have Opportunity   In all the
history of the world, comparatively few women have had an opportunity to an education beyond the sheer level of literacy, and many
have not even had that opportunity. Only in comparatively recent
times, and then only in some favored places, has the female of the
species been regarded as worthy of an educational investment.

The Colonial View   The American colonists
brought to this country the prejudices and limitations of their
European background. England, which had so large a share in
determining this heritage, gave but little attention to education of
girls. True, an Elizabeth I might be taught by as famous a master as
Roger Ascham, and some girls from favored families might be given
a polite, if superficial, education; yet the mass of females was passed
by. If they achieved sufficient literacy to read the Bible, that was
considered quite enough. We have no knowledge of what percentage
of the female colonists were literate throughout all the colonies, but
one study has revealed that of the 48 women who conveyed property
in 1653 to 1658, 58% made marks instead of signing their names,
and 38% of 130 women made marks in 1686 to 1697. The per-
centages for men at these times were 11% in each instance. In
Virginia, about the same time, illiteracy among women was found
to be 75%, and among men, 40 to 46%.

The force of the Protestant ethic would seem to indicate that
many women probably could read, but the early introduction of the
dame school here would seem to indicate that many mothers were
unable or unwilling to supervise the mastery of the alphabet and
reading in books of the *New England Primer* type. The fact that
some women did keep these schools proves, of course, that at least a
few were regarded as sufficiently literate to be paid to teach small
children in their own homes.

213

There were some basic inherited views which militated against any serious concern for the education of girls. Thomas Woody, who has prepared a monumental two-volume history of the education of women in the United States, cites reasons for this lack of attention to their education in colonial times:

1. Woman was regarded as intellectually and physically inferior to man.

2. The sphere of woman was considered to be the home, not any activity requiring formal education.[1]

When the first schools were established in the New England colonies, the towns considered that allowing girls to attend would be "inconsistent with the design"of the institution, so they were rigidly excluded. By the time of the Revolution, some towns relaxed their regulations enough to allow girls to attend early in the morning before the boys came to school, and again in the late afternoon after the boys had been taught. Generally, the Quakers were more liberal from the beginning, so it was not unknown for a girl to attend school in the Philadelphia area. This liberality did not rub off on the German immigrants in that area, for a contemporary account characterizes the "Pennsylvania Dutch" women and girls as unable to read or write. Generally, in the colonial era, education for girls was a scarce commodity.

The Female Academy   As soon as the academy had established itself as a worthy institution for the education of boys, some enterprising individuals opened comparable institutions for girls. Several female academies were chartered by legislatures, and many others developed without ever being chartered.

Among the most notable academies for girls were the school at New Haven, established in 1789 by Jedediah Morse, the geographer; one at Medford, Mass.; another at New Haven conducted by William Woodbridge who styled himself "the Columbus of Female Education"; an Ursuline convent school established in New Orleans in 1727; a boarding school opened by Countess Benigna Zinzendorf in Philadelphia in 1742 and moved to Bethlehem in 1749. This latter school attracted students from great distances: New York, Connecticut, South Carolina, Georgia, Nova Scotia, and the West Indies. In the first hundred years, more than 7000 girls attended.

[1] Woody, Thomas: *A History of the Education of Women in the United States.* Science Press, 1929. 2 vol.

In John Poor's academy at Philadelphia, "young ladies" were instructed in reading, writing, rhetoric, grammar, composition, and geography. In this particular school, some of the girls had strong feminist convictions, as shown by this selection from an oration made by one of them in 1792:

> Our high and mighty Lords (thanks to their arbitrary constitutions) have denied us the means of knowledge, and then reproached us for the want of it. Being the stronger party they early seized the sceptre and the sword; with these they gave laws to society; they denied women the advantage of a liberal education; forbid them to exercise their talents on those great occasions, which would serve to improve them. They doom'd the sex to servile or frivolous employments, on purpose to degrade their minds, that they themselves might hold unrivall'd, the power and preeminence they had usurped. Happily, a more liberal way of thinking begins to prevail. The sources of knowledge are gradually opening to our sex. Some have already availed themselves of the privilege so far as to wipe off our reproach in some measure.

It should be remembered that academies frequently maintained preparatory departments in which elementary school subjects were taught. One should not, therefore, conclude that attendance at an academy meant that a particular girl was getting an education on the secondary school level. Polite families with some economic substance preferred to send their children, both boys and girls, to the preparatory division of an academy rather than to the early district school. The Richards girl who learned an addendum to Zaccheus' fall from the tree (in the first chapter) was attending an academy preparatory department at the time.

After the Revolution, certain academies admitted girls and boys on an equal basis. This procedure was more common on the frontier and in other sparsely populated areas, where two academies could hardly be supported. Generally, in the cities, boys and girls continued to attend separate academies.

Except in the academies for girls, and in the summer sessions of district schools attended by girls and small boys too young to work, all the teachers were men. It would have been unthinkable for a woman in colonial America to teach a class of larger boys.

The Normal School   The open frontier
and tremendously expanding opportunities in manufacturing and

seafaring offered a wide range of vocations and opportunities to young men after the Revolution. Thus fewer of them were attracted to teaching, which was only ill-paid and seasonal work.

Women were beginning their long climb to emancipation. To help them, the new normal schools were a great boon. Elementary school teaching, both in the city ward schools, and in the rural district schools, soon fell into their possession. Teaching was one of the few discreet, genteel vocations offered to a young woman throughout much of the nineteenth century. Her poorly educated sisters might become housemaids or spindle-tenders in the mushrooming factories, but a girl with schooling could find nothing more attractive than teaching. For some mobile maidens considering matrimony, teaching would be but a stop-gap vocation until they obtained husbands. For others, to whom the opportunity never came—or who rejected it when it did come—teaching was a dignified calling by which one could support oneself modestly.

The women early recognized the attractiveness of the normal school, and they flocked to it in constantly increasing numbers. The three who were accepted the day that the first normal school was opened at Lexington, Massachusetts, in 1839, soon swelled to thousands as other normal schools were established. For one thing, the normal school was usually free. In some instances, as in the normal school at Albany, small allowances were made from state funds to help defray the cost of room and board. At Albany, each student also received three cents per mile allowance for travel from his county seat.

As long as the normal schools confined themselves to the preparation of teachers for elementary schools, these normal schools were predominantly feminine in constituency.[2]

Indeed, the school at Lexington restricted admission to women only. The socio-economic groups from which early students came is indicated by a report that 23 were daughters of laborers, 16 of farmers, 14 of tradesmen, 4 of captains of merchant vessels, 3 of clerks, 2 of newspaper editors, and 2 of railway inspectors. Three were orphans, and there were 29 widows.

Godey's Lady's Book,[3] a popular magazine for women, in 1853 published a memorial then being presented to Congress on the need for free normal schools for female teachers. In petitioning that 3 or 4 million acres of the public domain be set aside to establish normal

---

[2] Visiting the normal school at New Haven, Connecticut in 1934, the author noted there were no men students. He asked Lester Ade, the principal, what he would do if a young man applied. The principal replied, "I'd tell him to go somewhere else!"

[3] This magazine was edited by Sara Josepha Hale, the first woman to make her mark in American journalism.

schools "for the benefit of the Daughters of the Republic," the memorial listed these propositions:

1. That to find 20,000 young men, who would enter on the office of pedagogue, would be utterly impossible, while the great West, the mines of California, and the open ocean, laving China and the East, are inviting them to adventure and activity.

2. That, therefore, young Women must become the teachers of Common Schools, or these must be given up.

3. That young women are the best teachers has been proved and acknowledged by those men who have made trial of the gentle sex in schools of the most difficult description (see Reports of the "Board of Popular Education," "Reports of Common Schools in Massachusetts," &c.), because of the superior tact and moral power natural to the female character.

4. That female teachers are now largely employed, on an average five of these to one male teacher, in New England, New York, Pennsylvania, Ohio, and wherever the common school system is in a prosperous condition; and everywhere these teachers are found faithful and useful.

5. That, to make education universal, it must be moderate in expense, and women can afford to teach for one-half, or even less, the salary which men would ask, because the female teacher has only to sustain herself; she does not look forward to the duty of supporting a family, should she marry; nor has she the ambition to amass a fortune; nor is she obliged to give from her earnings support to the State or Government.

6. That the young women of our land, who would willingly enter on the office of teacher, are generally in that class which must earn their livelihood; therefore these should have special and gratuitous opportunities of preparing them for school duties; thus the Normal Schools, in educating these teachers of Common Schools, are rendering a great national service.

7. That, though the nation gives them opportunity of education gratuitously, yet these teachers, in their turn, will do the work of educating the children of the nation better than men could do, and at a far less expense; therefore the whole country is vastly the gainer by this system.

8. That it is not designed to make a class of celibates, but that these maiden school-teachers will be better prepared to enter the marriage state, after the term of three or four years in their office of

instructors, than by any other mode of passing their youth from seventeen or eighteen to twenty-one. That earlier marriages are productive of much of the unhappiness of married women, of many sorrows, sickness, and premature decay and death, there can be no doubt.

Though the memorial pointed out that there were 2,000,000 children and youth "destitute, or nearly so, of proper means of education" requiring at least 20,000 additional teachers, Congress took no action.

Mary Lyon

Emma Willard

Emma Willard, Mary Lyon   With the exception of the Moravian School at Bethlehem, which in time came to be Moravian College for Women (still later, joined with Moravian College, a men's institution, to form the present coeducational college), most of the early academies and seminaries for girls were short lived, being private ventures and not having corporate existence. Two schools which were destined to have a permanent influence on women's education were shortly to be established by Emma Willard and Mary Lyon.

Emma Willard taught for a time in a rural school at the age of sixteen, then attended an academy. She opened her own boarding school in 1814 and moved it to Waterford, New York, in 1818, upon the encouragement of DeWitt Clinton. When Troy, New York, offered a building and grounds in 1821, she again moved. At first she hoped for a state subsidy, but soon turned to private sources for funds. In time, she used much of her own income from textbook royalties for supporting her school. At one time it enrolled 400 students, a phenomenally large number. The curriculum was the first extension into higher education for women. The school served to place the education of women in a favorable light, for it was widely publicized. Mrs. Willard covered more than 8000 miles in a Southern and Western trip in 1846, everywhere carrying her message on the educability of women.

Mary Lyon, too, attended a district school and an academy, where, it is said, she mastered the Latin grammar in three days, to the amazement of the master. She then taught rural school near Buckland, Massachusetts, at seventy-five cents a week and "boarded round." For ten years, she was an associate of Zilpah Grant in conducting an academy. She founded her own school on these principles: it was to be for middle class girls, much less expensive than the usual academy or seminary; it was to require domestic labor by the students; it was to have a strong religious influence on the students. It was opened as the Mount Holyoke Female Seminary in 1836. Gifts ranged from three cents to a thousand dollars. Eventually, the seminary metamorphosed into Mount Holyoke College.

Catherine Beecher

Catherine Beecher   While Mrs. Willard and Mary Lyon were founding their seminaries in New York and Massachusetts, another New England woman, Catherine Beecher, was founding similar institutions in the West. She and her family were much interested in saving the people of the West to Christianity, and they knew that educational institutions under Christian influence were necessary to this cause. In 1833, she helped found the Western Female Institute in Cincinnati. In 1850, she went to Milwaukee to help found the Milwaukee Female Seminary. In 1853, she was in Dubuque for a similar purpose. Her correspondence with persons founding seminaries was heavy, and whenever she had an opportunity, she arrived in person to encourage the believers in her cause.

Girls' High School   When public high schools were established, the question immediately arose as to whether or not girls might attend. The first one, the English Classical School, founded in Boston in 1821, was opened to boys only. It was renamed the High School in 1824, apparently by the principal without any authorization by other authority. Girls and their parents sought admission for the females, but it was not permitted. In 1825, the Boston school committee, faced with persistent requests, agreed to open a separate "public school for the instruction of girls in the higher departments of science and literature." As a measure of economy, it was decided to use the monitorial plan of instruction. The city council appropriated $2000 for the school. The school opened in 1826 with 130 pupils. The school was such an "alarming success," according to contemporary accounts, that it was abolished in 1828. The report was made that the school was closed because "a single school of this description would not accommodate more than one fourth of those who ought to attend such an institution." Since all could not attend, it was decided that none should have the opportunity.

Worcester, Massachusetts, preceded Boston with the establishment of the First Female School in 1824. It was established to placate girls who had been denied admission to the municipal Latin School. It was of secondary rank, claiming to maintain standards equivalent to those of the Latin School.

The New York High School Society opened a secondary school for boys in 1825 and one for girls the next year. Bridgeport, Connecticut, opened one school with separate departments for the two sexes, in 1826. In certain towns that were unwilling to establish public high schools, private ones were opened. They were, of course, very similar to the academies which then dominated secondary education.

High Schools: Expansion and Coeducation   Until after the
Civil War, the academy was the common secondary school, with high
schools for either boys or girls found in only a few cities. William T.
Harris said in 1860 that there were only forty high schools in the
whole United States. By 1870, the number had grown to 160; by
1880, to 800; by 1900, to 6005.

As the high school movement spread, these schools frequently
became coeducational, except in a few of the larger or more conservative cities. Many towns which wanted secondary education for
both boys and girls found they could not afford two separate schools.
Here, economics and expediency overcame any lingering prejudices
against coeducation.

What first appeared as an expedient was soon rationalized into a
positive good. Reasons cited in support of coeducation were its
economy, its accordance with the laws of nature, the alleged refining
influence the girls would have on the boys, the hope that it would
render school government easier, that it would serve as a stimulus to
study, and that "it enables the sexes to form a just estimate of each
other." History has indicated that the first and the last of these reasons
have proved true. There has been some doubt about the other claims.

Higher Education   When girls achieved
success in the common schools, they assaulted the secondary schools,
and the academies and a few high schools surrendered to them.
Having achieved a secondary education, they next moved on the
colleges. Here the resistance was stronger and able to hold out longer.
A few early attempts were easily rejected, as in the case of Lucinda
Foote, age 12, who was examined "in the learned languages, the
Latin and the Greek" in 1783 and found to have made "commend-
able progress" and to be fit for admission to Yale College except for
one consideration, her sex. Admission of females to college, it was
said, would cause them to forsake having children, so charmed
would they be by quadratic equations!

Woody points out that two conditions had to exist before women
could aspire to college educations: first, they had to progress through
the secondary school in sufficient numbers; and, second, they had to
attract the attention and sympathetic help of influential men to
change the mores of the society. This they promptly set out to do.
Fortunately, they began their campaign at a time when the humanitarian spirit was abroad, not at a time of conservative retrenchment.

Modestly, they tried to allay hostility by avoiding the name "college." They were content, for a time, to have their institutions known as seminaries or institutes. The Tennessee Female Institute, chartered in 1848, was renamed in honor of Mary Sharp, a contributor, and issued diplomas bearing a seal inscribed "Maria Sharpius Collegium." The catalog said the college aimed to give women an education "as thorough as their brothers have been acquiring at their colleges and universities."

Elmira College   New York, in
1852, chartered the Auburn Female University, but it was soon moved to Elmira and renamed Elmira Female College. The charter specified that "no degree shall be conferred [until] a course of study equivalent to a full ordinary course of study as pursued in the col-

College girls studying physics at the turn of the century.

leges of this state shall have been completed." The college was to be subject to visitation by the Regents of the University of the State of New York "in the same manner and to the same degree as the other colleges of the state." This college conferred its first degree upon women in 1859. The degree was called "Artium Baccalaureata"— that is (female) bachelor of arts. After comparing the Elmira admission and graduation requirements with those of Amherst, Columbia, and Oberlin, Woody concludes that though there were differences in scope and number, the Elmira courses "formed a justifiable basis for issuing the Bachelor's Degree."

The college continues to this day as a college for women but "Female" has been dropped from the name. It is now known as Elmira College. It admits men to its evening sessions, it being the only college in the area.

Oberlin College

Like many new institutions in the West, Oberlin, at its beginning in 1833, found that many aspiring students were not ready to pursue college studies. In the first year, President James H. Fairchild reported, the college was mainly a high school with more than 100 pupils, of whom a third were women. By 1834, college-level classes were operating, but women were not ready for the college courses until 1837, when four girls were accepted. By 1866, the college had granted the A.B. degree to 84 women. The college was pleased, at a later date, that most of the graduates had married, though three had become "somewhat distinguished lady lecturers," being indeed "strong-minded women."

Antioch College

From the very opening in 1852, it was the avowed purpose of Horace Mann, president of Antioch College "to secure for the female sex equal opportunities of education with the male, and to extend those opportunities in the same studies, and classes, and by the same instructors, after the manner of many academic institutions in different parts of the country." The first student body was described as "motley," and most of those who enrolled were consigned to the preparatory department. The preceptress had difficulty explaining to one female student why a visiting male cousin could not share her room.

Southern Colleges and State Universities

A number of institutions for women in the South assumed the name of "college" when they were opened or soon thereafter. While these certainly focussed attention on the need for higher education for women, Woody concludes that they were scarcely collegiate in grade, being more typically like existing seminaries.

The developing state universities of the West admitted women from their opening or a few years thereafter. Iowa was open to women immediately. Wisconsin, Washington and Michigan admitted women at early dates.

Cornell University

When Ezra Cornell founded the great university which bears his name, he proposed to have an institution which would offer to "any person" the opportunity to pursue "instruction in any study." He said he hoped the university would prove "highly beneficial to the poor young men and the poor young women of our country." A building and an endowment from Henry W. Sage facilitated the early admission of women. The university, in one of its publications, defended the admission of women by saying "the difference between a college where ladies are not admitted and one to which they are admitted is the difference simply between the smoking car and the one back of it." Some men students, abetted by certain of the faculty who felt that men should have the advantage of "congenial savagery," resisted the administration's endeavor to admit women, but succumbed. The faculty even consented to appointment to the faculty of "a woman scholar."

A Matter of Degrees

Though a poem in *Blackwood's Magazine* in 1869 asked why a woman should want an academic degree,[4] the women generally did want the customary reward for a college course. Then the question arose as to what degrees would be appropriate. Could a woman be a *bachelor* of arts? A *master* of arts? Though Catherine Beecher had earlier held that the granting of "titular degrees to females" would be in "bad taste," which would cause "needless ridicule" and "painful notoriety," the colleges tried various expedients. Some awarded the "first degree"; some called the women "graduated pupils of the college"; some gave "certificates of proficiency"; some conferred the degree of *mistress* of arts, *maid* of arts, *sister* of arts, *mistress* of English literature, *mistress* of polite literature, *mistress* of teaching, *mistress* of liberal learning, etc.

4 The poem ends:
    "A Ministering Angel in Woman we see,
    And an Angel should covet no other Degree."—

Graduate and Professional Study　　　　Having gradually worked their way up through college graduation with a baccalaureate degree, some women endowed with a high degree of feminism next laid siege to the graduate and professional schools.

Even without any formal education beyond study at the State Normal School at Albany, Kate Stoneman had studied law privately and had been admitted to the bar by a special act of the New York legislature in 1886. So strong a feminist was she that the president of the normal school was directed by the executive committee to "explain to Miss Stoneman that any expression of her views in regard to women's rights and cognate subjects" to the students "was contrary to the wishes of the committee."

A speaker at Mary Sharp College in 1855 pointed out to the graduates that schools of law, theology, and medicine offered "a thousand inducements" to a young man but barred their doors to women. Gradually, however, these doors opened, though reluctantly. By 1885, very few women college graduates were in any of the professions except teaching. In 1907, a study of 3800 alumnae of two colleges revealed only 33 doctors, 7 lawyers, 2 ministers, and 2 architects. In four large colleges with 1258 faculty members, there were only 25 women on the staff in 1911. One institution reported that the president believed "we must in time have women on our faculty." Those women who were appointed found their academic advancement to professorships slower than men's.

All graduate instruction in America is relatively young, dating only from the last part of the nineteenth century.[5] Real emphasis on research as a part of graduate study began in the United States at the new Johns Hopkins University in 1876. Still, most Americans who wanted graduate study went abroad, especially to the German universities. There were 411 Americans at Prussian universities in 1894.

Bryn Mawr University offered graduate study to women in 1885 and had awarded 18 doctorates by 1900. Pennsylvania admitted its first candidates for the Ph.D. degree in 1885, two men and two women. Two women were enrolled in the graduate program of Columbia in 1890. Yale condescended to admit women for graduate work in 1891, "not as a rival or opponent of the colleges for women, but an ally and helper to them." Hopkins accepted women, "provided there is no objection on the part of the instructor concerned." In 1900, the doctorate was won by 312 men and 31 women in all American universities.

[5] It is true that Yale granted the first American Ph.D. in 1861, but this would scarcely be considered of true graduate quality today. Harvard's graduate school was established in 1872, Pennsylvania's in 1882, and Columbia's in 1890.

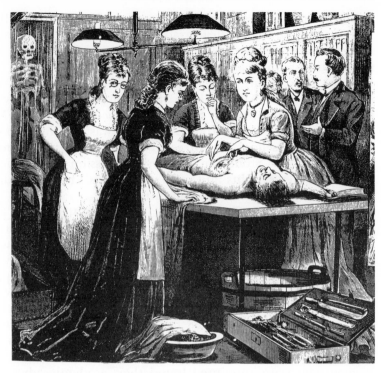

Anatomy lesson at Female Medical College,
New York. Circa late 1800's.

Women in Medicine   Throughout history, women
have had special responsibility for the ill and injured, but the professional study of medicine was something quite different. Some few
women were taught obstetrics privately by a Dr. Shippen in Philadelphia at the time of the Revolution, but this seems to have been
primarily a short course for midwives.

The *Buffalo Medical Journal* said that study of medicine would
make women estranged from men and "loathsome and disgusting,"
but Elizabeth Blackwell persisted to win the first M.D. degree
awarded to a woman in the United States, in 1849, by the small
medical school at Geneva, New York. Harvard admitted three Negroes to its medical school in 1850, but persuaded one woman, whom
they had accepted in a moment of weakness, to withdraw her acceptance. Even after medical schools admitted women to lectures, they
would not permit them to observe clinical cases with men students,
on the grounds of "decency." When they persisted, male students
threw tobacco quids at them.

Women as Lawyers The first law
degree to a woman was granted in 1871 by the law school of Washington University, St. Louis. By 1890, so few women were in law schools that they were not reported separately in the total of 5,252 students. By the turn of the century, most law schools admitted some women, but Harvard, Yale, Columbia, Washington and Lee, and Virginia still excluded them. When Myra Bradwell sought admission to the Illinois bar in 1869, she was refused, and the United States Supreme Court sustained the refusal. Even in 1902, fewer than half the women with law degrees were in practice.

Present Status With a few
exceptions, all graduate and professional schools are open to women at the present time, but proportionately fewer American women are engaged in law, medicine, and other professional work than in certain European countries. The number of women physicians in the Soviet Union is greater than in the United States. While legal and educational impediments to professional training have largely been eliminated, family and social pressures still exist to exclude all but a relatively small number of women from professional study and practice. Even in college teaching, where the hostile family and social pressures are mitigated considerably, there are relatively few women Ph.D.'s available.

For Further Reading

Boas, Louise S. *Women's Education Begins: The Rise of Women's Colleges.* Wheaton (Mass.) College Press, 1935.
Social conditions underlying the beginnings of education of women.

Gilchrist, Beth B. *The Life of Mary Lyon.* Houghton Mifflin, 1910.
Life and works of one of the pioneers.

Goodsell, Willystine. *Pioneers of Women's Education.* McGraw-Hill, 1931.
Emma Willard, Catherine Beecher, Mary Lyon—their trials and triumphs.

Komarovsky, Mirra. *Women in the Modern World: Their Education and Their Dilemmas.* Little, Brown, 1953.
"The history of higher education of women in the United States is a record of violent controversies." The anti-feminist "vogue." Can college educate for marriage and parenthood?

Newcomer, Mabel. *A Century of Higher Education for American Women.* Harper, 1959.

Women's colleges vs. coeducation; the beginnings in the United States; what women students were like; education and employment; women as scholars and artists.

White, Lynn T. *Educating Our Daughters: A Challenge to the Colleges.* Harper, 1950.

Should educational opportunities for women differ from men's?

Woody, Thomas. *A History of Women's Education in the United States.* Science Press, 1929.

A monumental two volume history of the rise of education of "females" in the United States.

13

The Education of Teachers

What Teachers Were Like Though schools of various sorts had existed from earliest colonial days, no attention was paid for a long time to the education of teachers. Along with the concept that education was a matter for the home, church, and charity, went the idea that anyone could teach.

Sometimes the assumption is made that all colonial teachers were of pretty poor stuff. There is a certain degree of valid evidence for this assumption, particularly in court records and colonial newspapers. The first president of Harvard, Nathaniel Eaton, flogged his students unmercifully and fed them bad food. Fired by the board of trustees, he departed with a substantial portion of the college's funds, according to the testimony of Cotton Mather. A Dutch master in New Netherlands was charged with paying "more attention to the tavern than to the school." Another was "too intoxicated at times to know what he was doing or saying." Of a teacher of the Society for the Propagation of the Gospel in Foreign Parts, it is recorded that "he is much given to drink and don't attend the church."

The first schoolmaster in New Amsterdam, Adam Roelantsen, was frequently in and out of the courts, particularly in slander suits. Other teachers were involved in cases of profanity, which was considered a grave offense in a society where piety was so highly esteemed; in financial manipulations, including charging items to the pastor, then selling them to a pawnshop; indebtedness; running away from contracts as indentured servants; gross immorality; lapsing from the true faith, even joining with the Quakers.

While we must admit that teaching was not an impressive or attractive vocation during colonial times, still all the accounts of teachers' shortcomings must be balanced against the number about whom no complaints were made. The total number of persons who got drunk, stole, violated the commandments, and slandered is not excessively large. If one were to compile an account of present-day teachers from court records and newspaper columns, the conclusion

229

he could draw, while correct, would not provide a warrantable basis for a conclusion more sweeping. Records of some towns bear glowing testimonies to the upright character and pedagogical skill of the local schoolmasters.

Teaching in Colonial and early national schools was not a very arduous or challenging occupation. Lesson hearing was the most important part of one's responsibilities. In the discussions of schools, we seldom run across any mention of methodology, except memoriter recitations and caning as discipline.

Need for Teacher Education   When schools were small and relatively unimportant, society did not expect its teachers to have high attainments or special preparation. Indeed, schools existed for decades in America before we find the suggestion that some emphasis be placed upon special education of teachers. One of the first mentions of the education of teachers is the incidental reference by Benjamin Franklin in his prospectus for the establishment of an academy in Philadelphia. Among other reasons for such a school, Franklin said that perhaps

> a number of the poorer sort will be hereby qualified to act as Schoolmasters in the Country, to teach children Reading, Writing, Arithmetic, and the Grammar of their Mother Tongue, and being of good morals and known character, may be recommended from the Academy to Country Schools for that purpose; the Country suffering at present very much for want of good Schoolmasters, and obliged frequently to employ in their Schools, vicious imported Servants, or concealed Papists, who by their bad Examples and Instructions often deprave the Morals and corrupt the Principles of the children under their Care.

Whether Franklin meant by "the poorer sort" those who had difficulty keeping up with their school subjects or those from economically less favored circumstances does not appear clear. There is some evidence for either point of view: persons who failed in the higher studies did accept refuge in teaching,[1] and again teaching appealed especially to those who came from relatively underprivileged homes.

A more extended argument for the special preparation of teachers was made in the *Massachusetts Magazine* for June, 1789. In an unsigned article (which, it is conjectured, was written by Elisha Ticknor) the writer says

> There should be a public grammar school established in every county in the state, in which should be taught English grammar,

---

[1] Hence the adage "those who can, do; those who can't teach."

Latin, Greek, rhetoric, geography, mathematics, etc., in order to fit young gentlemen for college and for school keeping . . . No man ought to be suffered to superintend ever so small a school except he has first been examined by a body of men . . . We should have a worthy class of teachers, regularly introduced and examined, and should soon see the happy effects resulting from this noble plan.

In 1816, Denison Olmsted delivered at Yale College, upon the occasion of his receiving a Master's degree, an address in which he outlined his plan for "a seminary for schoolmasters." In this he stated that, in his opinion, "nothing was wanted in order to raise all our common branches to a far higher level . . . but competent teachers and the necessary books." Mr. Olmsted was then led to the idea of his "seminary for teachers," to be established by the state, with instruction gratis. "The pupils were to study and recite whatever they were themselves afterwards to teach, partly for the purpose of acquiring a more perfect knowledge of these subjects, and partly learning from the methods adopted by the principal the best modes of teaching." Ample instruction was also to be provided in school organization and government.

Yale College again figured in the early advocacy of institutions for the training of teachers, when Professor James L. Kingsley in 1823 suggested the establishment in each county of a "superior school, intermediate between the common schools and the university" for the preparation of common school teachers. He declared that under the existing system, teachers seldom had any preparation for teaching other than that which they had received "in the very school where they afterwards instruct."

Professor Kingsley's article was warmly endorsed in a pamphlet by William Russell, then principal of an academy in New Haven. This pamphlet shows that as early as 1823 American leaders were accustomed to place tremendous faith in education as a means of improving the social, political, and economic order. "The information, the intelligence, and the refinement which might be diffused among the body of people would increase the prosperity, elevate the character, and promote the happiness of the nation to a degree perhaps unequalled in the world," he declared.

Once abroad, the idea of special preparation of teachers made rapid headway among the citizens of New England. Samuel R. Hall, a clergyman who had been sent to Concord, Vermont, by the Domestic Missionary Society, opened the first seminary in America, exclusively for the training of teachers. This was in March, 1823. It was a private venture, without state aid, and was conducted with little more equipment than the enthusiasm and experience of the Rev. Mr. Hall. He appears to have been a person of forceful personality, capable of securing the introduction of new ideas, for he is credited with persuading the pupils of a Maine school district, in which he was a teacher, to write compositions—a then unheard-of innovation.

The superintendent of common schools of the State of New York ordered 10,000 copies of Hall's publication, *Lectures on School Keeping* for distribution in the common school districts throughout the state. This order received the approval of the state legislature, April 26, 1832. Kentucky took similar action.

Hall's book was the first professional book in English on the subject of school keeping to be published in America. While it is impossible at this date to estimate the influence of this little book in molding public opinion in New York in favor of state-supported teacher training institutions, it must have carried considerable weight, for it was circulated during the rise of public interest in the professional preparation of teachers. With the prestige of the state superintendent behind it, and with Governors DeWitt Clinton and Martin Van Buren endorsing higher standards, it may be assumed that the book was widely read in the state.

Hall pointed out in the "lectures" that the decline in the status of the public education at the time was due to several factors: inadequately trained teachers, parsimony in support, division of community opinion, non-patronage of the public schools by the wealthy, inadequate compensation for teachers, and improperly constructed and poorly located schoolhouses.

The curriculum of Hall's school, in a three-year course, was based upon a common school education, with a thorough review of the subjects to be taught in the common schools; some mathematics, book chemistry, natural philosophy, logic, astronomy, evidences of Christianity, and moral and intellectual philosophy. In the third term of the third year, Hall presented a new study called "the art of teaching." The subject matter in the seminary appears to have been a typical academy curriculum of the time, with the addition of the work in pedagogy.

Hall sent forth from twenty to fifty teachers each year with "certificates of approbation." Similar experiments were made at Amherst Academy and at the female seminary at Ipswich, Massachusetts.

In 1830, the Rev. Mr. Hall was called to Phillips Academy at Andover, Mass., where a teachers' seminary was provided for the preparation of teachers for common and higher schools. When he was engaged in the furthering of the state normal school movement in Massachusetts, Horace Mann visited Andover and inspected the teacher training work done there. Hall later removed from Andover to Plymouth, N.H., and for three years carried on work in teacher training there.

The Rev. Thomas H. Gallaudet, then principal of the American Asylum for the Education of the Deaf and Dumb, in 1825 published a series of essays in the *Connecticut Observer,* over the signature, "A Father." In these articles he said that institutions existed for the training of "able divines, lawyers and physicians," but that teachers had to grope their way "through a long and tiresome process." He then asked why an institution should not be provided for the "training up of instructors." Gallaudet's plan was notable in that it proposed instruction in the "Theory and Practice of the Education of Youth," the development of a course of lectures on the subject, the furnishing of a library, the establishment of a practice or "experimental" school, and the preparation by the faculty "of the best books to be employed in the early stages of education." The presence of even one such institution would arouse wide public interest, Mr. Gallaudet declared. The very "conflict of opinion would keep alive the public interest in the general subjects." In view of the lack of widespread interest in his plan, Gallaudet applied the principle of gradual adjustment, suggesting that the experiment should be undertaken on a small scale. If once begun, it would before long demonstrate its practical utility.

In 1824–25, James G. Carter published a series of essays in the *Boston Patriot,* setting forth the crying need for the establishment of normal schools. His plan provided that these schools, if established, should give a thorough grounding in the subjects to be taught in the common schools, should provide a course in the science and art of teaching, and should have available a practice school for purposes of experimentation and observation. These essays were subsequently published in pamphlet form.

The series of articles attracted favorable attention throughout the country, particularly in Massachusetts. It was this series, with Carter's subsequent efforts at propagandizing the movement, that earned him the title of "Father of Normal Schools," and warranted Henry Barnard's saying that to him, "more than to any other one person, belongs the credit of having first arrested the attention of the leading minds of Massachusetts to the necessity of the immediate and thorough improvement in the system of free or public schools and of having clearly pointed out the most direct and thorough mode of procuring this improvement by providing for the training of competent teachers for these schools."

In his series, Carter outlined the purpose of normal schools, suggested means of organization and management, proposed a course of study to be followed, and set forth the advantages to ensue from founding such institutions. Carter argued that it would be of little avail for a legislature to make large appropriations directly for the support of schools until "a judicious expenditure can be assured." Such a judicious expenditure could be assured only by competent teachers. Furthermore, it would "do absolutely no good to constitute an independent tribunal to decide on the qualifications of teachers, while they have not had the opportunities necessary for coming up to the proper standard. And it will do no good to overlook and report upon their success, when we know beforehand that they will not have the means of success." It would be equally futile, the argument continued, to build schoolhouses and put in them young teachers directed to teach specified subjects "while it is obvious that they can not know how, properly, to teach any subject."

Teaching, Carter said, was "the only service in which we venture to employ young and, often, ignorant persons without some previous instruction in their appropriate duties." While it was true that the state required the prospective teachers to be examined and certified by the minister of the town, this was in reality "a perfect farce" which resulted in "no efficient check upon the obtrusions of ignorance and inexperience," for the ministers were under strong local pressure to license practically any applicant.

In 1827, Carter opened at Lancaster, Massachusetts, a normal school as a private venture. His petition to the state legislature for aid was rejected by a single vote in the senate, despite the favorable report of the education committee, to which the request had been referred. Massachusetts thus lost to New York the opportunity of being the first state to inaugurate a permanent policy of rendering financial aid in the professional preparation of teachers. The people of Lancaster rendered valuable assistance for a time, but because of a misconception of the aims of the school, soon turned against it and forced Carter to abandon the experiment. He continued, however, to give instruction privately to certain pupils, many of whom later became successful teachers.

In 1830, Carter assisted in the founding of the American Institute of Instruction, whose members and lecturers constituted a veritable honor roll of American educational leadership in this period. At the 1831 meeting of this society, Carter gave a lecture on "the necessity and most practical means of raising the qualifications of teachers." In January, 1837, this institute sent to the legislature of Massachusetts a memorial petition for the better preparation of the common school teachers of the Commonwealth. In the words of Harlan H.

Horner, "This memorial was an able document and deserves a permanent place in the history of American education." It was drawn up by George B. Emerson, chairman of the committee appointed for that purpose, and for many years secretary and then president of the Institute.

Emerson's biting indictment of the qualifications of common school teachers reads, in part:

> They are often without experience in managing a school: they have no skill in communicating. Instead of being able to stimulate and guide to all that is noble and excellent, they are, not seldom persons of such doubtful respectability and refinement of character, that no one would think for a moment, of holding them up as models to their pupils. In short, they know not *what* to teach, nor *how* to teach, nor in *what spirit* to teach, nor what is the nature of those they undertake to *lead,* nor what they are *themselves,* who stand forward to lead them.

As a member of the Massachusetts legislature after 1835, Mr. Carter continued to manifest an intense interest in popular education. As chairman of the committee on education in 1836, he again recommended the founding of a seminary for the professional education of teachers. In 1837 he made a vigorous effort to secure the appropriation of half of the state's share of the United States surplus revenue fund for the education of common school teachers, but he failed to win legislative approval. In 1838 his enthusiastic speeches probably turned the scale in favor of the passage of the normal school act.

The American Lyceum at a meeting in 1831 resolved "that this Lyceum consider the establishment of seminaries for the education of teachers a most important part of every system of public instruction." The members of this society included such men as Alexander Proudfit of Salem, N.Y., Professor Olmsted of Yale, Henry Barnard, S. R. Hall, Edward Everett, Stephen Van Rensselaer, Thomas S. Grimke of South Carolina, William C. Woodbridge, and George Emerson.

In his treatment of "Observations on the Improvement of Seminaries of Learning in the United States: with Suggestions for Its Accomplishment," Walter R. Johnson of Germantown, Pennsylvania, in 1825 arrived at the conclusion that the principal improvement should be the establishment of schools for the preparation of teachers. Such a school "ought not to be an insulated establishment," but should be "connected with some institution where an extensive range in the sciences is taken." The course of study would require at least a year, and should comprehend a series of lectures and practical illustrations on the subject of "intellectual philosophy as connected with the science of education"; a study of physical education; a course in methods of "conveying instruction" in science and the manual arts, and another methods course in "all those branches classed under the Philological department."

No one of the earlier advocates of teacher training institutions seems to have been conversant with the European normal school systems. The year 1825 apparently marks the first extant reference, in an American treatise on teacher preparation, to the Prussian system. Johnson, in that year, referred to the Prussian schools in his pamphlet. The next year, William C. Woodbridge said that "Seminaries for Teachers must be founded, devoted exclusively to this object, as is done in the most improved countries of Europe."

As early as 1829, Woodbridge and Gallaudet projected a teachers seminary after the Prussian model for Hartford, Connecticut. In the same year, there was published in New York a book of travels by Henry E. Dwight, who had visited certain of the normal schools of Germany, and who in this volume advocated American adoption of the plan. "Were such seminaries established with us, by increasing the compensation of the instructors we might easily persuade them to make it (teaching) the employment of their lives."

An article in the *American Annals of Education* in 1831 said that "in those of the countries of Europe where education has taken its rank as a science, it is almost as singular to question the importance of a preparatory seminary for teachers, as of a medical school for physicians." Woodbridge, the editor, in the same year reprinted a translation of an article on the Prussian normal schools.

Victor Cousin's celebrated report on public instruction in Prussia, including a section on the preparation of teachers, was made available in translation in this country in 1825, and an account of three Prussian normal schools, prepared from data taken from Cousin's report, was published in 1836 in Philadelphia.

"Unquestionably, the man who did most to disseminate the knowledge of the Prussian teachers' seminaries among the people of Massachusetts and New England, and to convince them of their fundamental importance, was Charles Brooks." Mr. Brooks, a Unitarian minister, settled in Hingham, professed that he "fell in love with the Prussian system." It seemed to possess him "like a missionary angel" when it was first explained to him in the course of a forty-one day passage from Liverpool to New York in 1834. His informant was a Dr. H. Julius of Hamburg, his cabin mate, whom he had met at a literary soirée in London. By the time he had reached the Gulf Stream, Brooks had "resolved to *do* something about *State* Normal Schools."

Fired with this missionary zeal—Brooks himself referred to his campaign for normal schools as a missionary movement—he studied the Prussian system for six months, and opened communication with Victor Cousin, whom he had met in Paris in 1833. Cousin supplied several books on normal education, and was Brooks' "comfort and strength."

Brooks adopted Cousin's name for these institutions, and popularized the term "normal schools." Mangun has shown that before Brooks' missionary efforts, such terms as "institutions for educating teachers," and "seminaries for teachers" were generally used. For years, even after Brooks' work, the term "normal school" was often misunderstood, the institutions often being called "Norman schools" or "Mormon schools."

Brooks launched his campaign with a sermon at Hingham, stating here for the first time the famous, and now trite, expression: "As is the teacher, so is the school." This slogan was used to substantiate the argument for the establishment of teacher training institutions. The sermon not having been welcomed so enthusiastically as Brooks expected, according to his own account, he then proceeded to write "three enormously long lectures" of two hours each, describing the Prussian system, showing how it could be adapted to Massachusetts, and demonstrating that "great, practical, Christian results" could be obtained through the system and through it only. Brooks felt that there were grave objections to private normal schools and insisted from the beginning upon state control.

He called a convention to meet in Plymouth, advertising it widely. At a crowded meeting-house, he elaborated his plan. Ichabod Morton, a deacon, offered $1000, and at the next meeting of the American Institute of Instruction introduced a resolution which Brooks regarded as "equal to a three-hundred-pound Parrot gunshot" in his cause. Invitations to lecture poured in to Brooks, and the crusader covered more than 2,000 miles in his chaise, lecturing free of charge. One week he lectured eight times. Brooks, by his own account, seems to have been adept at attaining considerable space in print, free if possible, but paid for if necessary, and such activity, with its resultant publicity, attracted widespread attention.

There is some evidence that historians of the Massachusetts normal schools, particularly Gordy in his brief treatment, have been inclined to over-emphasize Brooks' part in the establishment of these state institutions. It should be noted that most of these opinions were based upon Brooks' reminiscences, published some years after the campaign for normal schools. Edward Everett wrote in his journal, July 13, 1864, that "a most absurd document appears in the *Transcript* this afternoon, being a pretended account by Reverend Charles Brooks of the introduction of normal schools in Massachusetts, of which he takes the entire credit to himself. My agency is as much ignored as possible. Whoever knows Mr. Brooks knows that he is a person wholly destitute of influence, and few things retarded the introduction of the normal schools more than the circumstance that he was riding them as a hobby." Again, on December 20, 1864, Everett recorded that President Sparks of Harvard concurred with him in the opinion of Brooks' "ridiculous pretensions" which were "one of the greatest pieces of charlatanism ever attempted."

This extreme view is manifestly unfair to Brooks, and is not substantiated by similar expressions elsewhere. Albree has stated that "as far as the history of normal schools in Massachusetts is concerned, there are three men who will stand out above others in history of that time: Carter, who showed the need; Brooks, who offered the remedy and aroused public attention so that the law was established, and Horace Mann, who put the law into practice." With the inclusion of the names of Governor Everett and several other minor leaders, this is probably as fair an estimate as can now be arrived at.

In 1836 and 1837, Governor Levi Lincoln touched upon education in his annual messages, mildly and hesitatingly. Brooks was "grateful for a little dew, though the state was ready for a copious shower." The creation of the Board of Education in April, 1837 was a good omen for the normal school propagandists, for it demonstrated that Massachusetts was becoming conscious of its educational responsibility. When Horace Mann, the first secretary of the board, asked Brooks to continue lecturing on normal schools until they were secured, the latter replied that "they were already secured, and no power could stop them." However, Brooks continued his efforts, and secured the commendation of both John Quincy Adams and Daniel Webster who "emphatically approved" of the movement and "hoped that Normal Schools would be established, not only in Massachusetts, but throughout the United States." Adams, "the old man eloquent," who, as a member of the national House of Representatives, was then deep in his contests over the right of abolitionists to submit petitions to Congress, took time to attend a convention at Hanover, in September, 1838. Among the points he made was this: "We see monarchs expending vast sums in educating the children of their poorest subjects, and shall we be outdone by kings?"

Edward Everett, the statesman-orator, must be assigned a share of the credit for the first successful introduction of state normal schools in America. As governor, he was a member of the first state board of education, and in that body advocated state aid in teacher training. As a doctor of philosophy from Göttingen, probably the first American to be awarded the degree there, Everett took more than an amateur interest in the Prussian system of normal schools. He knew about the university standards of Germany, "and the idea of a seminary or preparatory school to teach teachers especially appealed to him."

It was doubtless fortunate that a man of his vision and scholarship was in the state house during this period. As governor, Everett wrote the annual reports of the newly established Board of Education, and he took particular interest in the development of the normal schools. The first report, made in February, 1838, spoke of the "happiest results" obtained in foreign countries where schools for teachers were a part of the educational system. "The art of imparting instruction," it said, "has been found, like every other art, to improve by cultivation in institutions established for that specific object. . . . The board cannot but express the sanguine hope that the time is not far distant when the resources of public or private liberality will be applied in Massachusetts for the foundation of an institution for the formation of teachers."

William E. Channing, another influential New Englander, in 1837 declared, "We need an institution for the formation of better teachers; and, until this step is taken, we can make no important progress. An institution for training men to train the young would be a fountain of living waters sending forth streams to refresh present and future ages."

A share of the immediate credit for the establishment of the Massachusetts normal schools must be given to Edmund Dwight, who gave $10,000 for that purpose, provided that the legislature would match it with an equal sum. The legislature acquiesced when Horace Mann placed Dwight's offer before it. The act for the establishment of the first normal school in America was passed on April 18, 1838. Brooks recorded that his "cup of joy was full" that the Prussian system had been "transplanted to America."

Not everyone concurred that normal schools were needed. Then, as now, pedagogy was suspect in certain circles. Professor Adams of Dartmouth was quoted as saying that though he had had 42 years of experience in teaching in different schools and seminaries, he believed he "should be able to communicate in an hour and a half all that could profitably be communicated by way of precept to aid one in acquiring the art of teaching."[2] This is an opinion that seems to persist in some minds up to the present day.

Normal Schools Established   Normal schools were established at Lexington, Barre, and Bridgewater, all in Massachusetts, in 1839. Fortunately journals describing the early days of one Normal School were kept by Cyrus Peirce,[3] the principal at the first school in Lexington, and by one of his pupils, Mary Swift. Peirce's journal begins:

> This Day the Normal School, the first in the Country, commenced. Three pupils, Misses Hawkins, Smith and Damon were examined by the Board of Visitors—viz Messrs. Sparks, Rantoul & Putnam, & admitted—

> July 8. Monday School opened this day with 3 pupils Hawkins, Smith & Stowe—one Miss Ralph added during the day Exercises Conversation—Grammar & Arithmetic. Three of the Scholars promise well.

> July 10. This Day Mary Swift of Nantucket joined the School.[4]

Miss Swift's journal gives a day-to-day account of the school, reporting on lessons received and commenting on Peirce's lectures. Some of the flavor of the period is conveyed by these random quotations:

> Mr. P. read over the portion of Peirce's Grammar on the subject of the verb, which part of speech he calls *asserters*.

> After copying some lessons on the globe school was dismissed.

> The lessons for this morn were N. Philosophy, Physiology, N. History. The subjects of the first were Light & Refraction.

> We punctuated some sentences.

> Mr. P. made some remarks on the manner in which the words prevent & let were used in the Bible, as differing from their present use.

> Part of the time was passed in explanation of the Trade Winds.

> I asked the cause of Aurora Borealis.

---

2 *Boston Recorder.* April 19, 1839.
3 The name is spelled *Peirce*, not *Pierce*, and is pronounced "Purse."
4 Norton, Arthur O. (editor): The First State Normal School in America: *The Journals of Cyrus Peirce and Mary Swift.* Harvard University Press. 1926.

The Albany Normal School   New York was
the second state to establish a state normal school, but did so only
after a ten-year experiment of subsidizing academies to prepare
teachers. As a consequence of persistent agitation on the part of
educational reformers, the legislature in 1834 passed an act providing
for use of state funds to subsidize teacher training in certain academies. This was the first legislative appropriation in the United States
for the establishment of teacher training institutions, antedating the
Massachusetts normal school act by five years.

For years, the governors—notably DeWitt Clinton and William
L. Marcy, the state superintendents of common schools, other professional leaders, the Regents of the University of the State of New
York, and many private citizens had demonstrated the inadequacies
of the hit-and-miss means of providing teachers for the common
schools. Marcy, in 1834, called for ample funds and the "establishment of seminaries of a more elevated rank" because "upon them we
must, in a great measure, depend for competent teachers of the common schools." Four months later, the act subsidizing the academies
was passed. The governor hoped it would "have an auspicious influence upon our system of common school education," but by 1838 he
thought that normal schools would better serve the purposes of the
state.

His successor, William H. Seward (who later was Lincoln's secretary of state), however, thought the system of "engrafting" normal
departments upon the academies the only practicable means of introducing normal schools into the United States. Shortly thereafter, the
Regents expressed their disappointment in the results. At first eight
academies were designated, but the number was increased to sixteen
within a few years. At the same time, the state subsidy for teacher
training was reduced from $400 to $300 per academy, though the
schools which were really trying to be effective in teacher training
reported that even $400 did not cover the expenses of these depart-
ments. The length of the required term was likewise reduced, from
eight to six months, on the grounds that very few prospective teachers would stay for more than half a year, "the remaining half being
devoted by them to the teaching of winter schools."

Colonel Samuel Young, secretary of state and ex officio superintendent of common schools, called a convention of district superintendents in 1842, and invited to it some of New England's leading
educators who favored normal schools—Horace Mann, George B.
Emerson, and William Gallaudet. Resolutions in behalf of a state
normal school resulted, after Mann had declared he could wish for
New York no better fortune than that she should "crown all her
noble education works" with one or more normal schools.

**Minnesota State Normal School at Winona, a typical teachers
college of the latter part of the Nineteenth Century.**

**Many Normal School students came from elementary schools,
even one-room rural schools such as this.**

Colonel Young wrote a recommendation to the Regents in behalf of a normal school. The Regents referred it to a special committee consisting of three men, one of whom was the Colonel. Thus Colonel Young, as secretary of state and ex officio a Regent, helped to consider the report which he, as secretary of state and ex officio superintendent of common schools, had proposed. Not surprisingly, this committee concurred with the superintendent's proposal!

In 1844, the legislature established a state normal school at Albany, in the recently abandoned railway station of the Mohawk and Hudson railroad. The first president was David Perkins Page, a protegé of Horace Mann's, who subsequently wrote a book on teaching which went through many editions. This was his *Theory and Practice of Teaching*.[5]

From this normal school at Albany the first class was graduated in 1845—eight months after they had enrolled. Since that time this institution (under a variety of names: State Normal School, State Normal College, New York State College for Teachers, State University College of Education) has sent forth thousands of teachers who have assumed roles in American education, from teaching in the simple one-room country schools to college presidencies. Many of the principals and teachers in normal schools subsequently established in western states came from Albany and the Oswego State Normal School.[6]

More Normal Schools

With the success of normal schools in Massachusetts and New York, other states embraced the idea. Some of the schools were state institutions, some were county normal schools, and others were municipal institutions. For many years most of them were exceedingly modest institutions on the post-elementary school level. The students came from elementary schools—often from one-room rural schools—and stayed for only a year or two. Well into the present century, the typical normal school offered only a two-year course, but frequently students did not stay that long, for even with a short term in a normal school, they found their services as teachers very much in demand. Not until late

---

[5] Of this book, Winship said, in 1889, "No other book on the subject of education has been read by so many American teachers through so many years . . . No other book has had so great influence in helping teachers, and to this day it remains the best book of its kind ever written."

[6] D. Franklin Wells, an 1852 graduate from the school at Albany, was the first professor appointed at the new State University of Iowa in 1855. His appointment as professor for the training of teachers antedated appointment of a president. Since Wells had no degree, the Iowa trustees conferred upon him the degree of bachelor of arts.

in the nineteenth century did even the best of the normal schools require high school graduation for entrance.

The early normal school curriculum consisted of a review of elementary school subjects, some small exposure to secondary school subjects, lectures on school-keeping, and student teaching in a model or practice school under the direction of the normal school faculty.

The curriculum at Albany, in 1845, included orthography, reading and elocution, writing, geography and outlines, English grammar with composition, history of the United States, human physiology, mental arithmetic, elementary and higher arithmetic, elementary algebra, six books of plane geometry, some trigonometry, land surveying, natural philosophy, chemistry with experimental lectures, intellectual philosophy, moral philosophy, science of government, rhetoric, theory and practice of teaching, experimental school and lectures, drawing, music and elementary astronomy. Two days after this curriculum was adopted it was decided "that the females be excused from studying plane trigonometry and surveying," in keeping with the idea that the minds of women were not so strong as men's.

By the time of the Civil War, a thin line of normal schools stretched westward over the northern states. After 1865, the number of schools increased rapidly, and the system extended into the southern states, sometimes with the financial encouragement of northern philanthropies. Many states also adopted the earlier New York pattern of teacher training classes in academies and high schools. But even when the normal schools grew to more than 150 by 1900, they still could not meet the demand for teachers. Since most of the normal schools were small, often with less than 100 or 200 students, they just did not supply teachers in the numbers needed. Well into the present century, the typical rural teacher (and often the city teacher as well) was a person who had taken one course devoted to teaching while he was still in high school, or else he was a rural school graduate without any formal study of pedagogy who had taken an examination set by a county superintendent of schools. Many of these persons were devoted, consecrated teachers, but, lacking exposure to learning beyond the elementary level, and lacking adequate exposure to professional skills, they were often routine teachers whose method was largely memoriter and catechetical in nature. The teacher dared not depart from the textbook because his own knowledge went no further.[7]

7 The author recalls that his class, in a small rural school in Northern Pennsylvania, was studying the geography of the Andes. Mention was made of Lake Titicaca, the highest in the world. One of his classmates asked the teacher if there were any fish in Lake Titicaca. The teacher, not knowing any more than the text set forth, exclaimed in an angry manner, "Walter, this is a lesson in geography, not in fishing!" How differently a professionally prepared teacher would handle the question!

Various states undertook efforts to promote the in-service education of teachers. Three principal agencies were employed—reading circles, teachers' institutes, and summer sessions.

The Reading Circle   The reading circle, a semi-formal class for reading and discussion on topics of value to teachers in service or in training, was customarily administered by a state board. Sometimes, too, the reading circle was subsidized by the state department of public instruction or by the state teachers association. By 1887, the federal bureau of education estimated that 75,000 teachers were pursuing systematic off-campus courses of study in both professional and general cultural subjects. The courses of study, sometimes four years in length, led to a certificate or diploma. Such diplomas were helpful in obtaining or in renewing a license to teach. In more recent times, the increased opportunity for teachers to attend normal schools and the institution of correspondence courses for university credit have served to diminish the need for reading circles. In a way, too, the in-service workshops developed by many city school systems and larger union or consolidated rural districts have served also to reduce the attractiveness of reading circles.

Teachers' Institutes   Teachers' institutes, for a span of nearly a century, were a powerful factor in the in-service education of teachers. Institutes were temporary assemblages of teachers for special drill and mutual improvement in all matters pertaining to the profession. They differed from present-day meetings of state and district education associations in that they were a temporary school with the specific aim of improving the teacher in everything pertaining to the discharge of his professional duties. They sought to increase the scholarship of the teacher by presenting subject matter on either elementary or more advanced levels. They sought to acquaint teachers with principles and methods of teaching and school management and with the principles of an emerging new subject, psychology. They sought to develop a professional spirit by bringing teachers together, taking them from their isolated districts for a few days or even a few weeks, and convening them in meetings with their fellow teachers. They seem to have been a peculiar cross between teachers' conferences and the later-day summer session or extension class, but they were designed to meet the special needs of their times.

There is some uncertainty as to which was the first teachers' institute in the United States. The two principal claimants for the honor of originating institutes are J. S. Denman of Ithaca, New York, and Henry Barnard of Hartford, Connecticut. Even before these men conducted institutes, however, teachers had been accustomed to gather in informal sessions, where the better-trained teachers took charge of a class of novices. Simple drills and presentation of subject matter were common, and time was often given to the discussion of practical schoolroom problems.

Denman's first institute, apparently the first one to use the name "institute," was conducted in 1843 at Ithaca, where Denman was county superintendent of schools. It was held for two weeks and was said to be "a revelation of the new agent in school improvement." Twenty-eight rural teachers attended. It was at once seen that teachers who were financially unable to enroll in a training class in an academy for a term or two would be willing and often eager to take advantage of an economical and short-term opportunity near at home. Other institutes were soon held in New York at Auburn and Rochester.

In the meantime, Henry Barnard had asked the Connecticut legislature for funds "to be expended so as to reach, if practicable, every teacher in the state." He felt that institutes would be preferable to normal schools at that time in Connecticut, for institutes were both cheaper and more widespread in their immediate influence. When the legislature refused the requested $5000, Barnard conducted such institutes at his own expense. Several public-spirited citizens and experienced teachers helped him. Barnard's first institute was for men; one for "females" was organized in 1840. Neither of these classes was called an institute, but the description of the work clearly places them in that category.

By 1844, the year the normal school was established in Albany, the number of institutes in New York had jumped to twenty. Some of these were actually called "normal schools." All these early institutes were voluntary, without any semblance of state subsidy. Teachers not only paid their own fare, board and room, but also hired the hall and paid the man conducting the institute. Appropriately, he was called the institute conductor. When we consider that the expense per teacher was reported as five dollars a week (yes, including room, board, and tuition!) and that the average salary of men teachers was fifteen dollars a month and women teachers seven dollars a month, we can appreciate their zeal and sacrifice for professional improvement. Naturally, the institutes were promoted earnestly by the county superintendents of schools.

Salem Town, one of the early "conductors" in New York, recorded these as typical subjects offered in institutes: orthography, English grammar, arithmetic, geography with the use of globes, analysis of words, "reading by sentences and paragraphs in an easy and elegant manner, and giving some general exposition of what was read," "principles and rules of mensuration of superfices and solids," algebra (as an elective), music "largely for social enjoyment," and such professional subjects as schoolroom policy, discipline, mental training, and "instilling virtuous and honorable principles of action." Gradually, some science found its way into the programs. Considerable emphasis was placed upon the three R's. One call for an institute cautioned all teachers to bring two or three slates.

William J. Milne, president of the State Normal College at Albany (successor to the State Normal School) listed these as subjects frequently discussed:

What are the best methods of securing order in school?

What are the best means of exciting an interest in study?

What can be done to interest parents in the school? (PTA's had not been "invented.")

Ways to prevent whispering.

How to teach reading without monotony and drawling.

Means of securing early and regular attendance.

The best way to teach the alphabet.

The day at an institute was full from nine in the morning until five in the afternoon, and then there were evening lectures.

New York and several other states granted subsidies to institutes, New York allowing $60 per institute at first and then $120. One of the arguments for the establishment of the normal school at Albany was that it would furnish institute conductors, and records of the institution show that graduates of the school did "bestow on the less favored recipients of government bounty, the affluence of (their) acquisitions." In 1847, David P. Page, the first president, visited eleven counties in thirty days and lectured 47 times before institutes. Another powerful lecturer was William F. Phelps, an early graduate, who later became principal of the normal school at Winona, Minnesota.

Salem Town reported in 1849 that the institute idea had spread to half the states in the union, that he personally had organized the first institutes in five other states, that he had taught in 33 institutes in New York, that more than 10,000 teachers had attended 69 institutes in New York, and that primary schools were more advanced in counties conducting institutes. In 1860, the state superintendent in New York said institutes were "the most potent influence in our educational system."

Moral persuasion not being enough to get all teachers to attend institutes, some states required local schools to pay salaries while teachers attended. Such a regulation in New York increased attendance to 3,500 more than the previous year.

General meetings were the most prominent part of early institutes, but as they grew in size, the criticism was made that they were mass meetings, too unwieldy and repetitious from year to year. Then sectional or "graded" sessions were held in many states. Even summer institutes, forerunners of summer sessions, were organized in 1896.

Eventually, the better preparation of persons before they entered upon teaching, the institution of a better system of professional supervision, and the institution of district meetings by professional associations for teachers diminished the importance of institutes. The name still lingers on in some rural areas for these teachers' association meetings, but the historic institute has served its day and has passed away.

Summer Sessions   Summer sessions are so common now in universities, colleges, and teachers colleges that one might never question whether there was a time when they were considered a startling innovation. The first summer school in America, philanthropically subsidized, was conducted in 1873 by the scientist Louis Agassiz at Buzzards Bay. Only a few teachers attended and the project was soon abandoned. North Carolina University conducted a summer school for teachers in 1877 and other temporary and sporadic ventures have been recorded. The Lake Chautauqua Institute, established in 1874 in western New York, was the first notable success. Beginning as a Sunday School assembly with strong emphasis on the teaching of the Bible, it gradually evolved into a rich educational and cultural institution, using "modern" normal school methods. Francis W. Parker, principal of the Cook County Normal School, Chicago, sponsored the "teachers' retreat" which emphasized "the principles of psychology and pedagogics," with practical applications to schoolroom situations. Chautauqua also maintained a school of music and a school of physical culture, both of which were popular with teachers. A genteel lady could combine study and vacation in cultural surroundings of impeccable moral standards.

Massachusetts educators set up a rival and flourishing summer session at Martha's Vineyard, and another, established at Saratoga, was later moved to Glens Falls, New York. All these ventures were outside the universities, but they soon saw opportunity for service and for summer income for their faculty members. Summer sessions were established in the late 1880's and early 1890's by the University of Wisconsin, Indiana University, and Cornell. Many other institutions, including colleges and normal schools, followed in their footsteps. As many as 2000 students enrolled at a "Summer School of the South" sponsored by the University of Tennessee in 1902. Andrew Sloan Draper, commissioner of education in New York, was an early advocate of summer sessions for teachers. He showed that the investment of more than $2,000,000 in normal school buildings and equipment stood idle for at least 25 per cent of the year. (This has a contemporary flavor but was pointed out in 1910.) The first New York normal school to conduct a summer term was Oneonta in 1912, at an expense of $4000. Albany offered a summer session in 1917, with an enrollment of 253 students taking 29 courses, taught by 16 instructors, at a cost of $6,100. By 1925, one teacher in every five in New York was taking a summer course at some institution, either public or private. Early normal school summer sessions were usually free, but after the 1930's, a small tuition fee was generally charged.

Many summer sessions have provided a splendid opportunity for teachers to upgrade themselves both in their subject matter and in education. Together with extension courses, some of these summer sessions have become a common route for teachers to meet degree requirements for the bachelor's and master's degree or to make up any certification deficiencies. Usually conducted for six weeks, they still allow the teacher a reasonable vacation before resuming teaching in the fall. Through "pre-session" and "post-session" and even "post-post-session," some colleges permit a student to gain as many as 15 semester hours of credit in the summer. Additional compensation for teachers with advanced degrees has been a strong incentive for enrollment.

Occasionally there are criticisms of summer sessions, on the grounds that they are tiring to the professors and students alike. One early criticism by W. B. Harlow (in *The Academy* in 1886) urged that teachers, for "two months at least, [should] flee from one another as if [they] were in danger of catching the plague." He wondered if true teachers after ten months of teaching were in a "fit condition to spend their vacations in brain work." Disregarding this warning, teachers have flocked to the professional meccas in increasing numbers. In 1962, more than 1,500,000 persons attended summer sessions in accredited colleges and universities. A large number of these were teachers, but others included persons trying to get back into the good graces of their deans and some who were attempting to cut their college exposure to three calendar years.

Changing Concepts in Teacher Education   Throughout the nineteenth century and well into the present century, America's greatest problem in teacher education was the challenge of providing the sheer number of teachers needed to "keep school." Standards were generally low. Though there were normal schools for the preparation of elementary school teachers, attendance at one of these institutions was not necessary to meet certification requirements. Many high schools offered "teacher training" classes and one could go straight from high school into elementary school teaching. College graduation was not necessary for a certificate to teach in high school. Indeed, many teachers went straight from their student days in the rural elementary school into elementary school teaching via examination, and then, after a few years of teaching in elementary schools, were "promoted" to high school teaching, without themselves ever having attended a high school. The testimony of Ambrose L. Suhrie, who went through this process, is recorded in his professional autobiography:

When I accepted the principalship of a high school, with an enrollment of two hundred, in a lumber town up in the wilderness of northern Pennsylvania at age twenty-one, my chief and about my only equipment for the undertaking were good intentions and the habit of industry.

I had no adequate basic education, either academic or professional, and no training in supervision or administration. The motive that had prompted me to accept the call was that I could not live, away from home, on a grade-teacher's salary. I had to have an administrator's salary or leave the "profession."

Education was, in those days, "the noblest of professions" in theory and "the sorriest of trades" in actual practice. In one county in which I had taught, there were two hundred sixty teachers and principals. Of these only one, a principal, was a college graduate, and only two, both principals, were two-year normal-school graduates. All the other two hundred fifty-seven teachers (and principals too) were, at best, little more than eighth-grade graduates, and were chiefly the products of the one-teacher rural school. By the age of twenty, I was a normal-school graduate with a life certificate, and so I had good "professional" standing in what was then in reality a layman's calling.[9]

Gradually, there was a demand for better professional preparation of teachers, both in subject matter and in professional studies. State after state raised requirements, though the pattern remains uneven to this day. In the 1930's certain states ceased issuing general licenses authorizing the holder to teach any subject in any grade of any public school, and began limiting the certificates to certain fields in which one had had special preparation. Often these standards, while better than in earlier years, were still lax. As late as 1963, one could get a certificate to teach all the sciences in Pennsylvania high schools if he were a college graduate with 18 semester hours of education and 18 semester hours of work spread over physics, chemistry and biology.

In many states, the prospective elementary school teacher could major in education, taking perhaps half his program in that field and spreading the remainder of his courses over elementary exposure in the other college departments.

After World War II, many critics of public education regaled the American public with tales of the absurdities practiced in the teacher preparatory institutions. Among these critics were Mortimer Smith, Arthur E. Bestor, Albert Lynd, and Admiral Hyman Rickover. Some of these critics formed an organization known as the Council for Basic Education. Rudolph Flesch's book *Why Johnny Can't Read* added fuel to the fire. The first reaction of teachers and professors of education was to denounce the critics as enemies of the schools. It appears now that some enemies of the public school took comfort from the criticisms and may even have publicized them, but eventually many educators, on second thought, came to see that certain reforms were necessary. Increasingly, superintendents insisted upon candidates who knew *what* they would teach as well as *how* to teach.

It should not be assumed that these reforms resulted entirely from the pressures of the lay public. Throughout the easy days when "progressive" education was in the saddle, there were respected fig-

[9] Suhrie, Ambrose L.: *Teacher of Teachers.* Richard H. Smith, Rindge, N.H., 1955.

ures in the profession who constantly insisted upon the importance of content. Among these figures, the most prominent was Professor William C. Bagley of Teachers College, Columbia University. He and his colleagues who insisted upon retaining a certain amount of content in education were known as the Essentialists. The lay critics have not uncovered any "shortcomings" in American education that Bagley and his associates had not recognized. Unfortunately, the Essentialists were apparently upholding an unpopular cause until the realities of the "cold war" and the Sputnik scare focused attention on American education.

A sound evaluation of Bagley's Essentialist position is set forth by William W. Brickman in *School and Society*:[10]

What Bagley and the Essentialists called for was an emphasis in education on effort, discipline, the heritage of the human race, the primacy of the teacher in the pedagogical process, the mastery of subject matter in a logical and sequential organization, and the importance of long-range goals. Bagley was a psychologist by profession, a scientist by sentiment, and a humanist by habit. To him, a teacher had to be one who knew what, why, how, and whom to teach. Neither in Teachers College nor in any other professional circle could he qualify as an organization man. There are those who still can recall his virtual one-man stand some four decades ago against the psychologists who would consign a portion of the human race to a status of perpetual intellectual inferiority on the basis of a pseudoscientific interpretation of the results of a test of factual information.

Dr. Bagley was too much a democrat and an individualist to set up a power structure with himself at the apex. The Essentialist Committee comprised at most no more than half a dozen or so individuals. But the principles of Essentialism were the property of innumerable teachers and educators on all levels of instruction and administration. Progressivism had the prophets, the public relations, and the prestige; Essentialism, the masses of men and women who quietly and realistically carried forth, to the best of their ability, the traditions and values of American education in a world that was being altered in an apparently aimless way. The Essentialist educator was less concerned with change for the sake of change than with the preservation and enrichment of the foundations of his civilization.

The ideas of Bagley and the Essentialists can be observed in many of the recent and current tendencies in American education. The

10 Brickman, William W. "Essentialism and American Education," an editorial in *School and Society*, April 20, 1963, p. 185.

Essentialist Committee is not functioning, but there are individuals and groups who generally believe as the Essentialists do, although they employ tactics which would not have made Dr. Bagley happy. The principles of Essentialism and the practices of its founder are still valid after a quarter of a century. They stand for the use of reason in education and humanity in relation with fellow men of differing views. They insist on solidity of subject matter, on scholarship, and on a sympathetic though not sentimental attitude toward those whose convictions lead them to contrasting conclusions.

Repudiation of the Normal School and Teachers College   After World War II, the normal school and teachers college, which had been launched in the previous century with high expectations, ran into unfortunate days. Partly because they did not change rapidly enough to meet new conditions, partly because their own students suffered a sense of inferiority, partly because the public had a poor image of the teacher, and partly because of the savage attacks of critics, the normal school and teachers college lost prestige rapidly. Many of them sought legislative permission for changing their status to all-purpose colleges. In Ohio, the state normal schools became state colleges and then state universities. In New York, the normal schools became state teachers colleges, then state colleges of education, then state university branches. In Pennsylvania, they were metamorphosed from state teachers colleges to state colleges, and so it went in state after state. If the legal sanction were accompanied by sufficient funds to raise the quality of the faculties and the educational facilities, the change was all to the good, but if the change was in name only, there was really no change at all.

Actually, generalizations made about the quality of work in normal schools and teachers colleges were unwarranted. These institutions (like any other institutions such as liberal arts colleges, or banks, or railroads) varied in quality from superior to very poor.

NCATE   Within recent years, the National Commission on the Accreditation of Teacher Education, commonly called NCATE, has assumed the function of accrediting the teacher preparatory institutions in the United States. This organization, an outgrowth of the American Association of Colleges for Teacher Education (a department of the National Education Association), has approved 385 colleges and universities for teacher education. These institutions prepare approximately 75

per cent of the nation's teachers. Many other colleges are in process
of seeking such accreditation. The accreditation is said to be voluntary, but subtle pressures are put upon an institution to seek
accreditation. For instance, the privilege of receiving a teachers
certificate by reciprocity among states may be limited only to the
graduates of an NCATE-approved college. There was considerable
criticism of NCATE in professional quarters when it denied accreditation to Carleton College and the University of Wisconsin. Whether
or not NCATE will become as potent a factor in teacher education
as the American Medical Association is in medical education and the
American Bar Association is in legal education remains to be seen.

New Plans in Teacher Education   The ferment of
recent years has brought many innovations in teacher education.
Liberally subsidized by grants from the Ford Foundation and other
philanthropies, several universities and colleges have launched experimental programs in teacher education. One of the first of these
was the master of arts in teaching program of Harvard University,
sponsored by President James B. Conant. Under this plan, Harvard
accepted liberal arts college graduates who had no professional
courses in education. These graduates were placed in a special program which provided them with professional courses, including student teaching and advanced courses in their content fields. Cornell
University, the Johns Hopkins University, Yale, Colgate, Temple,
and numerous other institutions of higher learning introduced similar plans. An attractive feature of these programs was the liberal
fellowship grants and the opportunity to earn a teacher's salary
during one semester of the academic year. Few people have questioned the desirability of recruiting the teaching late-comers who
decided on the profession in their college senior year. The question
arises over the matter of calling the program a master's program
since approximately one half of the courses taken (history of education, educational psychology, methods, student teaching, etc.) is generally taught on the undergraduate level.

Whether these experimental programs will set a new pattern or
whether they will disappear into the limbo of other experimental
approaches after the foundation grants run out, cannot now be
determined.

The Conant Proposals   James B. Conant,
whose studies of the high schools we have already noted, made a
study of teacher education which was published in September, 1963,

under the title, *The Education of American Teachers.* His major recommendations were that each state honor the teachers' certificates issued by any other state, that states should require only practice teaching for certification, that teachers should be limited to fields in which they have special preparation, that only those be licensed who have been approved by the college as a whole, that certificates in the secondary school should be for only one field of teaching, and that colleges preparing less than 25 elementary teachers a year should discontinue their programs. A reviewer in the *New York Times* suggested that Conant's report "may well turn out to be as revolutionary in the field of teacher education as was the 1910 report by Abraham Flexner" on medical education. The immediate response to the report seemed to indicate that this was too optimistic and too sanguine a prognostication. It will, however, form the basis for a re-evaluation of programs of teacher preparation both by states and by individual colleges.

For Further Reading

Barnes, Mary Sheldon (editor). *Autobiography of Edward Austin Sheldon.* Ives-Butler, 1911.

Biography of the "American Pestalozzi".

Dearborn, Ned H. *The Oswego Movement in American Education.* Teachers College, Columbia University, 1925.

Shows national influence of this normal school.

Elsbree, Willard S. *The American Teacher.* American Book, 1939.

The whole book is a gold mine of information from extensive sources on the preparation and status of the teacher from colonial times. Chapter 25, teachers' institutes; 26, summer schools; 31, tenure.

French, William Marshall and Florence S. French. *College of the Empire State.* New York State College for Teachers, 1944.

Centennial history of New York's first normal school at Albany and one of the first in the country to become a 4-year degree-granting institution. It is now a unit in the State University of New York. Students in other states may want to consult card catalogs in their libraries for parallel histories of normal schools in their own states.

Norton, Arthur O. (editor). *The First State Normal School in America: Journals of Cyrus Peirce and Mary Swift.* Harvard University Press, 1926.

Anecdotal material by the principal and one of the students in the first American normal school.

Page, David Perkins. *Theory and Practice of Teaching.* A. S. Barnes and Co., 1885.

A pioneer book in education, constantly in use in normal schools from the late 1840's until near the turn of the century. Numerous other editions of this book were also published.

Rogers, Dorothy. *Oswego: Fountainhead of Teacher Education.* Appleton-Century-Crofts, 1961.

A history of one of New York's normal schools—teachers colleges.

Sears, Jesse B. and A. D. Henderson. *Cubberley of Stanford.* Stanford University Press, 1957.

Biography of one of America's best-known professors of education of the first part of the present century.

Whitney, Allen S. "The First Chair of Pedagogy in an American University," *School and Society,* March 1, 1941.

Introduction of education into a university.

14

Informal Education Agencies

Education Without Schools So common are schools as an instrument of education today that many people, without much reflection, seem to think of the school as essential to education. Thus, one may hear even an educated person say, "I don't know anything about that. I never had a course in it."

And yet we know that people have become very well educated with little or no exposure to the school. In his whole life, Abraham Lincoln attended school for fewer days than the reader of this book had when he had finished first grade. Many a person who made a mark in American history had far less formal education than the eighth grade graduate. Obviously, then, education can be obtained outside the school; "without the book or licensed teacher," one can get a very good education. All we can claim for the school of any grade is that it will motivate and facilitate the process of education, if the learner is willing. Indeed, one of our contemporary problems may be that schools have become so much a part of the American scene that their true value is no longer appreciated. By way of illustration we may say that the daily orange juice of the modern child is not nearly so much appreciated as the orange the rural child found, once a year, in his Christmas stocking years ago.

There have been many agencies that contributed to the intellectual, social, political, and economic development of the American people in simpler ages than the present—and still do so contribute today. They are also educational agencies, though we do not place them in the locus of the school or refer to them with a capital E in the term "educational."

While we cannot give adequate treatment to all these agencies which have helped to provide vicarious as well as actual experiences to the American people, we can sketch briefly the contribution that some of them have made to our development.

Observation Many a person has received a good education merely by watching what others do and

257

adapting his response according to the pattern they set. Many an uncouth youth with the hayseeds still in his hair has seen how people of refinement conducted themselves and has adjusted his own behavior accordingly. Many a farmer or early industrial worker learned a better way to do his work by keenly observing others. To this day, farmers in remote areas become acquainted with strip and contour farming by seeing their neighbors practice it. County agents know that if they can persuade a few of the respected farmers to adopt a new practice, others will emulate them in time. Let a few people in a run-down area fix up their places and others will follow suit.

Lecturers and Shows   In frontier America, the printed word was scarce. People sought news and entertainment and information. The travelling lecturer was most welcome at homes and inns. When the circuit-riding preacher or lawyer came to town, people from miles around assembled to hear him discuss matters originating beyond the confines of their own little valleys. Even the Yankee peddler was welcome in the remote areas, for he brought news and entertainment as well as tinware, needles and pins, and wooden nutmegs. The success of that American phenomenon, the

The Yankee peddler brought with his wares news and entertainment to the frontier American.

medicine show, was built upon the hunger of the people for some diversion from their routine concerns.

P. T. Barnum made a great success of presenting strange animals to the rustic American public. He introduced rural America to the elephant, the lion, the rhinoceros, and the giraffe. Even his colorful posters spread all over the side of a barn were highly educational— to people who couldn't afford to attend his circus as well as to people who could. It is reported that Barnum had difficulty in getting people to leave his tent until he hit upon the inspiration of putting up a sign, "To the Egress," and people went in the indicated direction, expecting to find another strange creature from far across the seas.

People who have grown up in the present era of worldwide television coverage can little appreciate how starved previous generations were for any contact with the outside world. To these people, travelling lecturers and showmen alike brought new experiences to stretch their imagination.

War   War upsets and changes the way of life of a people. It was largely through their experiences in the French and Indian Wars and the Revolution that Eastern continental soldiers learned of the vast and rich lands of Western New York and the Ohio country. The Mexican and Civil wars took simple farm boys to far places. The occupation of the Philippines introduced Americans to the orient, and World Wars I and II took millions of Americans on their first trips abroad. In World War I, a popular song title asked, "How're you gonna keep 'em down on the farm, after they've seen Paree?" And the answer was that many did not return to the farm after having experienced a more cosmopolitan environment. Not only was the military involved but industry as well. World War II in particular churned up the American people by attracting them to war industries. The Navajos came off their reservations to work on the Santa Fe railway, and old English stock left their mountain fortresses in Kentucky and Arkansas to join the main stream of an industrialized society. More than one reader of this page is the product of a union of persons from diverse areas who would never have met except for the dislocations caused by the war.

Immigration   When America opened her doors wide to immigrants from all over the world, she imported many strange people from diverse lands. Each of these brought with him part of his heritage from the homeland—his religion, his music,

his folk literature, his art, his domestic economy, and his foods—
Swiss cheese, pizza, macaroni, smorgasbord, blintzes, and a host of
others. The resources of many lands have been tapped to enrich
the cultural traditions of America. While for a time the new immigrants were shunned and even feared, they stayed and soon became amalgamated into American ways. Much liberal thought was
brought to America by the Germans, who came here in great numbers after their 1848 revolution was repressed. In their first generation, the immigrants from Scandinavia were often called "dumb
Swedes"; a few generations later they were furnishing governors for
many of the mid-western states and professors for the universities.

Magazines   A free press
and a wide circulation of printed materials is a prerequisite to the
continued existence of a democracy. This was early recognized in
our history, for George Washington wrote to an early publisher,
"I consider such easy vehicles of knowledge as more highly calculated
than any other to preserve the liberty, stimulate the industry, and
meliorate the morals of an enlightened and free people." An editor
of *Harpers* could later say, with considerable veracity, that periodical
literature had done more than any other instrument to educate the
American people.

As soon as we became a nation, various people ventured to establish magazines. Many were started, but generally their lives were
short. Indeed. Noah Webster said in his *American Magazine* in 1788
that "the expectation of failure is connected with the very name of
a Magazine." In his exhaustive study, *A History of American Magazines*, Mott points out the hazards that so often led to failure. These,
he says, were the indifference of the public and of the writers, lack
of adequate means of distribution, losses in the collection of sub-
scription accounts, and manufacturing difficulties. It seems self-evi-
dent that there were just not enough subscribers who were willing
to pay the price. This was in turn due to two factors: economic conditions and the absence of a sufficiently large number of literate
and interested readers. *The Pennsylvania Magazine* had a circulation of perhaps 1500 copies for a brief time during the Revolution.
Mott thinks this was a record in the eighteenth century, and that
the total circulation of magazines at any one time then was not over
5,000 copies.

It was difficult to get sufficient readers among the 3,000,000 Americans. It was equally difficult to get writers, it appears, for frequently
the magazines inserted appeals for articles. The editor of the *Royal*

American Magazine asked "those gentlemen who will favor . . . with their lucubrations" to respond at once. The editor of the *New-York Magazine* asked readers to "lend a helping hand" by sending in manuscripts. Too, circulation was difficult, for Congress in 1792 refused to let the post riders carry magazines, though they were permitted to carry newspapers. Editors frequently indicated they would accept wood, cheese, butter, pork, corn or other produce in payment of subscriptions.

The history of magazines is littered with the corpses of early American publications. Franklin's *General Magazine, and Historical Chronicle, for All the British Plantations in America* survived only six months. Others were even shorter-lived. Tom Paine was for a short time an editor in Philadelphia. During the Revolution, a few magazines set forth the virtue of the American cause and made fun of the Tories. One pictured a repentant Tory, after the evacuation of New York by the British, as desiring to be pardoned, not wanting "to be roasted in Florida or frozen to death in Canada."

In the early National period, the magazines brought to the literate part of the American people excerpts from British literature which they pirated from their English contemporaries. Many began to introduce American writers to their constituents. Works of the "Hartford Wits," of Franklin, Washington Irving, Philip Freneau, James Brockden Brown, and Gouverneur Morris were published.

Matters of public concern were brought to the attention of the people. Some of the *Federalist Papers* were published. There were discussions of the need for a national university. Webster's *Compendious Dictionary* was reviewed, sometimes humorously. One reviewer suggested many Americanisms that Webster had not defined— "Hellniferous," "happify," "disengenus," "Engagedness," and "go betweenity," among others. Articles on medicine, particularly on the plagues of smallpox, frequently appeared.

These early publications were to be succeeded by others throughout the years, each making some contribution to the education of the people, and some of them exerting a profound influence over a great period of time. Among the latter were the *Southern Review* (1828–1832), *Godey's Lady's Book* (1830–1898), *Southern Literary Messenger* (1834–1864), *Merry's Museum* (1841–1872), *The North American Review* (1815–1939), *Scientific American* (1845–   ), *DeBow's Review* (1846–1880), *Harper's Monthly* (1850–   ), *Leslie's Weekly* (1855–1922), *The Atlantic Monthly* (1857–   ), *The Youth's Companion* (1827–1929), *The Nation* (1865–   ), *The Outlook* (1870–1935), *St. Nicholas* (1873–1935), *Collier's* (1888–

1957), *Ladies Home Journal* (1883–   ), *Literary Digest* 1890–
1938), *The Saturday Evening Post* (1821–   ), *The World's Work*
(1900–1932).

Journals of Education   Among the specialized
journals, those most directly influential in forming public opinion
about the schools were the *Academician,* "containing the elements
of scholastic science, predicated on the analysis of the human mind,
and exhibiting the improved methods of instruction"; journals
issued by the state superintendents in Michigan, Ohio, Connecticut,
Massachusetts, New York, Rhode Island, and Maine; William Russell's *American Journal of Education,* Woodbridge's *American Annals of Education,* the *Common School Assistant,* the *Common School
Journal,* the *District School Journal for the State of New York,* and,
most notable of all, Henry Barnard's *American Journal of Education,* acclaimed generally as the greatest treasure trove on the development of American education for the years 1855 to 1882. About
one third of its contents was devoted to the history of education
from ancient times to the 1880's. Faced with financial disaster in
1878, Barnard threatened to discontinue the *Journal* and melt down
the plates. To this, R. H. Quick, an educational historian, replied
that he would as soon hear "that there was talk of pulling down
one of our cathedrals and selling the stones for building material."
   Within the present century, many educational periodicals have
been started. Scarcely is there any sub-division of education without
one or more magazines devoted to its particular interests. There are
journals in elementary, secondary, and higher education; journals
for teachers and administrators; journals devoted to art, science,
mathematics, supervision, and curriculum development, audio-visual
education, and many other activities.

Specialized Magazines   The same abundance
of magazines holds true regarding all the professions, trades, and interests of various groups of the American people. The first medical
journal was the *Medical Repository* (1797–1824); the first law journal, the *American Law Journal* (1807–1817). There were numerous
magazines issued by the various religious denominations as early
as the 1820's. They spent many columns abusing other denominations. There were special journals in science, agriculture, mechanical
arts and, indeed, in nearly all fields of human activity. Somewhere
in the United States today is published a magazine which touches
upon the vocational, recreational, economic, and religious interests
of everyone.

Student Magazines The first college
magazine of which we have any record is the *Literary Cabinet*
published at Yale in 1806. Though the editor prophesied that it
would last "for years to come," it survived only a year. Harvard had
an equally short-lived publication in 1810–1811, with Edward
Everett as an editor. By the middle of the century, almost all colleges had a literary quarterly. By the twentieth century, many of
these had been transformed into weekly or even daily newspapers.
During the "roaring twenties," college humor magazines of doubtful
virtue were published on many campuses, often becoming embroiled
with the administration and the faculty. Not a few were suppressed
from time to time.

Significance of Magazines The rise of
the magazine of wide circulation coincided with the advancement of
literacy. As the school magazines developed a more literate reading
public, the circulation greatly increased. Even those mass media that
now pillory the schools would hardly exist if there were not people
trained in the schools to read what they publish.

These magazines have informed, amused, and entertained the
American people. They have often shaped their thinking on social,
political, and economic issues. Even their advertisements have been a
potent factor in developing what is called "the American way of
life." If it were not for the magazines and their journalistic companions, the daily and weekly newspapers, life in the United States
would undoubtedly be very different from what it is.

Newspapers The first known
newspaper in the English language was published in the Netherlands
in 1620, the very year the Pilgrims landed in America. Though
William Brewster, who came on the Mayflower, was a printer, he
found that there were too many priorities to warrant setting up a
press in the early years of the colony. The first American press was
set up near Harvard in 1638 and was soon busy printing almanacs,
sermons, religious tracts, and even a Bible. All the early presses were
strictly supervised by the authorities who were very distrustful of the
printed word. Sir William Berkeley, governor of Virginia, in 1671
thanked God that his colony did not have "free schools nor printing," for learning had brought "disobedience and heresy and sects
into the world" and "printing has divulged them and libels against
the government." God, he hoped, would spare Virginia from both
these sources of sedition.

Nonetheless, the people did want to know, and the printers did want to print. News letters and occasional broadsides appeared before the newspaper evolved. In 1689, an occasional paper entitled *The Present State of the New-English Affairs* appeared with the subtitle "Published to Prevent False Reports." This is an early acknowledgment of one function of a public press.

The first newspaper in America was *Publick Occurrences Both Forreign and Domestick,* printed by Benjamin Harris at Boston in 1690, but it was suppressed by the authorities. Harris then turned to safer materials and printed *The New England Primer.* By 1719, a change in the political climate had occurred, and the *Boston Gazette* was successfully published by the Boston postmaster. Benjamin Franklin, who later became Philadelphia's famous publisher, was introduced to journalistic work in his brother's *New-England Courant,* which Cotton Mather denounced as "a notorious, scandalous paper" as bad as the smallpox.

In the Revolutionary period, newspapers became rather common, chronicling all the stirring events of that era—the Boston Massacre, Lexington and Concord, the Declaration of Independence, and the important battles. Undoubtedly, the papers served to awaken the spirit of independence and patriotism. "The press hath never done greater service since its first invention," the *New Hampshire Gazette* declared. Newspapers had fast become a necessity to the American people. Their numbers grew rapidly. By 1800, there were perhaps 200 different papers, and by 1835 there were perhaps 1200. Many of these were intensely partisan in the age that Mott calls "the dark age of partisan journalism."

The presence of papers undoubtedly led many people to read. The teaching of reading in district schools, monitorial schools, and charity schools in turn produced more readers and made newspaper publication economically feasible. In addition to general news sheets and political papers, there were many special papers devoted to special causes—labor unions, temperance, abolition of slavery, the advance of the common school, and campaigns against the rate bill in education. Circulation of many was decidedly limited, often to only a few hundred copies each, but by 1860, the *New York Tribune* had a circulation of 200,000 and the *Ledger* had 400,000. These were national weekly papers. It is said that as far away as Kansas, farmers refused to make up their minds on public issues until they had read Horace Greeley's *"Try-bune."* Four factors accounted for these successes: the growth in the population, the development of a reading public through the work of the public schools, the growing interest in public affairs, and mechanical improvements which allowed the papers to be sold cheaply. Even

American women read the newspapers, Raymond of the *New York Times* noted. Dickens, in his *American Notes,* reported that the papers were "the standard literature of an enormous class, who must find their reading in a newspaper, or they will not read at all." He caricatured the American press in *Martin Chuzzlewit,* with newsboys shouting

"Here's this morning's *New York Sewer*" cried one. "There's this morning's *New York Stabber!* Here's the *New York Family Spy!* Here's the *New York Private Listener!* Here's the *New York Peeper!* . . . the last Alabama gouging case; and the interesting dooel with Bowie knives. . . ."

As commercial ventures, depending upon a huge volume of circulation to obtain remunerative advertising, the papers often pandered to the lowest taste of marginal subscribers, it is true. One sees the same phenomenon in the "pitcher papers" of mass circulation to this day. There is no gainsaying the fact, however, that the newspaper has broadened the outlook of the American people and has served to help form us into one nation.

Radio and Television   The American child and youth—indeed the adult as well—is far more knowledgeable and sophisticated than his counterpart of a generation or two ago. Better-equipped schools, better-educated teachers, a host of audio-visual techniques, travel, magazines, and newspapers have all helped to bring this education about. Within recent years, two additional media of education have made a great impact: radio in the days after World War I, and television after World War II. While both media have been exploited unmercifully to huckster all kinds of products of doubtful social utility, with detergent suds coming out the picture tubes all day and beer suds replacing them in the evening hours, it is still true that there have been programs of great educational value. All these new media have opened to a new generation many new windows onto the passing scene of man and his concerns.[1]

---

[1] When the author was twelve years old, he had not been outside his natal county in the fortress of the Pennsylvania mountains. His knowledge of the world was limited to what had been garnered from very scant sources: From the few basic textbooks in the district school, including a geography text that had two pictures on China—one showing a flooded rice paddy, and another presenting a forlorn group of females with bound feet; from the weekly *Williamsport Grit* with its strange tales of two-headed calves and three-legged dogs; and from occasional books that came his way. At the age of twelve, the author's son had been in thirty-eight states, Canada, and Mexico. Further, via a plentiful supply of books, motion pictures, and television, he had vicariously been to the top of Mt. Everest with Hillary and Tensing and to the far depths of the ocean with Beebe in his bathysphere.

While radio was at first conceived as an entertainment medium, it soon developed many educational characteristics. Often, of course, the entertainment was itself educational, as in the presentation of drama and good music. Some programs from commercial stations were designed primarily for use in schools. Notable among these were the Walter Damrosch Music School of the Air. For several years, the Ohio School of the Air broadcast regular school programs in the 1930's. Many state universities and independent colleges operated radio stations for educational purposes. At Ohio State, the broadcasts featured extension courses by radio, agricultural programs, drama and music, information, discussion groups, debates, and athletic events. An institute for education by radio was held annually at Ohio State, and its proceedings were published. Lessons in French, Spanish, and Italian were regularly conducted. Fifty-nine junior college courses were given for three years.

A practical demonstration of the interest in radio for education appeared in 1929. An eighth grade teacher at Walden, N.Y. had alerted her students to the forthcoming presidential inauguration of Herbert Hoover. The class learned the oath of office, then listened to the inauguration on a radio in the classroom. A student said Chief Justice Taft had made an error, that he said "preserve, maintain, and defend" whereas the prescribed oath said "preserve, protect, and defend." Fortunately, sound motion picture cameras had recorded the ceremony, and it was found that the student was right. Newspapers all over the nation used the occasion to comment on the use of radio in the classroom as a new departure.

When television first became readily available after World War II, there were prophesies that addiction to this medium would negate the work of the schools, for no one would do homework any more. Many research studies were made of the effects of TV on students of various ages, and many people wrote without having conducted research. It was soon discovered, though, that there were great educational potentialities in TV if it were properly exploited, for it could bring places and events from far away into the homes and classrooms.

In schools and colleges, two types of educational television were developed. Some programs, such as a year's series of lectures and demonstrations in physics, were made available through long-wave, commercial stations. Certain school systems and universities, often with financial resources supplied by foundations, developed their own short-wave television programs. Instructional television is now being developed in many parts of the country. The State of New York has undertaken to make many programs available daily to the schools. Hagerstown, Maryland, conducted a pioneering experiment in television instruction, with certain channels reserved for educational stations. One innovation was the Midwest Program of Airborne Television Instruction which provided programs for half a million students in a six state area, from an airplane flying 23,000 feet above the schools. In 1952, the Federal Communications Commission set aside 242 channels for educational purposes; later the number was raised to 267. While this medium has not been exploited as much as it should, (for schools are essentially conservative when it comes to innovations), practically every course in the school and college curriculum, from beginning reading to advanced physics, is being taught somewhere via television. Even post-graduate seminars in surgery are conducted by way of closed-circuit TV. The *Saturday Review* estimated in 1961 that at least 3,000,000 students in 7,500 elementary and secondary schools were receiving part of their daily lessons via TV. Colleges offer credit courses to more than 250,000 students.

It may be appropriate to say that TV will multiply superior teaching a millionfold; likewise, of course, it can multiply poor teaching to the same extent. One great asset is that the TV teacher is usually freed from all other responsibility and is given vast resources to support him in his lesson and in his role as instructor.[2]

Motion Pictures   The first experimental motion picture was made in 1888 in Edison's laboratory. A flickering show was opened on Broadway in 1895, and the first theatre exclusively for motion pictures was advertised in Los Angeles in 1902. The first films of "Life of an American Fireman," "The Great Train Robbery," and "Trapped by Bloodhounds, or a Lynching at Cripple Creek" were admittedly crude, but they were the forerunners of better films to come.

Motion pictures, like radio and television, were first conceived as a medium of entertainment, but it soon became apparent that they could be valuable adjuncts to an educational program. While there was some educational value to entertainment films, the educational emphasis was first felt when producers made documentary films regarding public questions. Of these, one dealing with water and soil conservation, called *The River,* was particularly notable. The photography was spectacular, and the script was sufficiently in the Walt Whitman vein to carry the concept of great power and drama:

2 In 1962, unions attempted unsuccessfully to assert jurisdiction over TV teachers as entertainers rather than instructors.

From as far west as Idaho,
    Down from the glacier peaks of the Rockies—
From as far east as New York
    Down from the turkey ridges of the Alleghenies—
Down from Minnesota, twenty-five hundred miles,
    The Mississippi River runs to the Gulf,
Carrying every drop of water that flows down two-thirds the con-
tinent,
    Carrying every brook and rill,
Rivulet and creek,
Carrying all the rivers that run down two-thirds of the continent,
    The Mississippi runs to the Gulf of Mexico.
Down the Yellowstone, the Milk, the White, and Cheyenne,
The Cannonball, the Musselshell, the James, and the Sioux;
Down the Judith, the Grand, the Osage, and the Platte,
The Skunk, the Salt, the Black, and Minnesota;
Down the Rock, the Illinois, and the Kankakee,
The Allegheny, the Monongahela, Kanawha, and Muskingum;
Down the Miami, the Wabash, the Licking, and the Green,
The Cumberland, the Kentucky, and the Tennessee;
Down the Ouachita, the Wichita, the Red, and Yazoo.
Down the Missouri three thousand miles from the Rockies—
    Down the Ohio a thousand miles from the Alleghenies—
Down the Arkansas fifteen hundred miles from the Great Divide—
    Down the Red, a thousand miles from Texas—
Down the great Valley, twenty-five hundred miles from Minnesota,
    Carrying every rivulet and brook, creek and rill,
Carrying all the rivers that run down two-thirds the continent—
    The Mississippi runs to the Gulf.

Soon certain companies began to produce films particularly for
the classroom. A historical series produced under the sponsorship of
Yale University was the pioneer. By the 1930's the major part of
educational films were being produced by three concerns, Coronet,
Encyclopaedia Britannica, and Young America (McGraw-Hill). In
addition, many trade associations and industrial corporations have
made available to schools and community organizations a large
number of sponsored films. Some of these are saturated with advertising, but others are entirely acceptable for educational use.

Film catalogs now contain thousands of titles ranging from reading readiness to advanced subjects to supplement college instruction.
The listing of film strips is even more exhaustive. To acquaint

teachers with the films available and the operation of projectors, as well as other audio-visual materials and techniques, Pennsylvania now requires a course in this field for permanent certification as a teacher.

"Adult Education"   To supplement the work of the district schools in the improvement of popular education, Josiah Holbrook started the lyceum movement in 1826. The name was taken from the Greek, indicating the place where Aristotle had taught. (The French *lycée,* or secondary school, gets its name from the same source.) The stated purposes of Holbrook's lyceum were to agitate for improvement of the common schools, to organize lectures and classes for the education of adults, and to stimulate the formation of libraries. In a few short years, 900 towns in the northern and western parts of the United States had local lyceum organizations, many of which were affiliated with the American Lyceum Association.

Most of the prominent men and women of the nineteenth century appeared on the circuit as lecturers before lyceum associations. Wendell Phillips gave his lecture on "The Lost Arts" two thousand times—a record that stood for many years, until broken by the Rev. Russell H. Conwell of Temple University with his "Acres of Diamonds" address.

Some of the local lyceums were known as institutes, and grew into permanent educational institutions. Among these were the Lowell Institute in Boston, the Franklin Institute in Philadelphia, and the Brooklyn Institute.

The first "Chautauqua" was organized at the lake of that name in western New York in 1874 under Methodist auspices. Its purpose was to provide at a summer resort, under Christian auspices, a measure of culture and refinement to people whose early educational opportunities had been limited. Thousands of eager people responded to informal conferences, recreation, and entertainment, all in the genteel environment of a Sunday School picnic.

Instruction in Greek and Hebrew was begun in 1875 under the direction of William Rainey Harper. Later, French, German, and English literature were added. To provide learning when the resort was not open, a home reading circle was organized. Its program extended over four years and was designed to give its participants an adult education with a college flavor. The first year, 7,000 people enrolled, and soon the number passed 60,000. Regular correspondence instruction was begun in 1883 and the institute was authorized

Culture under canvas. A Chautauqua meeting in 1908.

by the University of the State of New York to confer degrees. This authority was surrendered in 1902, when certain universities began to offer correspondence study.

At times, as many as 12,000 persons assembled at Chautauqua. In 1909, more than 2000 students took 188 courses from nearly a hundred visiting professors. Since the platform was open to "all sane, disinterested movements for social betterment," a wide variety of programs was presented.

The idea of similar meetings spread widely over the country, so much so that "Chautauqua" came to mean a series of lectures and entertainments provided anywhere for a week or two. Often the meetings were held in a tent in a meadow near a town. It has been estimated that perhaps two million participated each year, early in the present century. Aspirants for public office often appeared as speakers, both for the fees involved and to keep themselves before the public. William Jennings Bryan was an inveterate Chautauqua lecturer. Thus the term "the Chautauqua circuit" used by politicians. A list of Chautauquas conducted in 1910 showed eight in Alabama, thirty-nine in Illinois, thirty-four in Nebraska, six in Pennsylvania, and large numbers in several other states.

The increased sophistication of the American people, the introduction of the motion picture, the opening of hard-surfaced roads for tourist travel, and university summer sessions led to the decline of Chautauquas throughout the country, though the association still conducts meetings at its original site. In many areas, community lecture and artists' series are still conducted, but they are no longer called Chautauquas by any but a few oldsters with nostalgic memories.

Libraries   The first settlers
brought with them a small collection of books, mostly works on religion and occasional classics, but these remained in private hands and had very small circulation. The first attempt to found a library was in 1620, when a stranger, not identified, presented "fower great books" to the Virginia Company to be sent to the projected "Colledge in Virginia." These were probably destroyed in the Indian uprising in 1622 which doomed the proposed college.

John Harvard gave his books, along with his money, to establish a college in New England. The library had become quite extensive but was destroyed by fire in 1764.

Many of the early libraries outside the colleges were proprietary—that is, they were not public in our sense of the word, but were maintained by associations of people who paid annual dues. Such a library in New York City supplied valuable reference material to the new federal government during its stay in New York.

The Philadelphia Library was established in 1731 by Benjamin Franklin and associates. It was destined to grow into one of the largest libraries in the United States.

The national library was established in 1800 as the Library of Congress (or, as it was called in 1815, "the Library of the United States"), with the purchase of $5000 worth of books. Burned by the British in 1814, it was rebuilt around the private library that Thomas Jefferson sold to the government for $23,000. Since a copy of every publication to which the United States grants a copyright must be deposited there, it has become one of the world's most extensive libraries.

A small number of great libraries does not meet the needs of a people spread over vast territorial domain. There were early attempts to establish small, local libraries. Horace Mann's community in Massachusetts got a library by naming itself in honor of Benjamin Franklin, who responded by presenting books instead of a bell for the new church, with the comment that he thought sense would appeal more to the citizens than sound. Franklin asked a friend in London to send out "a parochial library for the use of a society of intelligent, respectable farmers, such as our country people generally consist of." Though these books were mainly old histories and theological works, they provided much of Horace Mann's early reading fare. It was in Franklin that Mann developed his interest in public libraries, a subject to which he was often to refer in his writings and speeches. In later years, he was particularly enthusiastic about state laws permitting or requiring the establishment of local libraries. New Hampshire was the first state to require the establishment of free public libraries, in 1849. Massachusetts soon followed. Now either mandatory or permissive legislation is common.

In many cities where libraries were lacking or inadequate, private associations were organized to make books available for their members. In colleges, the literary societies often maintained more books, available for more hours per week, than the official college library.

State libraries were usually formed to be of service to the legislature and other branches of the state government. In some states, they never advanced much beyond the service of a legislative library, but in other states they became very large and were noted for the liberality of their management. Of these, the New York State Library is notable. In 1893 this library instituted the policy of sending out books to other libraries throughout the state on a loan basis.

The philanthropies of such benefactors as Andrew Carnegie were instrumental in the development or improvement of many libraries throughout the nation.

Supposedly a function of the schools is to promote literacy and to build life-long interests in reading and study. If such be the case, then books must be readily available in public libraries.

The Arts   A pioneer people trying to wrest a living from a new land has little time to devote to the arts. Such was true in colonial America, where the few arts that existed were related to the simple life of the people. As an economic surplus began to be available, there was time and interest to be devoted to the aesthetic side of man's nature. Home furnishings became more elegant, a Georgian colonial architecture was developed, and there were even some indigenous artists in oil. Except for the public buildings which could be seen by all, most of the art forms were reserved to a limited few, and the general population was denied contact with artistic productions.

During the colonial period, any American who wanted to learn to paint went to England or Europe. Benjamin West, a Philadelphian, led a procession of young men abroad. At first, most went to England, but later Germany and France became training centers for American artists. Charles Wilson Peale attempted to found an art school in Philadelphia, without success, but the Pennsylvania Academy of the Fine Arts was launched there in 1805. The Cooper Union offered art instruction in 1857, and Yale opened its school of fine arts in 1864.

There were very few art objects in the country for many years, and often the custodians didn't know what to do with what they had. Several casts of antique art were purchased by Robert Livingston, ambassador to France, for the New York Academy of Fine Arts. For some years they remained in storage and then were open for display only intermittently. The successful founding of museums had to wait until there were sufficient people of wealth, leisure, and interest to concern themselves about art. With the increased prosperity after the Civil War, interest in art increased. At present, many relatively small cities have modest galleries to which are brought loan exhibitions from the more famous museums of the country. Men of great wealth have liberally furnished the great museums with masterpieces from all over the world, where they form a part of the cultural environment of the whole nation. Improvements in color printing have made it possible for large numbers of people to have excellent prints of masterpieces. Prized art objects are frequently reproduced in magazines of national circulation, literally bringing art to the millions.

For Further Reading

Elliott, William Y. *Television's Impact on American Culture.* Michigan State University Press, 1956.
Study of educational TV and commercial TV.

Frost, S. E., Jr. *Education's Own Stations.* University of Chicago Press, 1937.
Educational radio stations and their influence.

Hayes, Cecil B. *The American Lyceum.* Bulletin 12, United States Bureau of Education, 1912.
The development of this agency of adult education and its impact on American society.

Head, Sydney W. *Broadcasting in America*. Houghton Mifflin, 1956.
Influence of radio and televison in American society.

Henry, Nelson B. (editor). *Mass Media and Education*. Fifty-third Year-book of the National Society for the Study of Education. University of Chicago Press, 1954.
The role of mass media (the press, radio, television, motion pictures) and their relation to education.

Humble, Marion. *Rural America Reads*. American Association for Adult Education, 1938.
Emphasis upon reading as a means of cultural development in rural areas.

Institute for Communication Research. *Educational Television, The Next Ten Years*. Institute for Communication Research, 1962.
What may develop in the use of TV in education.

Mott, Frank Luther. *A History of American Magazines*. Harvard University Press, 1938–1957.
An exhaustive study of all major magazines published in America from 1741 to 1957. Their origins, influence and problems.

Mott, Frank Luther. *American Journalism*. Macmillan, 1941.
A standard history of newspapers in the United States.

National Society for the Study of Education. *Mass Media and Education*. Part II of the Fifty-third Yearbook. University of Chicago Press, 1954.
The role of mass communication in American society; the press, motion pictures, radio and television; the social impact of mass media. Relation of these agencies to classroom teaching.

Perry, Armstrong. *Radio in Education. The Ohio School of the Air and Other Experiments*. Payne Fund, 1929.
Experiments in the use of radio in the schools.

Schramm, Wilbur. *The Impact of Educational Television*. University of Illinois Press, 1960.
Influence of this medium upon education.

Shores, Louis. *Origins of the American College Library, 1638–1800*. Barnes and Noble, 1935.
The founding and growth of libraries in American colleges.

Spofford, Arnsworth R. *A Book for All Readers*. Putnam, 1909.
Chapter 15 gives a history of libraries.

15

The Non-Public Schools

A Persistent Question One of the persistent questions in the study of education is, "Who shall control education?" This is very much a live question today, as it has been in ages past. Through the study of the history of education and comparative education, we learn that different societies have arrived at different answers, at different times. Closely associated with this question is the corollary query: "For what ends shall education be controlled?" The answer to this second question determines, to a great extent, the answer to the first question.

Throughout history, there have been four answers to the question about the control of education: the family, the church, the state, or any combination of family, church, and state. In ancient times, control of the educative process rested primarily in the family, but in Athens, Sparta, and Rome the state came to assert its authority. This was particularly true in Sparta, where the state, to assure its survival, took over the education of boys at the age of seven, even taking them from their homes to live in a type of boarding school.

Concerned with the salvation of souls, the Christian Church could not ignore its responsibility for education. While pagan learning persisted for some centuries after the establishment of the church, more and more the church came to assert its right to direct the education of its young.

For centuries, of course, there was no concept of universal elementary education in our sense of the word. The church was content to direct the religious education of all its children and to provide for further education for only a select few. In a medieval society, this was sufficient. Though towns in the late medieval period maintained schools, there was no conflict with the church, for these town schools were subject to supervision of the universal church. Nor was there any conflict between the schools maintained by the

275

Renaissance princes in Italy, for again there was universal respect for the role of religious education.

Only with the Protestant Reformation did a conflict of authority arise in the modern sense. It was a fundamental principle of Protestantism that each child needed to be taught to read, for each man carried within himself a soul that must be saved, and this could be done only by knowing and doing the will of God as directly revealed in the Old and New Testaments. The Protestant belief was that each person must have personal access to the Biblical texts, rather than access through a priest.

Luther, one of the first Protestant writers on education, could not rely exclusively upon the family to provide this education. The newly reorganized church was not strong enough to do it alone. Since he had great respect for the authority of the princes who had protected him from the Pope and the Emperor, Luther naturally turned to these princes to sponsor and control the schools. He insisted that it was the moral obligation of the princes and the municipalities to maintain schools and to compel attendance. If the government could compel citizens to bear arms in time of war, he maintained it could compel people to send their children to school, "for we are warring with the Devil." It was the duty of the princes to see to it that there were always "preachers, jurists, pastors, scribes, schoolmasters and the like."

Early Protestant Patterns   This Lutheran advocacy of state control of education was not universally adopted by Protestants, however. In England, schooling was a family and church affair into which the state did not intrude until the nineteenth century after the effects of the industrial revolution had been felt. In the Netherlands, education remained primarily a family and church obligation, with some state direction. In the Catholic nations, the old traditions persisted; the government might be welcomed as a partner in the enterprise, but the church continued to assert its right to control.

Early American Patterns   We have noted that three patterns of control developed in the American colonies: a strict state mandate in New England, where the state and church were closely associated in a theocratic government; a church and charity system in the middle colonies; and a laissez-faire attitude in the plantation colonies, with some mission efforts by the established Church of England through its missionary societies. In New England, the state was the handmaid of the dominant church, and the schools were saturated with religion. Except in name, the colonial schools were essentially schools of and for the church.

Proposal for National Schools   After the Revolution, the tide of nationalism ran strong, and proposals were made by many writers for the creation of a national system of education directed toward the national ends of training for citizenship. Such proposals were much too revolutionary and contrary to the established patterns in the various states. By general accord, nothing was said in the Federal Constitution about education, and so by implication all authority was left to the states and to the people thereof.

Protestant Parochial Schools   The states were reluctant to set up strong state systems of education, so schooling went by default to the home or to the churches and their charitable societies. Even where state school systems existed or were established, there was no attempt to assert a state monopoly of education. Public, charity, and private schools existed side by side in many communities —and some communities had none at all.

Some of the Protestant churches made attempts to establish their own schools in association with their individual churches. Sometimes, these were conceived as schools for all the children of the particular faith, and sometimes they were thought of as schools conducted on a charity basis for children of the poorer classes.

The Episcopalians   The Episcopal Church maintained a small number of parochial schools in Maryland, South Carolina, Kentucky, Wisconsin, New Jersey, Georgia, and western New York in the years preceding the Civil War. In 1874, the general convention of this church received a report showing that there were 165 parochial schools with 7,500 students enrolled. The attitude of the church by that time had come to be that it should maintain schools where practicable, especially where the public schools were lacking or "deficient in number or thoroughness of training," but that elsewhere the public school was to be preferred or at least accepted. Indeed, some Episcopalians were now maintaining that there should be universal compulsory education in secularized public schools. Others were in favor of public education but insisted that the Bible must be taught in them. With the continued growth of the public school system, the Episcopalians accepted them and began to urge their members to exert an Episcopal influence on these schools. Eventually, a general convention endorsed public schools "for the sake of Christianity itself."

The Congregationalists The Congregational Church did not maintain parochial schools on the elementary level but applauded the public schools in the older parts of the Union. In the new territories on the Western frontier, the Congregationalists maintained a few church schools as a stopgap until public schools worthy of patronage could be established. In the West, the church was interested in schools to teach "true Americanism" as a safeguard against the educational endeavors of Mormons and Jesuits. In the East, the church warmly endorsed the public schools, the church's magazine, *The New Englander,* contending in 1867 that those who were opposed to public schools were "grumbling taxpayers, needy gentlefolk, disappointed place-men, ecclesiastical bigots, and selfish teachers of private schools." Parochial schools, it said, were "managed without responsibility to the public, liable to the most bigoted influences, and rife in sectarian gall." Since many of the public schools had been established in colonial days by the theocratic state with its Calvinistic Congregational influence, it is not surprising that the Congregationalists looked upon the public schools and found them to be good. The public schools through much of the nineteenth century still carried a Protestant Christian influence.

The Quakers The Quakers had early established schools in association with their churches, although William Penn had clearly stated that in his colony education should be a function of the government, not of the church. When the government did not act, the churches did. For many years the Quakers were opposed to public schools, particularly from 1800 to near the end of the century, insisting that their children should have "a guarded religious education" in Quaker schools. By 1900, however, most of their elementary schools had disappeared. The reasons for the decline seem to have been a shortage of teachers dedicated to parochial instruction, unwillingness of Quakers to support their own schools when they also paid taxes for the public schools, the small number of Quakers in many areas, and the realization that public schools were better than in former years. However, many nonsectarian private schools of Quaker origin are very active today.

The Baptists   For many years,
the Baptists recruited most of their members from the lower social
and economic classes, including a large number of Negroes. These
people did not have the same school-going tradition that existed in
the older Protestant churches, so they were less interested in any
type of elementary schools. Further, the Baptists lacked a strong
national organization, being committed strongly to the independence
of each local church. Until Roman Catholic parochial schools came
to be more numerous, the Baptists adopted a laissez-faire attitude
toward elementary education. With the rise of the Catholic "threat,"
they strongly endorsed the public schools and condemned parochial
schools.

The Methodists   Like the Baptists,
the early Methodists to a large extent came from the lower classes,
but instead of adopting the laissez-faire attitude of the Baptists, they
did express themselves on education. This may be because they had
a higher percentage of educated leaders and because they maintained
ties with the English Methodists who were interested in maintaining
dissenting schools in Britain. John Wesley and George Whitfield,
early leaders, attempted to establish schools in Georgia, where there
were no public schools. Bishop Francis Asbury in 1791 urged upon
the Methodists the establishment of schools for their own children
and "those of the poor in the vicinity of your small towns and villages," and urged the establishment of a parochial school by each
congregation. Very few such schools were ever organized, and by the
1830's the Methodists were endorsing the public schools. They soon
moved on to a demand for universal compulsory education. Some of
the leaders denied the right of any church to maintain parochial
elementary schools.

The Reformed Churches   In America, the
Calvinists from continental Europe were known as the Reformed
Church. The Dutch took the name of the Reformed Church in
America and the Germans called themselves the Reformed Church
in the United States. In the early 1800's, the Dutch church planned
a system of elementary parochial schools, but the schools were never
established in any significant number. While accepting the public
schools in the older states, the Dutch in 1843 urged their western
missionaries to establish schools. In 1846, the synod acknowledged
the supremacy of the state in public education by saying that "the

Synod should be careful not to interfere with the business of the State."

Whereas the Dutch Reformed members had been Americanized and were using the English language, the German Reformed congregations were largely composed of recent immigrants to whom English was a foreign tongue. Their interest in parochial schools was greater, for they wished to protect not only their religion but also their language. A church constitution in 1881 urged every congregation to maintain a parochial school "wherever such a school is practicable," but few were established. As the German members became integrated into American life, they also turned to the public schools for the education of their children.

Presbyterian Churches   The Presbyterians at various times before the Civil War had experimented with parochial schools. Approximately 300 such schools had been founded, but many of these were short-lived, and generally the Presbyterians came to share the view of their fellow Calvinists in the Congregational and Reformed churches that the public elementary schools were satisfactory. Presbyterians often joined with other Protestants in advancing the cause of public schools.

Lutherans   The Lutheran bodies in America derive from several European nations, primarily Germany, Norway, Sweden, and Denmark, but also from Finland, Hungary, and other countries to a lesser degree. Each group brought its own language and traditions, and each for a time had recourse to parochial schools. The German Lutherans in southeastern Pennsylvania were the first to immigrate in appreciable numbers. Both to protect their Lutheranism and their German language, they resorted to parochial schools almost exclusively. In the Ministerium (synod) of Pennsylvania, there were 240 parochial schools in 1820, but by 1860 the number had been reduced to 28, and the number continued to dwindle. Many of the German Lutherans were ardent opponents of Thad Stevens and Governor Wolf (himself of Pennsylvania German background) when they campaigned for free schools. Though Luther had been willing to assign education to the government in Germany, where the Lutherans were a majority, they felt committed to parochial schools in America, where they were both a religious and a linguistic minority. Henry Melchior Muhlenberg, patriarch of the Lutheran church, devoted much time to establishing schools. After the public schools had been in operation for a time, the Lutherans became reconciled to them, and their own separate schools dwindled away.

From the beginning, the Scandinavian Lutherans, most of whom settled in the new western states, patronized the public schools. Since most of them were farmers, living isolated from one another, it would not have been practicable for them to establish their own schools. There is no doubt that their patronage of the public schools greatly accelerated their absorption into the mainstream of American culture.

The German immigrants who came to the Mississippi and Missouri river valleys before and after the Civil War were strongly attached to the parochial school. While they might perforce attend a public school out of necessity, as the Roman Catholics also did, they hastened to build their own schools as soon as possible. Known as the Lutheran Church, Missouri Synod, they are still strongly attached to parochial schools and maintain the largest system of parochial schools in American Protestantism. The Missouri Synod, taking a stand contrary to the Roman Catholic position, declares that it does not want or will not accept any state or federal aid for education.

Other Parochial Schools   Two other smaller
Protestant denominations also maintain parochial schools. These are the Seventh Day Adventists and the Mennonites. When the public school was small and rural, the Mennonites were willing to send their children there, but when schools became larger and there was danger that their children would come into contact with worldly ideas contrary to their faith, especially in the upper elementary and junior high school years, they began to establish schools of their own.

Jewish   Within recent years,
there has been a numerical development of full-time Jewish day schools, both elementary and secondary. Whereas formerly Jewish children generally attended the public school for full time, then spent additional hours at a school in the temple to learn religion and Hebrew, many are now attending Jewish schools for both secular and religious studies. Jewish families, which have customarily attached great value to education in general and cultural tradition in particular, have certainly not withdrawn their support from good public education, but rather many families have moved to provide special education for children suited to it. In 1956, there were 172 elementary and secondary Jewish schools, with approximately half of them in the New York metropolitan area.

Secondary Schools and Colleges   Even when they abandoned the province of elementary education to the state, many of the Protestant churches continued an interest in secondary schools and colleges. Some even argued that the state had no right to tax the public for the support of public high schools. The Congregationalist *New Englander* maintained in 1873 that the state had no right to levy taxes for public secondary schools, but should leave this phase of education to churches and private bodies. At that time, of course, no one anticipated the growth of the secondary school that came about in the next century.

Some of the church-related secondary schools became fashionable and expensive and were thus limited to the richer members of their denominations and to other Protestant patrons. The poorer members of the denomination generally patronized the public schools.

Roman Catholic Position   The traditional Roman Catholic position is that education is primarily the responsibility of the church. The home and the state may share in this responsibility, but must recognize the primacy of the church's position and must give due consideration to the church's claim. Education belongs pre-eminently to the church, by virtue of God's will; the church's is superior to any other claim. The institution known as the school belonged to the family and to the church long before education was undertaken by the state. Since man is dependent upon God for his existence and possessions, it is clear that God must enter into all phases of man's life activities. All human rights and duties depend upon a divine source. Since the function of education is to develop the whole person, the task is incomplete unless knowledge of God and man's duties to Him are included in the educational program. A secular education is incomplete and therefore dangerous. The view of the church must be brought to bear upon all the activities of the school.

Catholics and Public Schools   Accepting the church's position, Roman Catholics could not and would not believe that the public school was a satisfactory means of education. Nothing but education directed by the church would be acceptable. While in an emergency a Roman Catholic child might attend a public school, as many have done and still do, this was not approved by the church. In fact, the church was strongly opposed to public schools on two grounds: the spirit of the public schools was primarily Protestant and therefore schismatic and heretical, because it was the King James

(Protestant) version of the Bible that was read; on the other hand, if the Bible reading and other Protestant doctrine were omitted, the school was secular and "godless."

In the early days of the Republic, the Roman Catholics were a small minority of the American people—only 30,000 persons in a population of 3,000,000. Being so small a portion of the population and being in many quarters regarded as a "foreign" institution, the church could not very well insist upon its point of view, strongly. Its only alternative was to provide its own schools in order to teach its doctrine and insure its prospective members against lapsing into Protestantism or agnosticism.

Catholic Parochial Schools   Roman Catholic schools were established soon after Catholic churches were erected in this country. In the East, there were parochial schools in New York, Philadelphia, and Baltimore; in the Louisiana territory, church schools had been founded during the Spanish and French regimes;

A Roman Catholic nun teaching children in a parochial school.

in California and neighboring states, there were mission schools, many of which had been founded by Father Junipero Serra in the latter part of the eighteenth century.

Nonetheless, parochial schools could not be founded as fast as they were needed. Many of the Catholic parishes were too poor to establish schools and to equip them. Teachers were in short supply, for there were yet no religious houses in America to prepare sisters and brothers to teach. The importation of religious orders from abroad ran into the practical problem of language, for most of the orders would come from France or Germany.

For a time, it appeared that Catholics and Protestants might cooperate in higher education. The board of trustees of the University of Pennsylvania had a Catholic member, while that grandiose project, the "Cathelopistemiad" University of Michigania, had a Sulpician, Father Gabriel Richard, holding the vice-presidency and six professorships in partnership with the Presbyterian Reverend John Monteith, holder of the presidency and seven professorships!

Immediately after the Revolution, the first Roman Catholic bishop of Baltimore, The Most Reverend John Carroll, founded church colleges to supply clergy to his churches and to provide nonclerics an opportunity in America for higher education under religious auspices. English-speaking Catholics previously had to go abroad to the English Catholic College at Douay, Belgium, which had been founded to keep Catholicism alive among the English-speaking people when they were not permitted to have their schools in England. The first Catholic educational effort after the Revolution was mainly directed toward higher education, and for the same reason that the early Calvinistic settlers founded Harvard and the Boston Latin School before they went about organizing common schools—namely, to assure a learned leadership for church and state. Many of these first colleges also included preparatory departments, as was common in the Protestant colleges at the time.

Mother Seton is regarded by Catholic historians as a principal founder of the parochial school system of her church. At Emmetsburg, Maryland, she established a school for poor children, with free tuition, free texts, and even free lunches. It was some years thereafter, however, before any considerable number of parochial schools were established.

For some time, the Catholics appear to have hoped that public school funds would be available for schools under at least nominal public control, but in which the Catholic version of the Bible could be taught. It will be remembered that the Public School Society in New York City had received public funds to conduct its free schools, even though these schools were admittedly Protestant in emphasis, even if non-denominational within the Protestant fold. We have seen also how the aid to this society was withdrawn when a Catholic society asked for a share.

Hostility to Parochial Schools   The 1830's to 1860's brought crowds of immigrants to the United States. They were needed to carry on the vast public and private works—the Erie Canal, the railroads, the factories, the mines all clamored for cheap laborers. They were eager to come, for there was overpopulation and a famine in Ireland, and threats of war and failure of a democratic revolution in Germany. Vast numbers of not easily assimilated persons came each decade—600,000 in the 1830's, 1,700,000 in the 1840's, and 2,600,000 in the 1850's. The most of these, and the most difficult to deal with, were the Irish. This "invasion" had profound sociological consequences. The Irish were predominantly Catholic and many were semi-illiterate, having been denied an education at home. Native Americans were alarmed by the threat to American mores by the large number of these "papists" who owed allegiance to an Italian pope. While economic motives entered into the matter,

A cartoon depicting the hostility and fear that some Americans had toward the Roman Catholics "invading" the public schools. Circa 1860's.

it appears that the "America for Americans" movement was primarily grounded in an attempt to keep America Protestant. It was claimed that no Catholic could possibly be a good American. Though they were despised, the Irish were also feared. Their commitment to parochial schools added one more ember to the flames, for the native Americans now were coming to believe that all classes of people should attend the common school which alone could assure continuance of the Republic.

In Charlestown, Massachusetts, which was later to become a stronghold of the Irish, a mob burned a Catholic convent in 1834, following a fiery sermon by the Rev. Lyman Beecher on an alleged papal plot to seize the Mississippi Valley. The teachers and the pupils had to flee in the middle of the night. The mother superior's warning that "the Bishop has twenty thousand Irishmen at his command in Boston" led to further hostility. Ten years later, a similar outbreak occurred in Philadelphia. In a raid on the Jesuit medical school in St. Louis, the cadavers used in medical instruction were alleged to be the bodies of Protestants who had been tortured by a local Inquisition. Tales by ex-nuns and fraudulent ex-nuns were circulated about the alleged horrors of convent life. Massachusetts went so far as to appoint a body to inspect the convents in that state.

The hostility toward parochial schools was, then, part of a larger hostility toward Catholicism. It was argued in the religious press that if the Catholics did not have the parochial schools, their children would be "Americanized" through the public schools, where they would be freed from superstition and "popery."

When Bishop Hughes petitioned the city council of New York for three hours to grant public funds for Catholic schools, Protestant opponents took two days for rebuttal. One minister said he would prefer to grow up an infidel rather than a "papist." The council refused to grant assistance to the Catholic schools. Soon the state legislature was to discontinue grants to the Public School Society and to require the city to operate public schools.

It was the request of the Catholics for state funds for their schools which precipitated the constitutional provisions or amendments to state constitutions forbidding the use of public money to aid any institution in which any denominational tenet or doctrine was taught.

Expansion of Parochial Schools   The Catholics now had to face squarely the question of whether they would send their children to the public schools, which still had a Protestant flavor, or whether they would sacrifice to build their own system of schools consistent with their educational philosophy. Unless they were to be reconciled to the possibility that many of their children might fall away from the faith of their fathers, they had to develop their own schools.

In some communities, temporary compromises were worked out. At Poughkeepsie, New York, the local public board of education leased the Catholic parochial school buildings and conducted "public" schools in them, paying the members of the teaching order, and reserving the right to inspect and control the schools. This system was continued until 1898, when the school superintendent refused longer to countenance it. A similar system was used in New Haven, Connecticut, until the 1930's.

The Third Plenary Council of the Catholic Church, meeting in 1884 at Baltimore, exhorted and commanded Catholic parents "to procure for their beloved offspring, given them by God, reborn in Christ in baptism, and destined for Heaven, a truly Christian and Catholic education." To check the zeal of some church authorities, however, the council forbade denying the sacraments to parents who continued to send their children to public schools. The council then went on to order the construction of a parochial school near each church within two years, unless the bishop allowed a postponement. The churches were exhorted to improve the quality of their schools where they were not of "the highest educational excellence."

The local churches feverishly entered into building schools, but only rarely were they able to keep pace with the growing numbers of children. Though there are now 10,631 Catholic parochial elementary schools enrolling more than 4,445,288 pupils, still half the Catholic children of elementary school age are enrolled in public schools. In 2,376 Catholic secondary schools in 1961, there were 937,671 pupils enrolled. The growth of Catholic schools has been at so great a pace that the teaching orders can no longer supply the needed teachers, so classes have become larger and larger, and lay teachers have increasingly been used. The number of lay teachers in elementary schools increased from 4,747 in 1950 (7.1% of the total) to 32,723 in 1961 (29.5% of the total). In the secondary schools, the lay teachers in 1961 were 26.7% of the total. The large classes, as in some public schools as well, have not been sound from an educational viewpoint.

Renewed Hostility   In the heyday of
the revived Ku Klux Klan after World War I, the nativist hostility to the Catholic Church again burst into flame. Now, there was also

considerable anti-Jewish sentiment as well. Michigan attempted to
insert into its constitution a provision to suppress parochial schools,
but the attempt failed. In Oregon, the legislature in 1922 passed a
law requiring attendance at a public school. Constitutionality of the
law was challenged by a Roman Catholic teaching order which conducted a parochial school, and by a private military academy. The
challenge was based upon several contentions, the chief ones being
that the law violated the religious rights of citizens by refusing them
the right to choose an education with a religious orientation, and
that it denied parents the right to make decisions regarding the education of their children. In 1925, the United States Supreme Court
in *Pierce v. Society of Jesus and Mary* declared the law unconstitutional. The decision, in part, reads:

> The statute in suit trespasses, not only upon the liberty of the
> parents individually, but upon their liberty collectively as well. It
> forbids them, as a body, to support private and parochial schools
> and thus give to their children such education and religious train-
> ing as the parents may see fit, subject to the valid regulations of
> the State. In that respect the enactment violates the public policy
> of the State of Oregon and the liberty which parents have hereto-
> fore enjoyed in that State.
>
> The legislative power of a State in relation to education does
> not involve the power to prohibit or suppress private schools and
> colleges. The familiar statement that education is a public func-
> tion means no more than that it is a function that the State may
> undertake, because it vitally interests and concerns the State that
> children shall be furnished the means of education and not be left
> to grow up in ignorance. But the power of the State to provide
> public schools carries with it no power to prohibit and suppress
> private schools and colleges which are competent and qualified to
> afford what the State wants, namely education. . . .
>
> No question is raised concerning the power of the State reason-
> ably to regulate all schools, to inspect, supervise, and examine
> them, their teachers and pupils; to require that all children of
> proper age attend some school, that teachers shall be of good moral
> character and patriotic disposition, that certain studies plainly
> essential to good citizenship must be taught, and that nothing be
> taught which is manifestly inimical to the public welfare.
>
> . . . we think it entirely plain that the Act of 1922 unreasonably
> interferes with the liberty of parents and guardians to direct the
> upbringing and education of children under their control. . . .

The fundamental theory of liberty under which all governments in this Union repose excludes any general power of the State to standardize its children by forcing them to accept instruction from public teachers only. The child is not the mere creature of the State; those who nurture him and direct his destiny have the right, coupled with the high duty, to recognize and prepare him for additional obligations.

Federal Aid to Church Schools?

There is a decided difference of opinion at present regarding the desirability and the constitutionality of federal aid to other than public schools. Even in the Catholic hierarchy these differences exist. Many bishops demand federal aid for their schools. On the other hand, the *Pittsburgh Catholic,* official organ of the Pittsburgh diocese, contends that

There are weighty reasons why Catholics should not seek the state contributions for the education furnished by their schools, to which, in all justice, they are entitled. These reasons have been repeatedly set forth by leaders of the church in this country; they have dictated the position taken by Catholics thus far, and their importance is strongly confirmed by recent developments. When state funds are accepted, some measure of state interference and control must also be accepted. State money for Catholic schools means close dealings with public officials; it means political connections; it means dictation regarding the manner in which the schools are to be conducted. . . .

Under favorable conditions, assistance from the public treasury is a handicap and a difficulty; under unfavorable circumstances it can become a catastrophe.

The entire history of the church, emphasized by recent events, shows that public funds come at too dear a price. Mexico had state aid, and so had Spain and Germany and Italy and France. And it proved a weakening, demoralizing connection. Better the sacrifice and the limitations which independence requires than the unsound edifice built on the deceptive, treacherous basis of state aid.

"Breaches in the Wall"

Great pressures have been applied and still are being applied upon Congress and the legislatures of various states to grant public funds to sectarian schools, primarily to Roman Catholic parochial schools. In some states, all except doctrinal textbooks are now furnished at public expense. In some states, free transportation to and from parochial schools is provided for. In Pennsylvania, the public school authorities are required to furnish health services to non-public schools within their boundaries. Where these forms of state aid have been tested in the courts and upheld, the reasoning has been that these are welfare services furnished equally to all citizens, not aid to the schools in which any denominational tenet is taught. Justice Rutledge of the United States Supreme Court, in a dissenting opinion in *Everson v. Board of Education of the Township of Ewing* declared, however, that more was involved than just bus transportation. He said that "distant as it may be in its present form from a complete establishment of religion, it differs only in degree, and is a first step in that direction." The first breach in the principle, he said, was upholding the use of public money for the purchase of textbooks; bus transportation was the second breach; if these were successful, further breaches in the principle of separation of church and state would be attempted.

Unsettled Questions   In relation to
a discussion of parochial schools, it is appropriate to discuss the role of religion in the public schools, for the interest of many people in parochial schools depends, in part, upon what happens to religion in public schools. It is an established fact that the public school in the United States cannot advocate any particular tenet of any denomination. While the schools of a homogeneous country such as Norway can be avowedly Lutheran, while the schools of Italy or Spain may be avowedly Roman Catholic in their teachings, our schools must be neutral.[1] Disestablishment of religion, acceptance of all religious beliefs, and refusal to grant preferment to any denomination are constitutionally established policies. But how shall these principles be interpreted and applied? There has been great variance from state to state. By their constitutions, most states forbid public aid to sectarian institutions; most prohibit sectarian influence in the schools. However, some have required the reading of the Bible daily in public schools; others have permitted it; still others forbid it. In some states, an elective course in Bible study is permitted in secondary schools; one requires study of the Ten Commandments. There have been many other variations, but all have recently come under an important ruling by the U.S. Supreme Court.

The Supreme Court   A justice of
the United States Supreme Court remarked that the court was fast

---

[1] Note, however, that public schools in France (an overwhelmingly Catholic country) are strictly secular and nonreligious.

becoming a national school board. Within recent years, many appeals have been made to the court on the issue of religion and the schools. In the case of McCollum, the court held that it was unconstitutional for a school board to permit clergymen to give religious instruction in a school under the so-called "released time" program; on the other hand, in a New York City case, the court upheld voluntary religious instruction given away from the school on "released time." The Educational Policies Commission held that the public school can teach "objectively about religion without advocating or teaching any religious creed," but who is to judge objectivity vs. subjectivity? Late in 1962, the Supreme Court had before it three questions: Was a Pennsylvania law requiring Bible reading in school constitutional? (A state court said it was not.) Was a similar Maryland law constitutional? (A state court said it was.) Was it constitutional for parochial school texts to be purchased with public funds? (A state court said it was not; but other state courts have said it was.)

These questions came fast upon a decision by the United States Supreme Court that a prayer prescribed by the Regents of the University of the State of New York (the state board of education) for use in schools was unconstitutional. Would the United States court find the insertion of "under God" into the Pledge of Allegiance unconstitutional? The court has already held that a student, for reasons of conscience, need not take the pledge.

The United States Supreme Court, early in 1963, ruled that Bible reading and the Lord's Prayer were unconstitutional. Apparently this decision had been expected, for this ruling brought forth much less popular expression of dismay and indignation than had the decision on the "Regents Prayer" in 1962. The earlier decision had brought forth an attempt to amend the constitution, severe attacks on the court in the halls of congress and in a portion of the public press, and even a proposal that Chief Justice Warren and his associates be impeached. Between the two decisions, the nation had an opportunity to examine the whole issue more calmly. A special bulletin issued by the American Association of School Administrators attempted to give guidance to members of the teaching profession and the pronouncements of civil and church leaders were helpful to the lay public.

There were pockets of resistance to the 1963 decision. State superintendents in several states had to caution local boards to act in the spirit of the decision. Having noted the Fabian tactics of certain boards in dragging their heels in racial desegregation, other boards attempted the same tactics in this instance. In a few cases, students picketed their own schools demanding the continuation of "opening exercises" of a religious nature.

A Completely Secular School?   Perhaps decisions will
make the school entirely secular, but this will not be satisfactory to
those who hold that education is incomplete and unsatisfactory
without religion. The net result may be an added impetus to the
further expansion of parochial schools, Roman Catholic and Protestant alike. On the other hand, the grave financial problem of expanding denominational and parochial schools gave these churches
pause.

Secondary Schools   The churches which
have maintained elementary parochial schools also conduct secondary
schools. The Roman Catholics have the largest number. These are
not parochial schools, in the strict sense of the word, for normally
they are conducted by the diocese rather than the parish. Some are
conducted by religious orders as boarding schools. Generally, the
founding of secondary schools came after the parochial elementary
schools, for two reasons: the church thought the education of the
younger children of more immediate importance, and further, it has
been only in recent years that any large number of Catholic church-
school pupils have persisted through the high school.

Independent Schools   From the early
days of the colonies there have been private schools of various kinds,
both on the elementary and secondary levels. Some of the present
schools began as academies shortly after the Revolution. Instead of
becoming public high schools, as many did, some elected to remain
independent and to concentrate upon a college preparatory function.
There are, in addition, a large number of county day schools and
military schools, both on elementary and secondary levels. In times
of prosperity, they are more generally patronized than in times of
financial retrenchment. Many private or independent schools fell
upon hard times in the depression of the 1930's; many failed, but
others persisted through the lean years to reap their harvest in the
present days of affluence. Recent charges that the public schools were
anti-intellectual, committed only to life-adjustment programs, have
turned some parents to the cause of the independent schools. Recently there has been an attempt to open independent elementary
schools to emphasize phonics in reading, to conduct classes on the plan
of Maria Montessori, and to follow various conservative or traditional practices. One private school emphasizes the fact that it uses
the McGuffey Readers as basic texts. In most states, it is relatively
easy for anyone with a particular educational objective to found an

independent school. Supervision by the state varies greatly throughout the country, but in no state is it particularly arduous.

For Further Reading

Beck, Walter H. *Lutheran Elementary Schools in the United States*. Concordia Publishing House, 1939.
Schools established and maintained by one of the major Protestant denominations.

Billington, Ray A. *The Protestant Crusade*. Macmillan, 1938.
Influence of Protestantism in America.

Boles, Donald. *The Bible, Religion and Public Schools*. Iowa State University Press, 1961.
Status of religious emphasis in public schools.

Burns, Rev. J. A. *The Catholic School System in the United States: Its Principles, Origin and Establishment*. Benziger Brothers, 1908.
Standard history of Roman Catholic educational efforts in America.

Burns, Rev. J. A. *The Growth and Development of the Catholic School System in the United States*. Benziger Brothers, 1912.
Revision of previously cited book, with more material.

Burns, Rev. J. A. and Bernard J. Kohlbrenner. *A History of Catholic Education in the United States*. Benziger Brothers, 1937.
Revision of Father Burns' first two books with newer developments.

Culver, Raymond B. *Horace Mann and Religion in the Massachusetts Public Schools*. Yale University Press, 1929.
Mann's controversies with those who wanted sectarian religion retained in the Massachusetts schools.

Curran, Francis X. *The Churches and the Schools: American Protestantism and Popular Elementary Education*. Loyola University Press, 1954.
A Catholic's evaluation of Protestant influence in church schools and public schools. Traces decline of Protestant schools.

Curti, Merle. *The Social Ideas of American Educators*. Littlefield, Adams, 1959.
Chapter 10 presents the educational philosophy and contributions of Bishop John Lancaster Spalding, perhaps the greatest Roman Catholic educator in the United States. (1840–1916.)

Dunn, William K. *What Happened to Religious Education?* Johns Hopkins University Press, 1958.
Decline of religious influences in education.

Fichter, Joseph H. *Parochial School, A Sociological Study*. University of Notre Dame Press, 1958.
A priest's sociological study of a Catholic parochial school.

French, William Marshall. *American Secondary Education*. Odyssey, 1957.
Chapter 11 for independent schools, and Chapter 12 for independent schools, both on the secondary level.

Johnson, Alvin W. *Legal Status of Church-State Relationships in the United States, with Special Reference to the Public Schools*. University of Minnesota Press, 1934.
Church-state relations in educational matters.

Johnson, Alvin W. and Frank H. Yost. *Separation of Church and State in the United States*. University of Minnesota Press, 1948.
Elaboration of the doctrine of separation and its application to education.

Maynard, Theodore. *The Story of American Catholicism*. Macmillan, 1948.
A history of this church in the United States. Mention of its educational efforts.

Melville, Annabelle M. *John Carroll of Baltimore*. Scribners, 1955.
A biography of the first Roman Catholic bishop in the United States. Mention of his interest in establishing parochial schools and colleges.

Moehlman, Conrad. *Church and State, the American Way*. Harper, 1944.
Emphasis on separation.

National Catholic Welfare Conference. *Summary of Catholic Education, 1960 and 1961*.
Statistics on Roman Catholic schools.

Sherrill, Lewis B. *Presbyterian Parochial Schools, 1846–1870*. Yale University Press, 1932.
Another study of church-related schools.

16

Incorporating the Minorities

Many Minorities in America   The people of
the United States belong to a pluralistic society, one made up of
people of many backgrounds, many traditions, many heritages, many
philosophies. In such a society, there are majorities and minorities.
Actually, almost any American crosses over from majority to minority
and back again in his daily life. One may be white (a majority member) but a Roman Catholic (a minority member), or he may be a
Negro (a minority member) but a Democrat (a majority member,
which might turn into a minority at a subsequent election).

One of the great contributions America has made to civilization is
a demonstration that persons with tremendously different social,
political, racial, religious, and economic backgrounds can work together for the common good. We have not demonstrated this proposition to its maximum, but we have demonstrated it with a reasonable
degree of success.

People from all over the world have come to America and have
been given the opportunity to join in a common effort. A common
system of education, with the acknowledged right of the individual
to dissent therefrom, has been a part of this grand scheme. In not
all cases have all these advantages been available at once. In many
instances, social attitudes had to develop before we could approach
the American ideal of a free, equal educational opportunity for all
the children of all the people. We have not yet attained this ideal.
Indeed, we may never completely attain it, but certainly great progress has been made.

We could, if we wished to be sufficiently comprehensive, deal with
the education of many minority groups. We have, however, selected
three—one on the basis of color, one on the basis of land of origin,
and one on the basis of physical condition. We shall here treat of the
education of the Negro, of the immigrant, and of the physically
handicapped.

Education of the Negro   Soon after Negro
slavery was introduced into the English colonies, the question arose
as to the role these people would play in the society into which they
had involuntarily been injected. In Virginia, a school was established
for Indians and Negroes in 1620, but it was destroyed in the Indian
wars. Nothing further was done until 1701, when an English missionary society sent a teacher, Samuel Thomas, who reported he had
taught twenty Negroes to read. A catechetical school for Negroes was
conducted in New York for some years after 1704. In Georgia, it was
resolved in 1747 that "the owners of slaves should educate the young
and use every possible means of making religious impressions upon
the minds of the aged." In 1790, a Methodist conference discussed
means of teaching "poor children, white and black, to read," and
resolved upon Sunday Schools as the proper agency, with a proper
textbook "to teach them learning and piety." It appears, then, that
the education of Negroes was undertaken as an extension of philanthropic and missionary endeavor, primarily for religious reasons.

By the middle of the 1700's, however, a marked change began, for
both Georgia and South Carolina passed laws forbidding teaching
slaves to read or write. Later other states imposed similar restrictions,
even forbidding the teaching of free Negroes. Some clandestine
schools were maintained for this purpose, however.

Until the rise of the abolitionist movement, there was similar
feeling in the North about the education of Negroes. When it was
proposed to open a manual labor school for them at New Haven, a
public meeting resolved by a vote of 700 to four that "the founding
of colleges for educating colored people is an unwarrantable and
dangerous undertaking to the internal concerns of other states and
ought to be discouraged." Because it admitted colored students, the
Noyes Academy was ejected from Canaan, New Hampshire by three
hundred persons using a hundred yoke of oxen. Prudence Crandall
was imprisoned at Canterbury, Connecticut, for opening her school
to colored girls. Nevertheless, a number of schools for colored children and youth were successfully maintained in the Northern states,
including schools in southeastern Pennsylvania at Cheney and at a
place now known as Lincoln University.

The Civil War increased the opportunities for education among
the Negroes. For one thing, the latent opposition in the North to
schools for them decreased, and active steps were taken in the South
by the Union armies to set up schools for "contraband of war," as
the Negroes released from slavery were termed. A school was opened
at Fortress Monroe in 1861 and similar schools were opened wherever
the Union armies went. The first teacher at Fortress Monroe was
Mary L. Peake, a "free woman of color" who had been educated in

England. From this very modest beginning developed Hampton Institute, which has had a distinguished record of more than a hundred years in the education of Negroes. Its most famous graduate was Booker T. Washington, who became an important leader in the education of his people.

In 1864, it was reported that there were 95 schools with 102 teachers and 9,571 students in Louisiana. In the Negro regiments, the men prevailed upon their officers to teach them reading, writing and the elements of arithmetic.

Freedmen's Bureau   Congress created the Freedmen's Bureau in 1865 and authorized it to cooperate with religious and philanthropic societies in the education of Negroes. The American Missionary Association and several church bodies furnished funds and teachers. There was a spontaneous movement to begin schools all over the South, often under a tree if no building was available. Night schools were established in great numbers. In 1866, there were 975 schools with 90,778 pupils. Ten years later the enrollment was 571,506. Teachers were recruited from colored people who had at least the elements of an education, from teachers sent into the South by Northern philanthropic and missionary societies, and from Southern whites as well.

Teaching the Freedmen.

The Freedmen's Bureau was instrumental in aiding several institutions of higher education for Negroes, including the institutions now known as Morehouse College, Atlanta University, Johnson C. Smith University, Fisk University, and Howard University.

Tax-Supported Schools   We have seen that some Southern states had made some progress toward free public schools for white children before the Civil War. The war left this rudimentary system in a shambles. Now the South was confronted with the problem of rebuilding and advancing a system of education for whites and also one for Negroes, for it was unthinkable at the time that children of both races would be sent to the same school. It was West Virginia, indeed, that set up the first system of separate schools. In its first constitution in 1863, provision was made for a dual system of schools.

While the state governments which were set up by a combination of Northern "carpetbaggers," native white "scalawags," and newly enfranchised Negroes, placed the education of Negroes and whites on an equal basis, this system lasted only as long as it was supported by Federal troops. In the border states, no such systems were projected. Kentucky, for instance, made no provision for Negro schools until 1871, and then provided for their support from taxes on property owned by Negroes, and from a poll tax of one dollar on each male Negro. Eventually, in the case of *Claybrooks* v. *the City of Owensboro,* such allocation of taxes to dual schools was declared unconstitutional, so then the Negro schools had access to a share of all public school funds.

Some white idealists, believing that separate schools would inevitably be unequal and undemocratic, attempted to cause the adoption of a system of mixed schools. H. M. Bond asserts that Negroes were less interested in having their children actually attend mixed schools than in their having the right to do so. He holds that they wished to use this right to force provision for their own schools of equal quality. The answer, which prevailed for many years, was a dual system of schools which turned out in some instances to be decidedly unequal. In 1932, one county spent $178 per white child enrolled and eight dollars per Negro child enrolled. The argument used to justify this discrimination was that the whites paid most of the taxes and their children were therefore logically entitled to most of the educational expenditures. Also, many persons asserted that the Negro was "fundamentally incapable" of profiting from an education.

Philanthropies

The cause of education for Southern Negroes was greatly advanced by Northern philanthropies. Among these were the Peabody Fund for the education of both races; the John F. Slater Fund for "uplifting the lately emancipated population of the Southern states and promoting their prosperity"; the Anna T. Jeanes Fund, to assist in providing elementary schools for Negroes in the South. The work of these funds was greatly supplemented in the early part of the present century by the Julius Rosenwald Fund, which furnished building plans and local leadership for schools for Negroes. By 1932, the Rosenwald Fund had been instrumental in the construction of 5,357 schools with a capacity of 663,615 students. Liberal aid was also given to Negro colleges. It is significant that Negroes themselves gave liberally to their own institutions.

Effects of Dual System

The Southern states were economically least able to support any system of public education, their total wealth being far less per capita than that of the more

The after-math of the War Between the States: a battered countryside, a shattered economy, and a wounded self-confidence.

industrialized sections of the country. This lack of funds for education in turn helped perpetuate the South's relative poverty, for there is an established relationship between the amount of education a people has and their economic well-being. Added to this financial problem was the fact that the Southern states were determined to maintain two separate school systems, a double burden that caused both systems to be sub-standard for many decades. In almost any statistical analysis of education state by state, it was the Southern states that stood at the bottom of the list.

Since the whites controlled the state and local governments, they often saw that the greater share of their funds went to white schools and the smaller share to Negro schools. Until recent years, it has usually been the Negro schools that were the oldest and the least equipped, and the Negro teachers who were least well paid. Under these circumstances, it is not surprising that relatively few Southern Negroes made any significant advance in education. What is remarkable is the fact that many individuals did rise to make their marks in the world.

What Kind of Education?

There were two viewpoints regarding education for Negroes on the part of those who believed in its importance. The radical point of view was that the Negro should have a chance to prove himself in the same type of education available to the whites. Many Negroes subscribed to this point of view: if a white man thought Greek and Latin and mathematics important, then it was important for the Negro as well. This explains the rush of newly emancipated colored people to study subjects for which they had no background of preparation.

A more conservative viewpoint was that the first responsibility of education was to enable the Negro to move from his existing status of illiteracy and economic inferiority into literacy and vocational competence. This was the program of Hampton Institute in its earlier years, where the emphasis on industrial and agricultural education antedated the introduction of manual training and agriculture into the public schools of the country. This was the ideal which Booker T. Washington took with him from Hampton to the new institution which he founded, Tuskegee Institute. This more modest aim, it must be admitted, found the more hospitable reception among both Southern and Northern whites.

Actually, both philosophies fortunately prevailed. And both had their handicaps, for this was the question: After a Negro had acquired either vocational skills or an academic education in the liberal arts, where would he use his education? In both the South and the North, society was reluctant to admit Negroes to positions commensurate with their education. This explains the phenomenon of Phi Beta Kappa keys on chests of railway Pullman car porters. It also explains the reply of a student at Hampton Institute to the author .in 1933. The student was complimented on a neat and plumb brick fence he was laying. His reply was, "Yes, sir, but when I graduate I'll be lucky to get a job carrying hod for a white bricklayer!"

"Separate but Equal" The practice of segregating children by races was not a practice limited to the Southern states. It had been practiced north of the Mason and Dixon line as well as south of it. In 1849, a Massachusetts court upheld racial segregation in schools. Though the legislature soon desegregated the schools by law, the judicial concept remained. In 1896, the United States Supreme Court upheld a Louisiana law which required separate railroad accommodations for the two races, and cited with approval the then generally accepted practice of segregation according to race in the public schools. This was the famous *Plessy* v. *Ferguson* case which gave rise to what came to be called "the Plessy doctrine." As late as 1927, the Supreme Court reaffirmed the doctrine in a case which did not interfere with Mississippi's sending a Chinese child to a Negro school. It seemed, at least superficially, that the matter was settled, and that maintenance of a dual system of education was constitutional, if the schools were equal.

Knowing that many schools in fact were not equal, several Southern communities moved fast to span the chasm between the two school systems. In some instances, new schools for Negroes were superior to equivalent schools for whites.

Supreme Court Decision, 1954 But conditions change as the times change, and the Supreme Court of the United States also changes in its social outlook. There have been numerous cases in which a later United States Supreme Court has reversed the decision of an earlier United States Supreme Court in an analogous case. In early 1954, it seemed that eventually the court would rule again on the constitutionality of the "separate but equal" doctrine, for the world had moved since the Plessy case.

First, the Negro had risen in American society to a place where his talents and potential contributions could not be ignored. Second, the Negro had made a decided contribution to the winning of World War II, and thousands of Negroes had been in parts of the world where segregation was not practiced. Third, the rising tide of independence among the colored races of the world placed the United States, the champion of democracy, in an embarrassing and anomalous position in world affairs. Fourth, many Americans were convinced that segregation was contrary to principles of their religion and their political faith.

There were evidences of the handwriting on the wall, for the United States Supreme Court had ruled that certain Negroes were entitled to attend the hitherto white state colleges. In 1938, the court ordered a Negro admitted to the law school of the University of Missouri, and it held that a hastily organized law school in Texas was not "equal" to the University of Texas. In Oklahoma, a Negro was ordered admitted to a classroom when the University tried to segregate him in an adjoining room.

In 1952, five cases were appealed to the United States Supreme Court, dealing with segregation in the public schools in Kansas, South Carolina, Virginia, Delaware, and the District of Columbia. On May 17, 1954, the final decision was announced by the court: all the school districts were told that separateness implied inequality and were instructed to proceed with desegregation "with all deliberate speed." The court retained jurisdiction of the cases to check on compliance.

Federal troops were employed at Little Rock, Arkansas, to seat Negro students in a hitherto all-white high school. United States marshals and Federal troops were used again to force the admission of James Meredith to the University of Mississippi in 1962.

Many threats were made, and some states even repealed their public school laws in their attempt to resist desegregation. In time, more moderate voices were raised in the South. It appears that the majority of the American people support the Supreme Court decisions. Admittedly, there will be some years of litigation and perhaps even more turmoil before this issue, like so many others, passes into history.

Great Number of Immigrants   When Congress was considering plans for the second census in 1800, it received two memorials, one from Thomas Jefferson as secretary of the American Philosophical Society, and one from President Timothy Dwight on behalf of the Connecticut Academy of Arts and Sciences, urging that an enumeration be included of persons not born in the United States. Unfortunately, Congress did not see fit to adopt these recommendations, and it was not until the seventh census in 1850 that such a

" FIRST WE CLOSED OUR SCHOOLS, THEN ONE THING LED TO ANOTHER!"

count was made. Approximately 2,225,000 persons of foreign birth were enumerated in 1850; by 1900, there were more than 10,000,000; by 1910, 13,500,000; and it reached more than 14,000,000 in 1930. Thereafter, the number declined. Foreign-born or first generation descendants of foreign-born constituted nearly forty percent of the total population early in the present century.

This tremendous flood of persons from other countries, often without any traditions of democracy, posed a great challenge to American democracy. That these huge numbers became Americanized and assimilated into the general population is a great tribute to them and to American institutions. Among these American institutions which made it possible to absorb so many people with diverse traditions and customs was the American public school. In the case of Roman Catholic immigrants, the parochial school made a marked contribution and, of course, many other social agencies did their part. Among these were churches, settlement houses, philanthropic societies, social organizations of all kinds, newspapers in English and in a host of other languages, the citizenship process, and many others. Nonetheless, it was largely the public school system which made the major contribution in this process, both through educating the children of the immigrants and through Americanization and citizenship classes for the adults.

The Early Immigrants   It was fortunate that most of the immigrants up to the Civil War came from the English-speaking lands, from Germany, and the Scandinavian nations, for their cultures were relatively easier to absorb into the colonial traditions of America. These were the days when the public school system was yet in its infancy. The fact that the Germans of colonial and early national periods in Pennsylvania remained a foreign island in an English commonwealth indicated what might have happened on a much greater scale in the latter part of the nineteenth century if the school had not been available to help in their assimilation. Not until recent years has English officially replaced German or the "Pennsylvania Dutch" version of German in certain areas of Pennsylvania. This shows the powerful influence of the public school and associated economic and social pressures.

The Later Immigrants   After the Civil War, many of the immigrants came from Southern and Eastern European areas, where the traditions were far different from those which the Americans had developed. Russians, Ruthenians, Ukrainians, Poles, Italians, Greeks, and others came in large numbers. They were harder to absorb, but by that time America had a public school system and various social agencies to accelerate the adaptation of these people and their children to American ways. These later migrants were more prone to settle in urban areas. This concentrated the problem into a smaller area. Fortunately, it was in these urban areas that the schools were relatively better equipped to handle the problem.

Whereas the earlier immigrants had largely settled on the land among Americans, the ones who came after 1880 were more prone—or forced—to live in areas among their own kind—in "little Italies," "little Polands," "little Ruthenias," etc. It should be noted that an act of Congress in 1818 had forbidden immigrants to purchase blocks of land in groups. Thus, they were forced into a mixed society. There were no such regulations about settlement in the cities; indeed, there were various pressures applied to get the immigrants to live in segregated areas. Living with people of the same national origin, speaking the language of the "old country," they became much harder to assimilate.

Nonetheless, their children were privileged to partake of the American educational system. They did this so effectively that by 1907 the degree of illiteracy among children of immigrants was lower than among children of native-born whites, for the nation as a whole. Less than one per cent of immigrant children between ten and fourteen years of age were illiterate, whereas the figure for children of native-born whites was more than four percent. The explanation for this is that immigrants came to northern and urban areas where public and other schools were more readily available, whereas the statistics for native-born children of old American stock included children in both rural and urban areas all over the country.

Early School Leaving   It is true that many immigrant parents tried to evade the compulsory education laws, for they did not, in many cases, have a school-going tradition in their background. Indeed, some of them even prided themselves on a heritage of illiteracy, and thought their children were putting on airs in getting an education. This attitude is shown in a peasant story from Poland:[1]

> I am a son of a peasant farmer. Until ten years of age I did not know the alphabet, or, exactly speaking, I knew only the letter B. Father did not send me to school. He was always repeating: "We have grown old, and we can't read nor write, and we live; so you, my children, will also live without knowledge." . . . Once my mother took me to church. I looked to the right, a boy, smaller than myself, was praying from a book; I looked to the left, another one held a book just like the first. And I stood between them like a ninny. I went home and said to my father that I wanted to learn from a book. And father scolded me. "And who will peel potatoes in the winter, and pasture the geese in summer?" Here I cried. . . . Once, while peeling potatoes, I escaped from my father and went to an old man who knew not only how to read, but how to write well. I asked him to show me (letters) in the primer, and he did not refuse. I went home and thought: "It is bad? Father will probably give me a licking." And so it was. Father showered a few strokes on me and said: "Snotty fellow! Don't you know that, as old people say, he who knows written stuff casts himself into

[1] Park, R. E. and H. A. Miller: *Old World Traits Transplanted.* Harper and Brothers, 1921, p. 7.

hell?" But I used to steal out to learn more and more frequently.
. . . Once I found on the road an old almanac. I looked at it,
and I read on the last page that there was in Warsaw a Gazeta
Swiateczna which people order and receive it by mail every Sunday. After that I said to one of the neighbors, not a young man,
"Do you know in Warsaw there is a Gazeta which everyone, even
if not educated, can read?" And that man said to me: "Look at
him, at the snotty fellow! He wants a newspaper!" "Do you know,
Kum," said he to my father, "your son will become a real lord,
for he says that he will order a newspaper." "Ho, ho!" said father,
"but where will he get the money?"

A second reason for the encouragement of early drop-outs was
economic. Often poorly educated foreign parents looked upon children as breadwinners who were expected to engage in employment
at the earliest possible age to bring in some money for the family
coffers until such time as they went into the world on their own.
In the old countries, children had been looked upon as an economic
asset in performing farm labor, as contemporary American children
were. Even though the family was now in a different environment,
this attitude persisted. Any readers of the Alger books will recall
that some Italian padrones brought orphan children to the United
States and put them out to work to shine shoes, sing on street corners,
and sell papers.

In some instances, it took two or three generations for an immigrant family to achieve a high school graduate. In other families,
particularly among people who had a high esteem for learning,
particularly Jews, this step was achieved in the first generation born
in this country, and often by young children brought from abroad.
It is, of course, true that families which had early been established
here also often went through many generations before having a son
or daughter graduated from high school.

Conflicts for the Children   Many sons and
daughters of immigrants were thrown into conflict with their parents
by their exposure to the American schools. In school they were
exhorted to be Americans, but at home the parents still spoke the
language of the old country and carried on the mores from abroad.
This conflict for one boy is poignantly told by John Fante:[2]

I enter the parochial school with an awful fear that I will be
called a Wop. As soon as I find out why people have such things

2 Fante, John: "The Odyssey of a Wop," *The American Mercury*, September, 1933,
XXX pp. 91–93.

as surnames, I match my own against such typical Italian cognomens as Bianci, Borello, Pacelli—the names of other students. I am pleasantly relieved by the comparison. After all, I think, people will say I am French.

Doesn't my name sound French? Sure! So thereafter, when people ask me my nationality, I tell them I am French. A few boys begin calling me Frenchy. I like that. It feels fine.

Thus I begin to loathe my heritage. I avoid Italian boys and girls who try to be friendly. I thank God for my light skin and hair, and I choose my companions by the Anglo-Saxon ring of their names. If a boy's name is Whitney, Browne, or Smythe, then he's my pal; but I'm always a little breathless when I am with him; he may find me out. At the lunch hour I huddle over my lunch pail, for my mother doesn't wrap my sandwiches in wax paper, and she makes them too large and the lettuce leaves protrude. Worse, the bread is home-made; not bakery bread, not "American" bread. I make a great fuss because I can't have mayonnaise and other "American" things. . . .

I am nervous when I bring friends to my house; the place looks so Italian. Here hangs a picture of Victor Emmanuel, and over there is one of the cathedral of Milan, and next to it, one of St. Peter's, and on the buffet stands a wine-pitcher of medieval design; it's forever brimming, forever red and brilliant with wine. These things are heirlooms belonging to my father, and no matter who may come to our house, he likes to stand under them and brag.

So I begin to shout at him. I tell him to cut out being a Wop and be an American once in a while. Immediately he gets his razor-strop and whales hell out of me, clouting me from room to room and finally out the back door. I go into the woodshed and pull down my pants and stretch my neck to examine the blue slices across my rump. A Wop! that's what my father is! Nowhere is there an American father who beats his son this way. Well, he's not going to get away with it; some day I'll get even with him. . . .

My grandmother has taught me to speak her native tongue. By seven, I know it pretty well, and I always address her in it. But when friends are with me, when I am twelve and thirteen, I pretend to ignorance of what she says, and smirk stiffly; my friends daren't know that I can speak any language but English. Sometimes this infuriates her. She bristles, the loose skin at her throat knits hard, and she blasphemes with a mighty blasphemy.

It is not surprising that out of situations such as this many first-generation Americans turned to delinquency and crime. Many a person became a social problem because of the factor which sociologists profoundly call "conflicts of biculturality."

Settlement Houses

A form of adult education found helpful in orienting the immigrants to American civilization was the settlement house, a philanthropic or charitable institution placed in an area of heavy immigrant congestion and staffed by social workers, either professionals or volunteers. Begun in the 1890's, these settlement houses undertook to integrate the newcomers into American ways. Of these, Hull House, operated "back of the yards" in Chicago, was the most famous. Under the direction of Jane Addams, attempts were made there to sustain the immigrants' respect for their old culture and to urge them also to an acceptance of American ways. Attempts were made to meliorate the harshness of the adjustment from the old to the new. The humanitarian approach of the settlement workers seems to have been more effective than the militant approach of the various patriotic societies which preached a loyalty that was primarily grounded in submissiveness.

Americanization

When World War I burst upon America, there was great concern about the loyalty of immigrants to this country. The term "hyphenated American" became a reproach. The goal now was to convert the immigrants into 100% Americans. All the fervor of a great crusade was brought to bear upon them, including all kinds of pressure. In one instance, a group of American ladies waited upon a Bohemian tenement dweller to "Americanize" her. She asked them to come back the next week. "What, you want to postpone your entrance into American life?" they protested. "No, no!" was the reply, "We're perfectly willing to be Americanized. Why, we never turn any of them away. But there's nobody home but me. The boys volunteered, my man's working on munitions, and all the rest are out selling liberty bonds. I don't want you to get mad, but can't you come back next week?"[3]

The desire to be accepted by others as real Americans prompted some of the immigrants with "foreign" names to change them, either by shortening them or by adopting an entirely different one. The Cabots of Boston unsuccessfully went to court to prevent the adoption of their name by the Kabotchniks.

[3] This and other anecdotes of the period appear in John Higham's *Strangers in Our Land* (Rutgers University Press, 1955, chapter 9).

Education for immigrants. A school for newcomers. Photograph circa 1900.

Americanization Schools   The desire to
convert the immigrants to American ways led to the establishment
of special evening school programs to teach them English and facts
about America. In 1914, a federal bureau of education found that
the education of immigrants was a local affair, uncoordinated and
often in the hands of questionable private agencies. Only two states,
New Jersey and Massachusetts, had made any effort on the state
level. By 1920, nine had mandated public evening classes for immigrants and eighteen others had passed permissive legislation. In
1932, there were 178,449 students enrolled in such classes.

Unfortunately, much of the educational effort was not well
planned to meet the needs of the pupils. An illiterate adult would
be put to work on an elementary school primer to read "I am a
yellow bird. I can sing. I can fly. I can sing to you."[4] A Polish mill-
hand was discovered reading, "I am a little buttercup!" Only after
several years of such ludicrous experience did especially prepared
books become available which dealt with adult matters in a simple
language. Since some immigrants would not attend evening school,
special schools were set up for them in their industrial plants.

With the termination of large scale immigration because of restrictive legislation after World War I, the need for Americanization

4 The equivalent today would be the "look, look, look, see, see, see!"

classes dwindled. Within recent years, some areas have reestablished classes to serve refugees of the Hungarian resistance movement and the large number of Puerto Ricans coming to this country.

Educating the Handicapped   A democratic philosophy of education implies that each shall be afforded the opportunity to become what he is capable of becoming. Consequently, a democratic society provides educational opportunity for the child who deviates from normal, for he also is capable of becoming something. This explains the current interest in what is called "the exceptional child"—the child who deviates significantly from the normal in mental, physical, or emotional characteristics to the extent that his education requires a modification of school practices or even special school services. (The term "exceptional" in theory refers to persons at either end of the scale—the gifted as well as the dull—but here we are concerned with the education of those persons who have physical or mental handicaps.)

Until the humanitarian movement of the 1830's there were no educational facilities for blind, deaf, or crippled children. Out of pity, they were cared for at home, but no schools were available to them. With the humanitarian movement, the first attempts were made to accept the handicapped and to integrate them, insofar as possible, into normal society. There are perhaps as many as 4,000,000 children with varying degrees of handicaps in our American society.

The two pioneers in the education of the handicapped were Thomas H. Gallaudet, who opened a school for the deaf in Hartford in 1817, and Samuel Gridley Howe, who began to teach the blind in Boston in 1832. Howe attracted international attention when he educated a little girl who was both deaf and blind. At first, the deaf child was taught by sign language and the manual alphabet, but the transition was soon made to lip reading and voice production. Most of the early techniques were adapted from practices in France.

As a result of the pioneer efforts of these men, with the warm encouragement of Horace Mann, state boarding schools for the deaf, the blind, and the mentally handicapped were established. Some private schools were also opened. In some cases, because of inadequate financing, these were little more than custodial institutions, but several did outstanding work in returning their students to society, able to live reasonably normal lives.

Until the early 1900's there were no public school provisions for children who differed markedly from normality. Then certain systems began to introduce special classes of various kinds. Now a well organized system has several special classes. In many instances, these represent the cooperative effort of neighboring school districts.

The widespread intelligence testing movement that was developed in the schools after World War I indicated that special classes were also necessary for persons of low intelligence. The concept of individual differences that grew out of intelligence testing and other psychological movements indicated that special adaptations had to be made for many children. This led to the preparation and hiring of speech correctionists, social workers, visiting teachers, remedial reading specialists, and physical therapists, as well as teachers with special interest in teaching retarded children. All these occupy the field known as "special education." In the case of children of normal intelligence who are homebound by various types of illness, there is now some provision for telephone connection with their peers in a regular classroom.

A class scene in a school for the deaf and dumb in New York in 1856.

Special programs are offered in some universities and teachers colleges to prepare teachers for all kinds of handicapped children.

For Further Reading

Ashmore, Harry S. *The Negro and the Schools*. University of North Carolina Press, 1954.
The picture of race relations and the schools to 1954.

Bond, Horace Mann. *Education of the Negro in the American Social Order*. Prentice-Hall, 1934.
The standard history of Negro education.

Bowers, David F. (Editor). *Foreign Influences in American Life. Essays and Critical Bibliographies*. Peter Smith, 1952.
Cultural influences brought to America by its immigrants.

Brickman, W. W. and Stanley Lehrer. *The Countdown on Segregated Education*. Society for the Advancement of Education, 1960.
Comprehensive, timely account of the history, current status and possible future of segregated education in the United States, in South Africa and elsewhere.

Brown, Francis J. and Joseph Roucek. *One America*. Prentice-Hall, 1946.
A sociological study of immigrants.

Clift, Virgil A., Archibald W. Anderson and H. Gordon Hullfish. *Negro Education in America*. Harper, 1962.
Education of Negroes, viewed historically; anthropological and sociological factors; striving toward educational equality; Supreme Court decision and its aftermath; problems of desegregation; goals and plans for the future.

Commons, John R. *Races and Immigrants in America*. Macmillan, 1913.
Influence on America from many lands abroad.

Curti, Merle. *The Social Ideas of American Educators*. Littlefield, Adams, 1959.
Chapter 7 for "Education in the South" and Chapter 8 for "The Black Man's Place."

Davie, Maurice R. *World Immigration*. Macmillan, 1936.
A standard history of the migrations of people.

Fairchild, Henry Pratt. *Immigration*. Macmillan, 1919.
An older history of American immigration.

Higham, John. *Strangers in the Land*. Rutgers University Press, 1935.
A study of newcomers to America.

Hutchinson, E. P. *Immigrants and Their Children, 1850–1950*. John Wiley, 1956.
Relates problems of education and assimilation.

Shoemaker, Don. *With All Deliberate Speed*. Harper, 1957.
Dispassionate account of desegregation in the South after the Supreme Court decision.

Wallin, J. G. W. *The Education of Handicapped Children*. Houghton Mifflin, 1925.
A history of America's growing interest in affording educational opportunity even to the handicapped.

17

Control and Administration

An Evolutionary Process   There are more
than fifty million persons now enrolled in American schools from
the kindergarten through the university. This is more than one-
fourth of all the American people. To get these people into school,
to see to it that a school is there to serve them, to make provision
for the teachers and the teaching requires control and administration. Operating the schools is an important business function; likewise, it calls for educational statesmanship and administration of
the highest character.

The modern educational system is a marvel to behold. It is a
thoroughly complex structure that was never planned as a systematic
unit. Rather, like Topsy, it "just growed." It is a product of nearly
two centuries of evolution, extemporization, adaptation, improvisa-
tion, and sometimes just patching the roof when it rained. Often,
a procedure adopted in one age, which may have served its purpose
well at the time, has lingered on to become an incubus and a handicap in a later age. In the process of evolution, many compromises
have been worked out between conflicting interests. What we have
today, then, is perhaps not the best conceivable system of education,
but one that works with a reasonable degree of success and efficiency.
Since there is no traditional system which must remain "as it was in the
beginning, is now, and ever shall be," it becomes the duty of each
generation to make such additional revisions and adaptations as
changing circumstances or changing philosophies dictate from time
to time. To adapt a Jeffersonian phrase, the schools belong always
to the living generation.

Simple Control and Administration   When the educational
needs of a generation were simple, as in colonial Massachusetts and
its neighboring colonies, the matter of control and administration
was also primitive. The colony was convinced that literacy was a
good, so the general court (legislature) enacted laws requiring the

314

establishment of schools, as we have seen. No cumbersome bureaucracy was necessary. Establishment and supervision of the schools was made a responsibility of existing agencies, the town government. The administration and supervision became the duty of the board of selectmen or their committee. Matters of the smallest detail were discussed in the town meeting. When the towns were divided into parishes or school districts, a similar simple pattern of control now existed, for the authority rested in the school board or committee in each district. Within limits set by the scanty state laws, the local district was in effect sovereign. Many states had no general school laws for well into the nineteenth century, and those that did have them had only one state board secretary or superintendent to administer them.

State School Funds   To encourage the establishment and maintenance of schools, certain Eastern states early in the national period founded permanent state school funds. The interest was to be used by the state to help support the expense of education on the local level. Where no public schools existed, the fund might be made available to voluntary and charitable organizations such as the Public School Society of New York City. Where public schools existed, as in New England and some parts of New York, the local apportionment went to the school district.

Such state funds do not administer themselves, so a state officer was necessary. New York was the first state to appoint such an officer, called state superintendent of common schools. New York could have assigned the responsibility to the Regents of the University of the State of New York, thus avoiding many decades of divided authority, but at that time the Regents considered their province to be limited to the academies and colleges of the state. The new superintendent was Gideon Hawley, an attorney. In addition to making an equitable distribution of the state school fund, he required reports from the local districts and occasionally sent them letters about what the schools should be accomplishing.

The Massachusetts state board of education, established in 1837, was the first state board in the United States. This was a board of laymen. They engaged Horace Mann as their executive officer to distribute the state fund, receive reports, and compile statistics. Mann enlarged upon his duties and came to be the conscience of the state in educational matters. His series of annual reports were a mixture of statistics and educational essays or reports. He aroused the state to the need for educational reform, encouraged a revision of the curriculum, led in professionalizing teaching, obtained additional funds, and carried on little wars with those content to rest on the status quo. His imaginative leadership, combined with high idealism and a practical sense of what was politically obtainable, served as inspiration for many other state superintendents in following decades.

Connecticut needed a state officer to administer its school fund, which had largely come from sale of land in that state's "Western Reserve" in Ohio (land to which the state had retained legal title when it renounced any claim to sovereignty based upon its colonial charter). It was thought at the time that Connecticut's well managed school fund of nearly $2,000,000 would produce a large enough annual income to pay a substantial part of the cost of operating local schools. Finding that less than half the children of school age were in school, Barnard attacked the problems in his state much as Mann had done in Massachusetts. When the state board was abolished in 1842, Barnard went to Rhode Island in a similar capacity, but returned to Connecticut in 1851 as principal for a normal school and ex officio secretary of a re-created state board.

State school funds were greatly augmented in many states by the distribution of surplus federal revenue to the states by an act of 1836. It may seem strange in this day of deficit budgets that a century and a quarter ago the federal treasury was embarrassed by having too great a surplus, but such was the case. The surplus was distributed to the states, theoretically on deposit, but it was understood that it would not be recalled, nor has it ever been. In some states, it made nice pickings for corrupt officials, but in many others it was wisely invested, and the yearly interest was used for schools.

It was a naive assumption that income from permanent state school funds could be expected to pay any considerable amount of the expense of operating schools throughout the state. For a time, when schools were small, inexpensive, and few in number, the state grants were helpful, but the time soon came when most of the burden of supporting the schools had to be assumed by the local districts through a property tax. Later, state aid was increased from general state funds. In some states at present, the majority of all expenditures for public schools now comes from state sources; in others, it still is only a small proportion of the total amount.

County Superintendents   It soon became

apparent that the state superintendent of common schools (or superintendent of public instruction, as the office was often called) could hardly exercise any reasonable degree of supervision or control over the large number of district schools throughout the state. There were hundreds and often thousands of such small districts within a given state. Some type of intermediate administration was needed. The gradual evolution of the county superintendency met this need. Either through state school law or constitutional provision, many states adopted the system of county supervision. The early duties of such superintendents were generally clerical and statistical, but also included visiting the schools and certificating teachers. By 1870, most of the states had county superintendents.

In most cases, these superintendents were chosen at a popular election, for these were the days of the Jacksonian direct election of officers on the long ballot. Because the better politician (not necessarily the best professional candidate) often won the election, weak administration was frequently a characteristic of the county level. There were many instances of unconscionable violations of school regulations by the county superintendents to perpetuate themselves in office. In one instance, the county superintendent issued a teacher's license to a two-year-old girl and in another case a teacher's certificate was issued to a collie dog. Many a superintendent found it politically expedient to be a safe compiler of statistics, a gracious dispenser of professional favors, and an affable visitor to the district schools. Some of the superintendents were competent, professional leaders who transformed the schools of their counties by rigorous inspection, by intensive teacher education through supervision and county institutes, and by awakening the public conscience regarding education.

In some states, the intermediate unit was not the county but a supervisory district which might include two or more counties, or only a part of a large and populous county. In the twentieth century, certain of the smaller states made the county the basic unit of administration by abolishing the small local districts.

The City Superintendency

There were very few large or even medium-sized cities in the United States when the free school system was inaugurated. In most cases, the schools were established in rural areas, in villages, or in small cities. Even in these small cities, the schools frequently were not integrated into one system, but rather they were a number of independent schools, each subject to its own district board. In Buffalo in 1837, there were seven 'districts, each maintaining a one-room, one-teacher school. Chicago at about the same time had five independent districts, each maintaining its own school. Such a system was seen to be disorganized, so special legislation was enacted to merge the districts under the direction of a single municipal board of education.

To bring certain uniformity into its schools, Buffalo in 1837 appointed a superintendent of schools. It was the first American city to do so. By 1870, only twenty-seven cities had established superintendencies.[1] After 1870, the city superintendency was rapidly established in most of the other cities of the nation. In several instances, the superintendency was regarded merely as a glorified clerkship, but under the leadership of certain strong superintendents it began to take on the coloration of professional status.

Not all the early superintendents rose from the ranks of the teachers. Nowhere were any qualifications stated for the position. Dr. Frank Spaulding, a distinguished figure in American education, recounted in his autobiography that he had never attended a public school except a rural ungraded school, and had seldom visited one before he was appointed superintendent at Ware, Massachusetts in 1895. Later, in turn, he was to become superintendent at Passaic, New Jersey; in Newton, Massachusetts; in Minneapolis, Minnesota; and in Cleveland, Ohio. In 1920, he became chairman of the department of education in the graduate school of Yale University. Speaking of eligibility for a superintendency, Dr. Spaulding wrote:

> The answer to any such incredulous question regarding my certificate is simplicity itself. There was then in Massachusetts no such thing as an educational certificate. Every school Committee appointed whomsoever it pleased to any type of position; there was no legal bar to the appointment of illiterates even to the highest public school posts. And yet at that time, under these conditions of local and lay responsibility, leadership in the improvement of schools in many ways, and especially through advancing the professional qualifications of teachers, was generally credited to the State of Massachusetts.

Professionalization

The early city superintendents of schools, often themselves at first strangers to the problems they would meet and the policies they would establish, were largely responsible for the development of school administration as a professional rather than as a lay vocation. Frank Spaulding,

[1] These cities were (in addition to Buffalo), Louisville, Providence, Springfield (Mass.), New Orleans, Rochester, Columbus, Syracuse, Baltimore, Cincinnati, Boston, Gloucester, New York City, San Francisco, Jersey City, Newark, Brooklyn (which was not then united with New York City), Cleveland, Chicago, St. Louis, St. Joseph, Indianapolis, Worcester, Milwaukee, Albany, Kansas City, and Washington, D.C.

William T. Harris in St. Louis, John D. Philbrick, in Boston, Andrew Sloan Draper in Cleveland, and others, gave a professional color to what had hitherto been a layman's calling. Draper, for example, taught the board of education in Cleveland that boards legislated but did not administer. He jealously reserved administration to himself.

The organization of the city superintendents into a professional society affiliated with the National Education Association did much to advance the prestige of the superintendency and to pioneer in the development of professional study in this field. Known first as the Department of Superintendence of the NEA, the organization is now the American Association of School Administrators. It now includes in its membership nearly all the local chief school administrators in the United States. Membership is now restricted to persons who have done approved work in professional preparation for school administration, a condition which the founders of the association could not have met.

Professional Literature The demand for preparation by superintendents and prospective superintendents led to the inauguration of courses in school administration in both undergraduate and graduate schools. In the early 1900's a thin trickle of books on the subject began to emerge. Of these, the series by Elwood P. Cubberley on school administration, supervision of instruction, organization and administration of a school, and other topics were particularly notable. Those were the pioneering days when one author could encompass nearly the whole field of public education in his writings. Soon the trickle of books on administration became a flood. Several are now published every week. Two magazines designed primarily for administrators, *The Nation's Schools* and the *American School Board Journal,* have grown prosperous from a large volume of advertising. When the AASA holds its annual meeting at Atlantic City there is a huge exhibit of all types of school equipment and publications.

The Principalship The elementary and secondary school principalships have gone through a professional evolution comparable to the superintendency. When the one-room school grew into a graded school of several rooms, someone had to be placed in charge of supplies and immediate problems. This was at first a head teacher who might have been paid a token stipend for these extra duties. From this humble beginning developed the principalship. For some decades, the possession of a teacher's certificate was enough to qualify one for a principalship, but in recent years many states have required a special administrative certificate based upon successful experience as a teacher and graduate study in professional subjects. These requirements vary greatly from state to state.

Expansion of State Departments

Often, the early state superintendents did their own clerical work. Gradually, as the state assumed more and more control over the schools, this one-man office expanded into a wonderful bureaucracy of associate superintendents, assistant superintendents, division chiefs, directors of bureaus, etc. etc. Every new function authorized for the state department of education necessarily meant the expansion of the administrative and supervisory staff. In the better organized states, staff members have the security of civil service status, but in others there is a great turnover following elections.

The extent of the personnel and the services provided varies greatly from state to state. In several states, the staff is relatively small and the services are limited. On the other hand, the more populous states have greatly expanded staffs and services.

Superintendents and Commissioners

The first chief state school administrators were appointed or elected officers to whom the state's general school responsibilities were assigned ex officio, as part of their administrative job. Gideon Hawley in New York, Horace Mann in Massachusetts, and Henry Barnard in Connecticut and Rhode Island were appointive officers. Barnard, when he returned to Connecticut from Rhode Island, had an ex officio assignment as superintendent, along with his appointment as state normal school principal. After Hawley was dismissed in 1821, the duties of the office were assigned ex officio to the secretary of state until 1854, when a new state office, superintendent of public instruction, was created. This office existed until 1904, when the legislature unified the department of public instruction and the Regents of the University of the State of New York into one body. The new chief professional officer in New York was then known as the commissioner of education and president of the University of the State of New York. The first commissioner was Andrew Sloan Draper, who was superintendent of public instruction from 1886 to 1892, until he became superintendent of schools in Cleveland, Ohio, and then president of the University of Illinois.

The chief officers of other states are variously known as commissioners of education, state superintendent of public instruction, or state superintendent of schools. Some, as in California and several western states, are still elected on a political ballot. Some, as in Pennsylvania, are appointed by the governor. Some are appointed by a state board of education, somewhat removed from direct political influence. Many authorities agree that the last method calls forth abler persons and results in the best kind of administration. The New York commissionership is much less political than the office in other states.

Growing State Aid

Except for relatively small grants from permanent state school funds, most of the schools in the nineteenth century were supported primarily from local funds raised principally by real estate taxes. As the states continued to raise their educational standards, it was discovered that some areas were too poor to afford the schools that the state required. In order to assure all the children of the state, wherever they were, a reasonably acceptable grade of education, state aid was greatly expanded. Often these grants were dependent upon certain matching funds from the local sources, or they were dependent upon the adoption of certain practices. To encourage the centralization or consolidation of small districts into larger units, the states made it financially tempting for local units to combine.

Elaborate formulae for the distribution of state funds were worked out with the aid of such experts as Professor Paul Mort of Teachers College, Columbia University. Many such terms as "foundation program," "reimbursement fraction," and others came into common usage.[2]

The amount and proportion of state aid varies greatly from state to state. In the agrarian states of the Great Plains and of the South, where most of the wealth is still in land and buildings, the percentage of state aid remains small. In states where much of the wealth is in industry, securities, and wages, the state aid is larger, for taxes on these sources are more effectively administered by a state than by a smaller community. State subsidies are often accompanied by state income or sales tax levies.

[2] A new state aid program in New York in 1962 was designed so that a district of average wealth would receive 49% of its operating expenses up to $500 per weighted average daily attendance. The formula was

$$\text{aid ratio} = 1.00 - \frac{\text{valuation per resident child in district}}{\text{state average valuation per child}} \times .51$$

U.S. Office of Education   Up to 1867,
the United States was one of the few major nations of the world
without a national ministry of education. The reason for this lack
was the fact that here education was a state rather than a national
responsibility. With the support of the National Association of State
and City School Superintendents and the National Teachers' Association, Congress in 1867 created a department of education, but
the next year this was reduced to a bureau in the department of
the interior. Subsequently, it shifted from one status to another, and
is now designated as the Office of Education in the Department of
Health, Education, and Welfare. From the beginning, the chief has
been known as the commissioner of education.

In the early years of the bureau, its work was primarily statistical.
Its meager appropriation permitted only the gathering and dissem-
inating of information. As first commissioner, Henry Barnard (1867–
1870) began this tradition. Neither he nor William T. Harris was
successful in coping with the political situation in Washington.
Their successors over the years have also had their difficulties with
Congress and the administration. There is little tenure or stability
in the commissionership. Within recent years no one has held the
office sufficiently long to make any impression on the schools of the
nation. Agitation for the establishment of a separate department of
education with cabinet status has never produced results. Within
recent years, the federal grants to education through the Smith-
Hughes act, the federal assistance to federally influenced areas, the
National Defense Education Act, and grants for research have multiplied the work of the office and resulted in its expansion. Nonetheless, it does not rank in importance with national ministries of
education abroad.

Federal Aid to Education   While federal aid
to the general education programs of the states is still a very controversial issue, there have been a growing number of precedents
for such a policy. All the precedents, however, have been piecemeal
grants for specific purposes. Instances of federal aid for specific purposes include the land-grant provisions for common schools and
higher education, as instituted in the Northwest Ordinance and subsequently applied to new states upon their admission to the union;
the distribution of surplus revenue in 1837; the Morrill Act granting
federal land to provide for agricultural and mechanical colleges; the
second Morrill Act of 1890 granting cash subsidies to the A. and M.
colleges; the Smith-Hughes and related acts to subsidize vocational

and home economics instruction in secondary schools; the educational subsidy of returned veterans after World War II and the Korean War; and the National Defense Education Act to upgrade the teaching of mathematics, science, and the foreign languages.

There have been various other proposals for federal aid and control for education. The most radical was a bill introduced into Congress by George F. Hoar, representative from Massachusetts in 1870, to provide for federal control of education in the states of the late Confederacy. The president would be authorized to appoint a state superintendent in each state, and federal officers would be empowered to prescribe texts, select teachers, and collect local taxes. This bill was so contrary to any precedent that even a vindictive Congress refused to inflict it upon the former enemy states. In 1881, Senator Henry W. Blair introduced a bill to grant federal aid to the states in proportion to their degree of illiteracy, but this was never passed.

The issue of federal aid then became somnolent until World War I showed glaring deficiencies in American education, as measured by the performance of draftees on intelligence tests. The National Education Association then began to agitate the issue of federal aid. Bills for this purpose have been introduced into nearly every Congress since, but have never passed both houses. Opposition has largely centered in the Chamber of Commerce of the United States, the National Association of Manufacturers, and some Roman Catholic organizations. Generally, Southern legislators (whose areas would get proportionately more federal aid) have been enthusiastic supporters of federal aid, while representatives from the industrial areas of greater wealth have more frequently been opposed. The federal activities in the desegregation of racial schools have spurred a resistance in the South to federal aid, for there is fear that it might be associated with desegregation. Some form of general aid from federal funds seems inevitable, but it may continue to be blocked for some years. By consulting current lay and professional periodicals (indexed in *Readers' Guide to Periodical Literature* and in *Education Index*) the reader may bring history up to date, for there is much current writing and discussion of this subject.

Who Controls Education?

What is done in a school and how it is done is a product of several influences: the state education laws and the regulations made to implement these laws; local regulations not contrary to the state laws; court decisions which interpret the laws and at times declare them unconstitutional;

and local customs and traditions. Each of these is a potent factor. Sometimes, of course, local regulations and customs are contrary to state laws and court decisions, but they persist until they are challenged in each individual instance. It is obvious now that the segregation of pupils into separate schools on the basis of race is unconstitutional, for the United States Supreme Court has so decreed, but segregation still persists in many areas.

Many persons are not fully aware of the fact that laws say what the courts declare that they say. We have had many instances throughout American educational history in which the tides of education have been dammed or released by court decisions. The best known of these cases are the Dartmouth College case, decided by the United States Supreme Court, and the Kalamazoo case, decided by the Michigan Supreme Court.

There have been many additional cases, including the decision of 1954 by the federal high court declaring racial segregation at any level of public education unconstitutional; the *McCollum* v. *Board of Education* case in which religious instruction in a public school was declared unconstitutional; cases in which free bus transportation of pupils to parochial schools was permitted; other cases in which purchase from public funds of nonreligious texts for use in parochial schools was found constitutional; numerous cases in state courts regarding the liability of school districts for accidents suffered by children, and many others.

Since courts often reflect the social climate in which they function, a subsequent court in another case may reverse the decision of a previous court. The most notable example was the reversal of the educational implication of *Plessy* v. *Ferguson* by the 1954 desegregation decision. Another example is the reversal of an 1854 decision by a Maine court that a child could legally be expelled from school for refusing to read the Bible, against which he or his parents had an objection.

Principle of Lay Control   It is a
fundamental principle of American school administration that the schools are controlled by laymen, not by professional educators. This is a principle that students often find hard to understand. The laws governing education are made by legislative bodies composed of laymen. State boards of education are composed of laymen. Local boards are similarly constituted. The school administrators and the teachers are bound by these laws and local regulations not contrary to them. A local board still has authority to set reasonable and non-

discriminatory regulations in excess of the minimum mandated by state law. If the state law states that school shall be in session for at least 180 days, the local board has the right to require a reasonable number beyond that. The local board can set certification standards for its teachers higher than those set by the state.

. The principle of lay control, which grew up unplanned out of the peculiar localism prevalent in the early national period, is at once a democratic safeguard and also a hindrance to educational progress. Since the professional group is controlled by the lay authority, the interest of the people in their schools is safeguarded. Not uncommon, however, is a local district's refusal to improve its schools, or its insistence on legislating what is the "truth" to be taught. If the majority on the lay board favors isolationism, any mention of the United Nations may be prohibited in the schools. A member of the Indiana state textbook commission, a few years ago, proposed to forbid any books mentioning Robin Hood or the Quakers, on the grounds that Robin was a Communist (in that he stole from the rich and gave to the poor), and that the Quakers were un-American in their pacifism. Another board in 1962 restored the McGuffey readers to the elementary schools of their district.

State Sovereignty Though the state has seen fit to create school districts and to endow them with considerable authority, the state remains educationally sovereign. If the

A cartoon depicting the possibility of selfish lay groups forcing their pet educational theories upon the schools by coercion.

legislature saw fit, it could change district boundaries or abolish districts as it saw fit. A practical illustration of the state's asserting its sovereignty was in the Watervliet, New York, case in 1897. Because of a factional dispute, the board of education was deadlocked, two to two, and the school did not open. The state superintendent, maintaining that school had to be kept, sent in his own staff to run the school. The court upheld this action on the grounds that the state constitution placed the state government in the position of insuring education to all the children of the state. Further, it said that since common schools were the concern of all the people of the whole state and not of the districts alone, the state was obligated to see that this matter of common concern was implemented. Since the local authority had failed in its duty, the state's responsibility was clear and unmistakable. In Pennsylvania, the state superintendent has sent in deputies at various times to administer schools which have been unable to meet their financial obligations.

For Further Reading

Babbidge, Homer D. and Robert M. Rosenzweig. *Federal Interest in Education.* McGraw-Hill, 1962.

A survey of federal interest and participation in education.

Conant, James B. *The Child, Parent, and the State.* Harvard University Press, 1960.

Relation of government to public education, our national needs in education, the citizen's responsibility; prophesy that a century hence the American high school will be regarded as a great contribution our age made to American democracy.

Council of State Governments. *The Forty-Eight State School Systems.* Council of State Governments, 1949.

The role of the continental states in education. Status of education and policies in the various states.

Gross, Neal. *Who Runs Our Schools?* John Wiley, 1958.

What Massachusetts superintendents say about the power structure in the control of education. Who supports the schools? Who blocks them? What are the pressures? Why do people aspire to be members of school boards?

Marsh, Paul E. and Ross A. Gortner. *Federal Aid to Science Education: Two Programs.* Syracuse University Press, 1963.

The federally aided programs in science. History, operation and results.

Miner, Jerry. *Social and Economic Factors in Spending for Public Education.* Syracuse University Press, 1963.

Socioeconomic characteristics of communities and their relation to community spending for education.

Munger, Frank J. and Richard F. Fenno, Jr. *National Politics and Federal Aid to Education.* Syracuse University Press, 1962.

Controversy over federal aid to education, the issues, special interests involved, various congressional actions, why a broad bill has not been passed, prospects for the future.

Reeves, Charles E. *School Boards: Their Status, Functions and Activities.* Prentice Hall, 1954.

Legal status of boards, methods of selection, board organizations, functions, development of local control, relation of board to school personnel.

Reeder, Ward G. *School Boards and Superintendents.* Revised. Macmillan, 1954.

A manual on problems they may face, written for school board members.

Reller, Theodore L. *Development of the City Superintendency of Schools in the United States.* The author, 1935.

A thorough study of the establishment of superintendencies in several American cities. Pioneers in this office and their contributions to the development of school administration.

Sufrin, Sidney C. *Administering the National Defense Education Act.* Syracuse University Press, 1963.

Application of NDEA to public elementary and secondary schools.

Sufrin, Sidney C. *Issues in Federal Aid to Education.* Syracuse University Press, 1962.

Problems of administration, goals and standards, which will face federal, state and local districts in any federal aid program.

Wasserman, William. *Education Price and Quantity Indexes.* Syracuse University Press, 1963.

Application of price-quantity indices to education at local, state and national levels.

White, Alpheus L. *Local School Boards: Organization and Practices.* U.S. Office of Education Bulletin, 1962, No. 8.

Latest study of school directors: membership characteristics, board organization, meetings, policies, compensation, problems, their education, occupations, etc.

18

Professional Organizations of Teachers

Present Organizations The annual directory of national and state education associations published by the United States Office of Education contains more than 100 pages of type smaller than that used in this volume. The list contains only the names of the associations, their office addresses, the names of the president and secretary, and the titles of their official publications. To these should be added an even larger number of local associations. It is apparent that there is no shortage of organizations, general and specific, to serve all the diverse interests in education at the present time. The broad distribution of these organizations reflects the widespread tendency for persons with similar interests to join together to serve their mutual interests. We cannot, in the space of one chapter, enter into the history of each of these organizations, nor would it be profitable for us to do so. We can, however, make some general observations and trace certain trends showing how these organizations have brought their influence to bear upon educational institutions, educational procedures, and educational philosophies.

In general, these organizations separate themselves into various categories. First, there are national and state associations, comprehensive in character, which are general organizations. Second, there are national and state associations limited to a particular segment of the educational process. Third, there are local associations, sometimes independent, and sometimes affiliated with a national or state association. Fourth, there is a category of honorary societies, some of which carry on active programs and some of which rest on their laurels.

American Institute of Instruction While there were some early voluntary associations of teachers on local levels, the first significant association in the United States was the American Institute of Instruction, organized in 1830. It was organized by "teachers and friends of education" at Boston. More than 300 persons, representing various education interests in eleven states, assembled for a four-day meeting in August. The constitution stated the purpose of the association as "the diffusion of useful knowledge in regard to education." At first, the annual meetings were all held in Boston, forty-nine of the first fifty being held there or elsewhere in New England.

The list of leaders in the institute is an honor roll of the men and women who were the pioneer propagandists and explorers in American education: Amos Bronson Alcott, the Concord philosopher and founder of the Temple School which followed Pestalozzian procedures; Henry Barnard, the scholar of the common school revival and editor of the *American Journal of Education*; James G. Carter, the protagonist of free common schools and of normal schools; Samuel J. May, abolitionist and principal of a normal school; Horace Mann, secretary of the Massachusetts board of education; Lowell T. Mason, who introduced music into the public schools; Julia Ward Howe, author of "Battle Hymn of the Republic"; Samuel Gridley Howe, founder of institutions for the blind; Elizabeth Peabody, who conducted the first English-language kindergarten; John D. Philbrick, superintendent of schools in Boston; David P. Page, principal of the first normal school in New York, and many others.

The American Institute of Instruction was a meeting place of practicing teachers and of public-spirited men and women who were interested in education as a part of the great humanitarian crusade. The fundamental purpose of the organization was advocacy of educational reform, both in expansion of the schools and in curricular development. Much of the leadership came from the members who were not practicing as professional teachers. Only incidental mention was made of teacher status or welfare.

American Lyceum Association   Josiah Holbrook had organized a series of lyceums in Massachusetts and Connecticut to agitate for improvement in the common schools, to provide for adult education through lectures and classes, and to organize libraries and museums. By 1831, there were more than 900 local lyceum associations in the United States. Movements toward a national association of these local groups culminated in the founding of the American Lyceum Association in 1831. Its constitution stated that the purpose of the national association was to secure these conditions for good education: better legislative provisions for free schools, improvement of qualifications of teachers, closer relationship between schools and colleges, improvement of instruction and discipline, introduction of natural science into the schools, encouragement of better education for "females," and the supplying of books and teaching apparatus to the schools.

At the first national meeting in New York City, Stephen Van Rensselaer, founder of the institution which later grew into Rensselaer Polytechnic Institute, presided over representatives from seven states. This and succeeding meetings discussed such topics as school discipline, use of the Bible in common schools, the monitorial system of instruction, introduction of natural science into the common schools, and the study of physiology. There being no text in physiology suitable for schools, the lyceum offered $300 as a prize for the best manuscript. Comparative education was the topic at a later meeting. Congress was petitioned to insert a question in the next census to find out how many children between the ages of seven and sixteen had received no elementary education.

There is no record of meetings of the American Lyceum Association after 1840. Apparently, individual local lyceums continued primarily as sponsors of lecture series for some years, and then gradually merged into the comparable Chautauqua movement.

Both the American Institute of Instruction and the American Lyceum Association were organizations of persons with broadly humanitarian views, who saw education as an agency of social amelioration and moral regeneration. Both organizations enrolled teachers, but they were not primarily associations of practicing teachers.

Two Other Associations   Two other associations designed to be national in character showed some signs of becoming significant influences, but their contribution was only temporary. The first of these was the Western College of Professional Teachers, organized in 1831 at Cincinnati. (Here "college" was used in its historic sense meaning association, as in college of cardinals, for example.) Unfortunately, it never transcended sectional interests, being too remote from eastern centers of population. In 1849, the American Association for the Advancement of Education[1] was formed in Philadelphia under the presidency of Horace Mann, but it never succeeded in enlisting actual teachers in any responsible number.

[1] Not to be confused with the Society for the Advancement of Education which publishes *School and Society,* a biweekly magazine in education.

State Associations   In 1845 and
1846, the grammar school teachers in Massachusetts and Connecticut
withdrew from the American Institute of Instruction to form their
own associations. In 1845, Rhode Island and New York teachers
also organized state associations. By 1857, there were fifteen state
associations including (in addition to Massachusetts, Connecticut,
Rhode Island, and New York) organizations in Ohio, Vermont,
Michigan, Pennsylvania, Wisconsin, Illinois, New Jersey, Iowa, New
Hampshire, Indiana and Missouri. In relation to the total number
of teachers, the membership was small. Many teachers had not yet
become sufficiently interested in their calling to feel any obligation
to be members. This was particularly true when teaching was easy to
enter and easy to leave. The development of a professional attitude
had to await the preparation of a professional corps of teachers. To
some extent, too, the county institute served as a substitute for a
teachers' association, and there was the advantage of not having dues.

With indifferent success, most of the state associations attempted
to maintain journals. Few, however, assumed any financial responsibility, leaving it to the editor to make out as best he could.
In some instances, the state superintendent of public instruction
designated the journal of the state association as his official publication.

National Teachers Association   None of the
four pioneer associations having fulfilled their early expectation of
becoming national associations for teachers, persons interested in
a national movement tried again. Thomas W. Valentine and Daniel
B. Hagar, presidents of the New York and Massachusetts state
organizations, along with presidents of eight other state associations,
issued a call for a convention to meet in Philadelphia in 1857 to
organize a national association. The invitation was issued to "practical school men"—meaning those with a direct connection with the
schools. The call read:

> The eminent success which has attended the establishment and
> operations of the several teachers' associations in the states of this
> country is the source of mutual congratulations among all friends
> of popular education. To the direct agency and the diffused in-
> fluence of these associations, more, perhaps than to any other
> cause, are due the manifest improvement of schools in all their
> relations, the rapid intellectual and social elevation of teachers
> as a class, and the vast development of public interest in all that
> concerns the education of the young.

That the state associations have already accomplished great good, and that they are destined to exert a still broader and more beneficent influence, no wise observer will deny.

Believing that what has been accomplished for the states by state associations may be done for the whole country by a National Association, we, the undersigned, invite our fellow-teachers throughout the United States to assemble in Philadelphia on the 26th day of August next, for the purpose of organizing a National Teachers' Association.

We cordially extend this invitation to all practical teachers in the North, the South, the East, and the West, who are willing to unite in a general effort to promote the general welfare of our country by concentrating the wisdom and power of numerous minds, and distributing among all the accumulated experiences of all; who are ready to devote their energies and their means to advance the dignity, respectability, and usefulness of their calling; and who, in fine, believe that the time has come when the teachers of the nation should gather into one great educational brotherhood.

As the permanent success of any association depends very much upon the auspices attending its establishment, and the character of the organic laws it adopts, it is hoped that all parts of the Union will be largely represented at the inauguration of the proposed enterprise.

The first constitution contained this noble statement of the proposed objectives of the association:

To elevate the character and advance the interests of the profession of teaching, and to promote the cause of popular education in the United States, we, whose names are subjoined, agree to adopt the following constitution.

Forty-three members signed the constitution thus forming the parent organization to the modern National Education Association. While membership was limited to "gentlemen," two women were, inexplicably if chivalrously, allowed to sign. Women were allowed to be honorary members, but if they had anything to say, they had to submit it "in the form of written essays" which would then be read by the secretary or by some male member selected by the writer. Nearly half the founders went home as officers: there were a president, a vice president, a secretary, a treasurer, and one counselor from each state represented.

The second meeting of the National Teachers Association was held at Cincinnati in 1858. Only five members attended, but a new membership to the extent of seventy-five was recruited from the invited guests. One of the speakers summarized educational progress to date. The twelve most important developments, he said, were the founding of state departments of education, normal schools, and teachers institutes; the work of the state teachers associations; the multiplication of books on education; publication of educational journals; improvement in textbooks; construction of better schoolhouses; grading of schools; education of women; steps in the training of the deaf, blind, and feeble-minded. Horace Mann attacked parochial schools, but the members resolved "that all teachers, whether in colleges, academies, public, private, or parochial schools . . . be regarded by us as brethren and fellow laborers in a common cause." The association was invited to the wine cellars of Mr. Longworth, a leading citizen; whether to look or to imbibe, the record does not say.

A Small Association   When one thinks of the National Education Association, he thinks of a vast organization with nearly 1,000,000 members, an extensive headquarters staff and a magnificent headquarters building in Washington, D.C. costing more than $5,000,000. This is the association today, but its beginnings were very modest. It took sixteen years for the membership to pass the 200 mark; sixty-one years to pass the 10,000 mark. Only in 1922 did the membership pass 100,000. For many years, there was no permanent office; the secretary, whoever it might be, maintained it in his own home. Foundation of a journal had been discussed in 1859 but the motion was tabled and it lay on the table until 1920.

The National Education Association   After some years under the name of the National Teachers Association, the members in 1870 voted to change the name to National Educational Association. Later the "Educational" was changed to "Education." The scope of the association was expanded by the admission of three other organizations as departments, namely the American Normal School Association, which became a department; the National Association of School Superintendents, which became the Department of Superintendence, only to change its name in 1937 to the American Association of School Administrators; and the Central College Association, which became the Department of Higher Education. In addition to these absorbed departments, the NEA created a new one for elementary education.

Annual Conventions   Except for the
war years of 1861 and 1862 and the postwar years of 1867, 1878,
and 1906, the association met each year. During the period 1943 to
1949, only the representative assembly or the board of directors met.

At the Indianapolis meeting in 1866, the word "person" was substituted for the word "gentleman" in regard to eligibility for membership, so women were now able to become full-fledged members.
Eventually, in 1911, Ella Flagg Young, superintendent of schools
in Chicago, was elected president of the association. Arrangements
have been made since 1918 for the election of male and female presidents in alternate years. In recent years, of course, the main executive has been an executive secretary who normally holds office for a
long period of years. Indeed, there have been only three secretaries
since 1918.

Proceedings   The published reports
of the NEA, entitled the *Proceedings*, are a good mirror in which
to view the passing educational scene. Edgar B. Wesley in his authorized history of the association entitled *NEA: The First Hundred
Years* has drawn many interesting aspects of educational problems
from these *Proceedings* and other association papers. One can view
the rise and fall of various methods of teaching. One can see the
association campaign for a national university, advocate simplified
spelling and temperance, campaign for higher salaries and a single
salary schedule, promote international cooperation, and develop an
interest in educational research. In the proceedings are preserved the
educational views of outstanding educators of the generations succeeding one another: Horace Mann, Amos Bronson Alcott, William
Holmes McGuffey, Francis W. Parker, James P. Wickersham, Nicholas Murray Butler, Charles W. Eliot, John Dewey, John D. Philbrick, G. Stanley Hall, Elwood P. Cubberley, George D. Strayer,
William T. Harris (he addressed the association's conventions 145
times), and a host of others.

Affiliated Organizations   Throughout the years,
various educational organizations have affiliated with the NEA, and
new departments have been established within the organization.
Eighteen departments use the word "association," thirteen use "national," and four use "council" in their names, then adding "departments of the NEA." From time to time the departments change
their names and functions. Others are dropped when their emphasis

is no longer needed or when social and professional conditions change. Twenty-one of these departments maintain permanent staffs at the NEA headquarters in Washington. An assistant executive secretary of the NEA for professional relations coordinates the work of the NEA and the departments.

Among the interests of the various departments are school administration (chief administrators, elementary school principals, secondary school principals, administrative women, and women deans and counselors) , health and physical education, industrial arts, supervision and curriculum, home economics, vocational education, music, art, journalism, social studies, mathematics, science, speech, business education, teacher education, higher education, kindergarten-primary, rural education, exceptional children, adult education, research, audio-visual education, public relations, and classroom teaching. There are divisions for educational secretaries and for retired teachers.

Since the NEA sponsors Future Teachers of America on the secondary level and the Student Education Association on the college level, one could maintain a membership from one's teens to death.

National Education Association headquarters in Washington, D. C.

The largest department is the department of classroom teachers. Perhaps the most influential in American education is the American Association of School Administrators, whose annual meeting (usually in February at Atlantic City) is larger than the annual general NEA meeting.

State Associations   There is at least one state association affiliated with the NEA in each state. In some states, there are two—one for whites and one for Negroes. These state associations vary greatly in size, since the number of teachers vary in proportion to the population of the states. In the states with large memberships, the state association has a pattern of departments only less formidable than the NEA itself. Most of the state associations have headquarters as near the state capitol as they can get, so that the influence of the association can be felt when educational legislation is pending.

Local Associations   In many school districts there are local associations of teachers, often but not necessarily affiliated with the state association and the NEA. In urban areas, there are often two or more local associations, not necessarily proceeding in harmony. One of the principal functions of the local association is to represent the teachers in salary negotiations with the board of education. Some local associations maintain credit unions.

Zone Meetings   When membership of state associations became large, it was found desirable to have several meetings in various parts of the state so that more members could participate in the programs of the associations relatively near their homes. To some extent, these district meetings take the place of the old teachers' institute, providing general sessions for the presentation of well known speakers, and sectional meetings along the lines of special interests. In some states, these subdivisions are known as "zones," and in others as "convention districts."

Legislative Activities   *   From their early days both the NEA and the affiliated state associations have attempted to influence legislation, often with a high degree of success. The present major activity of the NEA is to secure enactment of national legislation for federal aid to the public schools. The state associations have had a major role in the establishment of minimum salary laws, tenure laws, teacher welfare legislation, and in general educational improvement.

Committees and Commissions The reader is already aware of the role of the NEA in appointing several committees and commissions to study problems in education and to recommend solutions. Particularly noteworthy have been the Committee of Ten on secondary education, the committee on the articulation of high school and college, and the commission on the reorganization of secondary education.

Not previously mentioned is the Educational Policies Commission, organized in 1935 to plan for education in the depression years and to speak the voice of education to the general public. The commission has issued a series of publications on the relation of education to public issues. Two volumes issued in 1944 and 1948 were entitled *Education for All American Youth* and *Education for All American Children.*

American Federation of Teachers Some teachers felt that the NEA was too genteel when times demanded more aggressive action. They charged that the NEA was founded by superintendents of schools and was used by them to keep teachers in line. They further charged that the NEA never developed a sufficiently vigorous program to improve the financial status of teachers. There was a feeling that a teachers' union rather than a professional association might be the answer.

In 1916, teachers from six cities met to form the American Federation of Teachers, which soon received a charter from the American Federation of Labor. When the AFL affiliated with the Congress of Industrial Organizations, the AFT joined the new affiliation, the AFL-CIO. Membership grew to perhaps 10,000 persons by 1920. This growth in membership seemed to threaten the NEA, which then undertook more aggressive representation of teachers. Undoubtedly, too, superintendents in some areas exerted influence to channel teachers away from the AFL viewpoint and into the NEA. By 1927, membership in AFT fell to about 3500.

The depression caused general unrest among teachers, and this was reflected in a gain in AFT membership, which grew to 55,000 in 1958. National legislation had opened the way to industry-wide bargaining over wages in industry, and apparently the labor union approach appealed to many teachers, particularly those in communities where there was a strong labor sentiment or where teachers

**Some of New York City's 40,000 school teachers demonstrating
during a strike called by the United Federation of Teachers.**

felt unjustly treated by the administrator or the board of education.

While the AFT constitution renounces the right of teachers to strike, the New York City members did participate in a strike against the schools in the early 1960's. While condemning this action, the NEA became more firm in its attitude and discussed employing "sanctions" against school districts which do not treat teachers justly.

In the next few years, there may be more conflict between the NEA and the AFT. Ultimately the teachers of America will have to decide whether they will follow the approach of a professional organization or the approach of a union, or some compromise between them.

American Association of University Professors   Though the NEA and the state associations affiliated with it aspire to represent all levels of education, they have made little appeal to college and university teachers. True, the NEA and various state associations have departments of higher education, but these enroll few members beyond professors of education and faculties of schools of education. Historically, college professors had had little concern with the public schools; they might think that college teaching was a profession, but they were quite sure that elementary and secondary school teaching were not. The fact that elementary and many secondary teachers were prepared in state normal schools and teachers colleges also widened the gap.

The orientation of most college professors seems still to be toward the learned societies in their own disciplines, such as chemistry, history, or mathematics. Apparently many of them prefer to be regarded as chemists or historians or mathematicians rather than as teachers.

Until 1915, there was no national organization in the professional field of education that appealed to these professors. In that year, the American Association of University Professors was organized, primarily to protect academic freedom of the professors and to encourage tenure protection. It has announced stands on these issues and will come to the defense of a professor summarily discharged without just cause. The only weapon the association has is the censure of a college board of trustees, the administration, or the college as a whole. Unless the college cares what the AAUP thinks about it, this is not a strong weapon.

Within recent years, the association has become more aggressive on the issues of faculty salaries. It now "grades" institutions each year in its *Bulletin* according to the amounts of faculty compensation, the grades ranging from AA to F. The association has never succeeded in enrolling a majority of the college faculty members in the country. The reason is hard to find. Some obviously think the association is too slender a reed. Some may be too timid to belong, fearing they might be considered liberal agitators. Others apparently see no need to join. The association's extreme timidity and caution during the McCarthy attacks on academic freedom alienated some.

There are state chapters of the AAUP, but they are loose organizations with little actively demonstrated power. There are local chapters on many campuses, but they do not enroll a majority of the teaching staffs.

Insurance, Annuity, and Retirement Plans   While they are not strictly professional organizations, some associations have become related to the profession through the development of various teachers' benefits; these are the Teachers Insurance and Annuity Association and the College Retirement Equities Fund. Their function is to provide annuity and insurance protection to teachers in institutions which have entered into contractual relationships with the association. Since teachers in public schools and public universities are generally covered by programs of state teachers' retirement systems or state employees' retirement systems, most of the patrons of TIAA and CREF are found in independent colleges and universities, independent schools, and educational foundations.

The beginnings of TIAA have their genesis in the philosophy and philanthropy of Andrew Carnegie. He had amassed a very great fortune, but came to believe that a man who died excessively rich died disgraced. He had already given $43,000,000 for more than 2500 library buildings, and was now searching for some other educational agency that needed financial support, for he believed that there was a vital link between education and democracy.

As a trustee of Cornell University, Carnegie was shocked "to find how small were the salaries of professors" and concluded that it would be extraordinarily difficult for a professor to set aside funds for his old age. All his money would not be enough to raise professors' salaries to any extent, but Carnegie believed he could furnish them pensions. He established the Carnegie Foundation for the Advancement of Teaching "to provide retiring pensions for the teachers of Universities, Colleges and Technical Schools" in the United States, Canada, and Newfoundland. The corporation drew up a list of institutions which met its criteria and announced it would grant pensions to the retired professors of these ninety-five colleges and universities.

It soon became apparent that Carnegie's grants of even $15,000,000 would not be sufficient to continue expanding the list. By 1958, the foundation had paid out more than $72,000,000 in free pensions, and many of the beneficiaries were still living and drawing funds.

With the advice of representatives of the American Association of University Professors, the Association of State Universities, the Association of American Universities, and the Association of American Colleges, the foundation decided that the proper solution would be a system of insurance and annuities available to all teaching employees in American higher institutions of learning. The program would need contributions of the teachers and of the colleges; it had to be on a contractual basis; it had to allow for teachers to move from one institution to another; and it had to be reasonably economical. In 1918, under the auspices of the Carnegie Foundation, a new corporation known as the Teachers Insurance and Annuity Association was founded. The Carnegie Foundation has supported the work of TIAA by grants to the total of $17,159,000.

An institution that meets its criteria enters into a contract with TIAA for insurance and retirement annuity coverage of its staff. Both the individual and the institution contribute toward the fund, on a regular basis, and when the individual reaches a stated retirement age, he draws his annuity in regular monthly installments. If he dies before retirement, the value of the accumulation is paid to his beneficiaries or to his estate. The amount of contribution varies from college to college. For years, the standard payment was five percent of one's salary, matched by another five percent paid by the institution. More generous contributions are now common. Many now total fifteen percent of the annual salary. Among the better colleges, the institution may pay the whole contribution. Each individual has a contract which remains his property if he moves to another college or if he leaves teaching altogether. Nearly 1000 junior colleges, colleges, universities, independent schools, and scientific and research foundations afford TIAA benefits.

All TIAA contributions and benefits are in terms of dollars. Since significant changes in the cost of living have been the rule in our free economy, there has been no assurance that the purchasing power of the dollar at retirement would be worth what one expected or hoped. In a time of depression, the dollar would purchase more than one expected; in a period of inflation, less. Since the fixed-dollar retirement income would, in an expanding economy, buy less, the TIAA hit upon the idea of allowing a portion of the contributions to be used in purchasing variable annuities, purchased and paid out in units based upon the fluctuating values of certain sound common stocks. To provide this type of contract, an affiliated organization known as College Retirement Equities Fund was established in 1952. One may not put more than half his contribution into this equity fund. Together, TIAA and CREF afford reasonable assurance of a retirement with an adequate income. In addition, TIAA sells life insurance and major medical insurance to qualified members of the teaching profession.

State Retirement Systems State and local retirement systems for teachers are relatively new in American education. Writing in Monroe's *Cyclopedia of Education* in 1918, two authors declared that relatively little had been done in the United States in pensioning teachers, in comparison with what had been achieved in leading European nations. Four types then in vogue in the United States were classified as private-voluntary, quasi-public, semi-public, and public. The private-voluntary were mutual benefit associations which were little more than sickness and burial associations operating through small membership dues, initiation fees, and special assessments. The quasi-public systems were based upon legislative authorization of the creation of funds through assessments equal to a percentage of teachers' salaries. Many municipal systems operated upon this principle in their formative years.

In the semi-public system, there were also deductions from teachers' salaries, but these deductions were supplemented by appropriations of public funds. A Wisconsin law of 1911, following this principle, required teachers to contribute one percent of their salaries for the first ten years of service and two percent thereafter. From the state mill tax, ten cents per capita of the school population was added to this fund. Annuities amounted to $12.50 for each year of service, with a maximum of $450.

The public system was a "true" pension system, operating automatically for all public school teachers. There were no contributions by the teachers. Both Maryland and Rhode Island had this system. After 35 years of service, a Rhode Island teacher could receive an annual pension of 50% of his annual salary up to $500.

In 1918, some type of pension or retirement system existed in 23 states. In some instances, they were state-wide, and in others they were limited to cities only.

Following the pioneering work of the Carnegie Corporation in the establishment of the Teachers Insurance and Annuity Association, pressures developed for the establishment of actuarily sound retirement systems for public school teachers as well. While there are variations from state to state, the better systems now provide that a teacher who has served 35 years and has reached the age of 65 may retire on approximately 50% of his salary over the five or ten best years of income. Generally, provision is made for earlier retirement by disabled teachers and for a joint annuity, at a smaller figure, for a teacher and his wife. In case of death prior to retirement, certain insurance provisions prevail. The funds are generally built up by contributions by the teachers, matched equally from local or state funds.

By 1961, sixty teacher retirement systems had invested funds of $7,300,000,000. Active members totaled more than 1,850,000. "Retirants"—that is, persons already receiving benefits—totaled just over 200,000. Annual income of these systems was more than $1,500,-000,000, and annual disbursements were more than $1,500,000,000. The median annual retirement allowance was $1,748. (Since this was based on salary scales lower than at present, the allowance may be expected to rise in ensuing years.)

Nearly a million members of state and local retirement systems were also covered by the federal social security system, with which many systems have been integrated.

Parent Teachers Association   With a membership of more than 12,000,000, the National Congress of Parents and Teachers is a potent allied organization of interest to teachers. This national organization, which has local associations in nearly every elementary school in the nation and in a smaller number of secondary schools, had its origin in the National Congress of Mothers, organized in Washington, D.C. in 1897. The name, National Congress of Parents and Teachers, was adopted in 1924.

Throughout the years, the association has been interested in all aspects of child welfare and education. Among the matters advocated by the association have been improvement of rural schools, international cooperation, aid to children during the depression of the 1930's, use of radio in education, automobile safety, citizenship education, juvenile delinquency, home-school cooperation, foreign relief, television, elimination of obscene literature from the mails, and many others.

The association's magazine, *The PTA Magazine*, helps to interpret the school and its changing program to the lay public. Programs are usually provided at the monthly meetings on the local school level. Many of these are very helpful in bringing teachers and parents together for the consideration of mutual problems. When the meeting is too much given to entertainment or to wrangling over small issues that should have been resolved by a committee, the effectiveness of the PTA disintegrates.

For Further Reading

Elsbree, Willard S. *The American Teacher*. American Book, 1939.

Chapter 33 for teachers' voluntary associations: NEA, AFT, state associations.

Lieberman, Myron. *The Future of Public Education*. University of Chicago Press, 1960.

Comparison of National Education Association and the American Federation of Teachers, by a partisan of the latter viewpoint. Chapter 9 deals with the records of the two organizations. Chapter 5 is entitled "The Myth of the Teaching Profession."

National Education Association. *NEA Handbook.*

An annual publication of the NEA containing detailed information about this association, its departments, and affiliated state associations. NEA charter, by-laws, code of ethics, directory, etc.

Wesley, Edgar B. *NEA: The First 100 Years.* National Education Association, 1957.

Founding, development and policies of the National Education Association.

19

Freedom in Education

Security vs. Freedom A democracy is constantly faced, in time of stress, with striking a nice balance between the need for national security and its historical aspiration for freedom of thought. We live in such a period at the present, so the freedom of thought and the freedom of teaching to influence that thought are vital national issues. However, this is not a new issue, for our history reflects many attempts, often very successful, to restrict the freedom of teachers.

Historically, the right of a member of the university world to conduct research and to disclose his interpretation of his findings to his students and to the general public has been known as academic freedom. By general usage, this term has also been applied to a correlative right on the part of teachers in schools of lower grade.

Teachers in elementary and secondary schools have never had unlimited freedom in the selection of their teaching materials, in the methods they employ, or in the emphases they wish to make. Because of the interrelatedness of the schools to the societies in which they exist, there have always been overt or implicit restrictions upon the freedom of the teacher. Such restrictions may be on his professional life or on his personal life, or both. While a changing society has been willing, when changing its mores, to accord more personal freedom to the teacher in his out-of-school life as a citizen, there has been great reluctance to grant equal freedom on the professional side.

Colonial Religious Orthodoxy From early colonial times, society insisted upon orthodoxy on the part of teachers at all levels. In the New England schools, only true believers in the Calvinistic Puritanism were allowed to teach. Even the first president of Harvard, Henry Dunster, was removed from office because his views on the baptism of infants varied from the views of the dominant clergy of Massachusetts. Teachers in New Netherlands had to meet the religious tests of the Reformed Church. Teachers sent out by the Home and Colonial School Society and the Society for the Propagation of the Gospel in Foreign Parts had to have the approval of Anglican clergy as to their religious orthodoxy. Until comparatively recent times, even in the nonsectarian public schools, school board members in hiring teachers have been interested in the religious affiliations of the candidates. The passage of fair employment practices acts in several states have made inquiries into a candidate's race, color, religion, or politics illegal, but surreptitiously such inquiries are still made.

Political and Economic Pressures   Attempts to restrict a teacher's religious views were only one facet of the determination by society or sub-groups in the society to assure orthodoxy in the schools. Other orthodoxies involved were in the political and economic spheres.

The teachers in colonial America, of course, were expected to be loyal to the royal establishment. When the Revolution broke out, a new orthodoxy was enforced. Myles Cooper, president of King's College and a Loyalist, fled half-dressed over the college fence and and sought refuge on a sloop bound for England. Teachers of all grades were now supposed to support the cause of independence. Those who refused were not allowed to teach.

Following the Revolution, many of the writers in the essay contest of the American Philosophical Society believed that education should be designed to serve national ends by preparing people for republican citizenship. There was talk of using the schools to convert the populace into "republican machines."

The next attempt to suppress teachers came with the rise of the anti-slavery movement; the pressures were both political and economic. Conservative Northern businessmen who were profiting from a lucrative trade with the Southern states wanted no agitation or practice that would interfere with the status quo. This explains the forcible removal of the Noyes Academy, which admitted Negro students, from Canaan, New Hampshire, and the closing of Prudence Crandall's school for colored girls at Canterbury, Connecticut. It also explains the Connecticut law of 1833 prohibiting the setting up of "any school, academy, or literary institution for the instruction or education of colored persons who are not inhabitants of this State . . . without the consent in writing, first obtained, of a majority of the civil authority, and also of the selectmen of the town."

Three abolitionist professors were forced to resign at the Western Reserve College in Ohio. Benjamin S. Hedrick was dismissed from the faculty of the University of North Carolina for radicalism—i.e., membership in the Republican party. His fellow faculty members hastened to pass a resolution to the effect that "the political opinions expressed are not those entertained by any other member of this body." Dr. Lyman Beecher and his trustees forbade the holding of abolitionist meetings at the Lane Theological Seminary in Cincinnati, with the result that most of the theological students withdrew.

Horace Mann, who himself believed ardently in the abolitionist cause, cautioned the Rev. Samuel May, one of his normal school principals, never again to take his normal school students to an abolitionist meeting. Apparently he felt that their being seen there would cause a hostile reaction toward the normal schools.

During the Populist revolt of the 1880's, the whole faculty of the University of Kansas was dismissed for adhering to staunch Republican doctrine after the Populists had captured the state government. Elsewhere, faculty were dismissed for upholding the cause of the Populists.

Orthodoxy vs. Evolution During the latter part of the last century, the inroads on freedom of teaching centered around reaction toward the doctrine of evolution. In 1884, Professor James Woodrow was forced to resign from the South Carolina Presbyterian Seminary for teaching this doctrine. In the church colleges, many controversies arose, and dismissals were common. One of the last spasms was a case in the public schools of Tennessee in 1925. The state had a law forbidding the teaching of evolution:

Section 1. Be it enacted by the general assembly of the State of Tennessee, That it shall be unlawful for any teacher in any of the universities, normals, and all other public schools of the state, which are supported in whole or in part by the public school funds of the state, to teach any theory that denies the story of the divine creation of man, as taught in the Bible, and to teach instead that man has descended from a lower order of animals.

Section 2. Be it further enacted, That any teacher found guilty of the violation of this act, shall be guilty of a misdemeanor and upon conviction shall be fined not less than one hundred dollars and not more than five hundred dollars for each offense.

Section 3. Be it further enacted, That this act take effect from and after its passage, the public welfare requiring it.

A cartoon at the time of the John T. Scopes trial in Tennessee. "Gathering data for the Tennessee trial."

In the Dayton High School, a biology teacher, John T. Scopes, deliberately taught the theory as a test of the law. The American Civil Liberties Union, with Clarence Darrow and Dudley Field Malone (two liberal attorneys of national stature), came to his defense. William Jennings Bryan, perennial campaigner for the presidency and the strongest orator of the fundamentalists, hastened to the attack. Thus a trial in an obscure county seat became a great circus to divert the world in the summer of 1925. "The monkey trial," as it was commonly called, attracted international attention. Scopes was found guilty and resigned from teaching. Twenty-five years later, Judge John T. Raulston, then at the age of 84, said the statute (still on the books) (now taken off the books) was wholesome and should be strictly enforced.

The Fear of Socialism
The latter part of the nineteenth century and the first years of the twentieth witnessed a tremendous growth of capitalism. Small industries mushroomed into great industrial giants. Combines and trusts, often ruthless in the exploitation of labor and in the amassing of great

wealth, became interested in protecting their rights and privileges against social criticism. When this criticism arose in the colleges and, to a modest extent, in the public school texts, repressive measures were brought to bear against these alleged "anarchists" and "revolutionists." There are numerous indications of such attempts to influence teaching. The president of Brown University was so severely criticized for his monetary views that he found his position untenable and resigned. A professor at Stanford University was forced to resign because Mrs. Stanford disapproved of his economic opinions. In 1914, Scott Nearing was dismissed from the University of Pennsylvania because he had irritated manufacturers by campaigning against child labor. The number of such dismissals led to the organization of the American Association of University Professors to protect academic freedom in institutions of higher education.

The dismissal of college professors usually attracted wider attention than the discharge of public school teachers. The dismissals were not the most serious consequence; probably of even graver import was the timidity and colorless teaching induced by fear of dismissal. Some teachers are sufficiently timid that they discard their professional integrity and bow to all kinds of pressures to "keep them in line."[1] They are not necessarily conscious of professional hypocrisy; sometimes they rationalize their conduct as good judgment.

Historically, the power to examine teachers before employment (a necessary and desirable right) has put into the hands of school boards and administrators the power to select "safe" candidates or to give subtle indications that only conforming teachers will be retained. The most extreme case, many years ago, involved a candidate who had been asked by a school trustee whether he taught that the world was flat or round. The candidate, desperate for a job, replied "I know *both* ways. Which one do *you want* taught here?" Teachers of the social studies have often been queried as to their social, economic, and political views.

Teacher Tenure   It was unconscionable pressures upon the teacher's professional integrity and upon his rights as a citizen that led the National Education Association and its affiliated state associations to demand the enactment of teacher tenure laws. An additional contributing factor in some areas of the United States was corruption on the part of school directors who

---

[1] One critic said he didn't know whether they were rabbits because they were teachers, or became teachers because they were rabbits.

demanded bribes in return for their votes in the annual election of
teachers to positions. In the coal regions of Pennsylvania this was a
rather common practice. In 1962, two school directors in Bristol
Township, Bucks County, Pennsylvania, were convicted and sen-
tenced to jail for plotting to sell two school principalships. Had they
not been protected by tenure, the two teachers involved would
scarcely have dared to bring charges against directors on the board.

Within the present century, an increasing number of states enacted
teacher tenure laws. These laws normally provide for the attainment
of tenure after two or three years of satisfactory service, a public
hearing in case dismissal is contemplated, and the right of the teacher
to the services of counsel. Specific causes for dismissal are usually
stated. Such causes are immoral or unprofessional conduct, incompe-
tency, persistent refusal to obey state education law or regulations of
the board of education, neglect of duty, or dishonesty. There is no
doubt that teachers have greatly been protected by such tenure laws.
The laws, unfortunately, have another less healthy aspect, for some
teachers, protected by tenure, have abused the privilege by resting
on their oars and doing as little as possible. After one or two attempts
to remove a teacher for incompetence, some administrators give up
and tolerate slackness in their schools.[2]

Censorship of Textbooks   There have been
numerous protests against the textbooks used in the schools, resulting in pressures upon the authors to change what they have written,
and upon school boards to discontinue the use òf books which are
found offensive by certain groups in the community. This has been
particularly true in the realm of literature, biology, and the social
studies. Indeed, textbooks are sometimes selected not on the basis
of their merit but on the basis of their nonoffensive characteristics.
The result is a sort of bland pablum, sticking to noncontroversial
materials.

After the Civil War, pressure was put upon textbook publishers
to make sure that their books in the field of American History were
"correct." Of course, what was deemed "correct" depended upon
which side of the Mason and Dixon line the schools were on. In
the South, veterans' organizations and the Daughters of the Confederacy were active pressure groups. In the North, the Grand Army
of the Republic policed the books to make sure the victory they had
won in the field would not evaporate in the schoolrooms.

[2] An administrator said to the author: "I've been through it twice. In both cases,
the teacher's smart lawyer made me look like a fool. I'll put up with a lot before
I ever try it again."

Physiology texts of the 1890's and subsequent decades showed the influence of the Woman's Christian Temperance Union. Two widely used texts in biology in the 1930's made no mention of evolution. Books in community civics were rewritten under pressure of utility corporations.

Both the resurgence of Anglophobism and development of the "red scare" of the 1920's led to a movement to purify the history books. In a climate where the mayor of Chicago could win votes by declaring he would not receive the King of England if he visited that city, and where the attorney general of the United States was deporting hundreds of alleged radicals, the schools could not escape investigation. Sparked by a series of exposures in the Hearst press, which declared that historians were perverting history in the interests of England, patriotic societies attacked the history texts. Under pressure, respected historians such as Van Tyne, McLaughlin, and Muzzey rewrote their works to omit references to John Hancock's smuggling activities, Hamilton's reference to the people as "a great beast," and the settlement of Georgia by "poor debtors and criminals."

In both New York and New Jersey, bills were introduced to prohibit the use of books to which patriotic societies objected. The New York bill provided:

Section 680. Use of certain types of books prohibited. No textbook shall be used or designated for use in the schools of any city, union, free school district, or common school district of the state which

(a) ignores, omits, discounts, or in any manner belittles, ridicules, falsifies, distorts, questions, doubts, or denies the events leading up to the Declaration of American Independence, or connected with the American Revolution, or the spirit and determination with which the United States of America has established, defended, and maintained its rights as a free nation against foreign interference, encroachment, and aggression, or

(b) ignores, omits, discounts, or in any manner belittles, ridicules, falsifies, distorts, questions, doubts, or denies the deeds and accomplishments of the noted American patriots, or questions the worthiness of their motives, or casts aspersions on their lives.

Section 681. Enforcement of the provisions of the article.

1. The Commissioner of Education shall supervise the enforcement of the provisions of this article, and he shall withhold all

public-school monies from any city or district which, in his judgment, willfully omits and refuses to enforce the provisions of this article, after due notice, so often and so long as such willful omission and refusal shall, in his judgment, continue.

The New Jersey bill was similar and, in places, identical. Neither bill became law, but both threats did serve to make teachers more timid in their teaching. In some states, the chief educational officers were authorized to exclude books from the school if they found them to be "un-American."

Declaring that teachers of history were better judges of what should be in a book than news editors or professional patriots, the teachers of Washington, D.C. urged the National Education Association to take steps to defend teachers from threats to academic freedom and professional standing. The American Historical Association condemned the censorship tactics of newspapers, fraternal orders, patriotic societies and other like-minded bodies. Admitting that there were different purposes to the teaching of history at elementary, secondary and advanced levels, the American Historical Association said that honesty and sound scholarship demanded a truthful picture of the past. Books should be evaluated on fidelity to fact, not on grounds of spread-eagle Americanism. The association declared that it was ridiculous to say that reputable scholars were perverting history.

Not satisfied with the Americanism of current texts, the American Legion decided in 1922 to prepare a "pure" American history. This work in two volumes, *The Story of Our American People* was written, not by a historian, but by a professor of English. Van Tyne said it might more appropriately be called "The Marvelous Story of Us." Though it was endorsed by the Daughters of the American Revolution, the Daughters of the Confederacy, the Elks, the Knights of Pythias, and many other organizations, the book was not widely adopted.

In Wisconsin, a historian protested that the law would "put the clock back by substituting for the deliberate judgment of first-rate scholars, the prejudices of the uninformed, of those whose notions of American History have never advanced beyond the point at which they or their fathers were left, in the eighth grade, by the stale textbooks of an earlier time."

Even in smaller colleges, pressures were applied to the faculty to discontinue the use of books that allegedly reflected upon "the American way of life"—i.e., the most conservative interpretation of "rugged individualism." For years, Lucille Cardin Craine operated a publication called the *Educational Reviewer* which ferreted out and denounced books with a liberal approach.[3]

The Nation, a liberal magazine, was removed from the libraries of the schools in New York City after it published a series of articles by Blanchard critical of the political interests of the Roman Catholic Church. *The Merchant of Venice* was removed from the secondary schools there when Jewish groups protested that it taught anti-semitism. There have been many objections to the use of Christmas carols in the schools.

The fact that powerful groups are able to influence the selection or rejection of textbooks operates also to make writers and publishers careful. Not infrequently authors are told by publishers that the inclusion of such-and-such a statement would injure the sale of a book. Naturally, authors are interested in royalties and publishers are interested in profits. If one can get a greater sale by being inoffensive to all, here is a great temptation.

Curriculum Controls   In addition to trying to influence teachers and textbooks, various groups influence the school by attempting to control the curriculum. These attempts are made on the legislative level within the state and on the local level as well. Politicians on either level are scarcely the best persons to construct a curriculum. Through such state and local pressures, certain courses are prescribed as a prerequisite to graduation. Such courses or parts of courses as state and national history, the harmful effects of alcohol and narcotics, swimming, kindness to animals, etc. are frequently mandated. All these may be desirable courses, but the question involved is whether or not such prescriptions should be made by laymen or by professional educators. Prescription by laymen, subject to pressures from particular groups, are likely to be haphazard and piecemeal. Many a state that prescribes the study of alcohol and narcotics says nothing about English.

Other devices for influencing the curriculum and its content are the distribution of free and inexpensive materials, such as pamphlets, study guides, maps, supplementary readers, sponsored motion pictures, etc. A catalog of just one of several motion picture distributing agencies lists more than 4000 such films, each designed to influence the pupil toward a product, a service, or a cause. The National

[3] The conservative chairman of the board of trustees of Hastings College, Nebraska, ordered the president of the college to take away from the students at once a text in economics which had been in use for several years, without his having read it, after it was denounced in a circular from a reactionary organization. The president refused. Shortly thereafter, he resigned.

Association of Manufacturers has an extensive catalog of materials designed to influence students toward that association's particular version of "free enterprise." Contests sponsored by many organizations were for some years regulated by the National Association of Secondary School Principals, but recently the organization has recommended the elimination of the schools' participation in any contests.

Loyalty Oaths   During the Revolution, certain states imposed loyalty oaths upon their teachers. Massachusetts, New Jersey, and Pennsylvania had such laws designed to weed out any remaining Tories. Once the Revolution was over, oaths were not again required until recent times. The aftermath of World War I, the depression of the 1930's, World War II, and the continuing cold war have resulted in loyalty oath laws in more than half the states. There is no questioning the objective that the legislatures had in mind in passing the laws—insuring of loyal teachers for American children and youths. These oaths have been resisted by teachers and their professional organizations on the grounds that they are an unwarranted insult to the great body of teachers and are also futile, for they keep from the teaching profession only persons who have conscientious scruples about taking such oaths, not hidden communists who would not hesitate to take the oaths. It appears that their greatest value has been to the paper and file cabinet manufacturers. Certainly no communist, setting out to subvert an American school, would let an oath stand between him and his objective.

The most notorious of the loyalty oaths was prescribed by the Lusk Laws in New York in 1921. They let loose morale-shattering witch-hunts, particularly in New York City, where a board of five persons was set up to pass on all cases of doubtful loyalty. The resulting furor caused the repeal of the act. In signing the repeal law, Governor Alfred E. Smith declared:

> It is a confession of the weakness of our own faith in the righteousness of our own cause when we attempt to repress by law those who do not agree with us. . . . It is unthinkable that in a representative democracy there should be delegated to any body of men the absolute power to prohibit the teaching of any subject of which it may disapprove. . . . The Lusk Laws . . . are repugnant to the fundamentals of American democracy. . . . In signing these (repeal) bills, I firmly believe I am vindicating the principle that within the limits of the penal law every citizen may speak and teach what he believes.

When the threat of bolshevism, which had motivated the Lusk Law and similar laws in other states, died down in the roaring prosperity of the 1920's, the demand for loyalty oaths subsided. However, when the collapse of the American economy in the 1930's brought new threats of radicalism, there were many new enactments. By 1935, such loyalty oaths were required in twenty states. The outbreak of World War II gave added impetus to the movement.

The Ives Law of 1934 in New York was typical of such legislation. Under this act no one was allowed to teach in any school, college, or university whose real property or any part of it was exempt from taxation, until he took an oath of loyalty. A resolution was introduced in Congress to ask the states to require an oath to support the federal constitution on the part of all teachers, but it was not passed. Congress did pass, however, a provision of the appropriation act which came to be called "the little red rider." This required each teacher in the public schools of the District of Columbia to sign on each pay day an affidavit that he had not taught communism since the last pay day.

The continuing developments of the cold war vis-à-vis the Soviet Union has tended to cause the loyalty oath legislation to be retained in states where it was already established. Occasionally there have been demands for its introduction in other states. The last major movement in this regard was in the heyday of Senator Joseph McCarthy of Wisconsin, who seemed generally to suspect teachers and professors of subversive activities. There were extensive investigations of the loyalty of teachers and professors. Two of the most notable cases were at the University of California and at the University of Washington.

Reasons for Restrictions   There were several reasons for the restrictions placed upon the freedom of teachers at the various critical periods in our history. It is apparent from the previous presentation that orthodoxy and fundamentalism wanted to protect themselves from more liberal religious interpretations and sought enactments to keep children from being exposed to "heretical" ideas. Patriots who themselves knew only a limited amount of "pure" history wanted only that taught to the next generation. At times, industries attempted to suppress the development of public criticism which would whittle away their privileges. Minorities brought pressure to prohibit any teaching which would reflect on their ideas. A spirit of anti-intellectualism prevailed in some places, as in the mind of the Georgia legislator in 1925 who said that there were only three books worth reading—the Bible, which "teaches you how to act"; the hymnal, which "contains the finest poetry ever written"; and the almanac, which "shows you how to figure out what the weather will be."

To the above reasons for the restrictions, we must add one more: the inadequate education of many of the nation's teachers. When teachers could be certified to instruct in an elementary school, possessing only an elementary education oneself, and to teach in a high school with only an elementary education and a weak "normal" course, obviously the teacher could not be regarded as a professional worthy of professional freedom. Generally, though, it was not the inadequately educated teacher who was guilty of unpopular ideas. He hadn't ever been exposed to any. The troublemaker was the person who had been away to college and had learned new ideas contrary to the mores of the community in which he taught. Un-imaginative teachers bound to textbooks don't get into trouble. It is teachers with new ideas who do.

Personal Freedom of Teachers   Communities which are not loath to restrict a teacher's freedom to teach would hardly be reluctant to place restraints upon a teacher's personal freedom as well. Traditionally, the American teacher has been less free in his personal life than other citizens, for he has been placed upon a pedestal beside the minister—both expected to be of exemplary character and conduct. The Boston board of education expressed it thus in 1841:

If, then, the manners of the teacher are to be imitated by the pupils,—if he is the glass, at which they "do dress themselves," how strong is the necessity, that he should understand those name-less and innumerable practices, in regard to deportment, dress, conversation, and all personal habits, that constitute the difference between a gentleman and a clown. We can bear some oddity, or eccentricity in a friend whom we admire for his talents, or revere for his virtues; but it becomes quite a different thing, when the oddity, or the eccentricity, is to be a pattern or model, from which fifty or a hundred children are to form their manners. It was well remarked, by the ablest British traveller who has ever visited this country, that amongst us "every male above twenty-one years of age, claims to be a sovereign." He is, therefore, *bound to be a gentleman.*

In 1852, a young teacher wrote to the editor of the *New York Teacher* asking why he and his young lady assistant were not free to walk to and from school together without public criticism. The good people of the village held that this was contrary to all precedent, and the school trustees administered discipline. He went on to say:

This is another evil incident to teaching, that ought to be remedied. Our patrons—and wonderfully *patronizing* they are sometimes truly!—have generally altogether too much to say about our private affairs. Our business is everybody's business; and a lawyer or a gentleman of any other calling, subjected to such treatment as we often receive, would wring the proboscis of the offender, and perhaps administer a dose of the *cat*. I know this is a difficulty peculiar to country districts and small villages; but the mass of teachers are in just such situations, and consequently they as a body are interested in this question. Teachers should be men of

Discipline being administered to a professor in 1859.
Tarring and feathering has since been done away with.

refined feelings; and no person who has more appreciation of decent treatment than a human donkey, can tamely submit to all that we are sometimes obliged to bear. Teachers, while they faithfully and sedulously perform their duties, should boldly maintain their rights, and resist every attempt to encroach upon them.

I do not intend, for $35.00 per month, to resign all the privileges guaranteed to me by the social compact. I am a citizen, and I shall exercise the immunities of citizenship as I deem proper, the whole town of L———— notwithstanding.

The only advice the editor of the magazine could give him was that the best way to "shut the mouths of gainsayers is just to take one more walk with your assistant—down to the minister's—and secure her services for life. . . . We tried that once, and have never seen cause to regret it."

Before the broadening point of view that came as an aftermath of World War I, many teachers led very circumscribed lives. They dared not smoke in public, nor could they play cards. In 1929, eleven high school teachers were dismissed in Kansas for attending a country club dance. Drinking alcoholic beverages was strictly forbidden. Pennsylvania still requires applicants for a state teacher's certificate to declare that they do not use alcoholic beverages. Teachers were not expected to participate in social activities except on week ends, and then in sufficient moderation to permit them to teach Sunday School. Sixty-eight teachers in Chicago were discharged in 1916 for joining a teacher's union, but won reinstatement in a superior court case, only to lose in the state supreme court. In numerous places, women teachers were dismissed immediately following marriage—or, at least, at the end of the school term. Sometimes this dismissal was on the basis that it would be unwholesome to have a married woman in a school. In the depression years of the 1930's, dismissals were more often for economic reasons, two salaries for one family appearing almost immoral during that time of widespread unemployment. With a change in this folkway, and with the great shortage of teachers after World War II, many a superintendent has called upon a married woman whom he or his predecessor "fired" years before because she married, to persuade her to return to teaching.

There has been so great a relaxation of restrictions upon teachers as persons, in recent years, that present teachers do not face nearly so much interference with their personal lives as in former times. Even in rural areas, there is much less restraint.

Teaching about Communism Though communism is a great threat to American institutions and liberty, many teachers hesitate to teach about it in literature or the social studies classes, lest their honest attempts be misconstrued by ill-informed students or politically naive parents. Evangelistic attacks upon communism might be accepted, but an attempt to study it from an objective point of view, weighing its accomplishments and its sacrifice of the rights of individual freedom, might arouse antagonism. During the McCarthy era, in particular, this was a grave danger. Addressing the New Jersey Education Association in 1954, Governor Robert B. Meyner declared that teachers were afraid of controversial issues. He reported that in answer to the question "Do you believe that teachers hesitate to engage in comparison of the Russian system with the American system for fear of misunderstanding of their motives?" the majority of teachers queried replied "yes." He went on to say that there could be no such thing as real education unless teachers and pupils have the right of free inquiry. Teachers, he said, had been "the victims of demagogues who, under the guise of fighting totalitarianism, are instilling totalitarian ideas in the minds of our people." Teachers, he said, would perfer digging ditches, driving trucks, or taking in washing to a life of academic slavery.

The Fund for the Republic, a Ford Foundation subsidiary, conducted a survey to assess the amount of fear among teachers, and concluded that it existed in large measure. The National Education Association in 1954 tried to counteract the spirit of censorship with a pamphlet, *Your Child Deserves Fact and Faith,* designed particularly for the lay public. A second pamphlet, *What Policies Should Guide the Handling of Controversial Issues* was designed especially for administrators and teachers. An NEA film, *Freedom to Learn,* portrayed the difficulties of a veteran teacher assailed by reactionary parents who had been inflamed by an organizer for an ultraconservative political group.

When Charles Boehm, superintendent of public instruction in Pennsylvania, decided that the high schools in that state should teach a unit on communism in the problems of democracy course, he shrewdly obtained "clearance" from the Pennsylvania department of the American Legion.

The Vigilantes In the days of the pioneer West, when the processes of law were unavailable or inadequate, a volunteer committee of citizens would organize itself to suppress and punish crime summarily. Such committees were often effective, but at times they hanged entirely innocent people. In the troubled times in which we live, we sometimes find instances of private citizens constituting themselves as educational vigilantes to suppress teaching in schools and colleges. There have been several such cases, two of which have been more notorious and have attracted more attention than others. In 1952, a radio commentator in California attacked a teacher, Miss Fern Brunner, as a "communist." Supported by the California Teachers' Association, she filed suit against the commentator and the radio station and collected substantial damages. In 1963, Mrs. Virginia Franklin, a teacher in Paradise, California, who had recently won a Freedoms Foundation

Mrs. Virginia Franklin, shown with the tape recorder that her adversaries used in their attempt to trap her.

award as an outstanding teacher of "the American credo," was attacked by the American Legion post, some John Birch Society members, and others. The charge was that she subverted the patriotism of her students by exposing them to leftist ideas. She was accused of being a communist. Her adversaries tried to trap her by recording her classroom discussions on a tape recorder hidden in a book especially carved out to conceal it. Eventually, the teacher and the administrators who supported her were vindicated in a school board election, 1700 to 1200. It was reported that Mrs. Franklin had sued her detractors for libel.[4]

If our times continue to encourage political extremism, we may expect an increase rather than a diminution of such vigilantism. The teacher will either teach according to the dictates of his own conscience and possibly at his own peril, or he will meekly accept the role of purveyor of flavorless pablum.

For Further Reading

Commager, Henry S. *Freedom, Loyalty, Dissent*. Oxford University Press, 1954.
Loyalty purges, "smearing," public apathy, all of which endanger freedom.

Kallen, Horace M. *The Education of Free Men*. Farrar, Strauss, 1949.
Many pressures and influences of social, religious, economic and military groups as hostile to the free education of free minds.

Kirk, Russell. *Academic Freedom*. Regnery, 1955.
Definition of academic freedom; the enduring idea of special liberty associated with academic institutions, scholars and teachers.

Lazarfeld, Paul F. and Wagner Thielens. *The Academic Mind*. Free Press, Glencoe, 1958.
A report of the Bureau of Applied Social Research, Columbia University, on 2400 interviews with college professors: their social origins, their reaction to suspicions and criticisms from outside the campus.

MacIver, Robert M. *Academic Freedom in Our Time*. Columbia University Press, 1955.
A study prepared for the Academic Freedom Project of Columbia University.

McWilliams, Carey. *Witch Hunt, the Revival of Heresy*. Little, Brown, 1950.
Likens present situation to the days of witch hunting. Modern "inquisitions" to ferret out "bad" ideas.

4 For the Brunner case, see *Journal of the National Education Association*, October, 1953. For an illustrated account of the Franklin case, see *Life*, April 26, 1963.

Sellin, Thorsten (editor). "Freedom of Inquiry and Expression". *Annals of the American Academy of Political and Social Science.* Vol. 200. November, 1938.

A short history of academic freedom, with special articles on restraints in many fields—invention, medicine, the press, literature, art, teaching, etc.

Sinclair, Upton. *The Goslings.* Upton Sinclair, 1924.

An exposé of attempts to control the freedom of teachers to teach objectively, especially in science and the social studies. See especially 79 to 89. A companion volume (1923) by the same author, *The Goose-Step* deals with trespasses on academic freedom on the college level.

Van Doren, Mark. *Man's Right to Knowledge and the Free Use Thereof.* Columbia University Press, 1954.

A series of sixty panels of "illustrative material from many lands to the end that man's right to knowledge and the free use thereof shall be understood and practiced," with commentary by Van Doren. Panels 41 to 49 on the scholar and the teacher.

20

Today and Tomorrow

The Past as Prologue We have thus far traced the development of American education from its simple beginnings on the Atlantic coastline of a new continent to the present. What now of the present and the future? An optimist would say that the past, with all its glories, is but prologue, and that a new and golden day is dawning in American education. As we look at contemporary education, we can see that the present is conditioned by the past through which we have come and by our expectations of the future, however dimly discerned, still over the horizon. Whether the future holds the golden age or whether it is already past remains to be seen.

Enrollment One of the astonishing features of the American educational system is the spectacularly large number of persons encompassed in it. The total number enrolled in American schools and colleges for 1963 was 51,486,000—between a third and a quarter of the American people. Educational statistics become obsolete almost before they are printed. Nonetheless, nothing can better portray the magnitude of our educational enterprise than these statistics for 1963:

94,860	*elementary schools*
30,000	*secondary schools*
2,010	*universities, colleges, junior colleges*
35,000,000	*elementary school pupils*
12,100,000	*secondary school pupils*
4,600,000	*full-time and part-time students in higher education*
2,062,180	*teachers at all levels*
150,170	*administrators and staff members*
183,700	*local, state, and college board members*

When we add to these pupils, teachers, administrators, and board members all those who are indirectly involved in American education—through construction activities, through publication of books and the manufacture of equipment, through professional services, through driving the buses and dusting the erasers, and through the payment of taxes, then we touch almost the whole of the American people.

When we look forward to the future, we see that the enrollment will continue to increase. To what extent it will increase will depend upon many variable factors which cannot be determined with any demonstrable certainty at this time. Among these factors are the birth rate, the economic condition of the nation, developments in our international relations, the success of "don't be a drop-out" campaigns, and many other factors. Assuming that present enrollment trends may continue (and this is a bold assumption, for they may be retarded or accelerated by any of the factors mentioned), the Department of Health, Education, and Welfare has projected these enrollments for the future, in full-time public and nonpublic elementary and secondary schools:

1963–64	48,342,000
1964–65	49,623,000
1965–66	50,417,000
1966–67	51,338,000
1967–68	52,205,000
1968–69	53,123,000
1969–70	54,041,000
1974–75	63,156,000
1979–80	72,087,000

The reader is cautioned that these are merely projections or extrapolations built upon present trends. The actual enrollments may be smaller or substantially larger. In a publication entitled *The Impending Tide,* the American Association of Collegiate Registrars in 1955 made what then appeared to be reasonable projected estimates of enrollment in secondary schools and colleges to 1967, but the projections turned out to be much smaller than the number of persons actually enrolled in the early 1960's. The estimated secondary school enrollment for 1962–63 was 10,322,275. Actually, there were 11,700,000 pupils enrolled when the secondary schools opened that fall. With different environmental circumstances, they could have been too optimistic. Perhaps the projections of the United States Department of Health, Education, and Welfare may be no more accurate. The best we can say for them is that they are educated guesses about a highly volatile subject.

When one reads of millions of pupils enrolled, one accepts the statistics but sometimes fails to see that each of these units is someone's son or daughter who will need a classroom, a desk, books, and a teacher. Each is an individual, capable of being taught and molded. In a democracy, each is a moral obligation upon society.

The persistent gain of more than a million elementary and secondary pupils per year will continue to put a great strain upon the educational system. It implies a continued demand for schoolrooms, supplies, and teachers. It implies finding adequate financial resources to continue even the present quality of instruction. The situation would be sufficiently critical if the increase in enrollment were spread evenly over the whole nation, but the facts are otherwise. The increase is uneven, being much higher in some states and communities than in others. The suburban areas around the large cities are witnessing a phenomenal growth, and certain states are increasing in population much more rapidly than others. Some of the states in the South and the rural Midwest have witnessed an actual decline in population and school enrollment. California has recently become the most populous state in the Union, surpassing New York for first place.

The rapid increase in enrollment in certain areas poses a great problem of educational logistics. Where the growth is caused by the development of a defense installation or a space administration activity, federal funds are availabe to the federally impacted area, but where the growth is due to ordinary commerical development, the state and the community must carry the whole load.

Similar explosions in the enrollment in colleges and universities are being experienced. Whereas the total enrollment in institutions of higher education was only 238,210 in 1900, it had grown to 2,439,910 by 1950. By 1962, it had reached 4,600,000 and there were estimates that it would reach 7,000,000 by 1970.

Curriculum Development in the Elementary School   Because we live in rapidly changing times, because we are subject to the pressures of widely divergent educational philosophies, and because of the tremendous interest a free people takes in its educational system in a time of crisis, there is much discussion of curricular matters at the present time. This is true on all levels—elementary, secondary and higher. The development of knowledge proceeds at so rapid a pace that each generation must ask anew the question posed a century ago by Herbert Spencer, *What Knowledge Is of Most Worth?* No longer can any reasonable number of school years encompass all the knowledge available, or all that needs to be known. The schools are faced with the problem of selecting from the cultural heritage of the race the materials that need to be known as a part of our common, general education—materials that can be taught in a reasonable number of school years. But this is only a part of the monumental task the schools face. Since we can no longer assume that the conditions under which the race has lived thus far can be transmitted unchanged and unchanging to the next generation, it becomes a function of the schools at all levels to prepare students for changes which appear inevitable, and to help them develop intellectual and moral criteria for making decisions in the years ahead.

Traditionally, the school has been a conservative agency of society, primarily interested in the transmission of the cultural heritage, and reluctant to depart from the ways of the fathers. Ours is the first civilization in history to acknowledge that the schools must be oriented more to the future than to the past. When a computer can now solve more problems in mathematics in ten minutes than a man with an adding machine can work in fifty years, it is obvious that some re-evaluation of the conventional curriculum is in order.

In the elementary school, we may expect to see more emphasis on the basic skills of reading, for it has become apparent that the products of the schools cannot read as effectively as modern conditions demand. The day when simple literacy was sufficient has passed. Reading must include more than the mastery of a basic skill. It must also include the technique of getting abstract ideas and concepts from increasingly difficult matter. Instruction must aim also at the building of a life-long interest in reading, for it is now apparent that most vocations will call for life-time study. Reading, too, will be important as a worthy use of leisure and as a means of arriving at satisfactory solutions of the increasing number of political, economic, and social problems that will confront our society.

Since our age is so greatly oriented toward science, it seems evident that room will be found in the curriculum for an increasing body of science. Throughout most of the history of our elementary schools, this has been a weak spot, largely because the teachers themselves knew little science. Traditionally, very little science study has been included in the education of elementary teachers. Much that has been included has been in biological science and its fringes (conservation, bird study, kindness to animals, etc.), whereas the present interest is increasingly in the physical and space sciences. Children have an insatiable curiosity about scientific phenomena. If they are taught by teachers who look upon science as a means of solving problems, rather than as a bag of tricks to amuse pupils, great forward steps can be taken in this field.

Mathematics is in the process of revision to include the concepts of what is called "modern" mathematics. Some attempts have been made to introduce the study of foreign languages into the elementary school, but these have sometimes been hastily conceived, and often they lack adequate planning to integrate their study into a comprehensive program throughout the secondary school. The fact of the matter is that most elementary school teachers are not capable of teaching a foreign language, and frequently there are not enough competent teachers of a language to offer any degree of thorough instruction in the elementary schools without detracting from the none-too-strong language programs of the secondary schools.

Secondary School Curriculum   While there has been criticism of the elementary school, particularly of progressive education, within recent years the major criticisms have been focused upon the secondary school curriculum. Since the Russians orbited Sputnik, there has been an insistent barrage of hostile criticism in books and magazines. In the forefront have been such critics as Hyman Rickover, Arthur Bestor, Albert Lynd, Mortimer Smith and Paul Woodring.[1]

The criticisms allege that the schools are anti-intellectual in that they prefer a life-adjustment curriculum to a rigorous pursuit of intellectual excellence; that progressive education has resulted in a general deterioration of the quality of education; that there is a conspiracy of the teachers to fasten mediocrity upon the schools; that teachers have been subjected to an overemphasis on vapid courses in education at a sacrifice of competence in subject matter.

These criticisms, despite the outcry of wounded "educators," have some merit, for some college teachers in education and some school teachers have permitted a deterioration in the quality of American education. In the relaxed period after World War I, many innovations were introduced—not all of them good. There were many reasons for these innovations. First, pressures of society and the hu-

---

[1] The reader is referred to such books as Rickover's *Education for All Children;* Bestor's *Restoration of Learning* and *Educational Wastelands;* Bestor's *The Retreat from Learning in Our Public Schools;* Lynd's *Quackery in the Public Schools;* Smith's *And Madly Teach* and *The Diminished Mind;* and Woodring's *Let's Talk Sense About Our Schools.* For more recent criticisms in a similar vein, consult the *Education Index,* under the heading "Education, criticisms of."

manitarian interests of the school were serving to retain in school an increasing percentage of nonacademic students who were unable or unwilling to learn the materials in the conventional curriculum. Secondly, there were pressures both within the profession and in the community at large to bring the curriculum more in harmony with the Seven Cardinal Principles enunciated in 1918. Third, this was a relaxed era. We had just won a great war to make the world safe for democracy. The nations had agreed upon a limitation of armaments. They had signed the Kellogg Pact renouncing war as an instrument of national policy. An expanding economy at home and the introduction of many labor-saving devices had promised an easier, fuller life for all. Optimism regarding the future abounded. Both society as a whole and the schools as its instrument could apparently take it easy. Fourth, a new emphasis upon psychology seemed to indicate that personality development of the individual was more important than solid learning. Doing enough to get by respectably came to be an accepted goal, both in school and in business. Many students tended to develop an attitude that the best way to succeed in business was not through conscientious work but through some such maneuver for status as "marrying the boss's daughter."

Not only were achievement levels dropped in the conventional academic subjects, but also many new subjects were now accepted as equivalent to the usual academic subjects. Some of these new subjects had a vocational orientation, and others were frankly acknowledged to be chiefly recreational in character. Increasingly, the school took unto itself responsibilities in health, moral and character education, driver training, recreation, and a host of similar activities once thought to be the responsibility of the home, the church, and community agencies. The cult of "the whole child" became popular.

To one who lived and taught in this optimistic era between the two World Wars, it appears that there was indeed a relaxation of the demands of the schools for competent performance. It appears further that this was not a conspiracy on the part of the educational profession to subvert the traditional way of education, but it was rather an indication of the unwillingness of the profession to stand against almost irresistible community pressures. Even colleges, allegedly the citadel of liberal learning and the cultural heritage, so much gave way to the pressures that Robert M. Hutchins could denounce them as mere educational service stations. His attempt to turn the colleges back to the study of fifty great books was notably unsuccessful. Frankly, America wanted degrees and diplomas more than learning, the shadow more than the substance, and the schools gave way.

Neither the Great Depression of the 1930's nor the Second World War made much change on the relaxed programs of the secondary schools. Indeed, the reports of the Regents Inquiry in the state of New York and of the American Youth Commission pointed the way toward further relaxation of standards. It was during World War II that Prosser was making his plea for a life-adjustment program and Harl Douglass was prescribing it not only for Prosser's protégés, but for all American youth. Looking forward naively to a return to a Harding type of "normalcy" and perhaps even to another economic recession, both the nation and its schools did not anticipate the Cold War. A federal bureau advised colleges to guide men away from careers in engineering on the grounds that there was an anticipated over-supply of personnel in this field.

The orbiting of Sputnik by the Soviet Union caught the nation off its guard. Anger replaced rationality. Surely someone was to blame for the softness of American life. It must be the schools with their relaxed program! The criticisms reached a crescendo in an avalanche of books, magazine articles (in such lay publications as *Colliers, The Saturday Evening Post, Life, Ladies Home Journal,* etc.), and newspaper columns. The schools which had recently been condemned for failing to relax their standards sufficiently now were excoriated for betraying a sacred trust by such relaxation.

Sensing a change in the spirit of America, the schools began to offer enriched or advanced courses for the gifted students. More mathematics and science were taught. Foreign languages came into their own. Schools which could find teachers even instituted courses in Russian. An alarmed Congress, still unwilling to provide for general federal aid to education, voted millions in a National Defense Education Act to subsidize the teaching of mathematics, science, and foreign languages. Special institutes in these subjects were offered, at government expense, to "retread" experienced teachers with new and modern concepts. So many millions of federal dollars were voted for educational research that state departments of education felt obligated to invent questionable research projects to use up the money before the appropriation expired. Foundations poured additional millions into research projects, particularly into new and sometimes exotic programs for the preparation of teachers.

The national emergency of the Cold War and space rivalry, together with the increasing number of high school graduates desiring to attend college, enabled colleges to raise their admission standards drastically. This in turn gave the secondary schools additional leverage in tightening up their standards. Many a high school graduate who would have been welcomed even by an Ivy League college in the 1930's or even in the 1950's was destined in the 1960's to receive a note rejecting his application for admission. Some admissions officers, on second thought, wondered if they were right in applying such rigid standards. Dossiers giving, under pseudonyms, the secondary school backgrounds and case data of Charles Darwin and Winston Churchill were rejected by American colleges.

In this period of international tension and philosophical pluralism, it is not surprising that confusion exists in American education, particularly on the secondary level. Until we know what kind of world we are preparing for and what our value judgments will be concerning that world, it is almost impossible to construct an acceptable curriculum. Until there is some reasonable synthesis, we may expect the confusion and the criticisms to continue.

In the meantime, the quality of education varies greatly from school district to school district and from school to school in the same district. Whether in public, private, or parochial schools, one can still find a full range from superior to mediocre to distinctly inadequate schools. To an observer, it appears that the quality of a school and its graduates is correlated more closely with the quality and the morale of the teaching staff than it is correlated with any other factor—finance, size, location, control, etc. In a rapidly changing time, one thing may still be immutable: Victor Cousin's dictum, so often quoted by Horace Mann: "As is the teacher, so is the school."

Methods of Teaching   Methods of teaching change from time to time, in keeping with changing environmental conditions. Unfortunately, however, there is often a cultural lag, for. one must cope with teachers in service who have been trained under previous methodologies and who become resistant to change. Further, there seems to be a tendency for teachers to teach as they have been taught, not as they have been taught to teach. Of America's nearly 2,000,000 teachers, there are not too many innovators. A large proportion appear to be relatively conservative and unimaginative persons who are content with conventional and routine procedures. In some cases, what is routinized becomes "*rut*-inized."

Despite the influence of educational reformers, many methods which might be employed to make teaching more meaningful and richly suffused with concepts remain untried. When the schoolroom was a barren place with only the teacher and a few basic texts as the educational resources, there may have been an excuse for the overemphasis upon routine questions and answers in a catechetical method. Now that our contemporary culture offers a rich supply of

Programed instruction, one of the many ways a teacher can enrich her professional procedures.

teaching aids in the form of supplementary books, pamphlets, magazines, models, charts, diagrams, graphs, phonograph records, tape recordings, motion pictures, and television, there is little excuse for routine teaching. Still, talking and even lecturing prevail, and the schoolroom is saturated with verbalisms.

Even the requirement in some states, as Pennsylvania for instance, that teachers must have passed a course in audio-visual education in order to qualify for a permanent teacher's certificate is not too effective, for there is no guarantee that the teacher will use the methods and devices covered in the course. When he taught a course in audio-visual education, the author told his class that he ought not give a final grade at the completion of the course, but ought to defer the grade until it became evident that the teachers used in their teaching what they had learned in the class.

Methods come and go, for fashions in educational procedure seem to change as much as in hair styles or length of skirts. At one time, after World War I, the Dalton plan of Harriet Parkhurst had some vogue. Under this plan, the student entered into a "contract" with the teacher to complete a planned project within a specified time, and he was released from conventional class activities to work on his own and at his own rate of speed. Conferences with the teacher to plan and to discuss activities and procedures were a part of the program. Unfortunately, the plan foundered upon the twin shoals of pupils' unwillingness to accept responsibility along with freedom and teachers' rigidity in expecting all pupils to work at the same pace.

The schools of America are littered with the corpses of methods which turned out to be passing fads rather than permanent improvements. The famous object-teaching, allegedly Pestalozzian in character, spread out from Oswego and had a thirty-year vogue, but by the turn of the century it was subject to derisive comment. The mechanistic Grube method of teaching arithmetic, imported from Germany, had a temporary vogue. The Morrison plan of unit-teaching, following the formal steps of exploration, presentation, assimilation, organization, and adjustment, though it was hailed as a new departure and panacea, soon became as formal as the Herbartian procedure which it resembled to a remarkable degree. The correlation of various disciplines into broader fields, as advocated by S. C. Parker, promised a new approach. Social studies replaced history, geography, and civics. General science combined basic elements of biology, earth science, physics, chemistry, and astronomy. Communication replaced reading, writing, composition, and speech. Sometimes this combination is called "language arts." The project method, as expounded by William Heard Kilpatrick, an interpreter of Dewey's educational philosophy, took the schools by storm. One was a very old-fashioned teacher if he did not engineer several projects a year. Even Latin classes took to the carving of Roman statesmen from giant bars of Ivory soap—more to the profit of Procter and Gamble than to the educational advancement of the pupils.

About 1950, many of the dissatisfactions with conventional teaching and the enthusiasms for newer methodology converged into the formation of the concept of "core" teaching and learning. Now, subjects as such were to be dismissed, and pupils were to work on "common learnings"—large, substantial bodies of concern to which the various subjects were summoned as their content or method was needed in the solution of a problem. Harold Alberty of Ohio State University learnedly discoursed on six types of "core," ranging from simple correlation of disparate subjects to a type of teacher-student planned activity without any reference to formal subject structure. Core programs had a considerable vogue, particularly in junior high schools, but schools employing them encountered many difficulties. The lack of teachers adequately prepared and hospitable to the idea was the greatest difficulty. Inability to communicate the philosophy of the core concept to parents and the public was another. More than any other state, Maryland espoused the core program. It was fairly common in certain schools in seven other states, but it failed to make a nation-wide impact. The general tightening up after Sputnik placed core programs on the defensive and led to their abandonment in certain systems. Though still espoused by certain schools of education, "core" does not seem to have a bright future, for teachers prepared as subject specialists find it difficult to conduct core classes around such topics as "The United States in the Contemporary World," "Juvenile Delinquency," "Collective Security," or "The People of Our Town." Whether right or wrong, present pressures are for increased competency in subject matter, and there is no apparent assurance that this is covered systematically in a core class.

Man's inventive genius has placed at the disposal of our teachers a whole range of mechanical marvels which they can use to supplement and enrich their professional procedures. The educational motion picture is widely used at all levels of instruction and in all fields of study. It literally extends the school into all parts of the world. Records and tapes are commonplace in courses in literature, drama, shorthand, and others. Programmed instruction (which can be taught with or without a teaching "machine"), allows students to work at their own pace, while saving teachers much labor in instruction for certain basic concepts. Opaque and overhead transparency projectors facilitate the showing of pictures, diagrams, and even themes. A growing number of educational television programs bring noted teachers and resource persons even to remote schools.

Some elementary schools are now experimenting with ungraded classes through which students pass at their own speed, in accordance with their individual interests and abilities. A growing number of secondary schools have adopted modifications of the Trump plan, sponsored by the National Association of Secondary School Principals. Financed by the Fund for the Advancement of Education and the Ford Foundation, the Association in 1956 began to develop experimental programs in nearly a hundred junior and senior high schools across the United States. Proceeding on the assumption that students need to develop individual responsibility and the skills of independent study and need to have satisfaction in learning, the commission tried to find more effective procedures more in keeping with present needs, using all available resources. J. Lloyd Trump and his associates advocated large group instruction for part of the program, using many mechanical devices. This large group instruction would be supplemented with small group discussions of fifteen or fewer students and by individual, independent study. Instead of attempting to provide the setting for all these diverse functions in a one-teacher, self-contained classroom, the school would develop team teaching and would readjust its rooms to provide for large lecture-demonstration halls, group discussion rooms, and independent study cubicles. Rigid schedules would become more flexible. Individual differences, both of teachers and of pupils, would receive more recognition than under conventional procedures.[2]

Financing the Schools   At the turn of the twentieth century, public schools were financed almost wholly from local funds, which were in turn derived primarily from the taxation of local real estate. True, state funds paid a small share of the educational costs, but the state share was relatively insignificant. This local support of education was in keeping with a long-standing tradition. When the states began to move toward higher standards of education, it immediately became apparent that some communities would have to strain themselves much more than others to attain even modest minimum standards, for there was no high positive correlation between the wealth of a community and the number of its children. Indeed, some areas of high wealth had few children, and many areas of low wealth had far more than their share of children. This inequity in the distribution of wealth and children pointed to the need for state funds, particularly for the less able districts. From modest beginnings, state aid has grown greatly, though its ratio to local funds varies greatly from state to state.

With the passage of the Smith-Hughes Act to subsidize education in agriculture and vocations, the principle of the granting of federal funds to subsidize special functions in the public schools was inaugurated. A study by the National Education Association revealed that of the total revenue and nonrevenue receipts of the public schools totalled $19,474,187,000 for the school year 1961–62.[3]

[2] The workings of the Trump plan in particular schools are described in *Focus on Change: Guide to Better Schools* by J. Lloyd Trump and Dorsey Baynham. Rand-McNally, 1961.

[3] Revenue receipts are funds from appropriations, taxes, permanent school funds and endowments, and other receipts which do not incur any liability; nonrevenue receipts, on the other hand, are funds from such sources as loans, sales of bonds, sale of property purchased from capital funds, and proceeds from insurance adjustments. Nonrevenue receipts either incur an obligation or change the form of an asset from property to cash and thus reduce the value of school property.

Of this nearly twenty billion dollars, the revenue receipts totalled $16,646,781,000. The funds came from these sources:

Local and intermediate	$9,337,562,000
State	6,700,585,000
Federal	608,634,000

Still, in many states, there were demands that state aid be increased, not only in amount but also in percentage of the total amount expended for education. Likewise, the demand for substantial federal aid to education continues. Eventually, one may prophesy, Congress will pass a general aid-to-education bill and the president will sign it. Had it not been for entanglement of federal-aid questions with such controversial issues as support for nonpublic schools and racial desegregation, such a bill might have been adopted earlier.

School District Reorganization   Another significant trend in American education is the reorganization of school districts into larger units. As a result of consolidation and the annexation of districts, great progress has been made in reducing the number of basic administrative units. The number of school districts in 1962 was less than half the number ten years before. From 37,475 districts in 1961, the number was reduced to 35,330 in 1962. Even more significant is the reduction in the number of districts since 1931–32, as shown by this tabulation:

1931–32	127,422
1939–40	116,999
1949–50	83,642
1959–60	40,605
1961–62	35,330

After many years of trying to "bribe" districts to consolidate, the Pennsylvania legislature in 1962 mandated a drastic reduction in the number of districts. It required each county board to submit a plan for the union of districts; if a county failed to submit a satisfactory plan, the state council of education (i.e., the state board) was empowered to make its own plans for larger units. The aim was to have districts of 4000 or more pupils, though it was acknowledged that some districts in rural and mountainous areas of sparse population would necessarily be smaller than this stated minimum.

Notwithstanding the substantial reduction in the number of districts, five states in 1962 still had more than 2000 school districts each. Further consolidation of districts was still needed, and it began to be apparent that this would become a matter of legislative compulsion if districts were unwilling to unite voluntarily to receive larger state subsidies.

Resistance to consolidation centers largely around the desire to keep the school near the children's homes, the mystic aura of the "little red schoolhouse," tradition, and the natural desire of school board members to perpetuate themselves in office. State school board associations have resisted consolidation because they did not want to reduce membership in their organizations.

Diminution of Local Control   One of the hallowed shibboleths of American education is the principle of local control of education. Local control has been an integral part of American education since our free schools were established. One must recognize that schools directed by local boards of education have made a significant contribution to American life. One must also recognize the selfless spirit and great effort of thousands of board members all over the nation. Generally, but not universally, they have been motivated by the high and noble consideration of assuring to American children and youth an ever-increasing educational opportunity.

It is apparent, however, that local control is passing from the scene. The threat to local control comes from contemporary conditions beyond the province of the local boards. Let us examine some of these conditions.

First, there is a demand for national standards of education. The strongest advocate of this point of view is Admiral H. G. Rickover. His thesis is that the teachers colleges have produced a generation of administrators who know nothing about teaching and who cannot therefore hold reasonable standards of education in local communities; that only a national system of educational examinations, with national subsidies to the schools producing the best results, and with federal standards, can restore quality to American education. He does, indeed, stress that his federal intervention will *at first* be voluntary and optional, with only prestige and subsidy as the incentives for adoption of his proposals. The reading of educational history, however, indicates that many innovations which began as optional and voluntary have in a short time become mandatory, either through legislation or public pressure. In New York, there were 3 stages in the development of free, public schools:

Rear Admiral Hyman G. Rickover, Ret.,
founder of our nuclear navy
and critic of American Education.

1. The legislature passed special bills enabling certain communities that had petitioned to do so to establish free schools. Numerous such laws were enacted.

2. Tired of such individual legislation, the state enacted permissive general legislation allowing any community, under certain circumstances, to establish free schools.

3. After most areas of the state had provided for free schools by the above two procedures, legislation mandated free schools everywhere.

Accreditation by a regional accrediting agency is not required by law. It is voluntary. But are there any districts that have not volunteered for such accreditation? Pressures can coerce "voluntary" procedures.

There may be merit to Rickover's proposal for national examinations. Certainly there have been values in the state-wide system of Regents examinations in New York. With persons being graduated from thousands of local high schools, holding only to local standards set up by local teachers hired by local boards, no one knows what a diploma signifies. It can mean merely a certificate of attendance. A national examination system would force a national curriculum and perhaps a national methodology. From the study of national systems abroad, we can find both merit and disconcerting elements in such a system. The English found disadvantages to their "payment-by-results" program when school subsidies depended on the test performance of pupils.

Edgar Fuller, executive secretary of the Council of Chief State School Officers, has pointed out that "if local and state professional and legal authorities do not learn better how to evaluate and accept or reject proposed curriculum changes, such changes may be imposed eventually by national forces and their state and local allies." He objects strongly to having a central control employing power, prestige, and money to achieve even commonly agreed-upon purposes. But his objection and others like it will not stand in the way of a manifest educational destiny if conditioning political and social factors seem to make central control necessary or desirable. It appears, as Kandel said years ago, that "educational systems are in fact colored far more by prevailing social and political concepts than by psychological theories or educational philosophies"; in fact, one may suspect that we often derive our psychological theories and educational philosophies from social, political, cultural, and economic circumstances.

Second, changes in American life serve to diminish local authority. The revolution in transportation, the demand for specialized teachers, the inabilty of small districts to provide adequate education—all these make it seem desirable to consolidate school districts into larger units. Perhaps we may make a semantic interpretation that these are still *local* districts, but they are not *local* in the traditional sense of that word. England has reduced her school districts from 2500 to 146. They are called Local Education Authorities, but are they local? Pennsylvania is mandating local district organization. The goal is to reduce 2129 districts to perhaps less than 500. In Lehigh County there may be a county-wide district, or two or three districts, instead of the eleven which now exist. A few short years ago, there were 25. The question is, will the new districts be local? They may be good, they may improve our educational efficiency, but they will not fit former concepts of a district that is local.

Writing of the mandate of the Pennsylvania legislature, the Pennsylvania Economy League, Inc. points out the pros and cons of the proposed reorganization. These briefly summarized are:

Pros

1. Larger districts can provide enriched programs, taught by specialized teachers.

2. Larger districts are more economical.

3. Larger districts can offer more special services.

4. Larger districts provide an integrated 12-year program, with effective control.

Cons

1. Home rule is destroyed.

2. Since the program does not provide for local option, desires of local districts are not recognized.

3. Size is no guarantee of quality.

4. Higher taxes are indicated, because of increased administrative and transportation costs.

5. [and this is the significant "con" for this presentation:] The influence of parents, citizens, and school directors will be reduced and dispersed, while that of the professional educators and the Department of Public Instruction will be considerably increased.

Perhaps the school board member should read American educational history and find out how the local district system arose. It is not universal among the leading nations of the world. It arose here out of our peculiar geographical, political, and social conditions. These conditions have changed. Perhaps the local district should disappear. In fact, it is disappearing fast over the nation. In the last 30 years, there has been a 68% reduction in the number of districts in the United States.

The first New England districts were the towns (or as Pennsylvanians would say, the townships). When settlements spread out from the town center, the needs of these more remote areas were met by the "moving" school—that is, the teacher conducting a series of short schools in many hamlets. When this expedient proved inadequate, separate districts were erected, often several to a town. This was the pattern that was followed in most of the other states. At a time when public education was marginal and limited to the simple program of a one-room school, taught by a nonprofessional teacher, this was not too bad. But by the 1830's, Horace Mann could say that the district school law was the most unfortunate legislation that Massachusetts and New York had ever enacted. In all these years, we have been trying to put Humpty-Dumpty together again, and not with complete success. There is a kind of Parkinson's law which states that school districts abhor consolidation unless it is accompanied by lucrative financial inducements; that boards not infrequently prefer their power and prestige structure to the most adequate education of the children of a district.

Third, American egalitarianism is a challenge to local control. Since we move readily from one state to another, we are all concerned about the quality of education, even in the most backward school district in America. The question is sometimes framed this way: "Should not every child under the American flag have an equal educational opportunity?" Some argue that such equal opportunity does not and can not exist short of national subsidies and control.

Fourth, there are no constitutional guarantees of the sovereignty of local school districts. Some think the local district has a right to perpetual existence. This is pure myth, sanctioned only by tradition. Court after court has held that education is a state function, not a local one. Legally, a legislature could redistrict a state as it sees fit. It could even abolish all local districts and maintain a state system directed from the capital.

It is customary to think of education as a state function, for we have been taught this in schools of education and in law schools. But we must also consider the possibility that the United States could declare education a national responsibility. We have seen numerous examples of federal involvement in education—the land grant colleges, the Smith-Hughes Act, the National Defense Education Act, the Civilian Conservation Corps, research contracts with universities, etc., etc. The argument that a national system of education would not necessarily be found unconstitutional historically is set forth by Dr. John S. Brubacher, now professor of education at the University of Michigan. Writing in *School and Society* in 1937,[4] Dr. Brubacher observed that decisions on the constitutionality of the social security act might lead one to believe that there might conceivably be a "radically new interpretation of the constitution" regarding education, if there were a sufficiently great national emergency. He contends the constitution says nothing more explicit about social security than it says about education,

> . . . yet Mr. Justices Roberts and Cardozo have had sufficiently logical ingenuity between them to extend the protecting cloak of our fundamental law to this latest child of social regulation without rending the integrity of its fabric. With such a precedent perhaps a national system of education may yet find support within the framework of the national constitution. If this be the case, the generation of teachers who were trained to think a national venture in education would be unconstitutional may now find their learning obsolete. Our educational authors may have to rewrite their texts.

4 Brubacher, John S.: "The Constitutionality of a National System of Education in the United States." *School and Society*, October 2, 1937.

In his decision, Justice Cardozo declared that the concept of the general welfare is not static:

> Needs that were narrow or parochial a century ago may be interwoven in our day with the well-being of the nation. What is critical or urgent changes with the times.

Brubacher believes that a sufficiently great national emergency could lead the Supreme Court to interpret the Constitution in such a way as to authorize a national system of education. He concludes:

> The final impression to be left with students of education is that, in the future, objection to national activity in education will have to be fought on the point of fact or policy and not that of law or constitutionality. The constitution seems elastic enough if the facts warrant its stretching.

Many believe, with Myron Lieberman and Hyman Rickover, that the national emergency is already here. Our need to compete with the Russians, they claim, with the resulting need for physics and mathematics rather than life adjustment, has created the kind of emergency situation that makes a living corpse of local control. Such an emergency could make national control of education a reality—if a majority of Congress and the Supreme Court agreed.

So far, the Supreme Court has made several decisions affecting education: The Dartmouth College decision, the Oregon private and parochial school decision, the desegregation decision, the Regents prayer decision among others. But in all these cases, the decision was not primarily educational. In each case some recourse was had to direct provisions of the constitution or its amendments which affect the rights of citizens. Yet under the extraordinary stresses of the Reconstruction period, Congress hotly debated the Hoar bill providing for federal schools in the South. How the Court would have voted on such a law in that emergency we can only speculate. We might also wonder what a present Court would say if Congress declared education an essential part of national defense—as many people contend it is.

The Teachers   Any continued improvement in American education will hinge, to a large extent, upon the teaching personnel in our schools. The problem of supplying the number of new teachers each year to replace those who have died, retired, or resigned, and also to provide for the great increase in the public population, is no small one. Approximately 100,000 new teachers enter the profession each year, to teach in elementary and secondary schools. Most enter with the amount of preparation indicated by the bachelor's degree. Some have the master's degree, indicating five years of collegiate preparation, and a very few (less than 1%) have the doctorate. In some states, persons with less than four years of college preparation are accepted. In 1962, almost 2600 beginning teachers had less than 120 semester hours of preparation. Of these, 138 had only the equivalent of one year of college.

The class of 1962 produced an estimated 142,500 college graduates who had met requirements for standard teaching certificates. Of these 88,000 had prepared for secondary school teaching and 54,500 had prepared for elementary school positions. The need was just the reverse, eight being needed in the elementary school for every five in the secondary school. Nor were the new high school teachers distributed among the subjects in relation to the demand. In some fields, especially in physical education for men and in social studies, the supply exceeded the demand. There were great shortages of librarians and teachers of physical education for women, of home economics, English, foreign languages, and the sciences.

Sixty-eight percent of those qualified for secondary school teaching actually entered teaching. Approximately eighty-three percent of prospective elementary teachers entered teaching. The NEA estimated that if thirty percent of all college graduates each year continue to enter teaching, the total number will be sufficient, but it pointed out the need to strike a balance between supply and demand in relation to grade level and subjects.

Most of the new teachers came from state teachers' colleges and from liberal arts colleges and universities which maintain departments of education. The difference between the candidates from these two principal sources is not so great as it formerly was, for the teachers' colleges are now requiring more preparation in general or liberal education and less in strictly professional courses.

A limited number of persons now enter teaching through the experimental master-of-arts-in-teaching programs carried on by certain colleges and universities (Harvard, Johns Hopkins, Colgate, and others), some of which receive private-foundation subsidies. The Ford Foundation, in particular, has granted millions to such ventures. It professes to see "a revolution under way in the education of teachers," likening its influence in education to the impact of the Flexner report on the education of medical doctors. Granting that a fifth year of education in professional subjects and in one's teaching specialty is valuable, some persons question whether such a program is worthy of the master's degree, in view of the fact that half or more of the fifth year program is essentially undergraduate work in education.

There is a growing tendency to insist upon a higher quality of work in teacher preparation. It has been suggested that states issue teacher's certificates only to persons graduated from institutions which have met the standards of the National Commission on the Accreditation of Teacher Education. This commission has not met with universal approval by college administrations, but seems to be strengthening its position.

Continuing Education   The term "adult education" is much in vogue at the present time. It would seem that our professional terminologists might have arrived at a more useful designation for this activity. "Adult education" usually does not include the full-time education of persons in colleges and graduate schools; by definition it covers only formal and informal instruction and aids to study for mature persons, usually on a part-time basis. It includes such instruction as one may get in special schools, extension centers, settlement houses, churches, clubs, and associations. The objectives may be informational, cultural, recreational, vocational, professional, remedial, retraining, or just passing the time. There are now more persons enrolled in this welter of activities than in full-time instruction in all our schools, but the total number of hours they put in is considerably less, for many adult education sessions last only for a few weeks and for only a few hours at a time.

Lyceum and Chautauqua courses, which we have described elsewhere in this volume, were early experiments in continuing education in America. Other notable ventures were discussion clubs such as the Junto founded by Benjamin Franklin in Philadelphia; various working men's associations in Eastern cities, which often maintained extensive libraries and discussion centers; night classes conducted by YMCA's and YWCA's, some of which eventually developed into colleges—notably the George Williams College in Chicago and the New Haven College in Connecticut. Within recent years, the International Ladies' Garment Workers Union has conducted a notable series of short-term institutes for its members. These are often conducted on college campuses with college professors giving much of the instruction.[5] Some business corporations, too, have used college instructors for liberal-arts and professional courses for their employees at various levels. Many industries have vast programs of in-service education and training.

---

[5] Not all colleges welcome the ILGWU. In the 1940's, the president of Hastings College, Nebraska, entered into a tentative agreement for such an institute for the ILGWU, only to have it cancelled by an anti-labor chairman of the board of trustees.

Another form of adult education was developed to serve the rural population of the country when federal funds were made available for the creation of agricultural experiment stations and the employment of county farm agents. This was an activity promoted by the federal government, in cooperation with the states, when it was discovered that an agency was needed to bring more education in scientific agriculture to the farm people than the A. and M. colleges could do. There seems no doubt that such services, together with short courses in the winter months at the A. and M. colleges, have done much to upgrade agricultural production in the United States.

Under the direction of President Charles R. VanHise, the University of Wisconsin set itself the objective of carrying education on a part-time basis into every section of the state. Wherever a group of people wanted instruction in any subject, the university undertook to supply a teacher. While these extension courses were adopted elsewhere, Wisconsin long occupied a preeminent place in this field.

The displacement of workers in certain fields of work because of automation or the vagaries of the market has furnished a new opportunity for adult education. For example, the state and federal governments now subsidize the reeducation of miners who are no longer needed in Pennsylvania and West Virginia coal fields.

Despite the intense educational efforts put forth during the last century, there is still an appreciable degree of illiteracy in the United States. This handicap is usually found among immigrants, Southern rural Negroes, and poorer whites in isolated areas. It is estimated that approximately 2,800,000 Americans aged 25 or more have no ability to read or write, and that a total of 8,300,000 may be classified as "functional illiterates" (as defined by the Selective Service System), since they lack a fourth grade education. Of 15,200 school systems studied by the United States Office of Education, only 4,840 reported any type of adult education. Only 160 offered instruction in basic literary education. Alabama is attacking the problem through a literacy program via television, as are the cities of Memphis, New Orleans, and Philadelphia.

We have reached a stage in civilization where one cannot "finish" school. Formal school days may terminate, but one must continue to keep on learning both for vocational efficiency and for the responsibilities of citizenship, to say nothing of worthy utilization of increasing amounts of leisure.

Research in Education   The modern scientific environment has so conditioned our thinking that education has

James B. Conant, a respected critic
and researcher of American Education.

become greatly devoted to the value of research. Lectures are now
so studded with the phrase "research indicates . . ." that if one proposes a new departure, he is at once asked if it is based upon research
findings. 'Twas not always thus, for one finds scant mention of research or a scientific approach to education before 1897, when J. M.
Rice, a physician who had studied at Jena and Leipsig, published
his pioneer study in the teaching of spelling. He had set out to
ascertain whether there might be any correlation between the time
spent on the teaching of spelling and the ability of pupils to spell.
His report indicated that there was very little correlation. There
were violent attacks upon his conclusions and upon his presumption
to make objective measurement in education, but Rice had, perhaps
unwittingly, initiated a new movement.

Soon educators and psychologists were measuring everything about
a school and its program, from the intelligence of pupils to the
square feet of window panes. Survey specialists in university departments of education offered their services to school districts to make
comprehensive surveys of an entire school system. Initiated by Paul
Hanus in Montclair, New Jersey in 1911, the survey movement
swept the nation, with some profit to the schools, the survey specialists, and the teams of graduate students in education who did most
of the work. The school system profited from an outside view by
disinterested persons, the specialists received handsome fees, and the
graduate students received experience and credit toward a higher
degree.

Most educational research has been carried on in universities by candidates for degrees. From the quality of some, one might conclude that the candidates were more interested in the degrees than in adding significantly to human knowledge. Certainly, most graduate student research has had little influence on American education.

After World War I, various state departments of education and the United States Office of Education devoted more attention to research. It became an important activity of the state education department in New York. Perhaps the most exhaustive project was the state-wide Regents' Inquiry into the Cost and Character of Education, in the late 1930's.

As a part of the hastily enacted National Defense Education Act of 1958, millions of federal dollars became available for research. So much money was available that had to be allocated in a short time, that some esoteric investigations were authorized. From 1957 to 1962, the federal research grants in education amounted to $17,600,000. Projects were supported in 127 universities and in 17 state departments in education. Grants per project ranged from $1,000 to $1,000,000 with an average of $50,000 per project.[6]

Research and other investigations are frequently financed by tax-exempt foundations. The Conant studies of the high schools and of teacher education were financed by the Carnegie Corporation. A number of studies in teacher education have been financed by the Ford Foundation, and several smaller foundations have furnished funds for research in schools or colleges in their home areas. One critic has said that if all the educational research done since 1900 were laid end to end, it would "stretch a long ways—but wouldn't go very far!" Today and tomorrow, there seems to be a need to limit research to significant problems, to assure that the quality of the research is improved, and to find more effective ways to promote the diffusion of any significant findings.

Changing Economic Viewpoint   Since "the highly educated man has become the central resource of today's society,"[7] and since it is widely acknowledged that we must be an educated society to progress or even to survive, most economists have had to change their point of view in classifying expenditures for education. Traditionally, these have been classified as consumption expendi-

---

[6] Among the research projects authorized were these: "Multivariate Statistical Procedures in Predicting Teacher-Pupil Classroom Behavior" at $17,236; "Problem-Solving Proficiency Among Elementary School Teachers" at $47,471; "Effects of Group Counseling on School Adjustment of Underachieving Junior High School Boys Who Demonstrate Acting-Out Behavior" at $68,050; and many others.

[7] Peter F. Drucker: *Landmarks of Tomorrow.* Harpers, 1959, pp. 114–125.

tures. Now, economists are beginning to regard them as an invest-ment. Since a modern industrial society is dependent upon educated men's scientific research and technically skilled manpower, at least as much as it depends on natural resources, there is justification for regarding money put into education as an investment rather than as consumption.

In modern technological civilizations, there is clearly established a positive correlation between the amount and quality of education and the advancement of technological progress. There is therefore a relationship between education as an investment and the increased production and wealth of a society. A higher level of education en-ables the society to produce more and better products. The increased production, in turn, facilitates educational expansion, both by pro-viding resources to be taxed for the support of education, and also by providing the leisure for its cultivation. Naturally, as a society grows richer it can afford to spend more for education—not only more in actual dollars, but proportionately more in relation to total income. Jefferson, in proposing a democratic scheme of education for Virginia, limited secondary and higher education to a few, for in his day one could not conceive of a society sufficiently affluent to spare any considerable number of people from work to pursue an educa-tion. Even early in the present century, the United States commis-sioner of education could not envision universal secondary education. The industrial revolution, particularly its present phase of automa-tion, has enabled man to release more time for education than a previous generation could have wildly imagined. And we may still be merely on the threshold of this new era.

For Further Reading

Austin, Mary C. *The Torch Lighters*. Harvard University Press, 1961.
Report of a field study of problems of teaching reading, with 22 recom-mendations for its improvement.

Benjamin, Harold. *The Saber-Tooth Curriculum*. McGraw-Hill, 1939.
Under the pseudonym of J. Abner Peddiwell, Professor Benjamin tells the fable of why paleolithic man justified the retention of a worn-out curriculum. Why one should still teach tiger-scaring long after all the saber-tooth tigers were extinct.

Conant, James B. *The American High School Today*. McGraw-Hill, 1959.
The noted "Conant report" on the American high school, with 21 recommendations for its improvement. The focus of the study is the

"comprehensive" high school. Deals with matters of fact and presents specific recommendations. Deals with social nobility, cultural lag, social change, motivation.

Conant, James B. *Slums and Suburbs.* McGraw-Hill, 1961.

Conant shows that slum youngsters have less opportunities for meaningful secondary education than do their counterparts in suburbia.

Curti, Merle. *The Social Ideas of American Educators.* Littlefield, Adams, 1959.

Chapter 6 emphasizes "the school and the triumph of business, 1860–1914."

Department of Health, Education, and Welfare. *Cooperative Research Projects. Bulletin,* 1962, No. 18.

A digest of research projects sponsored by the Office of Education. Includes such gems as "Program Development for Longitudinal and Cross-Sectional Research in Shaping Intellectually Linked Motives," whatever that may mean.

Deterline, William A. *An Introduction to Programmed Instruction.* Prentice-Hall, 1962.

A general explanation of teaching machines and programmed instruction. Chapter 6 deals with the roles of the teacher and the students in such a program.

Education Summary.

A semimonthly report on new developments, trends, ideas and research in education. Published by Arthur Croft Publications, New London, Connecticut.

Education U.S.A.

A weekly report on educational affairs published by the National School Public Relations Association in cooperation with the Division of Press and Radio Relations of the National Education Association. Summarizes events in education.

Ehlers, Henry. *Crucial Issues in Education.* Henry Holt, 1955.

Outstanding educational problems of our times: loyalty, censorship, religions, education, racial segregation, progressive education.

First Commission on Life Adjustment Education for Youth. *Vitalizing Secondary Education.* Department of Health, Education, and Welfare Bulletin, 1951, No. 3.

Definition of life adjustment education and enthusiastic championship of its case.

Hall, Robert King and J. A. Lauwerys. *Education and Economics.* Yearbook of Education. World Book Co., 1956.

The issue of the Yearbook of Education devoted to the relationship of economic factors to education throughout the world. Some articles deal with the American scene.

Halsey, A. H., Jean Stroud and C. Arnold Anderson. *Education, Economy and Society*. Free Press of Glencoe, 1961.

A reader in the sociology of education. Sociological interpretations of influences on modern education.

Hansen, Carl F. *The Amidon Elementary School*. Prentice-Hall, 1962.

-A widely discussed experimental elementary school.

Henry, Nelson B. (editor). *Social Forces Influencing American Education*. Sixtieth Yearbook of the National Society for the Study of Education, Part II. University of Chicago Press, 1961.

Educational change in America related to conditioning sociological and economic factors.

Hodenfield, G. K. and T. M. Stinnett. *The Education of Teachers*. Prentice-Hall, 1961.

An account of three conferences to reconcile the differences between "educationists" and subject matter specialists, with "a capsule projection of things to come." Chapter 18 deals with "Healing the Schisms in Education."

Hodgkinson, Harold L. *Education in Social and Cultural Perspectives*. Prentice-Hall, 1962.

"Some new ways of looking at the schoolhouse, teachers, administrators and children." Application of the perspectives of social science research to educational problems in our contemporary society.

Kelley, Earl C. *In Defense of Youth*. Prentice-Hall, 1962.

Present day youth problems and their relation to education. Part 3 deals with "Our schools have many faults" and "What are the fundamentals?"

Knowles, Malcolm S. *The Adult Education Movement in the United States*. Holt, Rinehart and Winston, 1962.

A new history of adult education from colonial times to the present. Suggests that absence of formal controls has aided in extension of adult education into many areas.

Lieberman, Myron. *The Future of Public Education*. University of Chicago Press, 1962.

A projection of what will happen in public education, with particular emphasis on local control, education of teachers, professional organizations, philanthropic foundations. Critical of the NEA.

Markham, Edwin and others. *Children in Bondage*. Hearst International Library, 1914.

Child labor conditions.

Morse, Arthur D. *Schools of Tomorrow—Today*. Doubleday, 1960.

A report on educational experiments prepared for the New York State Education Department. Deals with team teaching; New York City's demonstration guidance project; the teacher aids plan of Bay City; television in Washington County, Maryland; the Harvard program of teacher education; improvement of rural schools, etc.

NEA Research Bulletin.

Published four times a year, this little magazine contains latest statistics on American education: number of school districts, educational finance, teacher education, teacher supply and demand, ranking of the states in educational service, salary schedules, etc. Published by the National Education Association.

National Education Association. *Finding and Educating the Academically Talented Students in the Secondary School.* (Pamphlet) National Education Association, 1962.

Prepared for popular consumption, this pamphlet makes recommendations about the talented, arrived at by an NEA conference under chairmanship of James B. Conant.

National Society for the Study of Education. *Social Forces Influencing American Education.* Part II of the Sixtieth Yearbook. University of Chicago Press, 1961.

Chapter 3, by Theodore W. Schultz, deals with education and economic growth.

Pennsylvania State University. *Newer Educational Media.* Pennsylvania State University Continuing Education Center, University Park, Pa., 1961.

Papers summarizing research in the newer educational media such as motion pictures, television, programmed learning, and the implications of research for curriculum change. The TV programs of Dade County, Florida, and of the state of North Carolina.

Porter, David R. *The Quest of the Best in Education.* Sowers Printing Co., Lebanon, Pa., 1960.

The kindling of character as the chief role of education.

Reinhart, Bruce. *The Institutional Nature of Adult Christian Education.* Westminster Press, 1962.

Part adult education plays in the life of the church and the church's' role in adult education. Reasons for the Protestant churches' conservative resistance to the adult education movement in the church.

Research and Policy Committee of the Committee for Economic Development. *Economic Literacy for Americans.* Committee for Economic Development, New York, 1962.

A plea for the teaching of economics in public schools, with recommended action.

School and Society.

A biweekly magazine of education with longer articles of scholarly impact in education and shorter articles on the newest proposals and achievements. Published by the Society for the Advancement of Education.

Scott, C. Winfield, Clyde M. Hill and Robert W. Burns. *The Great Debate: Our Schools in Crisis.* Prentice-Hall, 1959.

An anthology of criticisms of our schools and of proposals for action to bring about reforms.

Sexton, Patricia Cayo. *Education and Income.* Viking, 1961.

Relation of education to the income of a society. Inequality of educational opportunities in public schools.

Simon, Kenneth A. *Enrollment in Public and Nonpublic Elementary and Secondary Schools, 1950–80.* U.S. Office of Education, 1962.

Projection of enrollments based on the census data for 1950 to 1980. Total enrollment, K through 12, public and nonpublic, is projected as 62,569,000 to 72,087,000 (In 1960, it was approximately 42,529,000).

Trump, J. Lloyd and Dorsey Baynham. *Focus on Change: Guide to Better Schools.* Rand-McNally, 1961.

The "Trump plan" and how it operates. One of the newest approaches in secondary education.

White, Alphens L. *Local School Boards: Organization and Practices.* U.S. Department of Health, Education, and Welfare Bulletin, 1962, No. 8. Government Printing Office, 1962.

A study of school board organization and practices. School boards as the key to school improvement programs. How boards are chosen and what they do.

Woodring, Paul and John Scanlon. *American Education Today.* McGraw-Hill, 1963.

Present status of a "complex, diverse and enormous" educational establishment. Objectives, changing philosophies, current issues, innovations, education of teachers and administrators.

Index

A. and M. colleges, 188–190
Abecedarians, 78
Abroad, ideas from, 127–133
Academic departments, 148
Academic freedom, 345
Academy, 21; 88–96; alternate names, 94; curriculum, 93–94; female, 95–96; 214–215; influence, 94; method, 94.
Academy, The, 249
Accidence, Cheever's, 11
Accreditation, 164, 191–193
Adams, John Quincy, 61, 104, 238
Adams, Professor, 239
Administration, 314–326
Adolescence, 167
Adult education, 269–271, 383
Affiliated organizations, NEA, 334–336
Agassiz, Alexander 248
Agrarianism, 103n
Agricultural education, 168–169, 188–190
Albany Normal School, 80, 216, 241–243, 246
Alcott, Amos Bronson, 329, 334
Alexander II of Russia, 130
American Annals of Education, 236
American Association for Advancement of Education, 330
American Association of Collegiate Registrars, 203–204
American Association of School Administrators, 319
American Association of University Professors, 338–339, 349
"American City," 164
American Council on Education, 163
American Education Fellowship, 140
American Federation of Teachers, 337–338
American High School Today, 165–166
American Historical Association, 352
American Institute of Instruction, 328–329

American Journal of Education, 111–112, 262
American Lyceum, 235
American Lyceum Association, 329–330
American Missionary Association, 297
"American Pestalozzi," 131
American Philosophical Society, 40, 99, 346
American Preceptor, 70
American Youth Commission, 163
Americanism, 68
Americanization, 308
Andrews, Rev. William, 28
Anti-intellectualism, 355
Anti-Masonic Party, 113
Antioch College, 105–106, 223
Apparatus, teachers', 79
Apprenticeship, 7–10; articles of, 9
Arithmetics, 71–72
Armed Forces Institute, 184
Articulation, 159
Arts, the, 272–273
Association of Women Friends for Relief of the Poor, 49
Attendance, 79, 124, 152
Auburn Female College, 222

Bache, Dr. Alexander Dallas, 145
Bagley, William C., 183, 252–253
Baptist Schools, 279
Barnard, Henry, 81, 83, 111–112, 233, 246, 262, 316
Barnum, P. T., 259
Barto v. Himrod, 123
Battledore, 2
Beecher, Catherine, 72, 191, 219–220
Beecher, Lyman, 347
Bell, Reverend Andrew, 50
Bestor, Alfred E., 3n, 140, 251
Bible, 2, 291
Bible reading, 291
Bingham, Caleb, 70
Blair, Henry W., 323

393

Blow, Susan, 134

Blue-back speller, 68

Board of Education, Massachusetts, 238

Boehm, Charles, 359

Boston Latin Grammar School, see Latin Grammar School

Breckinridge, Robert J., 114

Brickman, W. W., 252

Briggs, Thomas, 168

Brooks, Charles, 236–238, 239

Brubacher, A. R., 181

Brubacher, John S., 380

Brunner, Fern, 360

Bryan, William Jennings, 270, 348

Bryn Mawr College, 191, 225

Buchanan, James, 189

Buffalo, New York, 81

Buffalo Normal School, 180

Burton, 80

Butler, Nicholas Murray, 155

Butterfield, 161

Calvinism, 1, 7, 24, 57, 74, 87, 101

Carleton College, 254

Carnegie, Andrew, 272, 340

Carpenter, Janet, 175

Carroll, Bishop John, 284

Carter, James G., 55, 99, 109, 145, 233–235, 329

Catechism, 10

Catholepistemiad, 179

Censorship, 350–353

Central High School, Philadelphia, 145

Certification, see Teacher certification

Chamber of Commerce, United States, 323

Channing, William Ellery, 53, 109, 239

Charity schools, 15

Chautauqua, 184, 248, 269–271

Cheever, Ezekiel, 10, 26

Chicago, University of, 196, 206

Child-Centered School, 129, 138

Child labor, 56, 63, 161

Chipman, Nathaniel, 38, 39

Church in education, 1, 275–290

Citizenship, education for, 55

City superintendents, 317–318

Civilian Conservation Corps, 162

Clark University, 196

Classics persistent, 185

Claybrooks v. City of Owensboro, 298

Clayton County High School, Iowa, 149

Clinton, DeWitt, 49, 51, 83, 218, 232, 241

Clinton, George, 54

Clinton Academy, 92

Coburn, Warren, 71

Coeducation, in academies, 95–96; in colleges, 191; in high schools, 221

College Entrance Examination Board, 155–156

College entrance requirements, 25

College Retirement Equities Fund, 339–341

Colleges, colonial, 16, 29–33; westward movement, 173

Colleges, first nine, 23, 29

Collegiate institutes, 94

Colonial inheritance, 36–37, 67

Columbia University, 23, 177, 186

Comenius, 75, 130

Commission of Education, U.S., 322

Commission on Life Adjustment Education, 165

Commission on Reorganization of Secondary Education, 159–160

Committee on College Entrance Requirements, 158–159

Committee on Economy of Time, 159

Committee of Nine, 159

Committee of Ten, 156–158

Common learnings, 164

Common school, 53, 83, 90; "revival," 98–124

Common School Journal, 101, 108

Common school leaders, 82–83

Communism, teaching about, 359

Communistic experiments, 53

Compayré, Gabriel, 108

Compulsory attendance, 79, 124

Compulsory maintenance, 11–14

Conant, James B., 165–166, 254–255

Condorcet, 40

Congregationalist schools, 278

Connecticut, 49, 316

Connecticut Observer, 233

Constitution, United States, 41–42

Continuing education, 383

Control of colleges, 176–178

Control of schools, 314–327
Controversial issues, 354, 359
Cook County Normal School, 137, 248
Cooley, Justice Thomas C., 150–151
Cooper, Myles, 346
Cooper, Thomas, 55
Coordinate colleges, 191
Copy books, 76
Coram, Robert, 38, 39
Corderius, 11
Core curriculum, 372–373
Cornell University, 190, 196, 199, 224
Correspondence study, 183
Cotton, Reverend John, 5
Council for Advancement of Small Colleges, 193
Council of Chief State School Officers, 378
Counts, Georges, 140, 163
County superintendents, 316–317
Cousin, Victor, 128, 236
Craine, Lucille Cardin, 352
Crandall, Prudence, 346
Crary, Isaac E., 114
Cremin, Lawrence A., 135
Crime, education to reduce, 54
Cubberley, Elwood P., 106
Curriculum, in academies, 93–94; in colleges, 185–190; in normal schools, 244
Curriculum, elementary, 365–367
Curriculum, secondary, 367–370
Curriculum-centered school, 127
Curti, Merle, 36, 137

Dalton plan, 371
Dame school, 7
Damrosch, Walter, 266
Darrow, Clarence, 348
Dartmouth College case, 177–178
Daughters of American Revolution, 352
Day of Doom, 6
DeGarmo, Charles, 132
Degrees for women, 224
De la Educacion Popular, 109
Deism, 33
Democracy in Education, 137
Democracy, spread of, 54–56
Democratic ideal, 37–38
Denman, J. S., 246

Denominational rivalry in colleges, 175
Department of Defense, 184
Department of Secondary School Principals, NEA, 162
Department of Superintendence, NEA, 319
Depression, 1930's, 162–164
Desegregation, racial, 15, 291, 375
Dewey, John, 137, 183
Dictionary of the English Language, 69
Dilworth, Thomas, 71
Dimitry, Alexander, 114
Diploma mills, 173
District school, 45, 67, 83, 127
District School As It Was, 80
District School Journal, 121, 147
Dix, Dorothea, 61
Dorr rebellion, 55
Douglas, Harl A., 165
Draper, Andrew Sloan, 249, 320
Drop-outs, 169, 305–306
Dual system, 299–300
du Courteil, A.L.R., de LaF., 6, 38, 39
Duke University, 197
Dunster, Henry, 345
Du Pont de Nemours, Pierre S., 38, 39
Dutch, 1, 13
Dwight, Edmund, 109, 239
Dwight, Henry E., 236
Dwight, Nathaniel, 70

Early school-learners, see drop-outs
Easton, high school in, 146
Eaton, Nathaniel, 229
Eclectic Arithmetic, 71
Eclectic Readers, 73
Economic interpretations, 386–387
Education for All American Youth, 164, 337
Education departments in universities, 182
Educational Policies Commission, 164, 337
Edward, Ninian, 114
Egalitarianism, 379
Eggleston, Edward, 80
Elective principle, 198–199, 201–202
Eliot, Charles W., 27, 139, 155, 187, 192, 200–202, 206

Elmira College, 191, 222–223
Emerson, George B., 79, 144, 235
Emile, The, 128
England, education in, 377
English Classical School, 143
"English" education, 87
English Grammar, 71
English heritage, 1, 213
English Reader, 70
Enlightenment, 186
Enrollment, college, 202–205; high school, 153, 161; statistics, 363–364
Enrollment data, 153, 364
Episcopalian schools, 277
Erasmus Hall Academy, 91
Essayists, 38–41
Essentialists, 252–253
Evaluative Criteria, 164
Evenson v. *Ewing,* 290
Everett, Edward, 55, 100, 238–239
Evolution, 347–348
Expansion of higher education, further need for, 202
Extension courses, 184

Fairchild, James H., 223
Farmer's Hall Academy, 91
Farmers High School, 190
Farmer's and Mechanic's Journal, 60
"Farmville," 164
Federal aid, 289, 322–323
Federated McGuffey Societies, 74
Female academy, 214
Finance, 374–375
Five formal steps, 132
Flesch, Rudolph, 251
Flexner, Abraham, 255
Foote, Lucinda, 221
Ford, Henry, 74
Fortress Monroe school, 296
Founding of colleges, 173
Franklin, Benjamin, 40, 88–91, 104, 145, 230
Franklin, Mrs. Virginia, 360–361
Franklin and Marshall College, 201
Free academies, 94
Free school campaign, New York, 120–124
Free School Society, New York, 49; see also Public School Society
Free schools, 54

Freedmens' Bureau, 297–298
Freedom to Learn, 359
Freedom of teachers, personal, 356–358
French Huguenots, 1
French and Indian Wars, 17
Froebel, 133–134
Fuller, Edgar, 378
Fund raising projects, 197
Fund for the Republic, 359
Future Teachers of America, 335

Gallaudet, Thomas H., 55, 112, 233, 236, 310
Garfield, James A., 77
Garland, Hamlin, 56, 75n
Gary platoon system, 138
Geography, 70, 127
Georgia, University of, 178
Germans, 1
Gettysburg College, 112
Gilman, Daniel Coit, 195–196
Girls' High and Normal School, 144
Girls' High School, Boston, 144–145, 220
Girls' high schools, 220
Godey's Lady's Book, 216
Goodrich, C. A., 72
Goodrich, S. C., 72
Gradgrind, Mr., 130
Graduate study for women, 225
Graduates, college, 203
Grammar school, English, 84
Grammars, 70–71
Grammatical Institute of the English Language, 69–70
Great Movements, Age of, 53
Griscom, John, 83
Guide to the English Tongue, 68, 70

Hagar, Daniel B., 331
Hale, Edward Everett, 67
Hale, Sara Josepha, 216n
Hall, G. Stanley, 167, 196, 334
Hall, Samuel, 231–232
Hamilton, Alexander, 54, 58
Hampton Institute, 297
Handicapped, Education of, 310–311
Hansen, Allen O., 40
Hard Times, 130

Harper, William Rainey, 137, 184, 206, 269
Harris, William T., 156, 221, 322, 334
Harvard College, 1, 12, 25, 30–31
Hastings College, 174–175
Hawley Gideon, 46–47, 81, 83, 110–111
Hawthorne Nathaniel, 134
Hedrick, Benjamin S., 346
Helvetius, 40
Herbart, 132
Herbartianism, 132–133
High School enrollments, 153, 161
High School and Life, 164
High School, Modern, 21
High School, Traditional, 21
High Schools, Legality of, 149–152
High Schools, New York, 147
High Schools, number of, 143, 363; first, 143–146
High Schools, origins, 147
History, 72, 127
Hoar, George F., 323
Holbrook, Josiah, 329
Home and Colonial Infant Society, 131
Hoosier Schoolmaster, 80
Horn Book, 2
How to Evaluate a Secondary School, 164
Howe, Julia Ward, 329
Howe, Samuel Gridley, 310, 329
Hughes, Bishop, 286
Humanitarianism, 61–62

Illinois, local option law, 149
Illiteracy, 37
Immigration, 58–60, 90, 259, 302–310
Impending Tide, 364
Independent schools, 292
Indiana, early high school, 149
Industrial Education Association, 187–189
Industrial revolution, 62–63
Institutes, 77, 94, 245–248
Instructions for the Better Government . . . of Schools, 110
Irish, 1, 59
Issues of Secondary Education, 162

Jacksonian concept, 81, 317
Jamestown, 10

Jeanes Fund, 299
Jefferson, Thomas, 42–43, 55, 114, 179, 180, 271, 314, 387
Jewish schools, 281
Johns Hopkins University, 195, 225
Johnson, Mrs. Marietta, 138
Johnson, Walter R., 235
Jones, Margaret E. M., 131
Journals of education, 262
Junior colleges, 206
Junior High Schools, 167–168

Kalamazoo case, 149–152, 324
Kandel, Isaac, 165, 183
Kilpatrick, William H., 139, 183
Kindergarten, 133–134
Kings College, 176–177, 186
Kingsley, James L., 231
Know-Nothing Party, 59
Knox, Samuel, 38–39
Koos, L. V., 168
Krusi, Hermann, 131
Ku Klux Klan, 287–288

Labor, child, 56, 63, 161
Labor movement, 60–61
Laboratory school, Dewey's, 137
Lag, educational, 22
Laissez-faire attitude, 15
Lancaster, Joseph, 50, 83, 144
Land grants, 48, 182, 188–190
Lane Theological Seminary, 347
Latin grammar school, 10–11, 21–29, 87
Law, education in, 227
Law of 1642, Massachusetts, 24; Law of 1647, Massachusetts, 12, 24; Law of 1827, Massachusetts, 145
Law of 1795, New York, 45; Law of 1812, New York, 45; Free School Act, 122
Law of 1834, Pennsylvania, 15, 112–113
Laws, compulsory attendance, 79
Lay control, 324–325
Lectures on School Keeping, 232
Lectures and shows, 258
Legal education, 208, 227
Leonard, Gardner Cottrell, 210
Levels of education, 16

Lexington Normal School, 216, 240
Libraries, 271–272
Libraries, district school, 103, 104
Life adjustment curriculum, 158, 165
Lincoln, Abraham, 189
Lincoln, Levi, 55, 238
Lindsley, 55
Literary among women, 213
Little red schoolhouse, 127
Little Rock, 302
Local control diminishes, 376–377
Local education associations, 336
Locke, John, 27
Log college, 23–24
Low, Seth, 210
Loyalty oaths, 354–355
Lutheran schools, 280–281
Lutherans, 280
Lyceum, 235, 269, 329–330
Lynd, Albert, 36n, 140
Lyon, Mary, 191, 218

McCollum v. Board of Education, 324
McCulloch, John, 72
McGuffey, Alexander, 73
McGuffey, Reverend William Holmes,
    72–75
McGuffeyism, 72–75, 135
McMurry, Charles and Frank, 132
Magazines, 260–262
Man Without A Country, The, 67
Mann, Horace, 54, 57, 80, 83, 100–110,
    191, 233, 238, 271, 315, 347
Manual training, 134
Manumission Society, 49
Marcy, William, 241
Marshall, John, 177
Martha's Vineyard, 249
Martin, George H., 12, 13
Mary Sharp College, 225
Maryland, University of, 184
Mason, Lowell T., 83, 329
Massachusetts Magazine, 230
Massachusetts normal schools, 215–218,
    232–240
Master of arts in teaching, 254, 382
Mather, Reverend Cotton, 11, 26, 31,
    229
May, Reverend Samuel, 61, 347
Mayo, Charles and Elizabeth, 130
Medical education, 207, 226

Memoriter learning, 67, 127
Merchant of Venice, 353
Meriam, Junius L., 138
Method, in Latin schools, 27–28; in
    colleges, 186–187; in district school,
    127
Methodist schools, 279
Methods, contemporary, 370–374
Miami University (Ohio), 178
Michigan Agricultural College, 190
Michigan, University of, 179
Middle class, 87
Middle States Association, 155, 192
Miller, George F., 92
Milne, William J., 181, 247
Ministry, education for, 208
Minority, education for, 21, 295–313
Monitorial schools, 50–51
Montessori, Maria, 292
Montieth, Reverend John, 179, 284
Morgan, Christopher, 120
Morrill Act, 182, 188–190
Morris, Gouverneur, 41
Morse, Reverend Jedediah, 70, 214
Motion pictures, 267–269
Mount Holyoke Seminary, 191, 219
Moving school, 44
Muhlenberg, H. A., 113
Muhlenberg, Henry Melchior, 281
Murphy, Archibald D., 114
Murray, Lindley, 70, 71
Muskingum College, 175

Nation, The, 353
National Association of Manufac-
    turers, 323, 353
National Association of Secondary
    School Principals, 162, 170
National Commission on Accredita-
    tion of Teacher Education, 253, 383
National Commission on Accrediting,
    193
National Defense Education Act, 57
National Education Association, 131,
    331–336
National examinations, 377
National Intelligencer, 38
National Survey of Secondary Edu-
    cation, 162
National Teachers Association, 331
National Youth Administration, 162

Nationalism, 57

Nearing, Scott, 63

Neef, Joseph, 131

Negroes, schools for, 1, 49, 295–362; admitted to Oberlin, 191; agricultural and mechanical colleges, 190

New England Association of Colleges and Secondary Schools, 192n

New England Primer, 2–5, 25, 68, 213

New England's First Fruits, 30–31

"New Fifty Percent," 161

New Haven Normal School, 216n

New Netherlands, 13

New York academies, 92

New York College for Training of Teachers, 183

New York High School Society, 146, 220

New York State College for Teachers, 181

Newburgh Telegraph, 121

Newspapers, 263–265

"Non-accepting" districts, 113

Non-public schools, 275–292

Normal schools, 215–218, 231–245

North Carolina Reader, 114

North Carolina, University of, 248

North Central Association, 162, 192

Northwest Ordinance, 48

Northwest Territory, 48

Northwestern Association, 192n

Noyes Academy, 346

Oberlin Collegiate Institute, 191, 223

Object teaching, 131

Office of Education, United States, 322

Ohio State University, 178

Ohio University, 178

Olde Deluder Satan, 12, 24

Olmsted, Denison, 231

One-room school, 81–82

Orbis Pictus, 75

Oregon school case, 228

Oswego, 59, 131

Page, David Perkins, 102, 243, 247, 329

Papists, concealed, 90

Parent-Teachers Association, 343

Parker, Francis W., 72, 137, 248

Parley, Peter, 72

Parochial school attitude, 14, 67, 277–290

Patroons, 13

Peabody, Elizabeth, 133

Peake, Mary L., 296–297

Peale, Charles Wilson, 273

Peirce, Cyrus, 104, 240

Penmanship, 76

Pennsylvania, 60

Pennsylvania College, 112

Pennsylvania "Dutch," 1, 68

Pennsylvania State College, 190

Pennsylvania, University of, 177, 186

Personal freedoms, 356–358

Pestalozzi, 128–132

Pestalozzianism, 128, 372

Petitions for free schools, 121

Phelps, William F., 247

Philadelphia Centennial Exposition, 134

Philanthropy, 49, 61, 196–197, 299

Philbrick, John D., 319, 329

Phillips Academy (Andover), 91

Phonics, 4

Physiology, 75, 127

Pierce v. Society of Jesus and Mary, 288

Pierce, Cyrus, see Peirce, Cyrus

Pierce, John D., 114

Pike, Nicholas, 71

Pittsburgh, high school in, 146

Platoon plan, 138

Play school, 138

Plessy v. Ferguson, 301

Polytechnical institutes, 188

Poor, John, 215

Population, changing in high school, 160–162

Pormont, Philemon, 23

Potter, 79

Pragmatic education, 87

Presbyterian schools, 280

Pressey, S. L., 79

Primary school, 84

Principalship, 319–320

Private venture schools, 7, 88

Proceedings of NEA, 334

Professional organizations, 328–344

Professors, education in, 207–268

Progressive Education, 139

Progressive education, 135–141

Progressive Education Association, 139
Project method, 139
Proliferation of courses, 201
Proposals for the Education of Youth in Pennsylvania, 89
Prosperity, 64
Protestant heritage, 1
Protestant parochial schools, 276–281
Prudential officers, 80
Prussian schools, 128, 236
Prussian teachers, 130
Public school, 84
Public School Society, New York, 49, 59, 67, 119

Quakers, 214, 278, 325
Quincy system, 137

Radio and television, 265–267
Ragged School, 59, 131
Randall, S. S., 54
Rantoul, Robert, 109
Rate bill, 115–123
Ray, Joseph, 71–72
Readers, 68, 72–75
Reading circles, 245
Reading and writing schools, 11
Realistic studies, 187–190
Redistricting, 378–380
Referendum on free schools, 122–123
Reformed churches, 279
Regents examinations, 154
Regents' Inquiry, 163–164
Regents' Prayer, 291
Regents of University of State of New York, 91, 177, 241
Regional accrediting agencies, 164, 191–193
Religious tests, 11–13
Renaissance, 10, 31
Rensselaer Polytechnic Institute, 188, 330
Reorganization of school districts, 375–376
Research in colleges, 205
Research in education, 384–386
Restrictions in colleges, 175–176
Retirement systems, 339–342
"Revival," common school, 98
Rhode Island, 13, 55

Richard, Pére Gabriel, 179, 284
Rickover, Hyman G., 140, 251, 377
Ritter, Joseph, 113
Robinson, Oscar D., 158
Roelantsen, Adam, 229
Rogers, Reverend John, 5
Roman Catholics, 57
Roman Catholic schools, 282–290
Roosevelt, Theodore, 75
Rosenwald, Fund, 299
Rousseau, 62, 128
Rush, Benjamin, 38, 39
Russell, William, 53, 231
Rutgers University, 178

St. Louis, kindergarten in, 134
Sarmiento, Domingo Faustino, 108–109
Scholay, 64
School and Society, Dewey's, 137
School and Society (magazine), 330n
Schoolhouses, 77–78
Schoolmaster's Assistant, The, 71
Schools, decline of, 43
Schools of Tomorrow, Dewey's, 137
Schurz, Mrs. Carl, 133
Science, 187–188; in universities, 199–200
Science instruction, 135
Scopes, John T., 348
Scotch, 1
Secondary schools, numbers of, 143, 363
Sectarian doctrine, 57–58
Sectarian schools, 275–292
Secularism, 292
Seminary, 77
"Separate but equal" doctrines, 301
Seton, Mother, 284
Settlement houses, 308
Seven Cardinal Principles, 159–160
Seventh Report (Mann's), 103, 107, 128
Seward, William H., 241
Sharp, Mary, 225
Sheldon, Edward Austin, 59, 131–132
Simpson, Stephen, 60
Sinclair, Upton, 197–198
Slater Fund, 299
Slums and Suburbs, 165, 167

Smith, Mortimer, 36, 140, 251
Smith, Samuel H., 38, 39
Smith College, 191
Smith-Hughes Act, 169, 380
Snowbound, 76–77
Social change, steps in, 120
Social order, improvements in, 53
Socialism, fear of, 348–349
Society for the Propagation of the Gospel in Foreign Parts, 15, 67, 229, 346
Space exploration, 1
Spaulding, Frank E., 77, 318–319
Special education, 311
Spellers, 68
Spencer, Herbert, 38, 159, 366
Sputnik, 165, 252
Stanford University, 197
State aid, 321
State departments of education, 320–321
State education associations, 331, 336
State retirement systems, 341–343
State school funds, 315–316
State sovereignty, 325–326
State superintendent, 45, 81
State teachers associations, 331, 336
State University of Iowa, 182
Steps in social change, 120
Stevens, Thaddeus, 77, 83, 112–113
Stoneman, Kate, 225
Stowe, Calvin E., 57, 83, 114, 128
Straight, Henry, 132
Stuart, 150
Student Education Association, NEA, 335
Suffrage, extension of, 54–56
Suffrage, manhood, 55
Suhrie, Ambrose, 76, 250
Sullivan, James, 38, 39
Summer sessions, 248–250
Superintendent of schools, 81
Supervision, 80–81
Supreme Court, United States, 42, 290–291, 301, 381
Surplus Revenue Act, 64–65
Swedes, 1
Swett, John, 114
Swift, Mary, 240
Syllabus, first New York, 110

Teacher certification, 67
Teacher education, 67, 229–256
Teachers colleges, 180–183, 250–255
Teachers, contemporary, 381–383
Teachers' institutes, 77, 245–248
Teachers Insurance and Annuity Association, 339–341
Technical institutes, 187–188
Television, 170, 265–267
Tennent, Reverend William, 23–24
Tenure, teacher, 349–350
Textbooks, 68–70
Theocentric government, 11
Theology challenged, 185
Third Plenary Council, 287
Ticknor, Elisha, 230
Ticknor, George, 186
"Tidal wave," 203–205
Town, Salem, 247–248
Town school system, 43–44
Traditional school, 127
Transformation of the School, 135–136
Triangular trades, 87
Trump, J. Lloyd, 169–170
Trump plan, 169–170, 373
Tulane University, 191
Tully, 25
Turner, Jonathan, 188
Tuskegee Institute, 300

Union College, New York, 175
Union colleges, 175
Union Free School Act, New York, 147–148
Unitarianism, 57
United States Military Academy, 188
United States Office of Education, 322
Universitas, 195
Universities, 195–211, 224
University inspection of secondary schools, 154–155
University regalia, 208–211
Urbanization, 56–57
Ursuline convent, 214

Valentine, Thomas W., 331
Van Kleeck, E. R., 122n
Van Rensselaer, Stephen, 188, 330
Vassar College, 191
Vigilantes, 359–360

Virginia, 24
Virginia, University of, 178
Vocational education, 168–169
Von Marenholtz Bulow-Wendhausen, Baroness, 133

War, 259
Warfield, President, 155n
Warren, Earl, 291
Washington, Booker T., 297, 299
Washington, George, 42
Washington Academy, 92
Watervliet case, 326
Wealth, education related to, 64–65
Webster, Daniel, 105–106, 177, 238
Webster, Noah, 38, 39, 57, 68–70, 72, 74
Wells, D. Franklin, 243n
West, Benjamin, 273
Western Association, 192n
Western College of Professional Teachers, 330
Western Reserve, 49
Western Reserve University, 191
What Knowledge is of Most Worth? 159
When Youth Leave School, 164
Whitman, Walt, 77
Whittier, James Greenleaf, 76–77

Why Johnny Can't Read, 251
Wickersham, 113n, 334
Wigglesworth, Reverend Michael, 6
Wiley, Calvin H., 83, 114
Willard, Emma, 191, 218
William and Mary, College of, 42, 178
Wines, E. C., 54
Winship, A. E., 243n
Wirt, William, 138
Wolf, Governor George, 15, 112
Women in colleges, 190–191, 213–227
Women in professions, 226–227
Women teachers, 240–250
Woodbridge, William C., 70, 83, 214, 236
Woodrow, James, 347
Woody, Thomas, 214n
Working Man's Manual, 60

Yale College, 25, 32, 188, 195, 227, 231, 272
Young, Samuel, 121, 241
Youth Tell Their Story, 163
Ypsilanti Normal School, 180

Zinzendorf, Benigna, 212
Zone meetings, 336

234567890